HIGH PERFORMANCE
SCIENTIFIC AND
ENGINEERING COMPUTING
Hardware/Software Support

THE KLUWER INTERNATIONAL SERIES
IN ENGINEERING AND COMPUTER SCIENCE

HIGH PERFORMANCE SCIENTIFIC AND ENGINEERING COMPUTING
Hardware/Software Support

edited by

Laurence Tianruo Yang
St. Francis Xavier University
Canada

Yi Pan
Georgia State University
U.S.A.

KLUWER ACADEMIC PUBLISHERS
Boston / Dordrecht / London

Distributors for North, Central and South America:
Kluwer Academic Publishers
101 Philip Drive
Assinippi Park
Norwell, Massachusetts 02061 USA
Telephone (781) 871-6600
Fax (781) 871-6528
E-Mail <kluwer@wkap.com>

Distributors for all other countries:
Kluwer Academic Publishers Group
Post Office Box 322
3300 AH Dordrecht, THE NETHERLANDS
Telephone 31 78 6576 000
Fax 31 78 6576 474
E-Mail <orderdept@wkap.nl>

 Electronic Services <http://www.wkap.nl>

Library of Congress Cataloging-in-Publication

HIGH PERFORMANCE SCIENTIFIC AND ENGINEERING COMPUTING:
Hardware/Software Support
edited by Laurence Tianruo Yang and Yi Pan
ISBN 978-1-4419-5389-6

Contents

Preface

The field of high performance computing has obtained prominence through advances in electronic and integrated technologies beginning in the 1940s. Current times are very exciting and the years to come will witness a proliferation in the use of parallel and distributed systems. The scientific and engineering application domains have a key role in shaping future research and development activities in academia and industry, especially when the solution of large and complex problems must cope with tight timing schedules.

This book contains selected best papers on hardware/software support for high performance scientific and engineering computing from prestigious workshops such as PACT-SHPSEC, IPDPS-PDSECA and ICPP-HPSECA with some invited papers from prominent researchers around the world. The book is basically divided into six main sections. We believe all of these chapters and topics not only provide novel ideas, new results and state-of-the-art techniques in this field, but also stimulate the future research activities in the area of high performance computing for science and engineering applications. We would like to share them with our readers.

Part 1: compilation and architectural support

In chapter 1, *Rufai et al.* present OpenMP shared memory programming as a viable alternative and a much simpler way to write multithreaded programs. *Guo* proposes a linear data distribution technique in chapter 2, which extends the traditional block or cyclic distribution for intra-dimension as in HPF, to permit partitioning the array elements along slant lines on distributed-memory machine. Chapter 3 studies the communication issue in parallel applications. *Byna et al.* present a methodology for classifying the effects of data size and data distribution on hardware, middleware, and application software performance. In chapter 4, *Shin et al.* propose an adaptive dynamic thread scheduling approach that partially schedules threads in the form of a detector thread at a nominal hardware and software cost.

Part 2: numerical computation

In chapter 5, *Liu et al.* describe performance analysis of a BiCGSTAB solver for Multiple-Marine-Propeller simulation with several MPI libraries and platforms. *Yamamoto et al.* present a new BLAS-3 based parallel algorithm for computing the eigenvectors of real symmetric matrices in chapter 6.

Part 3: load balancing

Chapter 7 by *Plastino et al.* deals with concepts and experiments related to load balancing in SPMD applications. *Bourgeade et al.* in chapter 8 present an efficient dynamic load balance strategy for the numerical computation of pulse propagation in nonlinear dispersive optical media. The work described in chapter 9 by *Cariño et al.* contributes a loop scheduling strategy to dynamically load balance the parallel computation of the trajectories for improving the performance of wavepacket simulations.

Part 4: performance evaluation

To address parallel performance evaluation, *Kerbyson et al.* describe an important use of predictive application performance modelling in chapter 10. The following chapter by *Nethi et al.* surveys some of the recent performance evaluation tools for large scale parallel and distributed systems. A new methodology of performance evaluation using mixed level modelling techniques is proposed and its advantages over other existing tools is discussed.

Part 5: grid computing

Chapter 12 by *Chandra et al.* presents an autonomic partitioning framework for grid-based structured adaptive mesh refinement (SAMR) applications. In chapter 13, *Aversa et al.* deal with the utilization of Web services technology to discover mobile grid resources and services, within a mobile agent based grid architecture. *Schikuta* presents xDGDL, an approach towards a concise but comprehensive data-grid description language in chapter 14.

Part 6: scientific and engineering applications

A case study on the parallelization of a classical molecular dynamics code for simulating the formation of carbon clusters is presented by *Hayashi et al.* in chapter 15. In another chapter, namely chapter 16, *Chaudhary et al.* compare various parallelizing approaches for tribology simulations. The aim of chapter 17 by *Martin et al.* is to provide a high performance air quality simulation. *Thulasiraman et al.* describe an ant colony optimization based routing algorithm in mobile ad hoc networks and its parallel implementation in chapter 18. *Bhalla et al.* present in chapter 19 how to parallelize serializable transactions based on transaction classification in real-time database systems. In the last chapter, *Joo et al.* propose the adaptive selection of materialized queries in a mediator for the integration of distributed information resources.

Acknowledgments

We would like to thank the authors for their excellent contributions and patience in assisting us. We are also grateful for Susan Lagerstrom-Fife and Sharon Palleshi of Kluwer Academic Publishers for their patience and support to make this book possible. Finally, the fundamental work of all reviewers on these papers is also very warmly acknowledged.

LAURENCE TIANRUO YANG AND YI PAN

I

COMPILATION AND ARCHITECTURAL SUPPORT

Chapter 1

MULTITHREADED PARALLELISM WITH OPENMP

Raimi A. Rufai, Muslim Bozyigit, Jarallah S. AlGhamdi, and Moataz Ahmed
Information & Computer Science Department
King Fahd University of Petroleum & Minerals, Dhahran 31261, Saudi Arabia
{rrufai, bozyigit, jaralla, mahmed}@ccse.kfupm.edu.sa

Abstract   While multithreaded programming is an effective way to exploit concurrency, multithreaded programs are notoriously hard to program, debug and tune for performance. In this chapter, we present *OpenMP shared memory programming* as a viable alternative and a much simpler way to write multithreaded programs. We show through empirical results obtained by running, on a single processor machine, a simple matrix multiplication program written in OpenMP C that the drop in performance compared with the single threaded version even on a uniprocessor machine may be negligible. However, this is well compensated for by the increased programmer productivity resulting from the ease of programming, debugging, tuning and the relative ease of OpenMP skill acquisition.

Keywords: OpenMP, Multithreading, Threads, OdinMP/CCp

1.   Introduction

A thread is a unit of execution within a process. A process typically would have a number of threads running within it. These threads share the same execution environment, including memory. In a uniprocessor system, multithreading provides an illusion of concurrency. On a multiprocessor system however, multithreading does provide true concurrency, with threads running on different process simultaneously. In either case, there are advantages that can be derived from it. For instance, in a multiprocessor system, multithreading makes it easy to better utilize the available processors. In a uniprocessor machine, multithreading makes it possible to maximize the use of the processor: input/output (I/O) operations that might block waiting for a device, do so on a thread while active threads keep running on the processor. Writing multithreaded programs have often been done by means of calls to a thread library.

Multithreaded programming by directly making calls to routines of a thread library such as the POSIX thread library is inherently difficult. This difficulty has been attributed to various reasons. The programmer has to explicitly handle thread synchronization and deadlock prevention in the code. Debugging a non-trivial multithreaded program is a difficult and time consuming task. Threads break abstraction and modularity. Callbacks can lead to deadlocks when used along with locks [8].

Ousterhout [8] has suggested events as an alternative to threads. In an event-driven system, a number of small programs called event handlers are called in response to external events. There is typically a dispatcher that invokes the event handlers, often using an event queue to hold events that are still to be processed. If an events blocks during processing, the next event in the event queue is handled. Event handlersThus, in a sense, events can achieve some of the goals of threads, such as high responsiveness of applications to the user and better utilization of machine processors. Nonetheless, events can not really replace threads, as there are still situations where only threads are needed, such as when concurrency is required.

The objective of this work is to show that we can have the best of both worlds: Concurrency at the cost of easy programming. This is achieved by writing OpenMP codes and compiling with an OpenMP compliant compiler, specifically, we have used the freely available OdinMP/CCp, developed at Lund University [3]. While OpenMP is primarily targeted at multiprocessor machines, we have shown here that even on single processor machines, the drop in performance is negligible.

OpenMP is a specification that defines a set of compiler directives and callable runtime library routines that extend a base language (FORTRAN, or C/C++) to express shared memory parallelism. When OpenMP directives are added to sequentially written code, an OpenMP compliant compiler like OdinMP/CCp parallelizes the code using a fork and join model. In the fork and join model, a program starts as a single thread of execution then splits into multiple threads at certain points during execution only to recombine again as illustrated in Figure 1.1.

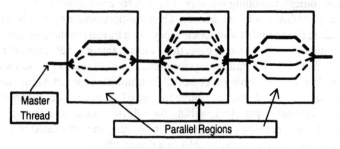

Figure 1.1.   Fork and Join Model.

The rest of this chapter is organized as follows: Section 2 gives a short introduction to OpenMP, a word on the OdinMP/CCp compiler and POSIX threads library, and discusses some related work. Section 3 describes the performance study we have done, and Section 4 concludes the chapter with some pointers towards areas of further work in a subsequent study.

2.   Background

This section provides background information on the technologies relevant to our study. Section 2.1 describes OpenMP. Section 2.2 discusses the open-source OdinMp/CC compiler. Section 2.3 overviews POSIX threads, while Section 2.4 gives some related work.

2.1   OpenMP

OpenMP [3] is a specification of a standardized set of compiler directives, which a programmer can add to the source code of an existing program, written with sequential execution in mind. The OpenMP directives allow the compiler to parallelize the code in question according to those directives, for execution on a shared-memory multiprocessor system. The OpenMP specification also includes library routines for accessing and modifying some of the execution parameters in the running program, such as the number of threads to be used [7]. Figure 1.2, taken from [9], sums it all up.

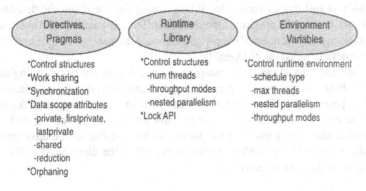

Figure 1.2.   Overview of OpenMP taken from [9]

Prior to the introduction of OpenMP, there was no standard way to easily parallelize a program for use on a shared-memory multiprocessor system. While a well-entrenched standard existed for message passing, programmers who wanted to use shared-memory systems had to either use non-standard, non-portable APIs or write cumbersome code for an underlying low-level multiprocessing API, such as POSIX threads. Such programs are often excellently portable, but in the process the programmers' attention and efforts are diverted from solving the main problem, to tending to the details of making the solution multiprocessing-capable. With OpenMP, however, the programmer focuses on solving the real problems at hand and the details of parallezing his programs reduces to merely adding a small set of directives and API calls to his program [7].

OpenMP is a widely accepted industry standard. Programmers developing to the OpenMP specification can expect their programs to be portable to a wide variety of different shared-memory multiprocessing systems, and makers of shared-memory multiprocessing systems have a well-defined API which, if they support it, makes their systems immediately viable for most of their prospective clients.

OpenMP is non-invasive - it does not force the programmer to radically change their programming style. Programs can be written for correct sequential execution first, and OpenMP directives and constructs can be added later, without influencing the execution of the program in the sequential case. Thus, programmers can separate the work they do on solving the actual problem from the work to parallelize the solution.

OpenMP defines a user-guided parallelization process. This means that the compiler does not have to perform vast analysis of the code, it can and should rely only on the information in user-supplied directives when parallelizing the code. This gives the user complete control over what should be parallelized and how, while at the same time making the compiler much less complex.

OpenMP is sufficiently complete. While freeing the user from the detailed labor of parallelizing the program, OpenMP still offers sufficient control over the parallelization and execution of the program, should the user have requirements above the default behavior of OpenMP.

OpenMP uses the #pragma C compiler extension mechanism, defining an OpenMP directive to have the form '#pragma omp directive-name [clause[clause] ...] new-line'. Each directive starts with #pragma omp, in order to reduce the risk for conflict with other pragma directives. Following that is the directive name (only one directive name can be specified in one directive), optionally followed by a number of clauses that affect the directive. Finally, a new-line concludes the directive [3].

2.2   OdinMP/CCp

OdinMP is a project at the Department of Information Technology at Lund Institute of Technology, with the goal of producing a set of freely available, portable implementations of the OpenMP standard for a variety of platforms. OdinMP/CCp is one of these implementations, implementing the OpenMP specification for the ANSI C programming language, producing code in C using the POSIX thread library, generally known as 'pthreads', as the underlying threading mechanism. The suffix 'CCp' is an acronym of 'from C to C with pthreads' [3].

OdinMP/CCp has the big advantage of being quite portable and platform-independent. All it requires of its target platform is that the POSIX threads library be available, which these days is more the rule than the exception for Unix-derived systems, as well as becoming more and more commonplace in other computing environments. Thus, a program written with OpenMP can be compiled and used on such systems, using OdinMP/CCp, even if no platform-specific OpenMP implementation is available.

OdinMP/CCp can also be used in development of a platform-specific Open-MP compiler, both for comparisons regarding execution, and as a prototype, since it is available with full source code.

One very simple example of where one might use OdinMP/CCp would be a home-built multiprocessor PC running Linux™. No OpenMP-capable C compiler is available for this platform, but Linux has good support for POSIX threads.

Likewise, an experimental multiprocessing system or one in development may have good use for an existing OpenMP implementation for evaluation or development purposes.

OdinMP/CCp can also be used to perform compiler-neutral performance comparisons between different platforms.

2.3   POSIX threads

The Solaris operating system contains kernel support for multiple threads within a single process address space. One of the goals of the Solaris Pthreads implementation is to make the threads sufficiently lightweight so that thousands of them can be present within a process. The threads are therefore implemented by a user-level threads library so that common thread operations such as creation, destruction, synchronization and context switching can be performed efficiently without entering the kernel.

Lightweight, user-level Pthreads on Solaris are multiplexed on top of kernel-supported threads called lightweight processes (LWPs). The assignment of the lightweight threads to LWPs is controlled by the user-level Pthreads scheduler. A thread may be either bound to an LWP (to schedule it on a system-wide basis) or may be multiplexed along with other unbound threads of the process on top of one or more LWPs. LWPs are scheduled by the kernel onto the available CPUs according to their scheduling class and priority, and may run in parallel on a multiprocessor.

2.4   Related work

OdinMP/CCp performance has been measured and compared to other implementations of the OpenMP standard for C/C++. However, these measurements were done on multiprocessor machines [3]. Also, the Solaris Pthread implementation has been profiled and its performance has been measured and compared against other thread libraries [5].

It is also interesting to note that OpenMP is being implemented over software distributed memory systems, such as TreadMarks [4] and an OpenMP Java language mapping is also being developed [2].

3.   Performance Studies

A program to multiply two square matrices and then store the result in a third one is prepared first as a sequential program. This is run with matrix sizes ranging from 100x100 to 600x600. Another version of the same program is prepared by adding OpenMP directives, to parallelize the loops (see source listing in the Appendix). The environment variable OMP_NUM_THREAD is set to 2 and then the OpenMP annotated version of the program is compiled using OdinMP/CC for matrix sizes ranging from 100x100 to 600x600 as done for the sequential version. The program is written to log the run times into a text file. Next, we repeat this for each value of each number of threads from 3 to 7. The resulting execution times and speedups are shown in tabular form in Tables 1.1 and 1.2 and in graphical form in Figures 1.3 and 1.4.

Table 1.1.   Execution Times

Matrix Size	Seq cc	Par cc 2	Par cc 3	Par cc 4	Par cc 5	Par cc 6	Par cc 7
200x200	4	6	6	6	6	6	6
250x250	9	12	12	12	12	12	12
300x300	17	22	22	22	22	22	23
350x350	30	37	37	37	37	37	38
400x400	44	54	54	54	54	56	57
450x450	66	82	82	82	82	84	83
500x500	88	109	109	109	108	111	111
550x550	125	153	153	153	153	156	156
600x600	164	201	201	202	200	210	205

Table 1.1 above shows gradual drop in performance as the number of threads are increased from two to seven relative to the single threaded version. This is to be expected because of the added thread management overheads. The drop in performance is shown again in Table 1.2 in terms of speedup. Speedup of a parallel algorithm is defined as the ratio of the execution time of the best known sequential algorithm for a problem to that of the parallel algorithm [1].

These runs were made on a Sun Workstation with a single 333MHz Sparc processor, 128 MB RAM and running SunOS 5.7 on a general-purpose network. Several runs were made and the average runtimes were taken. The algorithm is executed with higher number of threads ranging from 200 through 600.

Surprisingly, some speedups were recorded for large number of threads (200 threads and higher) in spite of the fact that the program profiled is a processor intensive one, as shown in 1.5 and 1.3. One would have expected that the se-

Table 1.2. Speedups.

Matrix Size	Seq cc	Par cc 2	Par cc 3	Par cc 4	Par cc 5	Par cc 6	Par cc 7
200x200	1.000	0.667	0.667	0.667	0.667	0.667	0.667
250x250	1.000	0.750	0.750	0.750	0.750	0.750	0.750
300x300	1.000	0.773	0.773	0.773	0.773	0.773	0.739
350x350	1.000	0.811	0.811	0.811	0.811	0.811	0.789
400x400	1.000	0.815	0.815	0.815	0.815	0.786	0.772
450x450	1.000	0.805	0.805	0.805	0.805	0.786	0.795
500x500	1.000	0.807	0.807	0.807	0.815	0.793	0.793
550x550	1.000	0.817	0.817	0.817	0.817	0.801	0.801
600x600	1.000	0.816	0.816	0.812	0.820	0.781	0.800
Ave.	1.000	0.784	0.784	0.784	0.786	0.772	0.767

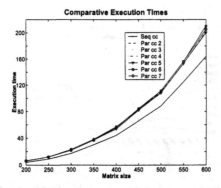

Figure 1.3. Comparative execution times with different number of threads, matrix sizes and C/C++ compilers.

quential version, which doesn't have any thread management overhead, would outperform the multithreaded version. This result can be explained by noting that the thread implementation in Solaris 2.x (SunOS 5.x) is a hybrid implementation in the sense that the kernel schedules LWPs (lightweight processes a.k.a. kernel threads), and the user-level thread library schedules threads onto LWPs. This means that since the kernel is aware of the LWPs, the multithreaded version of the program receives more processor cycles than the single-threaded version. Also, the fact that for small matrix sizes there was little difference in the run times for different number of threads, suggests that the overhead due to thread management is significantly low. Thus, the greater the number of threads, the greater the number of LWPs and thus the more the processor cycles that the multithreaded program receives.

It is yet unclear whether these unexpected speedups are peculiar to the Solaris operating system. Further experimentation on other operating systems will be

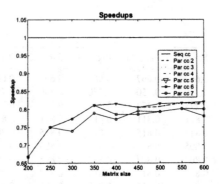

Figure 1.4.   Speedups for different number of threads and matrix sizes.

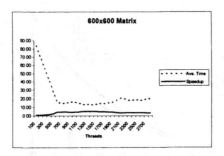

Figure 1.5.   Average running times and Speedups for a fixed matrix size.

needed to ascertain that. However, our basic premise is that where there is a drop in performance as in the case of a small number of threads discussed previously, the drop tends to be minimal. And for many applications, which are less processor-intensive, such as I/O intensive applications, speedups are possible.

4.   Conclusion and Further Work

We would want to conduct these experiments on a dedicated machine, so as to minimize the effect of other processes running on the machine. We would also want to profile more programs, with varying memory usage patterns, inter thread communication patterns, recursive programs, etc. This way we would better be able to characterize the behavior of the OdinMP/CC generated multithreaded programs. It would also be interesting to conduct similar readings on platforms other than Solaris. Further, we would also want to conduct similar performance studies on other OpenMP-compliant compilers in a future study.

Table 1.3. Readings for 600x600 Matrix.

Threads	Ave. Time	Speedup
1	72.00	1.00
100	84.00	0.86
200	70.00	1.03
300	56.25	1.28
400	42.75	1.68
500	28.17	2.56
600	15.80	4.56
700	15.25	4.72
800	15.00	4.80
900	16.57	4.34
1000	16.25	4.43
1100	15.44	4.66
1200	13.40	5.37
1300	13.78	5.23
1400	13.25	5.43
1500	13.50	5.33
1600	14.83	4.85
1700	14.60	4.93
1800	15.50	4.65
1900	16.00	4.50
2000	18.33	3.93
2100	21.00	3.43
2200	19.67	3.66
2300	18.00	4.00
2400	18.67	3.86
2500	19.00	3.79
2600	18.00	4.00
2700	20.00	3.60
2800	20.5	3.51

Acknowledgments

The authors wish to thank the Information & Computer Science Department at King Fahd University of Petroleum & for their support. The anonymous reviewers are also acknowledged for the valuable comments they proffered in improving this quality of this chapter. The authors will also want to Rob Neely for his comments on an earlier draft of this chapter.

References

[1] S.G. Akl, *Parallel Computation: Models and Methods* (Prentice-Hall, Englewood Cliffs, New Jersey, 1997).

[2] J. M. Bull and M. E. Kambites, JOMP - an OpenMP-like Interface for Java, Edinburgh Parallel Computing Center, UK, 1999.

[3] C. Brunschen, "OdinMP/CCp - A Portable Compiler for C with OpenMP to C with POSIX Threads", MSc Thesis, Dept of Info. Tech., Lund University, Sweden, 1999.

[4] H. Lu, Y C Hu and W Zwaenepoel, OpenMP on Networks of Computers, in *Proc. Super-computing '98: High Performance Networking and Computing*, November 1998.

[5] G. Narlikar and G. Blelloch, Pthreads for Dynamic and Irregular Parallelism, in *Proc. Supercomputing '98: High Performance Networking and Computing*, November 1998.

[6] The OpenMP ARB, "OpenMP: A Proposed Industry Standard SPI for Shared Memory Programming", Oct. 1997. http://www.openmp.org/specs/mp-documents/paper/paper.html.

[7] The OpenMP ARB, "OpenMP C and C++ Application Program Interface", Oct. 1998. http://www.openmp.org/specs/mp-documents/cspec.pdf.

[8] J. K. Ousterhout, Why threads are a bad idea (for most purposes). Invited talk at the 1996 USENIX Conference, 1996.

[9] K. V. Rao, Open MP Tutorial, A presentation given at Alliance 98, 1998.

Appendix: Source Listing

```
1.  #define MATRIXDIM 600
2.  #include <time.h>
3.  #include <sys/types.h>
4.  #include <stdlib.h>
5.  #include <stdio.h>
6.
7.  #ifdef _OPENMP
8.     #include "omp.h"
9.  #endif
10.
11. typedef struct matrix
12. {
13.   int dim1, dim2;
14.   int elements[MATRIXDIM][MATRIXDIM];
15. } matrixType;
16.
17. int mult(matrixType, matrixType, matrixType*);
18. void init(matrixType *m, int val);
19. void print(matrixType);
20. void parallelMult(matrixType *, matrixType*, matrixType*);
21.
22.
23. int main()
24. {
25. time_t startt, endt;
26. matrixType A = {MATRIXDIM, MATRIXDIM};
27. matrixType B = {MATRIXDIM, MATRIXDIM};
28. matrixType C = {MATRIXDIM, MATRIXDIM};
29. FILE * fp;
30. char * strstart = (char *)malloc(27);
31. char * strend = (char *)malloc(27);
32. int numthreads = 1, i;
33.
34. fp = fopen("outputfile.txt", "a");
```

```
35.
36.
37. for(i = 100; i < 2001; i += 500){
38.    #ifdef _OPENMP
39.        omp_set_num_threads(i);
40.        numthreads = omp_get_max_threads();
41.    #endif
42.
43.    startt = time(0);
44.
45.    parallelMult(&A, &B, &C);
46.
47.    endt = time(0);
48.    ctime_r(&startt, strstart, 26);
49.    ctime_r(&endt, strend, 26);
50.
51.    #ifdef _OPENMP
52.        fprintf(fp, "OpenMP Version with %d threads\n", numthreads);
53.     fflush(fp);
54.    #endif
55.
56.    fprintf(fp, "Start: %s \n End: %s\n", strstart, strend);
57.    fprintf(fp, "Time Taken to multiply 2 %d x %d matrices: %ld\n",
58.        MATRIXDIM, MATRIXDIM, (long)(endt - startt));
59.
60.    fflush(fp);
61.    #ifdef _OPENMP
62.        printf("OpenMP Version with %d threads\n", numthreads);
63.    #endif
64.
65.    printf("Start: %s \n End: %s\n", strstart, strend);
66.    printf("Time Taken to multiply 2 %d x %d matrices: %ld\n",
67.        MATRIXDIM, MATRIXDIM, (long)(endt - startt));
68.    fflush(fp);
69.
70. }
71. fclose(fp);
72. free(strend); free(strstart);
73. return 0;
74. }
75.
76. void parallelMult(matrixType * A, matrixType* B, matrixType* C){
77.    init(A, 1);
78.    init(B, 1);
79.    init(C, 2);
80.    mult(*A, *B, C);
81. }
82.
83.
84. void print(matrixType m)
85. {
86.    int i, j;
```

```
87. /*    printf("dim1 = %d, dim2 = %d", m.dim1, m.dim2);*/
88.    for(i = 0; i < m.dim1; i++)
89.    {
90.     for(j = 0; j < m.dim2; j++)
91.        printf(" \t %d ", m.elements[i][j]);
92.          printf("\n");
93.    }
94. }
95.
96. int mult(matrixType A, matrixType B, matrixType *C)
97. {
98.    int i,j,k;
99. #pragma omp parallel for
100.      for(i=0; i < C->dim1; i++)
101.       for(j=0; j < C->dim2; j++)
102.       C->elements[i][j] = 0;
103.
104.      if(A.dim2 == B.dim1)
105.      {
106.         /*matrices can be multiplied together*/
107.         /*initialise product matrix C*/
108.    #pragma omp parallel for
109.         for(i = 0; i < C->dim1; i++)
110.         for(j = 0; j < C->dim2; j++)
111.          for(k = 0; k < A.dim2; k++)
112.            C->elements[i][j]+= A.elements[i][k]*B.elements[k][j];
113.          return 0;
114.      }
115.      else
116.      {
117.         /*return error: matrices cannot be multiplied together*/
118.         return 1;
119.      }
120.    }
121.
122.    void init(matrixType *m, int value)
123.    {
124.        int i,j;
125.    #pragma omp parallel for
126.        for(i=0; i < m->dim1; i++)
127.          for(j=0; j < m->dim2; j++)
128.          m->elements[i][j] = value;
129.    }
```

Chapter 2

LINEAR DATA DISTRIBUTION BASED ON INDEX ANALYSIS

Minyi Guo

Department of Computer Software
The University of Aizu, Aizu-wakamatsu, Fukushima 965-8580, Japan
minyi@u-aizu.ac.jp

Abstract In this chapter, we propose a linear data distribution technique, which extends the traditional BLOCK or CYCLIC distribution for intra-dimension as in HPF, to permit partitioning the array elements along slant lines. The array distribution patterns are determined by analyzing the array subscript references in loop nests. If the data are distributed along the slant lines, then we show the conversion algorithm between global address and local address, and the conversion algorithm from global iteration space to local iteration space.

Keywords: Parallelizing compiler, Data distribution, Distributed memory multicomputer, Index analysis, Loop optimization

1.   Introduction

Distributed-memory multicomputers offer significant advantages over shared-memory multiprocessors in terms of both cost and scalability. Unfortunately, extracting all of the computational power from these machines requires users to write efficient software for them, which is a laborious process. One major reason for this difficulty is the absence of a global address space. As a result, the programmer has to manually distribute computations and data across processors and manage communication explicitly.

A data distribution is a mapping of array elements onto the local memories of a distributed- memory machine. A compiler uses this mapping to partition the arrays across the local memories of the distributed-memory machine and to generate message-passing code based on the array partitioning. Generally, distributing an array onto the local memories is done by a two-step process consisting of **alignment** followed by **distribution**. In the alignment phase, array elements are mapped to a template, which is an abstract multi-dimensional grid;

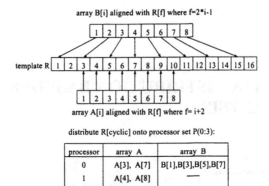

Figure 2.1.   Example of the array alignment and distribution steps

this allows one to relate members of different arrays, and specify replication if needed. The alignment is typically a function of the data access patterns in the program.

2.   Overview of Data Distribution

The distribution phase of the data mapping problem can be defined as the phase where the abstract template, and thus all the array aligned to it, are mapped onto the physical processors (see Figure 2.1). Distribution phase can be subdivided into static distribution and dynamic distribution.

The most commonly used distributions, which are the only ones currently available in the High Performance Fortran (HPF), are the cyclic, cyclic(size), block, and block (size) distributions, where size is a parameter which specifies the number of consecutive data items from a template to be assigned to a processor (see Figure 2.2). The cyclic distribution assigns one element to each processor in turn(the first element to the first processor and the second element to the second processor, etc.) until all the processors assigned to that dimension of the template are exhausted, and continues the same process from the next element until all the elements on that dimension of the template are assigned. This distribution is of special importance when load balancing needs to be achieved in the presence of iteration spaces where the lower or upper bound of an iteration variable is a function of an outer iteration variable, e.g., triangular iteration spaces. On the other hand, this type of distribution is not the best choice when there is a lot of nearest neighbor communication among processors, in which case a block distribution would be preferred [13]. The cyclic (size) distribution provides the programmer with the ability of specifying the number of elements which the compiler should assign as a unit to each processor in a cyclic manner. Thus, cyclic(1) produce the same effect as cyclic.

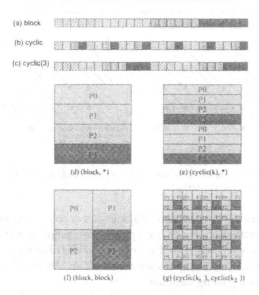

Figure 2.2.   Some schemes of the regular array distribution

The block distribution assigns n consecutive elements to each processor where $n = \lceil size\ of\ the\ array/number\ of\ processors \rceil$, for that dimension. Finally, the block(size) distribution assigns a programmer's specified number of elements to each processor. Examples are given in Figure 2.2. Note that both the block and the block(size) distribution can also be obtained from the cyclic(size) distributions. Block distribution are especially suited for rectangular iteration space and nearest neighbor (shift or offset) communication [13].

3.   Motivation

The traditional data distribution pattern used in most of the data-parallel languages is restricted to a method where arrays are distributed along intra-dimension with BLOCK or CYCLIC. However for some scientific applications, such a distribution fashion cannot guarantee the minimization of communication overhead.

Example 1 *Consider the following loop nest* L_1:

---

do $i = 1, n_1$
    do $j = 1, n_2$
        $A(i, j) = F(A(i + 1, j - 1), B(i + 1, j + 1))$ L_1
    enddo
enddo

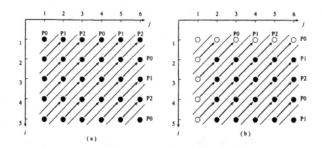

Figure 2.3. Communication-free data distribution for array A,B in loop L_1, the number of processors p=3. (a) Array A. (b) Array B

no matter how the array A is distributed along rows or columns over processors, the data communication among physical processors cannot be avoided when the SPMD program is executed. But if we extend the distribution pattern as anti-diagonal (Figure 2.3), no communication will occur. We call this distribution pattern as partitioning along slant lines.

Linear distribution is a more general class of distribution from which row, column, diagonal, parallelogram, etc., distributions could be derived. Both row and column distributions are one-dimensional distributions which can be obtained by skewing one dimension by a factor of zero with respect to another dimension. This factor has a non-zero value for diagonal distributions.

For this proposal, we suppose that, distributions of array elements over processors are not limited along intra-dimension, i.e. rows or/and columns. They can extend to inter-dimension, we call them linear data distributions. In other words, the array elements partitioned onto a certain processor satisfy linear equation $ai + bj = c_l$, where a, b and c_l are constants and i, j are array subscripts. For example, in Figure 2.3(a), $a = 1, b = 1$, and $c_l = 4, 7, 10, \ldots$ for the processor P_2.

4.   Linear Data Distribution

In the following discussion, we assume that array size is denoted as $n_1 \times n_2$ and the subscript starts from 1 while processors are numbered starting from 0.

4.1   Definition of linear distribution

Definition 1 *Let $P = \{P_0, P_1, \ldots, P_p\}$ be a virtual processor set, p is the number of processors. Each P_k also has a set whose elements are all data to be distributed over it. For linear distribution, given the values of constant a and b, an array A distributed onto virtual processor P_k can be represented as*

$$A_k = \{A(i,j) | ai + bj = c_l^k, 1 \leq l \leq L\}$$

where L is the number of linear lines distributed onto P_k.   ■

Example 2 *For loop nest appeared in Example 1, the communication-free data distribution is*

$$
\begin{aligned}
A_k &= \{A(i,j) | i + j = c_A^k, c_A^k = 2 + k + (l-1) * p, \\
    &\quad\ 1 \le l \le L \wedge (1,1) \le (i,j) \le (n_1, n_2)\} \\
B_k &= \{B(i,j) | i + j = c_B^k, c_B^k = c_A^k + 2, \\
    &\quad\ (2,2) \le (i,j) \le (n_1, n_2)\}
\end{aligned}
$$

Obviously, the traditional distribution such as BLOCK,CYCLIC can also be represented by linear distribution. For instance, (BLOCK,*) distribution can be expressed as

$$
A_k = \{A(i,j) | i = c \wedge k * B + 1 \le c \le (k+1) * B\}
$$

where B is the block size.
(*,CYCLIC) distribution can be expressed as

$$
A_k = \{A(i,j) | j = c \wedge c = l * p + k + 1 \wedge 0 \le l < L\}
$$

where

$$
L = \begin{cases} \lfloor \frac{n_2}{p} \rfloor, & k \ge (n_2 \bmod p) \\ \lfloor \frac{n_2}{p} \rfloor + 1, & k < (n_2 \bmod p) \end{cases}
$$

■

4.2   Distribution analysis

We distinguish two types of array references according to whether an array appears both on the left hand side and the right hand side of the loop body(refer to as the lhs and the rhs arrays respectively) or not. If an array is not only assigned its value(appearing as the lhs array), but also used as an operand (appearing as the rhs array), data dependence(flow or anti dependence) will occur in this loop. If a set of array elements which possess the dependence relation each other is partitioned on the same processor, communication among processors is not required. This and the next subsection describe how to compute the coefficients a and b, based on an analysis of two types of array references. We call these the *distribution analysis* and the *alignment analysis* respectively.

For an array appearing in a loop which has loop-carried dependence, we denote the existence of the dependence relations between $A(i_1, j_1)$ and $A(i_2, j_2)$ in the loop as follows:

---

do $i = 1, n_1$
    do $j = 1, n_2$
        $\delta(A(i_1,j_1), A(i_2,j_2))$ L_2
    enddo
enddo

where i_1, j_1, i_2, j_2 are linear function of i and j, respectively, i.e.,

$$i_1 = \alpha_{10} + \alpha_{11}i + \alpha_{12}j \tag{2.1}$$

$$j_1 = \alpha_{20} + \alpha_{21}i + \alpha_{22}j \tag{2.2}$$

$$i_2 = \beta_{10} + \beta_{11}i + \beta_{12}j \tag{2.3}$$

$$j_2 = \beta_{20} + \beta_{21}i + \beta_{22}j \tag{2.4}$$

We assume that the array A can be partitioned along

$$ai + bj = c \tag{2.5}$$

In order to eliminate the communication, the lhs array element and the rhs array element referred in a loop iteration (i, j) should be partitioned onto the same processor, which is satisfied if

$$ai_1 + bj_1 = c, \quad ai_2 + bj_2 = c'$$

where c and c' are constants assigned for the same processor. If we assign $c = c'$ then

$$ai_1 + bj_1 = ai_2 + bj_2 \tag{2.6}$$

should be true. Since i_1, j_1, i_2, and j_2 are given by (2.1), (2.2), (2.3), and (2.4), applying them to (2.6) we have

$$a(\alpha_{10} + \alpha_{11}i + \alpha_{12}j) + b(\alpha_{20} + \alpha_{21}i + \alpha_{22}j) =$$

$$a(\beta_{10} + \beta_{11}i + \beta_{12}j) + b(\beta_{20} + \beta_{21}i + \beta_{22}j)$$

which implies,

$$a\alpha_{10} + b\alpha_{20} = a\beta_{10} + b\beta_{20}$$

$$a\alpha_{11} + b\alpha_{21} = a\beta_{11} + b\beta_{21}$$

$$a\alpha_{12} + b\alpha_{22} = a\beta_{12} + b\beta_{22}$$

In matrix notation, we have,

$$\begin{pmatrix} \alpha_{10} & \alpha_{20} \\ \alpha_{11} & \alpha_{21} \\ \alpha_{12} & \alpha_{22} \end{pmatrix} \begin{pmatrix} a \\ b \end{pmatrix} = \begin{pmatrix} \beta_{10} & \beta_{20} \\ \beta_{11} & \beta_{21} \\ \beta_{12} & \beta_{22} \end{pmatrix} \begin{pmatrix} a \\ b \end{pmatrix}$$

Let

$$\alpha = \begin{pmatrix} \alpha_{10} & \alpha_{20} \\ \alpha_{11} & \alpha_{21} \\ \alpha_{12} & \alpha_{22} \end{pmatrix} \quad \beta = \begin{pmatrix} \beta_{10} & \beta_{20} \\ \beta_{11} & \beta_{21} \\ \beta_{12} & \beta_{22} \end{pmatrix}$$

and

$$\mathbf{a} = \begin{pmatrix} a \\ b \end{pmatrix}$$

Then the above system of equations can be abbreviated as

$$(\alpha - \beta)\mathbf{a} = \mathbf{0} \tag{2.7}$$

A nontrivial solution $\mathbf{a}$(at most one of a and b is zero) that satisfies (2.7) would imply zero communication. Such a linear distribution is known as a *nontrivial distribution*. We illustrate the use of the above sufficient conditions with the following examples.

Example 3 *Reconsider the loop L_1 in Example 1. For array A referred to in L_1, we obtain the following using the subscript reference analysis,*

$$\begin{pmatrix} -1 & 1 \\ 0 & 0 \\ 0 & 0 \end{pmatrix} \begin{pmatrix} a \\ b \end{pmatrix} = \mathbf{0}$$

which implies,

$$a = b$$

We select $a = 1, b = 1$ as a solution. This implies that A should be partitioned by anti-diagonals to achieve communication-free parallel execution, as shown in Figure 2.3(a). ∎

Example 4 *Consider a more complicated nested loop L_3*

---

do $i = 1, n_1$
    do $j = 1, n_2$
        $\delta(A(2i + j + 1, 3i), A(2j, i + j - 1))$ L_3
    enddo
enddo

For array A in L_3, we have

$$\alpha = \begin{pmatrix} 1 & 0 \\ 2 & 3 \\ 1 & 0 \end{pmatrix} \quad \beta = \begin{pmatrix} 0 & -1 \\ 0 & 1 \\ 2 & 1 \end{pmatrix}$$

applying them to (2.7), we have,

$$\begin{pmatrix} 1 & 1 \\ 2 & 2 \\ -1 & -1 \end{pmatrix} \begin{pmatrix} a \\ b \end{pmatrix} = \mathbf{0}$$

that is

$$a = -b$$

We select $a = -1$ and $b = 1$ as a solution. This shows that the diagonal partition of A is nontrivial distribution. ∎

It is possible that there only exists trivial solution for $\mathbf{a}$($a = 0$ and $b = 0$), which implies that there is no communication-free partition for A in this loop. We do not illustrate such instance due to limited paper space.

4.3   Alignment analysis

For a loop in which the assignment to array A uses values of array B, to ensure that the data elements are read in a statement residing on the same processor as the one whose data element is being written onto, the alignment between distributions of A and B must be specified. In the alignment analysis, although we can not determine how to distribute A and B onto the processors but we can specify the relationship of which elements of A and B get distributed on the same processor.

In this subsection, we will deal with the loop such as

---

do $i = 1, n_1$
    do $j = 1, n_2$
        $A(i_1, j_1) = F(B(i_2, j_2))$ L_4
    enddo
enddo

---

where $i_1, j_1, i_2,$ and j_2 are of the same functions as in Section 3.2. Similar to the distribution analysis, we specify that the arrays A and B are distributed along

$$a_1 i_1 + b_1 j_1 = c_1$$

and

$$a_2 i_2 + b_2 j_2 = c_2$$

respectively. Because the relation of elements of A and B is an alignment relation, we need not limit that they have the same value of c when A and B are distributed along the above formulas. After analyzing the subscript references for A and B similarly to Section 3.2, we should find a solution for the following system of equations to achieve communication-free partitioning:

$$\begin{pmatrix} -\alpha_{10} & -\alpha_{20} & 1 \\ \alpha_{11} & \alpha_{21} & 0 \\ \alpha_{12} & \alpha_{22} & 0 \end{pmatrix} \begin{pmatrix} a_1 \\ b_1 \\ c_1 \end{pmatrix} = \begin{pmatrix} -\beta_{10} & -\beta_{20} & 1 \\ \beta_{11} & \beta_{21} & 0 \\ \beta_{12} & \beta_{22} & 0 \end{pmatrix} \begin{pmatrix} a_2 \\ b_2 \\ c_2 \end{pmatrix}$$

Notice that there may be an infinite number of solutions, we are interested in the relationship between a_1, b_1, c_1 and a_2, b_2, c_2. Consider the loop in Example 5.

Example 5 *Compute the alignment relations of A and B in the following loop nest.*

---

do $i = 1, n_1$
    do $j = 1, n_2$
        $A(i + j, i) = F(B(i - 1, j))$ L_5
    enddo
enddo

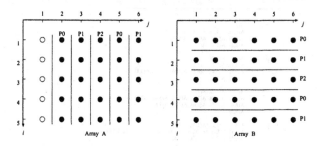

Figure 2.4. Communication-free data distribution for solution (1) of Loop L_5.

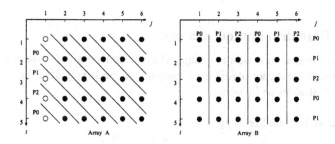

Figure 2.5. Communication-free data distribution for solution (2) of Loop L_5.

Communication-free partitioning is possible if the system of equations

$$\begin{pmatrix} 0 & 0 & 1 \\ 1 & 1 & 0 \\ 1 & 0 & 0 \end{pmatrix} \begin{pmatrix} a_1 \\ b_1 \\ c_1 \end{pmatrix} = \begin{pmatrix} 1 & 0 & 1 \\ 1 & 0 & 0 \\ 0 & 1 & 0 \end{pmatrix} \begin{pmatrix} a_2 \\ b_2 \\ c_2 \end{pmatrix}$$

has a nontrivial solution. The system of equations are reduced to the following set of equations:

$$a_2 = a_1 + b_1$$

$$b_2 = a_1$$

$$c_1 = c_2 + a_2$$

which has a solution (1) $a_1 = 0, b_1 = 1, a_2 = 1$, and $b_2 = 0$. This means that A is partitioned into columns and B is partitioned into rows (Figure 2.4). We also can select solution (2) $a_1 = 1, b_1 = -1, a_2 = 0$, and $b_2 = 1$, which implies that A is partitioned into diagonals and B is partitioned into columns (Figure 2.5). ∎

In practice, the type of partition selected will be determined through the distribution analysis of A(or B).

P0 :   A(1,1)
       A(5,1), A(4,2), A(3,3), A(2,4), A(1,5)
       A(8,2), A(7,3), A(6,4), A(5,5), A(4,6), A(3,7), A(2,8)
       A(8,6), A(7,7), A(6,8)

P1 :   A(2,1), A(1,2)
       A(6,1), A(5,2), A(4,3), A(3,4), A(2,5), A(1,6)
       A(8,3), A(7,4), A(6,5), A(5,6), A(4,7), A(3,8)
       A(8,7), A(7,8)

P2 :   A(3,1), A(2,2), A(1,3)
       A(7,1), A(6,2), A(5,3), A(4,4), A(3,5), A(2,6), A(1,7)
       A(8,4), A(7,5), A(6,6), A(5,7), A(4,8)
       A(8,8)

P3 :   A(4,1), A(3,2), A(2,3), A(1,4)
       A(8,1), A(7,2), A(6,3), A(5,4), A(4,5), A(3,6), A(2,7), A(1,8)
       A(8,5), A(7,6), A(6,7), A(5,8)

Figure 2.6. Array A's elements distributed to each processor for loop L_1, where A(8,8) and p=4.

4.4   Data distribution strategy

For our linear distribution technique, if coefficients a and b have been obtained through the subscript reference analysis, we can simply describe the data distribution strategy as follows:

Data Distribution Strategy

Say n arrays are used in a loop. For $i = 1, 2, \ldots, n$

(1) If $a_i = 0 \land b_i \neq 0$, select (*,BLOCK) or (*,CYCLIC). Practically, which of these two schemes is determined by other factors of the loop nest. For instance, if the bound of the inner-loop is the function of the index of outer-loop, selecting (*, CYCLIC) can achieve a good load balance. The same reasons are valid for (2).

(2) If $a_i \neq 0 \land b_i = 0$, select (BLOCK,*) or (CYCLIC,*).

(3) If $a_i \neq 0 \land b_i \neq 0$, select the linear distribution (a_i, b_i).

(4) If $a_i = 0 \land b_i = 0$, it only has *trivial distribution solution*. The good distribution scheme is determined by other factors of the loop nest.

(5) check the alignment relationship $[(a_i, b_i), (a_j, b_j)]$ so that no conflict occurs.

5.   Index Conversion and Iteration Space Conversion

For the traditional regular BLOCK/CYCLIC distributions, there exists a set of direct algebraic formula for conversion between local and global indices. But if linear distribution is selected, no such algebraic formula can be applied when parallelizing compiler generates SPMD programs. Therefore we should consider the index conversion algorithm between local and global and we also implement the conversion algorithm from global iteration space to local iteration space.

Let us first consider the distribution method from a global array to local arrays. With respect to the traditional regular distribution, the local array spaces

P0 : A'= A(1,1) A(5,1), A(4,2), A(3,3), A(2,4), A(1,5), A(8,2), A(7,3),
          A(6,4), A(5,5), A(4,6), A(3,7), A(2,8), A(8,6), A(7,7), A(6,8)
     bound[3] = { 1, 2, 7, 14}

P1 : A'= A(2,1), A(1,2), A(6,1), A(5,2), A(4,3), A(3,4), A(2,5), A(1,6),
          A(8,3), A(7,4), A(6,5), A(5,6), A(4,7), A(3,8), A(8,7), A(7,8)
     bound[3] = { 1, 3, 9, 15}

P2 : A'= A(3,1), A(2,2), A(1,3), A(7,1), A(6,2), A(5,3), A(4,4), A(3,5),
          A(2,6), A(1,7), A(8,4), A(7,5), A(6,6), A(5,7), A(4,8), A(8,8)
     bound[3] = { 1, 4, 11, 16}

P3 : A'= A(4,1), A(3,2), A(2,3), A(1,4), A(8,1), A(7,2), A(6,3), A(5,4),
          A(4,5), A(3,6), A(2,7), A(1,8) , A(8,5), A(7,6), A(6,7), A(5,8)
     bound[3] = { 1, 5, 13}

Figure 2.7.   The structure of the local arrays and their bound arrays for loop L_1.

are usually allocated to nearly $1/p$ of the size of the global arrays and data are distributed across processors with the same size for the row or column of each local array, whenever the distribution scheme is along the row or column. But in linear distributions, the sizes of each row in local arrays are different, since the global arrays are distributed along slant lines, and cyclicly partitioned to each processor in order to get a good load balance. Hence, we should allocate the local array space as (number of slant lines) × (maximum size of line length). Reconsider the array A in Example 1. Let $p = 4$ and A is an 8×8 matrix, A is partitioned along slant lines $i + j = c$. The local data are distributed to each processor P_0, P_1, P_2, and P_3, as shown in Figure 2.6. If we allocate the two-dimensional arrays for them, we must assign the local array space as 4×8, it consumes the 2 times the space of global array and half of the local space is useless.

We therefore allocate the local array space as one-dimensional array when the linear distribution is applied. The global array elements distributed along $ai + bj = c$ are cyclically partitioned by following the ascending order of the values of c, that is, the line whose value of c is minc(minimum c) is partitioned to P_0, next to P_1, and so on. For one processor, some parallel lines whose values are $c_1, c_2, \ldots, c_L$, where $c_i < c_j, i < j$, are partitioned over it, and the elements are also stored into the local array in the ascending order of the local values of c. Attached to each local array is a bound array which records the first position of each slant line in the local array. For the current example, the local alignment of the array elements and its bound array are shown in Figure 2.7.

It is clear that there exists greatly different structures between the global and local arrays, thus one should develop a special conversion algorithms between the local and global indices and a conversion algorithm from the global iteration space to the local iteration space for compiler generated SPMD programs. We

```
do i = 1, n
   do j = 1, n
      do k = 1, n
         C(i, j) = C(i, j) + A(i, k) * B(k, j);
      enddo
   enddo
enddo
do i = 1, n
   do j = 1, i
      T = A(i, j);
      A(i, j) = A(j, i);
      A(j, i) = T;
   enddo
enddo
```

Figure 2.8. The sequential source experimental program MULTRANS.

have developed the conversion algorithms from the global to local index, from the local to global index, and from the global to local iteration space respectively.

6.   Experimental Results for Linear Distribution

Here, we present an experimental evaluation for the linear data distribution techniques. All the experiments are implemented on CP-PACS, a 2048-processor MIMD distributed memory parallel computer developed at the University of Tsukuba. The node programs are written in C, using PARALLEL-WARE programming environment, a commercially available package that extends C and FORTRAN77 with a portable communication library.

The experimental programs are the latter half part of ADI, namely an alternating direction implicit solution for the two dimensional diffusion equation, and a program which includes a matrix multiplication loop nest followed by a matrix transposition loop nest, called MULTRANS.

The sequential source program MULTRANS is shown in Figure 2.8. We measured that the execution time of this sequential program is 201.76 seconds(with the data size 1024×1024) on a node of CP-PACS. We also implemented several versions of parallelized programs through determining different data distribution schemes for each program, to observe how performance is influenced by different data distribution schemes for the same program, and to verify whether the executions and the analytical results are consistent.

As widely known, based on the traditional BLOCK/CYCLIC distribution, we would better select the (BLOCK,*), (*,BLOCK) and (BLOCK,*) as the good distribution schemes for array A, B, and C respectively, in the program shown in Figure 2.8, for the matrix multiplication loop in the case of one-dimensional processor array. However, in the matrix transposition loop, $A(i, j)$ and $A(j, i)$

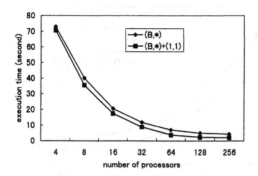

Figure 2.9. Performance of MULTRANS on CP-PACS (data size: 1024×1024).

have the data dependence relation in a loop iteration (i, j). Using the distribution analysis technique proposed in this paper, we obtained the coefficients of linear distribution (a,b) as $(1,1)$. That is, the linear distribution $(1,1)$ should be selected. Therefore, we implemented two types of distribution schemes for array A, where one is (BLOCK,*) for the entire program(denoted as (B,*) in Figures 2.9 and 2.10), another is (BLOCK,*) for the multiplication loop and $(1,1)$ distribution for the transposition loop(denoted as (B,*)+(1,1) in Figures 2.9 and 2.10). For the later case, it requires the redistribution of A between the two loops. We apply the naive redistribution approach [12] by using the global-local index conversion algorithms. The experimental results with the array size $n = 1024 \times 1024$ on CP-PACS are shown in Figure 2.9 Theoretically, the ideal speedup of a parallelized program run on p processors is p times as much as the execution time of sequential program, but due to the affect of communication, the ideal speedup cannot be achieved in practice.

Although the linear distribution version incurred the higher computation and communication overheads for converting the index and redistributing the array elements, due to the lack of communication execution in the transposition loop, it shows the better performance, especially when the number of processors is numerous. Figure 2.10 shows the details of the execution time of the program MULTRANS on the number of processors from 16 to 256. The curve denoted by "multiplication" represents the execution time of the matrix multiplication part of the program. In other words, the difference between the curve (B,*) and "multiplication" is the execution time of the matrix transposition with the distribution scheme (BLOCK,*), and the difference between the curve (B,*)+(1.1) and "multiplication" is the execution time of the matrix transposition with the distribution scheme $(1,1)$ and the redistribution cost from (BLOCK,*) to $(1,1)$. The curve denoted by "$(1,1)$ transposition" represents the execution times of the matrix multiplication and the redistribution. From the figure, we observed that the redistribution from the distribution scheme (BLOCK,*) to $(1,1)$ consumed most of the cost of executing the matrix transposition. In order to get more re-

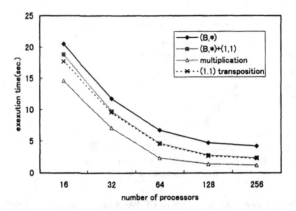

Figure 2.10.   The detail execution time of MULTRANS on CP-PACS(data size: 1024×1024).

markable improvement, we must develop the optimal redistribution algorithms between the traditional and linear distributions [12].

The technique proposed in this chapter seems to be independent of the underlying machine. Both machines seem to show the same order of improvement.

7.   Summary

In this chapter, we proposed a data distribution technique, called linear distribution. The advantages of our technique are

- Our technique extends the regular block/cyclic distribution scheme and can achieve good performance for some scientific applications.

- The regular block/cyclic distribution scheme can derived by our approach through index analysis in the loop.

- The determination of distribution schemes can be simply obtained by the index analysis.

To support the application of our approach, we developed some algorithms which make the conversion among the local, global indices and the local, global iteration spaces. The experimental results using our algorithms are obtained to evaluate the efficiency of our techniques. The main limitation is that we only deal with static array distribution in individual loops and do not consider dynamic distribution between several loops.

References

[1] Adve, V. S., Mellor-Crummey, J., Anderson, M., Kennedy, K., Wang, J.-C., and Reed, D. A.: An Integrated Compilation and Performance Analysis Environment for Data Parallel Programs, *Proceedings of Supercomputing '95*, San Diego, CA, Dec. 1995.

[2] Amarasinghe, S. P. and Lam, M. S.: Communication Optimization and Code Generation for Distributed Memory Machines, *Proceedings of the ACM SIGPLAN'93 Conference on Programming Language Design and Implementation*, Albuquerque, NM, June 1993.

[3] Anderson, J. M. and Lam, M. S.: Global Optimizations for Parallelism and Locality on Scalable Parallel Machines, *Proc. of the SIGPLAN '93 Conference on Program Language Design and Implementation*, ACM, 1993, pp. 112–125.

[4] Balasundaram, V., Fox, G., Kennedy, K., and Kremer, U.: An Interactive Environment for Data Partitioning and distribution, *Proc. Fifth Distributed Memory Computing Conference*, 1990.

[5] Balasundaram, V., Fox, G., Kennedy, K., and Kremer, U.: An Static Performance Estimator to Guide Data Partitioning Decisions, *Proceedings of the Third ACM SIGPLAN Symposium on Principles and Practice of Parallel Programming*, Williamsburg, VA, Apr. 1991.

[6] Banerjee, P., Chandy, J. A., Gupta, M., Hodges IV, E., Holm, J., Lain, A., Palermo, D., Ramaswamy, S., and Su, E.: The PARADIGM Compiler for Distributed-memory Multicomputers, *IEEE Comput.*, Vol. 28 (1995), pp. 37–47.

[7] Banerjee, U.: *Loop Parallelization*, A Book Series on Loop Transformations for Restructuring Compilers, Kluwer Academic Publishers, 1994.

[8] Bau, D., Koduklula, I., Kotlyar, V., Pingali, K., and Stodghill, P.: Solving Alignment Using Elementary Linear Algebra, *Proceedings of the 7th Workshop on Languages and Compilers for Parallel Computing*, Ithica, NY, 1994, Springer-Verlag, 1995.

[9] Chen, T.-S. and Sheu, J.-P.: Communication-Free Data Allocation Techniques for Parallelizing Compilers on Multicomputers, *IEEE Transactions on Parallel and Distributed Systems*, Vol. 5,No. 9(1994), pp. 924–938.

[10] Guo, M., Yamashita, Y., and Nakata, I.: An Efficient Data Distribution Technique for Distributed Memory Parallel Computers, *Transactions of Information Processing Society of Japan*, Vol. 39,No. 6, pp. 1718–1728 (1998).

[11] Guo, M., Yamashita, Y., and Nakata, I.: Efficient Implementation of Multi-Dimensional Array Redistribution, *IEICE Transactions on Information and Systems*, Vol. E81-D, No. 11, pp. 1195–1204 (1998).

[12] Guo, M., Yamashita, Y., and Nakata, I.: Improving Performance of Multi-dimensional Array Redistribution on Distributed Memory Machines, *Proceedings of the Third International Workshop on High-Level Parallel Programming Models and Supportive Environments*, Orlando, FL, USA, March 1998.

[13] Gupta, M.: *Automatic Data Partitioning on Distributed Memory Multicomputers*, PhD Thesis, University of Illinois, Urbana-Champaign, Sep. 1992.

[14] Gupta, M. and Banerjee, P.: Compile-time Estimation of Communication Costs on Multicomputers, *Proceedings of the Sixth International Parallel Processing Symposium*, Beverly Hills, CA, March 1992.

[15] HPF Forum: *High Performance Fortran Language Specification*, Rice University, Houston, Texas, version 2.0 edition, Nov. 1996.

[16] Kennedy, K. and Kremer, U.: Automatic Data Layout for High Performance Fortran, *Proceedings of Supercomputing'95*, San Diego, CA, Dec. 1995.

[17] Ramanujam, J. and Sadayappan, P.: Compile-Time Techniques for Data Distribution in Distributed Memory Machines, *IEEE Transactions on Parallel and Distributed Systems*, Vol. 2,No. 4 (1991), pp. 472–481.

[18] Wolfe, M.: *High Performance Compilers for Parallel Computing*, Addison-Wesley, 1995.

[19] Zima, H. and Chapman, B.: *Supercompilers for Parallel and Vector Computers*, Frontier Series, Addison-Wesley, 1990.

Chapter 3

QUANTIFICATION OF MEMORY COMMUNICATION

Surendra Byna, Kirk W. Cameron* and Xian-He Sun

Department of Compuer Science, Illinois Institute of Technology, Chicago, IL
{renbyna,sun}@iit.edu

Abstract   Communication in parallel applications is a combination of data transfers internally at a source or destination and across the network. Previous research focused on quantifying network transfer costs has indirectly resulted in reduced overall communication cost. Optimized data transfer from source memory to the network interface has received less attention. In shared memory systems, such memory-to-memory transfers dominate communication cost. In distributed memory systems, memory-to-network interface transfers grow in significance as processor and network speeds increase at faster rates than memory latency speeds. Our objective is to minimize the cost of internal data transfers. The following examples illustrating the impact of memory transfers on communication, we present a methodology for classifying the effects of data size and data distribution on hardware, middleware, and application software performance. This cost is quantified using hardware counter event measurements on the SGI Origin 2000. Our analysis technique identifies the critical data paths in point-to-point communication. For the SGI O2K, we empirically identify the cost caused by just copying data from one buffer to another and the middleware overhead. We use MPICH in our experiments, but our techniques are generally applicable to any communication implementation.

Keywords: Memory communication, Communication performance, Buffering

1.   Introduction

Computers continue to increase in complexity. Hierarchical memories, superscalar pipelining, and out-of-order execution have improved system perfor-

*Presently Department of Computer Science and Engineering, University of South Carolina, Columbia, SC, Email: kcameron@cse.sc.edu

mance at the expense of simplicity. Redesigned compilers allow applications to take advantage of new architectures and execute more efficiently.

Unfortunately, compilers are limited in their ability to increase performance. For instance, the compiler is often unaware of subtle characteristics of cache hierarchies. Optimal performance is typically achieved through a combination of optimized compilation and algorithm redesign through system dependent analysis.

Communication in parallel systems increases complexity tremendously. As a result, parallel compilation is even less fruitful than its sequential ancestor. Optimizing performance in such environments relies more heavily on the use of tools to provide performance data for analysis.

Distributed systems rely on middleware to address the interoperability of heterogeneous software and hardware implying additional complexity. The interaction between hardware, software and middleware is not well understood. Thus, the optimizing abilities of distributed compilers are very limited. Optimizing performance in such environments will greatly rely on tools for system dependent analysis.

Communication costs in such environments are a function of the critical data path (see Figure 3.1). A communicated message must be moved from the source's local memory to the target's local memory. *Memory communication* is the transmission of data to/from user space from/to the local network buffer (or shared memory buffer). *Network communication* is data movement between source and target network buffers. Communication cost consists of the sum of memory and network communication times.

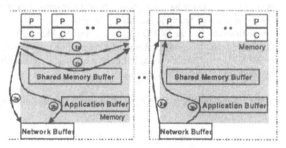

Figure 3.1. Memory communications within shared memory (1a-b) and to/from the network buffer in distributed communication (2a-b/3a-b) follow critical paths dependent upon data size, data distribution, and system implementation.

Unfortunately, the same layers of middleware that enable distributed processing (e.g. MPI, PVM) convolute the critical data path. Figure 3.1 illustrates the possible critical paths of data for communication in a simple distributed shared memory machine or cluster. The chosen path (and cost of the communication) depends on the destination, the data size and distribution, and the system implementation of the middleware.

Consider communication in a cluster of shared memory computers. Depending on the underlying communication scheme (e.g. MPI, PVM), the chosen implementation (e.g. MPICH [1]), and the system architecture design, different communication buffers will be used along the critical data path. For small data sizes, communication proceeds without application-level buffering. For large data sizes, data buffering at the application level will occur. Buffering will also occur at the network level.

The relative cost of memory communication is increasing. Processor speeds continue to outpace memory latency improvements. As the gap widens, memory performance becomes an even larger portion of overall execution time. It is very important to limit the cost of memory accesses. As mentioned, compilers can help, but given the complexity of present and future distributed systems the first step toward this solution is to identify the critical path of memory communication in a real system and quantify the cost.

Due to the increasing importance of memory, in this paper we seek to describe a scientific approach to empirically determine the critical path of memory communication. Our approach follows traditional methods of characterizing memory hierarchies applied to memory communication. We additionally apply a model of memory communication cost to characterize the effects of locality on observed buffer transmission. Our goal is to identify and quantify the costs of memory communication automatically. We test our methodology on a cluster of SMPs to show its usefulness and verify correctness.

2. Related Work

Gropp and Lusk provide the mpptest tool for measuring MPI message performance accurately [1]. This tool is currently part of the MPICH distribution and through experimentation can help tweak parameters in MPI implementations for specific platforms [2]. The mpptest tool can be used for limited buffer identification. Our work couples this basic approach with traditional methods of cache hierarchy evaluation to automate buffering cost identification.

Limited work has targeted the memory communication cost of non-contiguous data. Ashworth provides an application specific benchmark for non-contiguous communication in regular-partitioned, grid-based, distributed finite difference models [3]. This work is solely empirical and contextually specific, drawing no general conclusions regarding non-contiguous communication performance for message passing applications.

Much research has focused on the network communication cost of message passing for contiguous data. Dongarra et. al. provides a good overview of message passing performance issues and measurements [4]. Existing parallel communication models like LogP focus on network communication delay with limited consideration of memory communication [5]. Later derivates maintain this focus, extending LogP to long messages [6] and active messages [7].

More recently, LogP was extended to incorporate advanced memory communication cost. Similar to the aforementioned extensions, memory logP trades increased model complexity for improved model coverage of communication cost on evolving architectures [8]. Since this research focuses on enabling automated buffer identification, the additional model complexity is acceptable and necessary to quantify the individual contributions of contiguous and non-contiguous data.

Memory logP formally characterizes memory communication cost under four parameters: l: the effective latency, defined as the length of time the processor is engaged in the transmission or reception of a message due to the influence of data size (s) and distribution (d) for a given implementation of data transfer on a given system, $l=f(s,d)$. o: the overhead, defined as the length of time that a processor is engaged in the transmission or reception of an ideally distributed message for a given implementation of data transfer on a given system. During this time the processor cannot perform other operations. g: the gap, defined as the minimum time interval between consecutive message receptions at a processor. The reciprocal of g corresponds to the available per-processor bandwidth for a given implementation of data transfer on a given system. P: the number of processors per memory modules. Point-to-point communication in the memory hierarchy implies $P=1$.

The memory logP model additionally assumes: 1) the parameters are measured as multiples of the clock cycle, 2) the word size is 4 bytes for integer and 8 bytes for floating point, 3) the processor architecture is load/store, 4) any icache and branching effects are ignored, 5) any non-deterministic characteristics of memory access delay are not considered, 6) the receiving processor may access a message only after the entire message has arrived, and 7) at any given time a processor can either be sending or receiving a message. For memory communications involving data transfers across the memory hierarchy, these assumptions are reasonable

3.   Motivating Example

As mentioned, the compiler's ability to optimize performance is limited. Run-time characteristics coupled with system complexity inherently limit automated, a priori performance improvements. However, performance speedup can be achieved with the use of locality-conscious programming.

The SGI MIPSpro compiler offers a range of general-purpose and architecture-specific optimizations to improve performance including loop nest optimization, software pipelining and inter-procedural analysis [9]. -O2 optimization flag turns on all global optimizations (e.g. dead code elimination, loop normalization, memory alias analysis). -Ofast option turns on all optimizations related to loop nesting (e.g. loop unrolling, loop interchange, loop blocking, memory prefetch etc.).

We perform a series of simple experiments on an SGI system to quantify the limitations of current compiler technologies in the context of memory communication. We compare the performance of two programs that perform matrix transpose (MT): a simple MPI implementation with packing and unpacking of transferred data and a manual implementation using array padding and cache blocking. We compiled MPI source code with -O2 and -Ofast options in separate experiments. For all the implementations of MT we isolate and measure the memory communication cost by running the codes in a single processor system.

Our manual implementation uses external array padding, and cache blocking. In array padding, an array is transformed to reduce the number of memory system conflicts by adding a new column to the original array. Cache blocking is based on the idea of ensuring the best reuse of all the elements that are loaded into the cache before they are replaced by new elements. We choose a blocking size that guarantees the whole block fits into the cache.

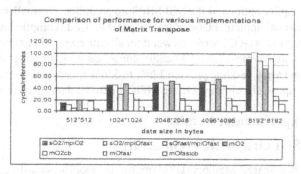

Figure 3.2. Performance gain with memory-conscious programming. The transpose operation with the use of array padding and cache blocking speeds up by 380% to 550% over the best MPI packing implementation.

We have chosen 5 sizes of square matrices (2-D arrays). These sizes are 512*512, 1024*1024, 2048*2048, 4096*4096 and 8192*8192 8-byte words. We measured performance for the following scenarios:

- Simple MPI implementation of MT using derived datatypes

    - compilation of MT using -O2 optimizations (default)

        * -O2 compilation of MPICH derived data type source code [sO2/mpiO2]

    - compilation of MT using -Ofast optimizations

        * -O2 compilation of MPICH derived data type source code [sO2/mpiOfast]

* -Ofast compilation of MPICH derived data types source code [sOfast/mpiOfast]

- Manual implementation of MT (default -O2 MPICH compilation)
  - compilation of MT using -O2 optimizations (default) [mO2]
  - compilation of MT using -O2 optimizations + cache blocking [mO-2cb]
  - compilation of MT using -Ofast optimizations [mOfast]
  - compilation of MT using -Ofast optimizations + cache blocking [mOfastcb]

As expected, the algorithm changes of the manual implementation outperform the simple compiler-generated code. Methods such as cache blocking and array padding exploit the system dependent characteristics of the memory hierarchy. Figure 3.2 shows the overall cost in cycles per memory reference for various compiler options of the SGI MIPSpro compiler. At smaller data sizes, MPI and manual implementations are comparable. Code compiled with the default optimizations (-O2) performs worst for all data sizes. -Ofast compiled MT performs better in most cases. Locality-conscious programming using cache blocking and array padding provide 380% to 550% speedup on average for this matrix transpose algorithm verse the MPICH derived data type version.

4.   Experimental Details

4.1   SGI Origin 2K architecture

Distributed Shared-Memory (DSM) multiprocessors provide the convenience of shared memory programming with a scalable design. The SGI Origin 2000 at NCSA utilizes a cc-NUMA architecture running the IRIX version 6.5.14 operating system. The interconnection network for 128 processors is a 5th degree hypercube with 4 processors (2 nodes) per router. High-speed, dedicated Craylink interconnects link nodes. The achievable remote memory bandwidth on Craylink interconnect is 624MB/sec in each direction, which adds a 165ns off-node penalty and 110ns per hop. As long as the communication is between nodes within a hypercube, per hop latency is zero, but the communication to an outer cube node causes increases in latency.

A directory based tree protocol maintains cache-coherence. A complex memory hierarchy reduces the impact of memory latency. Each node contains two MIPS R10000 processors [10]; each running at 195MHz, and 32kB two-way set associative, two-way interleaved primary (L1) cache. An off-chip 4MB secondary unified cache is present as well. Cache and page block sizes are 32 and 4096 bytes respectively. Load misses at L1 and L2 were measured as 12 and 90 cycles respectively. The MIPS R10000 is a four-way superscalar RISC processor. The machine used in testing has 48 195MHz MIPS R10000 processors, with 14 GB main memory. The available local memory access bandwidth is 680MB/sec in each direction. SGI O2K machine is selected as our platform due to availability and support of hardware counter libraries. As our study focuses on the effect of local memory references this can be generalized for commodity cluster architectures.

4.2 Hardware counters

All the commodity processors provide hardware performance counters to measure and validate the processor architecture. The MIPS R10000 processor has two on-chip 32-bit registers to count 30 distinct hardware events. In our experiments we have measured the events related to total cycles (event 0), graduated instructions (event 17), memory data loads graduated (event 18), memory data stores graduated (event 19), L1 cache misses (event 25), L2 cache misses (event 26). The overhead of cache misses on SGI Origin 2000 is measured [11] as 1 cycle for register access, 2-3 cycles for an L1 cache hit, 7-13 cycles for an L1 cache miss, 60-200 cycles for an L2 cache miss. A TLB miss costs more than 2000 cycles. This shows that the overhead increases massively as L2 cache misses occur. We have chosen these counters to study the memory effect on communication as they reflect the memory operations for any processor.

4.3 Performance measurement

We measure each experiment twenty times for all data sizes and hardware counter events. Accuracy is maintained by taking only the values with low standard deviation. In the next section we quantify performance degradation for non-contiguity of the data using the memory-logP model. For this we use a program that measures performance for sending a contiguous and a non-contiguous message with point-to-point blocking message passing under various data sizes and strides. We study point-to-point, blocking communication due to its prevalence in parallel applications. However, our methodology applies to any middleware implementation. In the third experiment, we use a matrix transpose algorithm to represent memory communication packing and unpacking. We measure the costs for simple contiguous message copying, non-contiguous message copying, and sending data to a remote processor.

5. Quantifying Communication Cost

Communication cost for sending a data segment depends on architectural parameters (e.g. cache capacity) and code characteristics (e.g. data distribution) as explained in the memory-logP model. Typically a message transmission involves data collection, data copying to the network buffer and data forwarding to the receiver. When a data distribution is not contiguous, typically it is collected into a contiguous buffer before copying to the network buffer (see Figure 3.1). This intermediate copying is costly as data sizes and strides increase resulting in additional capacity and conflict misses to the cache [12]. This can be done without extra buffer copying by directly copying to the network buffer. However the performance degrades further due to poor utilization of network buffer. Strided accesses decrease the efficiency of cache hierarchies designed to exploit locality (capacity misses). Caches with less than full associativity, often a small power of 2, suffer from mapping collisions under certain access patterns (conflict misses).

The parameters of the memory logP model capture architecture and code characteristics. Memory cost of transferring data of a specific size is a combination of unavoidable overhead (o), and effective latency (l) - a function of data size and distribution. Additional network latency after removing overlap exists in passing a message between two processors. Total communication time increases with memory latency (l). In our micro benchmark experiments, memory performance worsens with an increase in stride. We use the memory-logP model to enumerate the memory hierarchy performance so that a developer can improve the performance of those parts of code with locality-conscious optimizations. Quantifying the memory communication costs is the first step in bottleneck identification. Succeeding analysis can identify system buffer-related parameters.

Figure 3.3 and Figure 3.4 illustrate the communication cost and cause of 16-dword (16 x 8 bytes), strided data transfers using MPI Blocking Sends. The contribution of memory communication to total communication is obvious. As message sizes increase for fixed strides, data transfer time increases (Figure 3.3) from additional conflict and capacity misses (Figure 3.4) in the memory communication. The rate of cost increase is dependent upon the data distribution and the memory hierarchy characteristics.

Estimation of the o parameter of the memory logP model requires measurement of contiguous data transmission, a relatively simple task using micro-benchmarking techniques. We expect the o parameter increases proportionately as problem size and strides increase; that a scalable transmission method is chosen. Recent work [13] indicates that the overheads for packing and unpacking of MPI derived data types in implementations such as MPICH do not scale well.

Measuring the l parameter directly requires running experiments varying message size and contiguity. After subtracting the ideal overhead, the l function remains. In Figure 3.5 a comparison of various costs is shown. The first bar in each grouping quantifies overhead (o) of copying a contiguous data block. In the SGI O2K system measured, overhead remains constant as size increases. The second bar in each grouping shows the cost for packing a non-contiguous message into an intermediate buffer. This cost is similar to copying a contiguous message when the data fits totally into the cache. After the data size crosses this barrier, the costs increase due to cache and TLB misses. Sending a contiguous message includes a small fraction of memory copying cost (o) and network latency, but for non-contiguous messages, this memory cost increases with the data size as it includes the latency parameter (l).

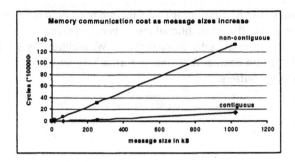

Figure 3.3. Total cost for sending contiguous (stride 1) and non-contiguous (stride 16) messages. The costs are similar at low data sizes and it increases a lot once the data does not fit into the cache or when TLB thrashing occurs.

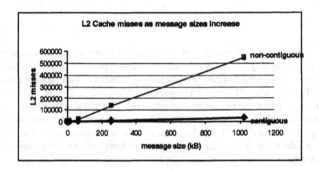

Figure 3.4. L2 cache misses for sending contiguous (stride 1) and non-contiguous (stride 16) messages. Each L2 cache miss costs between 60 to 200 cycles.

6. Identifying Memory Communication Buffers

Memory hierarchies are complex. System middleware (e.g. MPICH) provides abstractions (e.g. derived data types) to simplify distributed programming hiding the details of data transfer from the user. Determining the particular costs of memory communication is non-trivial due to the complex interaction between application, middleware, and hardware. However, to optimize performance, application developers must understand the full cost of communication. Using the quantifiable parameters of the memory logP model and micro-benchmark experiments, it is possible to identify buffer copies in shared memory architectures.

Specifically, we test various data sizes and strides iteratively and observe the largest gap among the successive hardware counter values after consideration of experimental variation. These gaps or significant changes pinpoint policy decisions in the case of MPI codes (application buffers) and memory hierarchy characteristics (implicit buffering). At the memory hierarchy level, our approach is similar to that of traditional micro-benchmarking techniques [14, 15] used to identify general cache characteristics. We additionally verify our analyses with hardware counter data; this is particularly important for identifying application-level buffers.

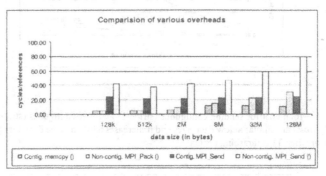

Figure 3.5.   Comparison of cost for various implementations of transpose algorithm. Contig.memcpy () : Copying data from one buffer to another using memcpy (). This is the basic overhead (o) to copy contiguous data. Non-contig. MPI_Pack () : This packs columns of matrix using MPI_Type_vector (). This cost is a combination of (o) and (l). Contig.MPI_Send () sends a contiguous message over network to another processor. This includes the cost of small contiguous copying overhead (o) and the cost for network transfer and software overhead of MPI_Send. Non-contig. MPI_Send () packs a non-contiguous data to transpose and sends to the receiver. This cost includes the packing overhead, copying data from memory to the network buffer and the network cost.

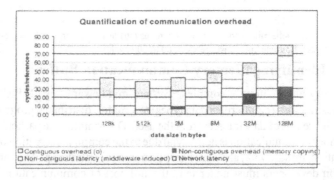

Figure 3.6.   From previous figure Contig. memcpy () = o, MPI_Send () contains the overhead due to copying of data from memory to the network buffer and network latency. Non-contig MPI_Send () has the additional buffer copying cost over MPI_Send () costs.

Inefficient memory communication is not limited to exploitation of the memory hierarchy. Figure 3.5 shows the increases in the latency parameter (l) with additional layers of overhead caused by middleware such as MPICH implementation is measured. It has been our experience that code developers targeting performance generally avoid certain abstractions such as derived data types since they understand the overhead resulting from such abstraction negatively and significantly impacts performance. Figure 3.5 affirms this intuition. Figure 3.6 shows the classification of various costs including (l), (o) and other latency. Collective costs of middleware are very high with the increase of message size. This depicts that the magnitude of the cost differential is truly system and application dependent. Hence, a more scientific approach to determine when to use abstractions such as derived data types would involve determining the exact cost for a specific application-architecture combination. This is the purpose of our techniques and the original motivation behind this work.

As discussed, the critical data path for communicating a message varies depending on the destination, data size, and distribution and the implementation of middleware (see Figure 3.1). For example MPI [16] uses three protocols in buffering: short, eager and rendezvous. In "short" protocol data is sent with the envelope of the message. This protocol is ideal for very small data sizes. With "eager" protocol, data is not stored in an application buffer at the sender, assuming the receiver can store the data (see Figure 3.1 2a/3a-b). This method is advantageous to reduce any synchronization delays. But buffering may require additional space for messages from an arbitrary number of senders. Memory exhaustion may occur at the receiver for large data. In "rendezvous" protocol, data is buffered at the sender until the receiver responds and posts a receive signal. This scheme provides scalability but comprises extra handshaking delays and stall for the cases of buffer exhaustion.

A standard-mode send function uses "eager" protocol while the message size is less than the available system buffer size. After the buffer size is surpassed, the system switches to rendezvous protocol. There are many implementations to deal with non-contiguous data. In a typical MPICH implementation [1] buffering is needed regardless of message size (Figure 3.1 2b) for strided datatypes. At the receiver, unpacked data requires an additional copy (Figure 3.1 3a); when unpacking is not necessary, no additional copy is made (Figure 3.1 3b). The CPU stalls when the buffer exhausts until the data is sent out of the buffer. Location of the receiver also impacts the overall communication cost in shared memory systems.

Comparing the performance of communication for contiguous and strided messages can isolate the overhead caused by additional buffering. The cost of sending a contiguous message between two processors is a combination of data transfer overhead (o) and network latency. Sending a strided message has extra overhead due to poor exploitation of memory hierarchy and additional buffer copying. Optimally, the cost of copying strided data into a contiguous buffer is the same as the cost of packing it using MPI implementation. Additional middleware induced overhead is separated by subtracting the costs of sending contiguous message and that of packing from the total cost of sending strided message. Figure 3.6 depicts the partition of these costs. This is an empirical method of separating all the costs in memory communication. Presentation of these costs provides a developer with an insight into exploiting the advanced memory hierarchies, and to decide which critical data path is optimal to use.

7.   Conclusions and Future Work

It was believed that data allocation is not a noticeable factor of communication in a parallel computing environment. All the existing parallel programming models consider cost of memory access either constant or negligible. Through our experimental testing, and case studies, in this research we have shown that memory communication is a function of data size and distribution. The performance degrades by a factor 10 times even with a small stride of 16. Communication performance can be improved more than 300% by using memory friendly optimizations external to compilers. This portrays a large scope for improvement of communication dominant applications and compilers.

Memory communication can be caused by many factors, under utilization fast CPUs with multiple levels of memory hierarchy, data distribution and various copying overheads between buffers. Application developers need to be aware of underlying architectures to develop high performance programs. But lack of documentation regarding the memory hierarchy and buffering schemes for various architectures is a source of difficulty in optimizing applications. Identification of these implementation based communication overheads is a part of enumerating the memory communication costs. In this paper we have presented an approach to determine the critical data path scientifically along with the memory access overhead as described earlier.

Towards modelling this memory communication, we have developed memory logP model [8]. We used the model to characterize, bound, and predict memory performance. The result of these techniques is a more accurate estimate of overall communication performance. We practically applied our techniques to two architecturally distinct systems, an IA32 Beowulf and the MIPS-based SGI Origin 2000. The resulting measurements for the o parameter quantified the scalability of the copying algorithm. Additionally, simple stack distance curve prediction was shown to be practically accurate (within +80% and -60%).

After recognizing the points of performance degradation, the next step is to optimize the performance. A program developer who is aware of all these details can be able to produce better solutions. But to achieve uniform and optimized performance there should be libraries and automatic development of these solutions to ease the burden on the programmer. Our future work is moving towards achieving these goals. One of our objectives is to improve the performance of MPI derived datatypes implementation, by observing memory operations. This work is progressing in collaboration with Argonne National Laboratory.

Acknowledgments

The authors wish to thank Dr. Bill Gropp, Argonne National Laboratory, and Dr. Eric Salo, developer of SGI MPI, who helped us in understanding MPI implementation. We would also like to thank National Center for Supercomputing Applications (NCSA) for access to the SGI Origin 2k machine at University of Illinois, Urbana-Champaign.

References

[1] William Gropp, Ewing Lusk, Nathan Doss, and Anthony Skjellum, "A High-Performance, Portable Implementation of the MPI Message Passing Interface Standard", *Parallel Computing*, 1996

[2] W. Gropp and E. Lusk, "High Performance MPI Implementation on a Shared Memory Vector Supercomputer", *Parallel Computing* 1996

[3] M. Ashworth, "The OCCOMM Benchmarking Guide, Version 1.2", URL: http://www.dl.ac.uk/TCSC/CompEng/OCCOMM/, March 1996

[4] J. Dongarra and T. Dunigan, "Message Passing Performance of Various Computers", *Concurrency: Practice and Experience*, Vol. 9 No. 10, pp 915-926, 1997

[5] D.Culler et al. "LogP: Towards a Realistic Model of Parallel Computation", *In Proceedings of Fourth ACM SIGPLAN Symposium on Principles and Practice of Parallel Programming*, pages 1-12, San Diego, California, May 1993

[6] A.Alexandrov, MF Ionescu, KE Schauser, and C. Scheiman. "LogGP: Incorporating Long Messages into the LogP Model - One Step Closer Towards a Realistic Model for Parallel Computation", *In Proc. Symposium on Parallel Algorithms and Architectures (SPAA)*, pages 95–105, Santa Barbara, CA, July 1995

[7] Csaba Andras, Moritz Matthew, I. Frank. "LoGPC: Modeling Network Contention in Message-Passing Programs", *IEEE Transactions on Parallel and Distributed Systems*, Vol. 12, No. 4, April 2001

[8] K. Cameron, X.H. Sun, "Quantifying Locality Effect in Data Access Delay: Memory logP", *International Parallel and Distributed Processing Symposium (IPDPS)*, 2003

[9] SGI MIPSpro family compilers, URL: http://www.sgi.com/developers/devtools/languages/mipspro.html

[10] National Center for Supercomputing Applications Archives, (NCSA) "Understanding Performance on the SGI Origin 2000" *NCSA Online document*, URL: http://archive.ncsa.uiuc.edu/SCD/Perf/Tuning/Tips/Tuning.html

[11] Shirley Moore, Nils Smeds, "Performance tuning using hardware counter data", *Presentation at SuperComputing*, 2001, Nov. 01

[12] Monica Lam, Edward E. Rothberg and Michael E. Wolf, " The cache performance of blocked algorithms", *Proceedings of the Fourth International Conference on Architectural Support for Programming Languages and Operating Systems*, April 1991

[13] J. Worringen, A. Gaer, and F. Reker, "Exploiting transparent remote memory access for non-contiguous and one-sided communication", *In proceedings of Workshop for communication architectures in clusters (CAC 02) at IPDPS*, 2002, Fort Lauderdale, FL, 2002

[14] R. H. Saavedra , R. S. Gaines , M. J. Carlton, Micro benchmark analysis of the KSR1, *Proceedings of the 1993 ACM/IEEE conference on Supercomputing*, p.202-213, December 1993, Portland, Oregon, United States

[15] R. Clint Whaley, Antoine Petiet and Jack Dongarra, "Automated Empirical Optimizations of Software and the ATLAS project", *Parallel Computing*, Vol. 27, Num. 1-2, pp. 3-25, 2001

[16] Message Passing Interface (MPI) Standard Specification, http://www.mpi-forum.org/docs/mpi-11-html/mpi-report.html

Chapter 4

THE NEED FOR ADAPTIVE DYNAMIC THREAD SCHEDULING*

Chulho Shin, Seong-Won Lee*
University of Southern California, Department of Electrical Engineering - Systems
{cshin,seongwon}@usc.edu

Jean-Luc Gaudiot
University of California, Irvine, Department of Electrical Engineering and Computer Science
gaudiot@uci.edu

Abstract   Earlier studies on Simultaneous Multithreaded (SMT) Architectures showed that performance of a realistic SMT architecture saturates early. This paper addresses our contention that a fixed hardware thread scheduling strategy cannot provide optimal results for various thread combinations. We propose an approach that partially schedules threads in the form of a detector thread at a nominal hardware and software cost. It offers the capability to adaptively switch thread scheduling policies depending on various situations. This article shows that there is much room for performance improvement for our adaptive dynamic thread scheduling approach. The results obtained by simulating a realistic SMT architecture show that 27% is approximately the upper-bound of the performance improvement for SMT with eight contexts. This demonstrates that our approach may significantly improve performance with good low-throughput detection and fetch policy selection heuristics.

Keywords: Simultaneous multithreading, Hardware thread scheduling, Detector thread

*A shorter version of this chapter appeared as "The Need for Adaptive Dynamic Thread Scheduling" in the special issue of Hardware/Software Support for High Performance Scientific and Engineering Computing at Parallel Processing Letters, 2004.
*Both are currently with Samsung Electronics Co.

1.   Introduction

Simultaneous Multithreading (SMT) or Multithreaded Superscalar Architectures [4, 11, 19, 18, 5, 9] can achieve high processor utilization by allowing multiple independent threads to coexist in the processor pipeline and share resources with support of multiple hardware contexts. Our work presented herein focuses mainly on multiprogrammed or multi-user environments where combinations of multiple threads that an SMT processor faces are significantly varied over time (*e.g.*, from a compute intensive set to a memory intensive set). For multiprogramming or multi-user workloads consisting of threads running on the processor independently of one another, no information about interactive behavior between threads is known in advance. Consequently, it is indispensable to adopt a more intelligent and more dynamic thread scheduling capability for sustenance of high throughput.

Performance of a multithreaded workload is bound by the critical path of the execution flow. Therefore, efforts to dynamically increase the performance of several threads that belong to one application might end up with no overall performance improvement at all. On the contrary, since independent threads do not share a common critical path of execution in SMT and a faster-moving thread can retire earlier, higher utilization more often means higher performance for workloads with multiple independent threads.

Studies by Tullsen *et al.* and Ungerer *et al.* [19, 14] have shown that when the number of threads allowed in the processor becomes more than four, performance saturates and in some cases even degenerates because of limitations in the shared instruction queue, fetch throughput, or contention in the L2 cache [18, 8]. In these studies, an attempt was made to overcome the saturation by finding a better fetch mechanism or increasing the number and availability of resources that would otherwise become bottlenecks (such as register files and instruction queues). It was also shown that increasing the size of the caches can result in higher saturation point.

We believe that one fixed thread scheduling that performs better than others "on the average" cannot deliver the performance we desire in SMT architectures which support more than four thread contexts. Instead, we claim that adding an adaptive dynamic thread scheduling is necessary to significantly improve the performance of SMT processors and to prevent them from saturating or letting performance degrade as the number of threads increases.

With adaptive dynamic thread scheduling, when a change in the system environment is detected, the next-interval fetch policy is decided and put into effect. However, having multiple fetch policies and decision-making algorithms in hardware could entail a high overhead. In this paper, we propose to exploit a detector thread approach which can help lower the hardware requirement and also make use of unused pipeline slots to run decision-making algorithms and fetch policies. This approach has the additional advantage that thread scheduling can be manipulated even after the chip has been produced because the detector thread is programmable. The detector thread can also help lower the overhead of the system job scheduler by shortening its stay in the processor and analyzing information before the job scheduler needs it.

2. Related Work

A study by Seznec [8] pointed out that L2 contention may limit the performance of SMT processors as the number of threads increases beyond four. Another study found out that adding threads above a four-issue bandwidth would give only a marginal return [14]. Various fetch policies were investigated as a remedy for saturation by Tullsen et al. in [18]. The focus of the study was on finding which fetch policy was optimal: on the average, *ICOUNT* turned out to produce throughput higher than all the others.

Detector thread idea itself is not entirely new. *DanSoft* [6] proposed the idea of *nanothreads* in which one of nanothreads is given the control of the processor upon the stall of a main thread. The idea was based on a CMP with dual VLIW single-threaded cores and its success hinges on the effectiveness of the compiler. *Assisted Execution* [16] extended the nanothread idea for architectures that allow simultaneous execution of multiple threads including SMT. It attempts to improve performance of a main thread by having multiple nanothreads perform prefetch and its success also hinges on compiler.

Another study that investigated the use of a special thread was undergone by Wang et al. which aims at realizing speculative precomputation in one of the two threads available on the Hyper-Threading architecture [20]. The study is targeted at improving the performance of single-threaded applications on two-context SMT processors.

Simultaneous Subordinate Microthreading (SSMT) [3] was proposed as an attempt to improve performance of a single thread by having multiple *subordinate microthreads* do useful works such as running sophisticated branch predication algorithm. The idea was not based on SMT architecture and also relies on effective compiler technology.

Our adaptive dynamic thread scheduling approach should not be confused with adaptive process scheduling [12] which addresses OS job scheduling issues for SMT processors: the goal of our approach is to offer more efficient thread scheduling at the level of instruction fetch in the SMT pipeline.

Parekh et. al. [13] investigated issues related to job scheduling for SMT processors. Another similar study [15] investigated job scheduling for SMT processors. The study proposed a job scheduling scheme called *SOS* where an *overhead-free* sample phase is involved where performance of various schedules (mixes) are sampled and taken into account for the selection of tasks for the next time slice.

A study to detect per-thread cache behavior using hardware counters and help job scheduling based on the information obtained on SMT was done by

Suh *et al.* [17]. This approach is similar to our idea of relating the detector thread with job schedulers.

3.   Adaptive Dynamic Thread Scheduling with the Detector Thread

3.1   Overview

As discussed earlier, having one single thread scheduling policy in an SMT processor can neither properly adapt to the varying system environments nor make full use of the unique opportunities presented by SMT architectures. With our adaptive dynamic thread scheduling (ADTS), we can tackle both problems. First, depending on what kind of application mixes are resident in the processor, a new fetch policy can be activated upon detection of low throughput. Second, unused pipeline slots can be used to detect changes in the system, identify threads that clog the pipeline and take actions to sustain high throughput rate; such threads will be suspended or excluded from fetch. Hereby, we propose the detector thread approach to realize ADTS without significant overhead.

A detector thread is a special thread which reads thread status indicators and updates thread control flags based on the current values of the indicators so that the thread control hardware can take any necessary action to improve performance of an SMT processor. The per-thread status indicators are updated by circuitries throughout the processor pipeline based upon specific events such as cache miss, pipeline stalls, population at each stage, *etc.*

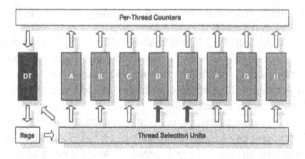

Figure 4.1.   How a Detector Thread works with normal threads.

The role of the detector thread is to check the values of the various thread status indicators and, based on the conditions dynamically defined in software, to properly update the thread control flags as shown in Figure 4.1. A thread will have its own set of flags. A flag will tell whether a thread can be fetched in the next cycle. Another example will be a flag that tells whether it should be suspended in the next opportunity. When the system thread is loaded, it will look at the flag and suspend the thread without going through the process of determining the thread to suspend. Then, the thread selection unit simply issues instructions from threads in their order of priority. Although the per-thread status indicators, thread control flags, and thread selection units are fixed in hardware, we can control the thread control behavior around those hardware resources by writing a different program code for the detector thread.

Depending on the values of the indicators that the detector thread watches, some threads can be given priority over others. This prioritization is put into effect by updating the thread control flags. One instance of thread control flag could be *suspend-thread*. If a flag of a thread is set, the hardware thread selection unit will stop allocating any new slots to the thread until the flag is reset. Later when the system job scheduler is activated, it will suspend the thread while bringing in a new *ready* thread whether that was previously suspended or is totally new.

The detector thread will have its own program cache sufficiently large (2 or 4KB) to fit its small program text and its data accesses should be mostly to special registers such as the per-thread counters and general-purpose registers. Consequently, it will not introduce a high degree of overhead. It will be the lowest-priority thread most of the time. The hardware dispatch logic should give the detector thread lowest priority to be chosen for new slots. It will give empty slots to the detector thread only when there are no other normal threads that can be assigned. The more wasted slots the thread selection unit finds, the more active the detector thread becomes by occupying more issue slots. When the slots are almost fully occupied, the detector thread will not obtain any more scheduling slots; this is acceptable because it means that the processor pipeline slots are enjoying high utilization.

Fetching the detector thread's instructions should not result in significant overhead either. Since instructions are coming from its own isolated program cache, it will not compete for fetch bandwidth with other normal threads. It should not affect the data memory bandwidth either because its data will be mostly coming from special registers.

3.2 Elements of adaptive dynamic thread scheduling with the detector thread

3.2.1 Per-thread status indicators.
Per-thread status indicators represent a set of counters that show the most recent state of the threads resident in the processor. Included are counters for cache misses (data and instruction), number of pipeline stalls, number of loads, number of long-latency operations, number of instructions in each stage, number of new instructions in each stage, *etc.*

3.2.2 Thread control flags and thread selection unit.
At each cycle, threads are selected and instructions of selected threads are chosen for fetch

and issue. In that selection process, the thread selection hardware looks at the thread control flags to make a decision as to whether a thread is to be chosen. This hardware unit represents the thread control provisions throughout the pipeline stages. For example, in the fetch stage, if a thread's *no-fetch* flag is set, no instructions will be fetched from the thread until the flag is reset. The thread selection unit watches thread control flags and takes appropriate action depending on the value of the flags. The flags could include *suspend, no-fetch, no-issue, etc.* However, flags that need immediate action are not included in this set of flags because, with the detector thread at the lowest priority, it cannot be guaranteed that the detector thread will update this flag early enough. The thread selection unit is not unique to our approach. Its equivalent is required even in SMT architecture with fixed thread scheduling. The difference is that the thread scheduling policy itself is hard-coded in conventional SMT whereas the scheduling policy is programmable in our proposed approach.

3.2.3   The detector thread.   As described earlier, the detector thread plays a major role in this process as shown in Figure 4.1. It keeps watching the per-thread status indicators and updates the flags based on its active policy. The indicators are updated by hardware on predetermined events in places spread across the pipeline. As described earlier, the detector thread has the lowest priority among threads. As long as the pipeline is well utilized, the detector thread will not often be activated. Can a detector thread experience starvation in such cases? This depends upon the the occupancy rate of the instruction fetch buffer. As long as the instruction fetch buffer is full, no instructions from the detector thread can be fetched. We examined the occupancy rate of the instruction fetch buffer and found that the average value is 7.7 with a deviation of about 0.1%. Because the fetch buffer size is 8 in our configuration, we can estimate that about 2400 detector thread instructions will be executed every 8K cycles which was used as the interval for experimentation. This seems to be more than enough to avoid starvation.

For this detector thread approach to work successfully, it has to be equipped with intelligent heuristics or algorithms to dynamically detect clogging (low throughput) and to choose a better fetch policy for the next time frame. However, since the resources allowed for the detector thread are quite limited in order to minimize hardware overhead, the algorithm is also limited in the data to which it can refer. It will be our next challenge to design good detection algorithms and policy selection algorithms. This will be beyond the scope of this paper because the main goal of this work is to present there are enough room in which the adaptive thread scheduling approach can play.

3.3   Why a detector thread?

It is true that what a detector thread does can be implemented as hardware. The advantage could be that an existing thread context need not be permanently assigned to the detector thread. However, the cost of hard-coding multiple policies might offset this advantage. Another likely advantage of the hard-coded approach is that scheduling actions will be taken faster because it would not depend on the availability of empty pipeline slots. However, as stated earlier, when the processor suffers from low throughput, empty pipeline slots will naturally be more easily available. The most significant advantage of the detector thread approach over its hard-coded counterpart is that because the detector thread relies on software, the algorithm is not fixed and it can be enhanced or corrected even after the processor is taped out. Thus, eventually, after an SMT processor is taped out, the same processor can be retargeted for two different applications (for example, for servers and desktops) by equipping it with two different detector thread algorithms.

3.4   Implementation of the detector thread

The detector thread can be implemented based on the idea proposed in the study of Simultaneous Subordinate Microthreading (SSMT) in [3]. The study showed that small program image of the *microthread* can be placed in a small on-chip RAM while preventing interference between the instruction fetch from the microthread and that from the primary thread. However, still there can be non-trivial overhead in the data path because the two threads will compete for access to it. This problem will become more severe when nine threads compete for access as in our case (the normal eight threads plus one detector thread). That is why we propose to have a separate data RAM for the detector thread as shown in Figure 4.2. DT DRAM and DT PRAM are both initialized upon reset by the OS through DMA and the DT DRAM is exclusively accessed by the detector thread. DT PRAM can be loaded with new codes by the OS via DMA if the OS determines that a new algorithm should be engaged to enhance the throughput.

3.5   Applications of the detector thread

The detector thread can be used for purposes other than dynamic thread scheduling. It can be used to alleviate the burden of the system job scheduler. A job scheduler is a part of many operating systems. It periodically checks system status and makes decisions on what jobs should be selected for the next time slice. Even in SMT, the job scheduler will have to periodically be invoked and run for a while to make decisions for the next time slice as long as more threads than contexts are available.

When a job scheduler is invoked, room must be made for it by suspending one of the threads. Then, the job scheduler will gather information by reading the hardware counters and then applying its policies to choose threads that will remain and the ones that will be suspended. Software context switching will be involved for those that are suspended. The job scheduler can shorten its stay by just checking the flags that the detector thread has updated and simply making

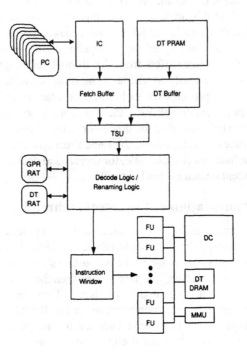

Figure 4.2.   Hardware Implementation of the Detector Thread (based on [3])

decisions based on that. The detector thread approach can also be used for other applications such as power monitoring where the pipeline is throttled so as to stay within the maximum power level.

4.   Methodology

To evaluate our ideas through realistic SMT simulation, we developed *SimpleSMT* simulator [10]. SimpleSMT is an SMT simulator based on the SimpleScalar tool set [1]. It thus inherits most architectural specifications of the superscalar model in SimpleScalar. SimpleSMT was developed by extending SimpleScalar to support separate integer and floating-point instruction queues and more pipeline stages to reflect the additional complexity of the SMT architecture. The simulation environment has been configured to have resources compatible with previous research on SMT [18] (for verification purposes). Table 4.1 shows the configuration used in our simulation.

Simulation has been performed with the Alpha EV6 binaries of the SPEC CPU2000 [7] benchmark suite which is compiled for a single Alpha 21264 processor. For simulation of multiple independent threads, the program com-

Parameter	Value
Fetch Bandwidth	2 threads, 8 instruction total
Functional Units	3 FP, 6 Int, 4 ld/st
Instruction Queues	64-entry FP, 64-entry Int
Inst Cache	32KB, direct, 64-byte lines
Data Cache	32KB, direct, 64-byte lines
L2 Cache	256KB, 4-way, 64-byte lines
L3 Cache	2MB, direct, 64-byte lines
Latency (to CPU)	L2 6 cycles, L3 12 cycles, Memory 62 cycles
Pipeline Depth	9 stages
Min Branch Penalty	7 cycles
Branch Predictor	2K bimodal
Instruction Latency	Based on Alpha 21264

Table 4.1. Simulator configuration

Mix Name	Applications
hiI-loM-mx	crafty, eon, equake, facerec, mesa, parser, sixtrack, vortex
hiI-hiM-mx	apsi, fma3d, galgel, gap, gcc, gzip, mcf, wupwise
loI-loM-mx	ammp, art, eon, mgrid, parser, sixtrack, twolf, vpr
loI-hiM-mx	applu, apsi, mgrid, gcc, gzip, lucas, mcf, swim
mxI-mxM-mx	ammp, crafty, equake, fma3d, gap, mcf, swim, twolf
hiI-loM-i	crafty, eon, gap, gzip, parser, twolf, vortex, vpr
hiI-hiM-i	crafty, gap, gcc, gzip, mcf, parser, vortex, vpr
loI-loM-i	eon, gcc, gzip, mcf, parser, twolf, vortex, vpr
hiI-loM-f	apsi, equake, facerec, fma3d, galgel, mesa, sixtrack, wupwise
hiI-hiM-f	applu, apsi, equake, fma3d, galgel, lucas, swim, wupwise
loI-loM-f	ammp, art, facerec, fma3d, galgel, lucas, mgrid, sixtrack
loI-hiM-f	applu, apsi, galgel, lucas, mgrid, sixtrack, swim, wupwise
mxI-mxM-f	ammp, art, equake, fma3d, lucas, mesa, swim, wupwise

Table 4.2. Various combinations of applications

bination was made of 4, 6, or 8 different programs which are selected from a total of 25 benchmark programs.

Since our study focuses on how various fetch policies affect processor utilization with different mixes of applications, we attempted to cover as broad a mix of benchmarks as possible. Three parameters were used for selecting various combinations: IPC on a single threaded machine model, memory footprint and integer, and the characteristics of the operations, floating-point or mixed. The result of this selection is shown in Table 4.2. Combinations with a mix of integer and floating-point applications were also made as even as possible. The name of a mix indicates three things: the first field indicates whether high-IPC applications were chosen, the second field indicates whether high-memory-footprint applications were chosen and the last field means whether integer, floating-point or mixed applications were chose. For instance, *hiI-loM-mx* means applications with high IPC, low memory footprint were chosen to form this mix and also a

Fetch Policies	
BRCOUNT	Number of total branches for a thread
LDCOUNT	Number of total loads for a thread
MEMCOUNT	Number of total memory accesses for a thread
L1MISS COUNT	Number of total L1 Cache misses for a thread
L1IMISS COUNT	Number of total L1 ICache misses for a thread
L1DMISS COUNT	Number of total L1 DCache misses for a thread
ICOUNT	Current Instruction Queue population for a thread
ACCIPC	Accumulated IPC for a thread
STALL COUNT	Number of total stalls incurred for a thread
RR	Round-Robin scheduling

Table 4.3.   Various Fetch Policies tested

mixture of integer and floating-point applications were selected. For simulation of 4- and 6-thread cases, a relevant number of applications were arbitrarily excluded from the 8-thread mixes.

The size of the memory footprint of each application was available from SPEC 2000 in [7] and the applications that take more than 100 MB of reserved memory were classified as the ones with high memory requirements. The throughput of each application as a singleton thread on our SMT model was available from [10] and it was used to determine whether the IPC of an application is relatively high or low.

4.1   Fetch policies modelled

We modelled ten different fetch policies as shown in Table 4.3. *BRCOUNT, L1DMISS COUNT, ICOUNT* and *RR* were proposed and evaluated in [18]. Additionally, we included in our list *LDCOUNT, MEMCOUNT, ACCIPC* and *STALL COUNT*. The description of each policy is found in the table. *L1MISS COUNT* and *L1IMISS COUNT* were added as well to have a closer look at the effect of the caches.

At each cycle, the simulator sorts out threads according to the fetch policy. Instructions are fetched from the first thread as long as the cache block boundary is not met. If no boundary is encountered, all eight instructions are fetched from one thread. Otherwise, instructions can be fetched from the next thread. We limited the number of threads that can be fetched in one cycle to two. A study [2] showed that fetching all eight instructions from one thread can adversely affect the performance due to fetch fragmentation. This mechanism was used in both fixed scheduling and adaptive scheduling.

Because of the huge size of the SPEC 2000 applications, it is almost impossible to run simulations until the end of all programs. Since the reference mode of a typical SPEC 2000 application has an average of 200 billion instructions, it would take about three months to completely run one application since our simulator executes about 25K instructions per second.

To lower the time requirement and yet get accurate simulation results, we ran simulation for a million cycles in ten randomly chosen different intervals by taking advantage of the *fast-forward* feature of the SimpleScalar simulator [1].

5. Experimental Results

5.1 Potential of adaptive dynamic thread scheduling

An attempt was made by Tullsen *et al.* to find out the best fetch policy in SMT [18]. Giving priorities to threads with fewer instructions in the instruction queues (*ICOUNT*) and the ones with newer instructions in the queues (*IQPOSN*) proved to produce higher throughput than other heuristics. The study concluded that *ICOUNT* performs better on the average except in some special cases where other policies can work better.

To verify this hypothesis, we ran simulations while keeping the record of the fetch policy that worked best in each interval (8K cycles). Figure 4.3(b) shows how many times each fetch policy was ranked as the best performer. (Note that the order of fetch policies shown in the legend is the same as the order each policy appears in each bar.) Undoubtedly, ICOUNT was ranked the first in more cases than any other single policy. However, it should be stressed that in about half of all cases, other fetch policies performed better than *ICOUNT* did. Fetch heuristics such as *LDCount, L1DMissCount, L1IMissCount* and, surprisingly, even round-robin are amongst them. These facts were not recognized by previous studies because they mostly relied upon an average analysis. Also, the main focus of the previous studies was on finding a fixed thread scheduling policy that would work best on average. We can infer that if we have the capability of switching thread selection heuristics, then we can significantly improve the throughput of the processor by using the heuristic that works better in each specific case rather than just one single hardwired fetch policy in all cases.

Another interesting point is found in Figure 4.3(a). It shows how many times each fetch policy was ranked as the worst performer. As the number of threads increases, it is more likely that *ICOUNT* becomes the worst performing fetch policy of all, reaching 20% of the time when eight threads are supported. This implies that simply balancing the number of instructions in the early stages of the pipelines does not work well when there are too many threads (eight) exist. When the number of threads is great, the effect of balancing the numbers does not translate well to effects of other policies such as BRCOUNT or L1MISSCOUNT. Detecting such conditions and preventing *ICOUNT* from being the fetch policy of choice in such cases thus should help sustain throughput of an SMT processor.

From the two figures, it appears that BRCOUNT is sensitive to the number of threads as well. BRCOUNT works better as the number of threads increases. It becomes more likely to become the best performer and at the same time less likely to become the worst performer as the number of threads increases.

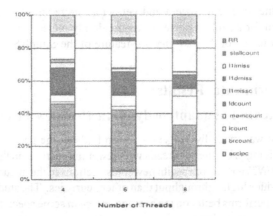

(a) How often each policy becomes the worst performer?

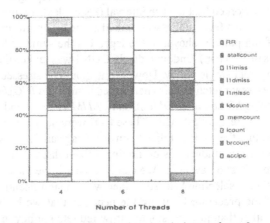

(b) How often each policy becomes the best performer?

Figure 4.3.   How often a fetch policy becomes the best or the worst of all?

However, note that BRCOUNT usually is not a good fetch policy for our mixes of applications.

Figure 4.4 shows the performance of the *MAX* strategy obtained using larger sets of data. Each data point in the graph represents the average IPC value of the thirteen different combinations of applications discussed in section 4 for each fetch policy. The line on top of the rest is for *MAX* in which the IPC of the pseudo fetch policy *MAX* was averaged over all thirteen mixes. For each mix, the IPC of *MAX* was obtained by averaging the highest IPC values found in each interval throughout the simulation lifetime. We find in Figure 4.4 that the IPC of *ICOUNT* presents an average IPC higher than all other real fetch policies

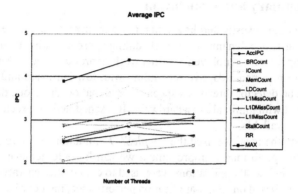

Figure 4.4. IPC of *MAX* and average IPC of various fetch policies

regardless of the number of threads. However, its IPC decreases as the number of threads increases from 6 to 8. This diminishing return in IPC as the number of threads increases was already discussed by previous studies [18, 8]. These studies recognized that inter-thread interference such as cache pollution account for such drawbacks of having too many threads simultaneously available on an SMT processor. The chart shows no such diminishing returns with the *MAX* pseudo fetch policy. Consequently, with eight threads, the throughput is more than one instruction per cycle higher than that of *ICOUNT* or 27% improvement.

It is obvious from Figure 4.4 that the adaptive dynamic thread scheduling will find more opportunity for performance improvement than a fixed scheduling approach as the number of threads increases. There are two reasons for this. The first lies in the fact that the overhead of the adaptive dynamic thread scheduling will be relatively small when there are more threads, for example, eight threads. The second reason is that an SMT processor will go through more adverse effects such as cross-replacement of blocks in the shared caches that may result in saturation observed in the studies described earlier. In such situations, fetch policies such as *LDCOUNT* or *L1MISSCOUNT* would work better than *ICOUNT* because they would give priority to the thread that relies less heavily on the performance of the cache.

We also observe from the chart that even with the *MAX* pseudo fetch policy, the IPC is saturated when going from 6 threads to 8 threads although it does not degenerate as *ICOUNT* does. This implies that one hardware context can be allocated to the detector thread without sacrificing performance in most cases. The possible paradox is if the detector thread becomes too effective, then it could delay the saturation point beyond seven, thereby creating the need for additional contexts.

6.   Summary and Conclusion

This paper has investigated how much more improvement can be made by allowing an adaptive dynamic thread scheduling approach rather than the fixed scheduling approaches employed in earlier work. It proposed the detector thread approach to implement adaptive scheduling with low hardware and software overhead. The detector thread is a special thread that occupies one designated thread context with minimal extra hardware. It is scheduled for execution when idle slots are available.

To validate the idea, we used the *SimpleSMT* simulator to derive an upperbound for the performance improvement we can hope to achieve using our approach. SPEC 2000 applications were used to create thirteen various mixes of applications based on single-application performance, memory footprint and type (integer or floating-point).

Simulation results showed that there still is significant room (27%) for performance improvement over fixed scheduling for eight threads on which adaptive scheduling can work. This paper stresses that adaptive scheduling is feasible because our platform is SMT where it is possible to have one thread resident in the processor with minimal overhead.

The results we obtained in this study are greatly encouraging. Since SMT was introduced, studies have repeatedly shown that having too many threads (usually more than four or five) will not return the expected throughput increase and sometimes even lower the throughput. Our study has shown that adaptive thread scheduling in combination with a detector thread can significantly extend the saturation point in terms of number of threads provided that the detector thread is programmed with effective low-throughput detection and fetch policy selection algorithms.

References

[1] T. Austin. The SimpleScalar Architectural Research Tool Set, Version 2.0. Technical Report 1342, University of Wisconsin-Madison, June 1997.

[2] J. Burns and J-L Gaudiot. Exploring the SMT Fetch Bottleneck. In *Proceedings of the Workshop on Multithreaded Execution, Architecture and Compilation (MTEAC99)*, Orlando, Florida, January 1999.

[3] R. Chappell, J. Stark, S. Kim, S. Reinhardt, and Y. Patt. Simultaneous Subordinate Microthreading (SSMT). In *Proceedings of the 26th Annual International Symposium on Computer Architecture*, pages 186–195, May 1999.

[4] S. Eggers, J. Emer, H. Levy, J. Lo, R. Stamm, and D. Tullsen. Simultaneous Multithreading: A Platform for Next-Generation Processors. *IEEE Micro*, pages 12–18, September/October 1997.

[5] M. Gulati and N. Bagherzadeh. Performance Study of a Multithreaded Superscalar Microprocessor. In *Proceedings of the 2nd International Symposium on High Performance Computer Architecture*, pages 291–301, Feburary 1996.

[6] L. Gwenlapp. Dansoft Develops VLIW Design. *Microprocessor Report*, 11(2):18–22, Feburary 1997.

[7] J. Henning. SPEC CPU2000: Measuring CPU Performance in the New Millennium. *IEEE Computer*, 33(7):28–35, July 2000.

[8] S. Hily and A. Seznec. Standard Memory Hierarchy Does Not Fit Simultaneous Multithreading. In *Proceedings of MTEAC'98 Workshop*, Feburary 1998.

[9] H. Hirata, K. Kimura, S. Nagamine, Y. Mochizuki, A. Nishimura, Y. Nakase, and T. Nishizawa. An Elementary Processor Architecture with Simultaneous Instruction Issuing from Multiple Threadds. In *Proceedings of the 19th Annual International Symposium on Computer Architecture*, pages 136–145, May 1992.

[10] S. Lee and J-L Gaudiot. ALPSS: Architectural Level Power Simulator for Simultaneous Multithreading, Version 1.0. Technical Report TR-02-04, University of Southern California, April 2002.

[11] J. Lo, S. Eggers, J. Emer, H. Levy, R. Stamm, and D. Tullsen. Converting Thread-Level Parallelism to Instruction-Level Parallelism via Simultaneous Multithreading. *ACM Transactions on Computer Systems*, pages 322–354, August 1997.

[12] Matthew McCormick, Jonathan Ledlie, and Omer Zaki. Adaptively Scheduling Processes on a Simultaneous Multithreading Processor. Technical report, University of Wisconsin - Madison, 2000.

[13] S. Parekh, S. Eggers, H. Levy, and J. Lo. Thread-Sensitive Scheduling for SMT Processors. Technical report, University of Washington, 2000.

[14] U. Sigmund and T. Ungerer. Evaluating a Multithreaded Superscalar Microprocessor versus a Multiprocessor Chip. In *Proc. of the 4 th PASA Workshop–Parallel Systems and Algorithms*, pages 147–159, April 1996.

[15] A. Snavely and D. Tullsen. Symbiotic Jobscheduling for a Simultaneous Multithreading Architecture. In *Proceedings of the 9th International Conference on Architectural Support for Programming Languages and Operating Systems*, pages 234–244, Cambridge, Massachussets, November 2000.

[16] Y. Song and M. Dubois. Assisted Execution. Technical Report Technical Report CENG 98-25, University of Southern California, 1998.

[17] G. Edward Suh, S. Devadas, and L. Rudolph. A New Memory Monitoring Scheme for Memory-Aware Scheduling. In *Proceedings of the High Performance Computer Architecture (HPCA'02) Conference*, Feburary 2002.

[18] D. Tullsen, S. Eggers, J. Emer, H. Levy, J. Lo, and R. Stamm. Exploiting Choice: Instruction Fetch and Issue on an Implementable Simultaneous Multithreading Processor. In *Proceedings of the 23rd Annual International Symposium on Computer Architecture*, pages 191–202, May 1996.

[19] D. Tullsen, S. Eggers, and H. Levy. Simultaneous Multithreading: Maximizing On-Chip Parallelism. In *Proceedings of the 22nd Annual International Symposium on Computer Architecture*, pages 392–403, June 1995.

[20] H. Wang, P. Wang, R. Weldon, and et. al. Speculative Precomputation: Exploring the Use of Multithreading for Latency. *Intel Technology Journal*, 6(1), Feburary 2002.

II

NUMERICAL COMPUTATION

Chapter 5

PERFORMANCE ANALYSIS OF A BICGSTAB SOLVER FOR MULTIPLE-MARINE-PROPELLER SIMULATION WITH SEVERAL MPI LIBRARIES AND PLATFORMS

Pengfei Liu
Research Officer, National Research Council Canada, Institute for Marine Dynamics
1 Kerwin Place, St. John's, NF Canada A1B 3T5
Pengfei.Liu@nrc.ca

Kun Li
Work Term Student, Department of Electrical and Computer Engineering
Memorial University of Newfoundland, St. John's, NF Canada A1B 3X5
Kun@engr.mun.ca

Abstract   Panel method, or boundary element method is widely used in marine hydro-dynamics computations, especially for lifting flows in which forces are to be obtained for foil or blade sections. For simulation of multiple propellers and foils, a couple of large, dense and asymmetric matrices are to be generated and to be solved a number of times during a numerical iteration process. A parallel BiCGSTAB matrix solver is developed for this engineering application and tested to run under four different MPI software libraries (MPICH, MPI/Pro, WMPI and Compaq Tru64 MPI) and three different operating systems (Windows 2000 Pro, Red Hat Linux 7.2 and Tru64) under a Compaq Proliant sever and a Compaq Alpha ES40 Server. Performance of the matrix solver, for this application case, for each configuration is evaluated in terms of computational time, speed, and price performance ratio for three different matrix sizes: 256MB, 1GB and 4GB.

Keywords: Panel method, BiCGSTAB, MPICH, MPI/Pro, WMPI

1.   Introduction

To solve problems and make performance evaluations in ocean and naval architectural engineering, various modelling simulations are performed. These simulations are often divided in to two categories: physical modelling and numerical modelling. Modern physical modelling requires large facilities (for example, an in-door towing tank could be as large as about 1000-m long), advanced data acquisition systems and intensive labour. Numerical modelling in hydrodynamics will not substitute the facilities, but can compensate some drawbacks of experimental set ups, thereby providing the most economical and feasible way for evaluation and design. In numerical hydrodynamics, numerical methods are divided in to two categories. They are potential flow based method and viscous flow based method. Typically in marine propulsion community, these methods are the panel method and the Reynolds-number Averaged Navier-Stokes (RANS) method.

In panel method, lifting and non-lifting bodies are represented only in terms of surface meshes as apposed to the RANS method, which uses volume meshes. The panel method requires a substantially smaller number of meshes, and hence, the computational time. For example, for a typical propeller simulation that requires downstream velocity prediction, the memory requirement of the panel method and the RANS method is about 0.5 GB and 50GB, respectively. For an offshore floating production storage and offloading (FPSO) platform with 6 dynamic positioning thrusters, the required memory storage for the arrays of a typical panel method and a RANS method code, with double precision, can be about 100 GB and 10000GB, respectively (see [4]).

Numerical modelling codes are often written with dynamic memory allocation to allow variations of input geometry and motion parameters. This requires heap memory allocation in a physical memory space to obtain an acceptable computing efficiency. For the above application cases, RANS code requires about 10TB of physical memory. This capacity of parallel computing hardware is not easily accessible. For the panel method, however, a PC cluster with a memory capacity of 100GB of DRAM would meet the minimum hardware requirement.

A serial panel method code for multiple thrusters was developed recently by the first author to handle multiple nozzle-propeller computations. This was the first attempt to use the panel method for a computation of multiple propellers. Due to hardware limitations, the maximum number of thrusters or nozzle-propellers to be evaluated cannot exceed 4, even if the mesh size was set to the minimum. This limitation is physical memory size of the Alpha ES40 server at the institute, which was only 16GB.

The matrix solver used here is the parallelized BiCGSTAB solver. A modified BiCGSTAB solver to improve the computational efficiency was presented by [7], which may require further work on initialization of the interactive parameters. In the present work, the standard BiCGSTAB procedure is used to test the performance of the MPI libraries and computing configurations. A detailed description of the solver can be found in [4]. As mentioned in their study, for dynamic positioning thruster simulation, a large size matrix, of an order of storage at about 30 GB, in each run, is to be updated and solved a million of times. Therefore, the numerical efficiency of the matrix solver and the computational efficiency of the software and hardware combination are important for the overall computational efficiency.

Many performance benchmark studies have been done in the literature. Most of which were conducted using the general NAS benchmark codes ([4]) to test the hardware performance. Comparison of different communication interface types was presented on the net ([6]). A comparison of three different MPI libraries on a Linux cluster was done by [5]. [1] compared three MPI libraries on an NT based cluster and a HP machine. In their study, WMPI had the best performance on NT, but documentation of the software was poor, as experienced by the authors of this present paper. NAS benchmark performance evaluation was presented by [3] on a cluster of PCs under NT and Linux. Performance evaluation for a few older machines for a CFD code on an Origin 2000, Pentium II cluster and Compaq Alpha cluster was presented by [2].

The problem was: for the above-mentioned particular numerical method and application, what is the computational performance of the solver, in terms of recent operation systems (Windows 2000 Pro, Red Hat Linux 7.2 and Tru64), up-to-date hardware configurations (PC server and Alpha Server) and MPI libraries (MPI/Pro, MPICH, WMPI, Compaq MPI)? In planning the required computational hardware infrastructure, what would be the best combination of MPI software, operating system and hardware for the particular engineering application? The present work is to answer these questions.

2.   Computational Configurations

2.1   Application geometry for the matrix solver

The above matrix solver was going to be used in the parallel version of the in-house panel method code Propella. In the application case, a dynamic positioning (DP) system of floating production storage and offloading platform consisted of four thrusters. The number of total body panels for the propellers and nozzles were 20160. The created doublet and source coefficient matrices took 4GB of memory for a matrix size of 20160×20160. In the code Propella, three such matrices took a total of 12 GB of memory storage. For far wake velocity prediction, a long wake history was required so that the wake matrix was in an order of 30GB of memory.

Figure 5.1 shows the surface mesh arrangement of this group of thrusters. The origins of the thrusters were located at (0.0,-0.2,0.0), (0.0,0.2,0.0), (0.6,-0.6,0.0), and (0.6,0.6,0.0), respectively. Each propeller had 4 blades with a rear hub. By varying the distances and relative locations of the thrusters, interactions between propellers in terms of hydrodynamic characteristics such as propeller and nozzle surface pressure, velocity, and thrust and torque coefficients can be predicted by the simulation code.

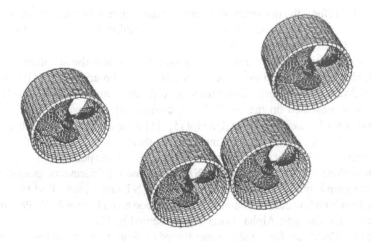

Figure 5.1.   Surface mesh presentation of a group of 4 thrusters.

2.2   MPI and hardware configurations

Computational hardware used was a Compaq Proliant server and a Compaq Alpha ES40. Their hardware and operating system configurations and are shown in Table 5.1. The CPUs in the Compaq Proliant server were the Intel Xeon 700MHz processors with 2 MB of cache memory each.

Machine/Specs	CPU (MHz)	Memory	OS	Cost
Alpha ES40	4 × 667	4 × 4 GB	Tru64	500k
Compaq Proliant	4 × 700	4 × 1 GB	Win 2000 Server Red Hat 7.2	38k

Table 5.1.   Hardware and operating system configuration of the two testing machines

Four MPI software libraries were tested. They were MPICH, MPI/Pro, WMPI and Compaq Tru64 MPI. A brief description for these libraries is as follows:

- MPICH: MPICH was developed by Argonne National Laboratory and Mississippi State University. It is probably the most popular MPI library at the time of the work. It was also free. MPICH allowed processes to communicate each other via either shared memory or over a network. At the time when this was written, the web page for MPICH was: http://www-unix.mcs.anl.gov/mpi/mpich/index.html. It is noted that this software, though free, is very user-friendly for installation and for code compilation.

- MPI/Pro: MPI/Pro was a commercial package by MPI Software Technology, Inc. The problem of communications performance bottleneck has been removed. In addition, MPI/PRO used Install-shield to install and set up the service daemon. MPI/Pro also supports both Intel and Alpha processors and was designed for Microsoft Visual C++ and Digital Visual Fortran. At the time of this work, the home page address of MPI/Pro was http://www.mpi-softtech.com. This MPI software requires Microsoft .NET Framework under Windows OSes.

- WMPI: WMPI was another commercial package by Instituto Supererior de Engenharia de Coimbra, Portugal. It was a full implementation of MPI for Microsoft Win32 platforms. WMPI was based on MPICH. WMPI package included a set of libraries for Borland C++, Microsoft Visual C++ and Microsoft Visual Fortran. The release of WMPI provides libraries, header files, examples and daemons for remote starting. WMPI trial version can be downloaded at www.criticalsoftware.com/wmpi. This MPI software would have been easy to install and to use with the Visual C++ compiler from within MS Visual Studio if the folder /documentation/user-manual have clear information on parallel code compilation settings under MS Visual Studio.

- Compaq Tru64 MPI: This MPI was described on the home page of HP, which merged the Compaq recently: "Compaq MPI is a version of MPICH from Argonne National Laboratory and Mississippi State University, concentrating on optimizing the most frequently-used code paths for performance on Compaq's UNIX clusters. Compaq MPI is functionally compatible with MPICH Version 1.1.1, with only minor differences..." Documentation and Compaq Tru64 MPI software can be downloaded on: http://www.hp.com/techservers/software/cmpisrc.html. This MPI software library was installed by the system administrator at the Institute. It was easy to use and compile, if a header file was included in the parallel code in addition to the ANSI C standard.

3.   Using the MPI Libraries

This section is an introduction to build and run MPI libraries under different operating systems. The MPI libraries used in this study are MPICH, MPI/Pro and WMPI and the operating systems are Windows 2000 Server and Linux Red Hat 7.2.

3.1   Windows system

For Windows compilation of the code, Microsoft Visual Studio was used. First, a new project was created (Win32 Console Application), then the necessary source files are written and added to the project. To use the MPI libraries, as with any other library, the preprocessor directive "#include <mpi.h>" is necessary.

3.1.1   MPICH.   Before starting any new MPI projects, or editing existing MPI application projects under Visual Studio, the locations to the MPI package directories must be defined. For high-performance program application, the authors suggest setting the active configuration first: Build → Set Active Configuration, then choose "program - Win32 Release". From the Visual Studio main window, go to project settings: Project → Settings → C/C++, then, select the category Preprocessor, and in the window for additional directories to include, type the path "C:/Program Files/MPICH/SDK/Include". The compiler must also be told where the MPI libraries are located: Project → Settings → Link. In the category General, add path "C:/Program Files/MPICH/SDK/lib/mpich.lib" with a space between it and any other adjacent entries.

To run the program, the syntax is:
⇒ mpirun -np # program [args..]
Where # is the number of processors that are going be used when running the parallel program. For example, if the parallel program is going to run on 4 processors, the command should look like the following:
⇒ mpirun -np 4 myprog.exe

3.1.2   MPI/Pro.   Similarly to MPICH, the MPI/Pro INCLUDE and LIB directories can be added directly in the project settings: Project → Settings → C/C++, in the category Preprocessor, the path is "C:/Program Files/MPIPro/Include". For the Link tab, the path is "C:/Program Files/MPIPro/lib/MPIPro.lib".

The command-line specification for mpirun varies depending on whether the user chooses a machines configuration or a procgroup file.

Machines File Format
The machines file is a simple list of machine names, the machines command-line specification for mpirun is as follows:
⇒ mpirun -np # [-mach_file | -mf <machines file>] program [args..]

Below is an example of a typical machines file for the Compaq Proliant machine which has 4 processors at IMD:
pc014014
Where pc014014 is the name of the Compaq Proliant machine. To run the code, just save this file with a name of "machines" and then run the command:
⇒ mpirun -np 4 -mf machines

Process Group File Format
The format of the procgroup mpirun command specification is as follows:
⇒ mpirun -pg_file | -pg <proc group file >

Below is an example of a typical procgroup file for Compaq Proliant machine at IMD.

pc014014 4 //fileserver/apps/program.exe

The example means run the program.exe on 4 processors. After saving this file with a name of "pg_4", the code can be run by executing the command as the following:

$\Rightarrow$ mpirun -pg pg_4

3.1.3 WMPI.

The WMPI INCLUDE and LIB directories can be added directly in the project settings: Project $\rightarrow$ Settings $\rightarrow$ C/C++. One needs to choose the Code Generation category and set the run-time libraries to use Multithreaded DLLs. Again, in category Preprocessor, the path is: "$(MPI_ROOT)/include". For Link Category, input the path "C:/Program Files/Critical Software/WMPI/lib".

Optionally, one may insert the path into Visual Studio and avoid this last addition in all of his WMPI projects (Tools $\rightarrow$ Options $\rightarrow$ "Show directories for" $\rightarrow$ "Library Files"). This is done by "double-clicking" on the empty box at the end of the list. This box will change to an edit gadget with a button to the right, with "..." on it. Click on the "..." button and a directory browser will appear. This browser can be used to locate the MPI home directory and the LIB subdirectory just underneath. Follow the same procedure for the INCLUDE directory. This option is also available for MPICH and MPI / Pro. To perform a computation with WMPI, it is necessary to set two configuration files: Cluster Configuration and the Process Group files.

Cluster Configuration

The cluster configuration file, named wmpi.clustercongf, in the current directory, indicates which machines may be used in a given computation, the communication devices that can be used to exchange data between processes, and the security context of processes for each machine.

It is possible to create a portable Cluster Configuration file by using the wildcard "." (period). Here we present an example of a portable configuration file for the Compaq Proliant machine at IMD:

/Machines
pc014014
startup address pc014014.imd.NRC.ca
shmem pc014014
/Connections
internal device shmem
external device shmem
/security
default user .
default domain .

String "/Machines" starts the machines section, which creates an entry for each machine of the cluster. In this case, only one machine pc014014 is used.

The line that includes
"startup address pc014014.imd.NRC.ca" indicates the IP address of the machine for starup. The string "/Connections" indicates how the processes of each machine communicate with all other processes. Default communication devices can be introduced for communication between processes that are running on the same machine (internal), and, for processes that are running on other machines (external). The string "shmem" means that internal communication is based on share memory.

Process Group File
The process group description file indicates which machines will be involved in the computation, as well as the executables. An example of a Process Description file for IMD Compaq Proliant machine is:
pc014014 3 X:/path/myprog.exe

It identifies the Windows Computer Name (the same as in the Cluster Configuration file), and then specifies the number of processes to run on this machine except the host processor. In this example, the computation uses 4 processors, the number "3" which in Process Description file means there are 3 processes to run in addition to the host processor. The executable path must be inserted from the point of view of the machine where the program is located. Finally, one may insert arguments for the processes that will run the executable.

To start, run myprog.exe in host processor. Then it will try to find a pg file with the name that is the same as that of the executable (myprog.pg), which should be present in the current directory.

3.2   Linux system

For Linux compilation, the same code that was used in Windows can be used after the command "dos2unix". This is an utility to convert characters in the DOS extended character set to the corresponding ISO standard characters.

3.2.1   MPICH.   To compile an MPI program, type the command:
⇒ mpicc -lmpich -lm program.c -o executable
To avoid having to type the full path of each command in /mpich-1.2.4/bin, the user can edit the file /.bash_profile to include the line:
PATH=$PATH:/mpich-1.2.3/bin
To run the program, the syntax is:
⇒ mpich -np # program [args..]
For example: mpich -np 4 program.exe

3.2.2   MPI/Pro.   To compile an MPI program, type the command:
⇒ mpicc -lmpipro -lm program.c -o executable
The syntax of running the MPI program in MPI/Pro is the same as MPICH:
⇒ mpirun -np # program [args..]

4. Results and Discussion

Figure 5.2 shows the performance in terms of execution time and speed for MPICH, MPI/Pro and WMPI libraries on the Compaq Proliant server under Windows 2000 Server OS for a small matrix size of 4434 × 4434. For this small matrix size, these three libraries gave about the same speed or execution time. A relatively straight line in the speed plot shows a good scalability of the overall computational performance.

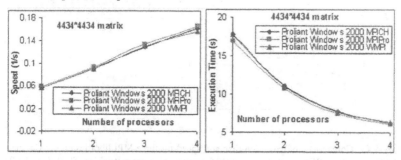

Figure 5.2. Comparison of execution time and speed for three MPI libraries on the Compaq Proliant server under Windows 2000 Server OS for a small matrix size of 4434 × 4434.

Figure 5.3 shows the performance in terms of execution time and speed for MPICH, MPI/Pro and WMPI libraries on the Compaq Proliant server under Windows 2000 Server OS for a medium matrix size of 9984 × 9984.

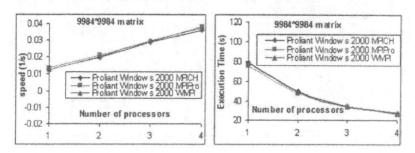

Figure 5.3. Comparison of execution time and speed for three MPI libraries on the Compaq Proliant server under Windows 2000 Server OS for a medium matrix size of 9984 × 9984.

For this size, the required memory storage for the matrix was 1GB with a double precision designation in C programming language. These curves also show little performance difference across these three libraries. The scalability is also as good as for the small matrix size.

Figure 5.4 shows the computational performance in terms of execution time and speed for MPICH, MPI/Pro and WMPI libraries on the Compaq Proliant

server under Windows 2000 Server OS for a relatively large matrix size of
20160×20160 (4GB memory with double precision). These three libraries
gave the same speed or execution time for the MPI software. The scalability
of the code and hardware for all MPI libraries seemed nearly linear, which is
good.

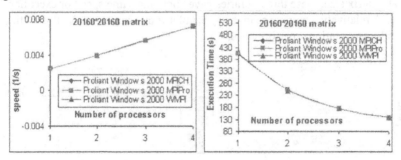

Figure 5.4.   Comparison of execution time and speed for three MPI libraries on the Compaq
Proliant server under Windows 2000 Server OS for a relatively large matrix size of 20160×20160.

Figure 5.5 shows the comparison of performance between MPICH and MPI/-
Pro under Red Hat Linux 7.2 on the Compaq Proliant server for a small matrix
size of 4434×4434. For such a small matrix size, MPI/Pro gave a much better
performance than MPICH. Both MPI software packages gave almost a linear
scalability.

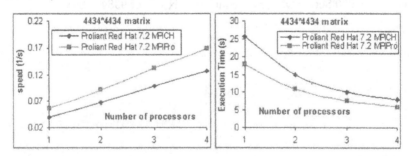

Figure 5.5.   Comparison of performance between MPICH and MPI/Pro under Red Hat Linux
7.2 on the Compaq Proliant server for a small matrix size of 4434×4434.

Figure 5.6 shows the comparison of performance between MPICH and MPI/-
Pro under Red Hat Linux 7.2 on the Compaq Proliant server for a medium matrix
size of 9984×9984. In this case, MPI/Pro had even better performance than
MPICH. The same as Figure 4, both MPI software packages gave almost a
linear scalability.

The larger matrix size of 20160 took about 4.0GB of memory storage and the matrix solver could not be executed under the Red Hat Linux. System hung up without giving an error message for an unknown reason. There might be a problem with the memory management in the Linux kernel.

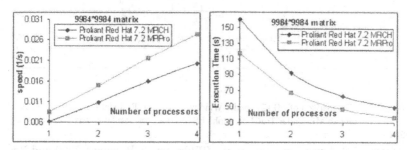

Figure 5.6. Comparison of performance between MPICH and MPI/Pro under Red Hat Linux 7.2 on the Compaq Proliant server for a medium matrix size of 9984 × 9984.

Figure 5.7 shows the comparison of MPICH under Windows 2000 and Red Hat Linux 7.2 on Proliant server and Compaq MPI under Tru64 on Alpha ES40 server for a small matrix size of 4434 × 4434. Alpha ES40 with Tru64 MPI gave the best performance with a large number of processors. MPICH gave a better performance under Windows 2000 Server OS than under Red Hat Linux 7.2.

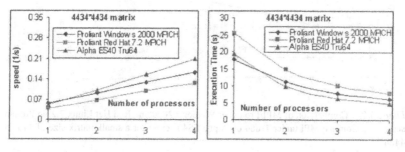

Figure 5.7. Comparison of MPICH under Windows 2000 and Red Hat Linux 7.2 on Proliant server and Compaq MPI under Tru64 on Alpha ES40 server for a small matrix size of 4434 × 4434.

Figure 5.8 shows the comparison of MPICH under Windows 2000 and Red Hat Linux 7.2 on Proliant server and Compaq MPI under Tru64 on Alpha ES40 server for a medium matrix size of 9984 × 9984. Alpha ES40 with Tru64 MPI gave the best performance at a large number of processors but poor performance when the number of processors was less than 2. MPICH yielded about the same performance under Windows 2000 Server OS as Compaq MPI under Tru64.

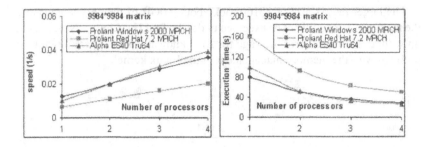

Figure 5.8. Comparison of MPICH under Windows 2000 and Red Hat Linux 7.2 on Proliant server and Compaq MPI under Tru64 on Alpha ES40 server for a small matrix size of 9984 × 9984.

Figure 5.9 shows Comparison of MPI/Pro under Windows 2000 and Red Hat Linux 7.2 on Proliant server and Compaq MPI under Tru64 on Alpha ES40 server for a small matrix size of 4434 × 4434. MPI/Pro yielded the same level of performance of the matrix solver on Windows 2000 Sever and Linux Red Hat 7.2. The Alpha ES40 had a better performance with number of processor great than 1.

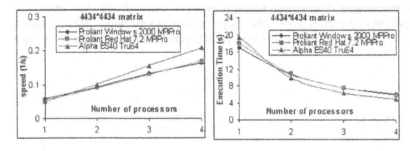

Figure 5.9. Comparison of MPI/Pro under Windows 2000 and Red Hat Linux 7.2 on Proliant server and Compaq MPI under Tru64 on Alpha ES40 server for a small matrix size of 4434 × 4434.

Figure 5.10 shows Comparison of MPI/Pro under Windows 2000 Server OS and Red Hat Linux 7.2 on Proliant server and Compaq MPI under Tru64 on Alpha ES40 server for a medium matrix size of 9984 × 9984.

It can be seen that MPI/Pro yielded a much better performance of the matrix solver on Windows 2000 Sever than on Linux Red Hat 7.2. MPI/Pro had the best performance under Windows 2000 Server OS with the number of processors greater than 2.

Figure 5.11 shows the comparison of WMPI under Windows 2000 Server OS on the Proliant server and Compaq MPI under Tru64 on the Alpha ES40 server for a small matrix size of 4434 × 4434. At the number of processors greater than one, the Alpha ES40 server had a better performance and the scalability.

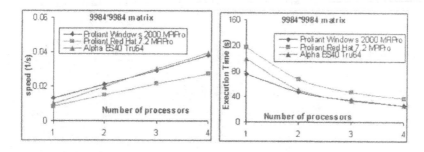

Figure 5.10. Comparison of MPI/Pro under Windows 2000 Server OS and Red Hat Linux 7.2 on Proliant server and Compaq MPI under Tru64 on Alpha ES40 server for a medium matrix size of 9984 × 9984.

The Alpha ES40 server was much better than the WMPI with the Windows 2000 Server OS.

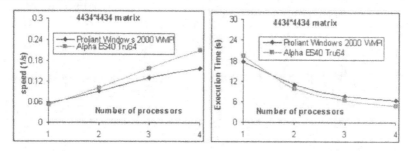

Figure 5.11. Comparison of WMPI under Windows 2000 Server OS on the Proliant server and Compaq MPI under Tru64 on the Alpha ES40 server for a small matrix size of 4434 × 4434.

Figure 5.12 shows the comparison of WMPI under Windows 2000 Server OS on the Proliant server and Compaq MPI under Tru64 on the Alpha ES40 server for a medium matrix size of 9984 × 9984. With the number of processors greater than two, the Alpha ES40 server had a better performance and the scalability. The Alpha ES40 server is again better than the WMPI with the Windows 2000 Server OS. For a computation of the larger matrix size of 20160, all the MPI software packages gave about the same speed under Windows 2000 Pro on the PC server. This comparison is not shown here but shown in the right plot of Figure 5.14.

Figure 5.13 shows price-scaled performance chart for different MPI software libraries on the Compaq Proliant sever for the small and medium matrix sizes of 4434 × 4434 and 9984 × 9984. The best performance was given by the MPI/Pro under Red Hat Linux 7.2 for the small size matrix and by the MPI/Pro under Windows 2000 Server OS for the medium matrix size, respectively. MPICH

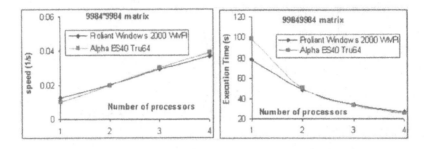

Figure 5.12. Comparison of WMPI under Windows 2000 Server OS on Proliant server and Compaq MPI under Tru64 on Alpha ES40 server for a medium matrix size of 9984 × 9984.

gave the poorest performance under both operations system for both small and medium matrix sizes.

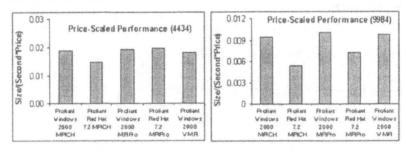

Figure 5.13. Price-scaled performance chart for different MPI software libraries on the Compaq Proliant sever for the small and medium matrix sizes of 4434 × 4434 and 9984 × 9984. MPI software price was neglected.

Figure 5.14 shows price-scaled performance chart for different MPI software libraries on the Compaq Proliant sever and Alpha ES40 sever for the medium and the large matrix sizes of 9984 × 9984 and 20160 × 20160. The best performance was given by the MPI/Pro under Windows 2000 Server OS for the medium size matrix. For all the sizes of a matrix mentioned above, Alpha ES40 gave the poorest performance. However, the performance comparison in Figure 14 for the Alpha sever was based on the total memory of 16 GB but in the tests, only 4GB was used. If the memory of the ES40 server was reduced to 4GB, the price performance index, as formulated by $\left\lceil \frac{N}{T} \right\rceil / P = \frac{N}{T \times P}$, where N is the number of rows of the matrix, T is the time in seconds and P is the price of the machine, would have been much higher, though it would be still far below that of the Proliant server.

Price of Windows 2000 Server OS software was not included in the price performance ratio in Figure 13 either when compared with Red Hat 7.2. This justification was made based on a reason that the price of the Windows 2000

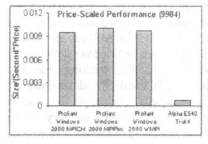 

Figure 5.14. Price-scaled performance chart for different MPI software libraries on the Compaq Proliant sever and Alpha ES40 sever for the medium and the large matrix sizes of 9984 × 9984 and 20160 × 20160.

Server OS may cancel out the inaccessibility of the Linux operating system in a typical company or institution, in which most workstations would be Windows driven. That is, the PC server machines when equipped with Windows operating systems, it can be utilized after working hours which are normally used by other Windows users.

From the above figures on the performance of the matrix solver, the following trends were observed:

- On the same hardware, say, Compaq Proliant server, the solver compiled with MPI libraries MPICH and MPI/Pro had a better performance under Windows 2000 than Linux Red Hat 7.2.

- On the Compaq Proliant server under Windows 2000 Server OS, the solver compiled with MPICH, MPI/Pro and WMPI showed almost the same level of performance.

- On the Compaq Proliant server under Linux Red Hat 7.2 operating system, the solver compiled with MPI/Pro showed better performance than with MPICH.

- On the Compaq Alpha ES40 server under Tru64 OS, the solver had better performance than on Compaq Proliant server under Windows 2000 Server OS and the Linux Red Hat 7.2.

- The solver on the Compaq Proliant server had much better Price-Scaled performance than on the Compaq Alpha ES40 server.

5. Conclusions

Experimentation to evaluate the computational performance of a parallel BiCGSTAB matrix solver for the marine propeller simulation code Propella was completed. The tests were performed under a combination of different MPI library software packages, operating systems, a multiple-CPU PC server and an Alpha server. Tests showed that MPI software packages did not make large differences. For the large size of matrix, which would be the normal case of parallel computing, three MPI libraries, MPICH, MPI/Pro and WMPI gave the same performance for the matrix solver under Windows 2000 Server OS on the Compaq Proliant server. As the matrix solver working under Red Hat Linux system was not successful, cluster of PCs under Windows operating system for this particular application seemed a better choice. As the solution of the matrix required distributing the storage of the matrix memory among the processors, shared memory configuration should give a better performance by reducing the communication overhead. Also too many processors for a relatively small matrix size (say 1000 CPUs versus a $10,000 \times 10,000$ matrix) will add communication overhead resulting in a degradation of the performance.

For simulations, a dynamic positioning system with multiple thrusters and a group of prop-fans (up to 12 propellers), a PC cluster with each PC having maximum possible processors and the fastest possible link with a total memory of 50-100GB, under a Windows OS environment, seemed to be the best configuration.

Acknowledgments

The authors would like to thank the National Research Council Canada for its support. They are also grateful to Mr. Paul Thorburn and Mr. Gilbert Wong in the computer support group at the institute for technical assistance. The director general of the insitute, Dr. Mary Williams is also appreciated for her comments and proofread of the manuscript.

References

[1] Baker, M. and Fox, G. (1998). MPI on NT: A Preliminary Evaluation of the Available Environments. *1st Workshop on Personal Computer Based Networks of Workstations (IPDPS 1998)*.

[2] Windows Clusters Resource Center. (2002). URL: http://www.windowsclusters.org.

[3] Hart, D., Lauer, D., and Stewart, C. (2000). Performance of Parallel Programs on PC Clusters: NT vs. Linux. *SIAM Conference on Computational Science and Engineering*. Washington.

[4] Liu, P. and Li, K. (2002). Programming the BI-CGSTAB Matrix Solver for HPC and Benchmarking IDM SP3 and Alpha ES40. *The 16th International Parallel & Distributed Processing Symposium (IPDPS)*, pages 15–19. Ft. Lauderdale, Florida USA.

[5] Ong, H. and Farrell, P. (2000). Performance Comparison of LAM/MPI, MPICH, and MVICH on a Linux Cluster Connected by a Gigabit Ethernet Network. *Proceedings of Linux 2000, 4th Annual Linux Showcase and Conference, Extreme Linux Track*, pages 353–362. Atlanta.

[6] tfcc-l archives (August 2000). http://www.listproc.bucknell.edu/archives/tfcc-l/200008/pdf00000.pdf.

[7] Yang, L.T. and Brent, R. (2002). The Improved BICG Method for Large and Sparse Linear Systems on Parallel Distributed Memory Architectures. *The 16th International Parallel & Distributed Processing Symposium (IPDPS)*, pages 15–19. Ft. Lauderdale, Florida USA.

Chapter 6

A NEW BLAS-3 BASED PARALLEL ALGORITHM FOR COMPUTING THE EIGENVECTORS OF REAL SYMMETRIC MATRICES

Yusaku Yamamoto*

Department of Computational Science and Engineering, Nagoya University, Japan
yamamoto@na.cse.nagoya-u.ac.jp

Mitsuyoshi Igai and Ken Naono

Hitachi ULSI Systems Corp. and Central Research Laboratory, Hitachi Ltd.
igai@hitachi-ul.co.jp & naono@crl.hitachi.co.jp

Abstract   We developed a new algorithm for computing the eigenvectors of a real symmetric matrix on shared-memory parallel computers. Instead of using the modified Gram-Schmidt orthogonalization, which is the bottleneck in parallelizing the conventional inverse iteration algorithm, we choose to hold the basis of orthogonal complementary subspace of the calculated eigenvectors explicitly, and successively modify it by the Householder transformations. This enables us to use the BLAS-2 routines instead of the BLAS-1 routines and reduce the number of interprocessor synchronization from $O(N^2)$ to $O(N)$. The performance of the algorithm is further enhanced with the blocking technique, which allows the BLAS-2 routines to be replaced with the BLAS-3 routines. We evaluated our algorithm on 1 node of the SR8000 (a shared-memory parallel computer with 8 processors) and obtained performance 3.1 times higher than that of the conventional method when computing all the eigenvectors of a matrix of order 1000.

Keywords: Eigenvector, Inverse iteration, Householder transformation, Parallel algorithm, Shared-memory, Blocking, BLAS-2, BLAS-3

*This work was done while the author was at the Central Research Laboratory, Hitachi Ltd.

1.   Introduction

The problem of calculating the eigenvalues and the corresponding eigenvectors of a real symmetric and complex Hermitian matrix is one of the most basic linear algebra calculations and has wide applications to scientific computing such as structural analysis and electronic structure calculation. One of the standard procedures for this problem is to tri-diagonalize the matrix by similarity transformations, calculate the eigenvalues and eigenvectors of the resulting real symmetric tri-diagonal matrix, and finally obtain the eigenvectors of the original matrix by back-transformation [7], [14], [15]. Within this procedure, the tri-diagonalization and the back-transformation can be efficiently parallelized both on shared-memory [12] and distributed-memory [2], [6] concurrent computers, and there are many high-performance implementations on modern supercomputers [3], [9], [10]. It is also easy to find the eigenvalues of the tri-diagonal matrix in parallel by, for example, using the bisection or multi-section methods.

Calculation of the eigenvectors of the tri-diagonal matrix is more difficult to parallelize, however, because one has to ensure orthogonality of the calculated eigenvectors. Many new algorithms have been developed to address this problem, including the divide and conquer method [4], [8], Dhillon's algorithm [5], and the multicolor inverse iteration method [11]. Among them, the divide and conquer method is very efficient and outperforms conventional methods such as the QL method and the inverse iteration method even on a sequential computer. But it is suitable only for the case where all the eigenvalues and eigenvectors are needed. Dhillon's method, which is an improvement over the conventional inverse iteration, obviates the need for explicit orthogonalization and still can produce orthogonal eigenvectors. This algorithm is implemented in the latest version of LAPACK (version 3.0) as a subroutine *dstegr*. But it does not always work well when the relative gaps of the eigenvalues are very small. In such cases, one has to use the subroutine *dstein*, which uses the conventional inverse iteration. The multicolor inverse iteration method reduces the number of orthogonalization to a minimum and thereby extracts parallelism in the computation of the eigenvectors. But it has the limitation that the level of available parallelism becomes quite low when the eigenvalues are clustered.

In this article, we propose another approach for computing the orthogonal eigenvectors of a real symmetric tri-diagonal matrix based on the idea given in Yamamoto et al. 2001. Like Dhillon's method and the multicolor inverse iteration, our method is based on the conventional inverse iteration. But instead of eliminating or reducing the orthogonalization, we choose to parallelize the orthogonalization process itself. To this end, we abandon using the modified Gram-Schmidt orthogonalization procedure, which is the bottleneck in parallelizing the conventional method, and instead, choose to hold the basis of the orthogonal complementary subspace of the calculated eigenvectors explicitly and successively modify it by the Householder transformations. When implemented on shared-memory multiprocessors, our method needs only $O(N)$

interprocessor synchronization to compute all eigenvectors of an N by N matrix. Moreover, in our method, two thirds of the total arithmetic operation can be performed with the BLAS-3 (matrix-matrix multiplication) routines. It is therefore especially suited for modern SMP machines with hierarchical memory.

The paper is organized as follows: In section 2, we briefly review the conventional inverse iteration method along with the difficulty in parallelizing it. We also give some assumptions and notations. The basic idea of our new algorithm, the Householder inverse iteration method, is given in section 3. The blocked version of this algorithm, which allows the use of the BLAS-3 routines, is discussed in section 4. Results of performance evaluation on the Hitachi SR8000, a shared-memory multiprocessor system, can be found in section 5. Concluding remarks are given in the final section.

2.   Review of the Conventional Inverse Iteration Method

2.1   The conventional inverse iteration method

Given an N by N real symmetric tri-diagonal matrix $\mathbf{T}$ along with approximations to its eigenvalues $\{e_i\}_{i=1}^{N}$ ($e_1 \leq e_2 \leq \ldots \leq e_N$), we consider the problem of computing the eigenvectors $\{\mathbf{v}_i\}$ corresponding to the eigenvalues $\{e_i\}$. In the conventional inverse iteration method (IIM), we perform the iteration

$$\mathbf{v}_i^{(m)} := (\mathbf{T} - e_i'\mathbf{I})^{-1}\mathbf{v}_i^{(m-1)} \tag{6.1}$$

for each i starting from the approximate eigenvalue e_i' and some initial vector $\mathbf{v}_i^{(0)}$. It is expected that if e_i' is sufficiently close to e_i, the component of $\mathbf{v}_i^{(0)}$ which is parallel to $\mathbf{v}_i$ is amplified during the iteration and $\mathbf{v}_i^{(m)}$ converges to $\mathbf{v}_i$.

But in finite precision arithmetic, the component parallel to other eigenvectors, say $\mathbf{v}_k$, remains in the calculated vector due to numerical errors. This causes the problem that orthogonality of the eigenvectors, one of the basic properties that the exact eigenvectors of a real symmetric matrix should have, is not guaranteed sufficiently. To remedy this problem, in the conventional inverse iteration method, $\mathbf{v}_i^{(m)}$ is orthogonalized against previously calculated eigenvectors after each iteration. This is usually done with the modified Gram-Schmidt (MGS) method [14], [15]. Because the magnitude of $\mathbf{v}_k$ component remaining in the calculated vector $\mathbf{v}_i$ is shown to be proportional to $(e_k - e_i)^{-1}$ according to error analysis [14], [15], orthogonalization is usually done only against those eigenvectors which belong to eigenvalues close to e_i.

The algorithm of the conventional inverse iteration with orthogonalization by the MGS method is shown in Figure 6.1. Here, the dot denotes the inner product of two vectors, and $\| * \|_2$ denotes the L_2-norm of a vector. In the practical algorithm, additional processes are necessary to deal with degenerate or tightly clustered eigenvalues, such as changing the initial vector or displacing some of the eigenvalues slightly. But these are omitted in the shown algorithm.

> *Grouping of the eigenvalues* : Define two eigenvalues as belonging
> to the same group when their distance is smaller than or equal to
> some criterion ϵ. Let the group to which the i-th eigenvalue belongs
> be denoted by $\mathbf{G}(i)$.
> **for** i=1: N
>   Set some initial vector $\mathbf{v}_i^{(0)}$.
> $m := 1$
>   **until** $\mathbf{v}_i^{(m)}$ converges
> $\mathbf{v}_i^{(m)} := (\mathbf{T} - e_i'\mathbf{I})^{-1}\mathbf{v}_i^{(m-1)}$
>   **for all** $k \in \mathbf{G}(i)$ $(k < i)$ **do**
> $\mathbf{v}_i^{(m)} := \mathbf{v}_i^{(m)} - (\mathbf{v}_i^{(m)t}\mathbf{v}_k)\mathbf{v}_k$
>   **end**
> $\mathbf{v}_i^{(m)} := \mathbf{v}_i^{(m)} / \parallel \mathbf{v}_i^{(m)} \parallel_2$
>   **end**
> $\mathbf{v}_i := \mathbf{v}_i^{(m)}$
> **end**

Figure 6.1.   The conventional inverse iteration method.

In the algorithm of Figure 6.1, the innermost loop over k corresponds to the MGS orthogonalization, in which the newly calculated vector $\mathbf{v}_i^{(m)}$ is orthogonalized against the previously calculated eigenvectors $\mathbf{v}_k$ within the same group $\mathbf{G}(i)$. An example of grouping of the eigenvalues is shown in Figure 6.2.

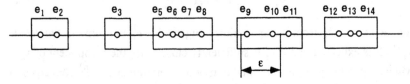

Figure 6.2.   Grouping of the eigenvalues in the conventional inverse iteration method.

2.2   Difficulty with the conventional algorithm

In the conventional IIM, the eigenvectors belonging to different groups can be calculated independently, for the orthogonalization of the calculated vectors is done only within each group. It is therefore natural in parallelizing this algorithm to exploit the group-level parallelism by allocating each group to one processor. In fact, the ScaLAPACK routine *pdstein* adopts this strategy.

But as the size of the matrix grows, the distance between adjacent eigenvalues becomes smaller, and the number of eigenvalues belonging to a group becomes large. In particular, it has been observed in many problems that if the criterion for grouping is set at $\epsilon = 10^{-3} \parallel \mathbf{T} \parallel_1$, which is a widely accepted value [14], most of the eigenvalues belong to one group when N is greater than 1000. If this is the case, most of the calculation has to be performed by one processor, and there is virtually no effect of parallelization.

When the group-level parallelism is not available, the modified Gram-Schmidt method itself has to be parallelized. Because the method is sequential about index k, the only possibility is to parallelize the BLAS-1 (vector-vector operation) routines that appear in the innermost loop, such as the inner product $c = \mathbf{v}_i^{(m)t}\mathbf{v}_k$ and the AXPY operation $\mathbf{v}_i^{(m)} := \mathbf{v}_i^{(m)} - c\mathbf{v}_k$. But this would cause as many as $O(N^2)$ interprocessor synchronization to compute all the eigenvectors, when most of the eigenvalues belong to the same group. Considering the fact that other parts of the eigenvalue solver such as the tri-diagonalization and back-transformation need only $O(N)$ synchronization, this is prohibitively expensive.

From the above discussion, we can say that there is no effective scheme for parallelizing the conventional inverse iteration method, when most of the eigenvalues belong to the same group.

3.   The Householder Inverse Iteration Method

In this section, we give the basic idea and the algorithm of the Householder inverse iteration method [16], which is a new eigenvector solver suited for a shared-memory concurrent computer. We also compare the arithmetic operation count of the new algorithm with that of the conventional method.

3.1   The basic idea

In the conventional inverse iteration method, the components of the newly computed vector that are parallel to the previously computed eigenvectors are removed by the modified Gram-Schmidt orthogonalization. However, because the MGS method is sequential about index k, the BLAS-1 operations such as $c = \mathbf{v}_i^{(m)t}\mathbf{v}_k$ and $\mathbf{v}_i^{(m)} := \mathbf{v}_i^{(m)} - c\mathbf{v}_k$ have to be parallelized when the group-level parallelism is not available. This brings about small granularity of $O(N)$ and extremely large amount of synchronization of $O(N^2)$.

To avoid this problem, we abandon using the MGS method for orthogonalization. Instead, we choose to hold the basis of the orthogonal complementary subspace of the previously calculated eigenvectors explicitly. Then we can make the newly calculated vector orthogonal to the previous eigenvectors by projecting it onto this subspace. After that, the orthogonal complementary subspace is updated so that it is orthogonal also to the newly calculated eigenvector.

Let $\mathbf{v}_i'$ be the newly calculated (i-th) eigenvector (before orthogonalization), V_{i-1} be the subspace spanned by the 1st to $(i-1)$-th eigenvectors, namely, $V_{i-1} = span\{\mathbf{v}_1, \mathbf{v}_2, ..., \mathbf{v}_{i-1}\}$, $V_{i-1}^\perp$ be the orthogonal complementary subspace of V_{i-1} in $\mathbf{R}^N$, $\mathbf{Q}_{i-1}$, an N by $N-i+1$ matrix, be the orthonormal basis of $V_{i-1}^\perp$, and $\mathbf{e}_j$ be an $N - i + 1$ dimensional vector whose j-th component is one and all the other components are zero. Then the orthogonalization process for v_i' can be described as follows:

(1) Calculate $p_i = Q_{i-1}^t v_i'$.

(2) Find a Householder transformation $H_i = I_{N-i+1} - \alpha_i w_i w_i^t$ which clears the second and the following components of p_i.

(3) Calculate $Q_{i-1} H_i$.

(4) Adopt the first column of $Q_{i-1} H_i$ as the orthogonalized new eigenvector v_i, and adopt the matrix that consists of the second and the following columns of $Q_{i-1} H_i$ as Q_i.

In the step (1) above, v_i' is projected onto $V_{i-1}^\perp$ and the resulting vector is expanded using the orthonormal basis Q_{i-1}. The vector of coefficients in this expansion is given by p_i. In step (3), The Householder transformation H_i is applied to Q_{i-1} from the right. Then, the first column of $Q_{i-1} H_i$ is parallel to the projection of v_i' onto $V_{i-1}^\perp$, because

$$
\begin{aligned}
(Q_{i-1} H_i) e_1 &= (1/\beta_i) Q_{i-1} H_i H_i p_i \\
&= (1/\beta_i) Q_{i-1} p_i = (1/\beta_i) Q_{i-1} Q_{i-1}^t v_i'.
\end{aligned} \tag{6.2}
$$

Here we used the fact that $H_i p_i = \beta_i e_1$ for some β_i, and assumed that β_i is not zero because $\beta_i = 0$ would imply that v_i' consists only of the components which are parallel to the previously calculated eigenvectors. We can also show that all the other columns of $Q_{i-1} H_i$ are orthogonal to v_i' because

$$
v_i'^t (Q_{i-1} H_i) e_j = p_i^t H_i e_j = \beta_i e_1^t e_j = 0 \qquad \text{for} \quad j > 1. \tag{6.3}
$$

So we can adopt the former as the orthogonalized eigenvector v_i and the latter as Q_i, an orthonormal basis of the new orthogonal complementary subspace $V_i^\perp$, in step (4).

As an initial orthonormal basis, we use the unit matrix of order N. In our algorithm, this initial matrix $Q_0 = I_N$ is successively updated by the Householder transformations, and is finally transformed to a matrix whose column vectors are the eigenvectors of T. Considering that the Householder transformations keep the orthogonality of a matrix to high accuracy [7], it can be expected that the eigenvectors obtained by this algorithm are highly orthogonal. Moreover, the main operations of this algorithm are projection of v_i to $V_{i-1}^\perp$ in step (1) and the Householder transformation of Q_{i-1} in step (2), both of which are the BLAS-2 (matrix-vector) operations. The number of interprocessor synchronization needed to parallelize the algorithm on SMP machines is therefore $O(1)$ for orthogonalization of one eigenvector and $O(N)$ for all eigenvectors.

3.2   The algorithm

Details of the Householder inverse iteration method are shown in Figure 6.3. The additional procedures for degenerate or tightly clustered eigenvalues are not shown in the figure, but are the same as for the conventional method.

$\mathbf{Q}_0 := \mathbf{I}_N$
$\mathbf{V}_0 := \phi$ (an N by 0 matrix)
for $i=1$: N
    Set some initial vector $\mathbf{v}_i^{(0)}$.
    $m := 1$
    until $\mathbf{v}_i^{(m)}$ converges
        $\mathbf{v}_i' := (\mathbf{T} - e_i'\mathbf{I})^{-1}\mathbf{v}_i^{(m-1)}$
        $\mathbf{p}_i := \mathbf{Q}_{i-1}^t\mathbf{v}_i'$ ($\mathbf{p}_i$ is a vector of length $N - i + 1$.)   (A.1)
        Find a Householder transformation $\mathbf{H}_i = \mathbf{I}_{N-i+1} - \alpha_i\mathbf{w}_i\mathbf{w}_i^t$
        which clears the second and the following components of $\mathbf{p}_i$.
        ($\mathbf{w}_i$ is a vector of length $N - i + 1$.)
        $\mathbf{q}_i := \alpha_i\mathbf{Q}_{i-1}\mathbf{w}_i$ '@($\mathbf{q}_i$ is a vector of length N.)   (A.2)
        $\mathbf{v}_i^{(m)} := (\mathbf{Q}_{i-1})_1 - \mathbf{q}_i(\mathbf{w}_i^t)_1$
        $((\mathbf{A})_i$ denotes the i-th column of matrix $\mathbf{A}$.)
        $m := m+1$
    end
    $\mathbf{Q}_{i-1}' := \mathbf{Q}_{i-1} - \mathbf{q}_i\mathbf{w}_i^t$
    (update $\mathbf{Q}_{i-1}$ by the Householder transformation)   (A.3)
    $\mathbf{V}_i := [\mathbf{V}_{i-1}|(\mathbf{Q}_{i-1}')_1]$
    Set $\mathbf{Q}_i$ to be the matrix obtained by eliminating the first column
    of $\mathbf{Q}_{i-1}'$.
end

Figure 6.3.   The Householder inverse iteration method.

3.3   Arithmetic operation count

The main operations of the Householder inverse iteration are equations (A.1), (A.2) and (A.3) in the algorithm of Figure 6.3. The equation (A.1) projects the computed vector $\mathbf{v}_i$ to the orthogonal subspace $V_{i-1}^\perp$, while (A.2) and (A.3) performs the Householder transformation. Assuming that the inverse iteration converges with single iteration, each of (A.1), (A, 2) and (A.3) needs $2N(N - i + 1)$ operations for the i-th eigenvector, and about N^3 operations for all eigenvectors. The total operation count is therefore $3N^3$. On the other hand, the conventional IIM needs $2N^3$ arithmetic operations when all the eigenvalues belong to the same group. This means that our method requires 1.5 times the operation count of the conventional method.

However, in contrast to the conventional algorithm, where almost all the operations are done in BLAS-1 routines such as inner-product and AXPY, our algorithm is based on BLAS-2 routines such as matrix-vector multiplication and rank-1 update of a matrix. Our method therefore leaves room for code optimization such as loop unrolling. By combining such techniques with reduced interprocessor synchronization, our new method has the potential to outperform the conventional method on shared-memory machines.

When the number of wanted eigenvectors is smaller than N, say N', the number of operations needed to perform each of (A, 1), (A, 2) and (A, 3) is

$$\sum_{i=1}^{N'} 2N(N - i + 1) = N^2 N' - \frac{1}{2}NN'(N' + 1) + NN'. \qquad (6.4)$$

So we need about $3N^2 N' - (3/2)N'^2 N$ total operations. Because the conventional IIM needs about $2NN'^2$ operations, our current algorithm is not competitive when N' is considerably smaller than N. However, by using the WY-representation, it is in principle possible to construct a modified algorithm which requires only $O(NN'^2)$ operations. We are now developing such an algorithm and will report on it in our next paper.

4.   The Blocked Algorithm

To attain high performance on a modern computer with hierarchical memory, it is important to increase the locality of data reference and use the data as many times as possible while it is in the cache. Such consideration becomes more important in shared-memory multiprocessor environment, because it helps preventing performance degradation due to bus contention between the processors, by enabling most of the data accesses to be done in the local cache associated with each processor.

In numerical linear algebra algorithms, locality of data reference can usually be increased by blocking, that is, by reconstructing the algorithm so that most of the computation is performed in BLAS-3 routines. The BLAS-3 routines can perform $O(L^3)$ operations on $O(L^2)$ data when the size of blocking is L, and thereby reduce the memory access by a factor of L when L is chosen so that all the necessary blocks can be stored in the cache.

In our algorithm described in the previous section, blocking is possible by deferring application of the Householder transformation on $\mathbf{Q}$ until several transformations are available, and then applying these successive transformations at once using the *WY representation* [7]. Let L be the size of blocking and i be an integer such that $1 \leq i \leq N$ and $\mathrm{mod}(i, L) = 1$. Then, in the i-th step of the blocked algorithm, after generating the Householder transformation $\mathbf{H}_i = \mathbf{I}_{N-i+1} - \alpha_i \mathbf{w}_i \mathbf{w}_i^t$, we skip its application on $\mathbf{Q}_{i-1}$ and instead accumulate it as WY representation for block Householder transformation as follows:

$$\mathbf{Y}^{(0)} = \mathbf{w}_i \qquad (6.5)$$
$$\mathbf{W}^{(0)} = -\alpha_i \mathbf{w}_i \qquad (6.6)$$

The following $L - 1$ steps are executed in a similar way. At the $i + j$-th step $(1 \leq j \leq L - 1)$, the matrices $\mathbf{Y}$ and $\mathbf{W}$ are updated as follows:

$$\mathbf{z} = -\alpha_{i+j}(\mathbf{I} + \mathbf{W}^{(j-1)}\mathbf{Y}^{(j-1)})\mathbf{w}_{i+j} \tag{6.7}$$

$$\mathbf{W}^{(j)} = [\mathbf{W}^{(j-1)}|\mathbf{z}] \tag{6.8}$$

$$\mathbf{Y}^{(j)} = [\mathbf{Y}^{(j-1)}|\mathbf{w}_{i+j}], \tag{6.9}$$

where $[\mathbf{A}|\mathbf{B}]$ denotes concatenation of two matrices. At the end of the $i+L-1$-th step, the block Householder transformation is applied to $\mathbf{Q}_{i-1}$, generating $\mathbf{Q}_{i+L-1}$ directly:

$$\mathbf{Q}_{i+L-1} = \mathbf{Q}_{i-1}(\mathbf{I} + \mathbf{W}^{(L-1)}\mathbf{Y}^{(L-1)})^t \tag{6.10}$$

As is clearly seen from eq. (6.10), application of the block Householder transformation can be done using only matrix-matrix multiplications, or BLAS-3 routines.

Of course, we also have to change eq. (A.1) in the non-blocked algorithm, because the matrix $\mathbf{Q}_{i+j-1}$ has not received necessary transformation at intermediate stages $i + j$ $(1 \leq j \leq L - 1)$. The correct formula to calculate $\mathbf{p}_{i+j}$ is

$$\begin{aligned}\mathbf{p}_{i+j} &= (\mathbf{I} + \mathbf{W}^{(j-1)}\mathbf{Y}^{(j-1)})\mathbf{Q}_{i-1}^t\mathbf{v}_{i+j}' \\ &= \mathbf{Q}_{i-1}^t\mathbf{v}_{i+j} - \mathbf{W}^{(j-1)}\mathbf{Y}^{(j-1)}\mathbf{Q}_{i-1}^t\mathbf{v}_{i+j}' \end{aligned} \tag{6.11}$$

Though the additional terms in eq. (6.11) increase the number of arithmetic operations slightly, the performance improvement due to the use of BLAS-3 will more than compensate for it.

We summarize the blocked version of our Householder Inverse Iteration method in Figure 6.4. Here, we assume for simplicity that N is divisible by L. In this algorithm, two thirds of the total operation can be done in BLAS-3, and the locality of data reference is greatly improved compared with the original algorithm given in the previous section.

5.   Numerical Results

5.1   Computing environments

We evaluated the performance and numerical accuracy of our Householder Inverse Iteration method on one node of the Hitachi SR8000, an SMP (shared-memory processors) machine with 8 processors per node [13]. Each processor has a peak performance of 1 GFLOPS and the total performance per node is 8 GFLOPS. We also used SR8000/G1, which has 14.4GFLOPS of total peak performance. For parallelization of the program, we used an automatically parallelizing FORTRAN compiler and specified the loops to be parallelized using compiler directives. As test matrices, we used the following two kinds of matrices:

$\mathbf{Q}_0 := \mathbf{I}_N$
$\mathbf{V}_0 := \phi$ (an N by 0 matrix)
for ib=1: N/L
$\quad i := (ib - 1) * L + 1$
$\quad$ for j=0: $L - 1$
$\qquad$ Set some initial vector $\mathbf{v}_{i+j}^{(0)}$.
$\qquad m := 1$
$\qquad$ until $\mathbf{v}_{i+j}^{(m)}$ converges
$\qquad\quad \mathbf{v}_{i+j}' := (\mathbf{T} - e_{i+j}'\mathbf{I})^{-1}\mathbf{v}_{i+j}^{(m-1)}$
$\qquad\quad$ if $j = 0$
$\qquad\qquad \mathbf{p}_i := \mathbf{Q}_{i-1}^t\mathbf{v}_i'$
$\qquad\quad$ else
$\qquad\qquad \mathbf{p}_{i+j} := \mathbf{Q}_{i-1}^t\mathbf{v}_{i+j}' - \mathbf{W}^{(j-1)}\mathbf{Y}^{(j-1)}\mathbf{Q}_{i-1}^t\mathbf{v}_{i+j}'$
$\qquad\qquad$ ($\mathbf{p}_{i+j}$ is a vector of length $N - i + 1$.)
$\qquad\quad$ end if
$\qquad\quad$ Find a Householder transformation
$\qquad\quad \mathbf{H}_{i+j} = \mathbf{I}_{N-i+1} - \alpha_{i+j}\mathbf{w}_{i+j}\mathbf{w}_{i+j}^t$
$\qquad\quad$ which clears the second and the following components
$\qquad\quad$ of $\mathbf{p}_{i+j}$.
$\qquad\quad$ if $j = 0$
$\qquad\qquad \mathbf{Y}^{(0)} := \mathbf{w}_i$
$\qquad\qquad \mathbf{W}^{(0)} := -\alpha_i\mathbf{w}_i$
$\qquad\quad$ else
$\qquad\qquad \mathbf{z} := -\alpha_{i+j}(\mathbf{I} + \mathbf{W}^{(j-1)}\mathbf{Y}^{(j-1)})\mathbf{w}_{i+j}$
$\qquad\qquad \mathbf{W}^{(j)} := [\mathbf{W}^{(j-1)}|\mathbf{z}]$
$\qquad\qquad \mathbf{Y}^{(j)} := [\mathbf{Y}^{(j-1)}|\mathbf{w}_{i+j}]$
$\qquad\quad$ end if
$\qquad\quad m := m+1$
$\qquad$ end
$\qquad \mathbf{Q}_{i-1}' := \mathbf{Q}_{i-1}(\mathbf{I} + \mathbf{W}^{(L-1)}\mathbf{Y}^{(L-1)})^t$
$\qquad$ Partition $\mathbf{Q}_{i-1}'$ as $\mathbf{Q}_{i-1}' = [\mathbf{Q}_{i-1}^L|\mathbf{Q}_{i-1}^R]$, where $\mathbf{Q}_{i-1}^L$ consists
$\qquad$ of the first L columns of $\mathbf{Q}_{i-1}'$.
$\qquad \mathbf{V}_{i+L-1} := [\mathbf{V}_{i-1}|\mathbf{Q}_{i-1}^L]$
$\qquad \mathbf{Q}_{i+L-1} := \mathbf{Q}_{i-1}^R$.
$\quad$ end
end

Figure 6.4. Blocked version of the Householder inverse iteration method.

(a) The Frank matrix: $\mathbf{A}_{ij} = \min(i, j)$.

(b) Matrices obtained from a generalized eigenvalue problem $\mathbf{A}v = e\mathbf{B}v$. Here $\mathbf{A}$ and $\mathbf{B}$ are random matrices whose elements were extracted from uniform random numbers in $[0,1]$. The diagonal elements of $\mathbf{B}$ were then replaced with 10^4 to ensure positive definiteness.

Both types of matrices were first tri-diagonalized by orthogonal transformations and then used as an input matrix for our algorithm.

5.2   Performance

First we show in Table 6.1 the execution times of the conventional inverse iteration method and the non-blocked version of the Householder inverse iteration method on the SR8000. The input matrices we used here are of type (a), but the execution times for matrices of type (b) were almost the same. The numbers in the parentheses show the execution time for computing the eigenvectors only, while those outside also include the time to compute the eigenvalues by the bisection method. We also show the execution time of the conventional IIM on the Hitachi S3800, a vector supercomputer that has the same peak performance of 8GFLOPS. Here, the time is for computing both the eigenvalues and eigenvectors, because the numerical library we used for this measurement did not have the function to compute only the eigenvectors.

Table 6.1.   Performance comparison of the Householder and the conventional IIM

Problem size	Conventional IIM (SR8000)	Householder IIM (SR8000)	Conventional IIM (S3800)
N=1000	4.21s (3.92s)	2.06s (1.64s)	2.15s
N=2000	18.84s (17.61s)	12.05s (10.68s)	12.40s
N=4000	98.46s (94.11s)	83.37s (78.68s)	80.65s

The figures show that the Householder inverse iteration method is more efficient than the conventional ones, especially when N is small, and achieves 2.4 times the performance when computing the eigenvectors of a matrix of order 1000. When comparing the execution time on the SR8000 and the S3800, one can see that while the conventional method fails to exploit the performance of the SMP machine due to a large number of interprocessor synchronization, our new method solves this problem and succeeds in attaining the same level of performance as that of the vector supercomputer even on the SMP machine.

Table 6.2 shows the execution times of the conventional and the Householder IIM on the SR8000/G1. In this case, the execution times of the blocked algorithm described in section 4 are also shown. It is apparent from the table that the blocking works well and increases the performance by about 50%. For the case of $N = 1000$, the blocked version of the Householder IIM achieves more than 3.1 times the performance of the conventional method.

As can be seen from tables 6.1 and 6.2, the superiority of our algorithm over the conventional IIM is large when N is small and decreases as N grows. This is natural considering that our algorithm reduces interprocessor synchronization at the cost of increased operation count. Note, however, that the cost of interprocessor synchronization is relatively low on the SR8000 [13]. For other SMP machines that have higher interprocessor synchronization cost, the effect of reducing the synchronization is larger and the effectiveness of our algorithm will remain for much larger value of N.

Table 6.2.   Performance comparison of the Householder and the conventional IIM (SR8000/G1, execution time for the inverse iteration part.)

Problem size	Conventional IIM	Householder IIM (non-blocked)	Householder IIM (blocked)
N=1000	2.20s	0.98s	0.70s
N=2000	9.93s	6.81s	4.36s
N=4000	49.84s	49.11s	30.76s

5.3   Numerical accuracy

To check the numerical accuracy of the new method, we evaluated the residual and orthogonality of the computed eigenvectors for the new and the conventional method. Here, the residual is defined as the maximum of the L_2-norm of $\mathbf{T}\mathbf{v}_i - e_i\mathbf{v}_i$ over all i, where e_i is the computed i th eigenvalue and $\mathbf{v}_i$ is the computed corresponding eigenvector. The orthogonality is defined as the modulus of the element of $\mathbf{V}^t\mathbf{V} - \mathbf{I}_N$ with the maximum modulus, where $\mathbf{V} = [\mathbf{v}_1, \mathbf{v}_2, \ldots, \mathbf{v}_N]$.

The results for the Frank matrices and the matrices from generalized eigenvalue problems are shown in Tables 6.3, 6.4 and Tables 6.5, 6.6, respectively. As can be seen from the tables, the residual for the non-blocked version of the Householder IIM is as good as that for the conventional one. As for the orthogonality of the computed eigenvectors, the method gives results that are better than or at least as good as those for the conventional method. It is also clear that blocking does not deteriorate the numerical accuracy either in terms of residual or orthogonality.

Table 6.3.   Comparison of the accuracy of the Householder and the conventional IIM (Residual, Frank matrices)

Problem size	Conventional IIM	Householder IIM (non-blocked)	Householder IIM (blocked)
N=1000	0.164×10^{-7}	0.164×10^{-7}	0.164×10^{-7}
N=2000	0.111×10^{-6}	0.111×10^{-6}	0.111×10^{-6}
N=4000	0.528×10^{-6}	0.528×10^{-6}	0.528×10^{-6}

Table 6.4.   Comparison of the accuracy of the Householder and the conventional IIM (Orthogonality, Frank matrices)

Problem size	Conventional IIM	Householder IIM (non-blocked)	Householder IIM (blocked)
N=1000	0.138×10^{-12}	0.400×10^{-14}	0.433×10^{-14}
N=2000	0.945×10^{-13}	0.622×10^{-14}	0.644×10^{-14}
N=4000	0.821×10^{-13}	0.124×10^{-13}	0.127×10^{-13}

Table 6.5. Comparison of the accuracy of the Householder and the conventional IIM (Residual, Matrices from generalized eigenvalue problems)

Problem size	Conventional IIM	Householder IIM (non-blocked)	Householder IIM (blocked)
N=1000	0.881×10^{-12}	0.858×10^{-12}	0.895×10^{-12}
N=2000	0.478×10^{-11}	0.475×10^{-11}	0.478×10^{-11}
N=4000	0.195×10^{-10}	0.197×10^{-10}	0.196×10^{-10}

Table 6.6. Comparison of the accuracy of the Householder and the conventional IIM (Orthogonality, Matrices from generalized eigenvalue problems)

Problem size	Conventional IIM	Householder IIM (non-blocked)	Householder IIM (blocked)
N=1000	0.824×10^{-11}	0.867×10^{-11}	0.837×10^{-11}
N=2000	0.932×10^{-11}	0.976×10^{-11}	0.892×10^{-11}
N=4000	0.119×10^{-10}	0.118×10^{-10}	0.155×10^{-10}

6.   Conclusion

In this article, we proposed a new algorithm for computing the eigenvectors of a real symmetric matrix on shared-memory concurrent computers. In our algorithm, we chose to hold the basis of the orthogonal complementary subspace of the previously calculated eigenvectors and successively update it by the Householder transformations. This obviates the need for the modified Gram-Schmidt orthogonalization, which is the bottleneck in parallelizing the conventional inverse iteration, and reduces the number of interprocessor synchronization from $O(N^2)$ to $O(N)$. The performance of the algorithm is further enhanced with the blocking technique, which allows the use of BLAS-3 routines. The orthogonality of the computed eigenvectors is expected to be good because the Householder transformations keep the orthogonality to high accuracy.

We evaluated our method on one node of the Hitachi SR8000, an SMP machine with 8 processors, and obtained up to 3.1 times the performance of the conventional method when computing all the eigenvectors of matrices of order 1000 to 4000. The orthogonality of the eigenvectors is better than or at least as good as that of the conventional method.

Our future work will include application of this algorithm to distributed-memory parallel computers.

Acknowledgments

We would like to thank Dr. Mendelsohn for many valuable comments on the first version of this paper. We are also grateful to Mr. Ioki and Mr. Tanaka at the Software Development Division of Hitachi Ltd. for providing the environments for our computer experiments.

References

[1] Berry, M.W. and Browne, M (1999). *Understanding Search Engines*, Philadelphia, PA: SIAM.

[2] Chang, H.Y., Utku, S, Salama, M. and Rapp, D. (1988). "A Parallel Householder Tri-diagonalization Strategem using Scattered Square Decomposition", *Parallel Computing*, Vol. 6, No. 3, pp. 297–311.

[3] Choi, J et al. (1995). "ScaLAPACK: A Portable Linear Algebra Library for Distributed Memory Computers – Design Issues and Performance", LAPACK Working Notes 95.

[4] Cuppen, J.J.M. (1981). "A Divide and Conquer Method for the Symmetric Tri-diagonal Eigenproblem", *Numerische Mathematik*, Vol. 36, pp. 177–195.

[5] Dhillon, I. (1997). *A New $O(n^2)$ Algorithm for the Symmetric Tri-diagonal Eigenvalue/Eigenvector Problem*, Ph. D. Thesis, Computer Science Division, University of California, Berkeley, CA.

[6] Dongarra, J.J. and van de Geijn, R.A. (1992). "Reduction to Condensed Form for the Eigenvalue Problem on Distributed Memory Architectures", *Parallel Computing*, Vol. 18, pp. 973–982.

[7] Golub, G.H. and van Loan, C.F. (1989). *Matrix Computations*, The Johns Hopkins University Press.

[8] Gu, M. and Eisenstat, S. (1995). "A Divide-and-Conquer Algorithm for the Symmetric Tri-diagonal Eigenproblem", *SIAM Journal on Matrix Analysis and Applications*, Vol. 16, pp. 172–191.

[9] Katagiri, T. (2001). *A Study on Large Scale Eigensolvers for Distributed Memory Parallel Machines*, Ph. D. Thesis, Information Science Division, University of Tokyo, Tokyo, Japan.

[10] Naono, K., Yamamoto, Y., Igai, M and Hirayama, H. (2000). "High Performance Imlementation of Tri-diagonalization on the SR8000", *Proc. of HPC-ASIA2000*, Vol. I, pp. 206–219, IEEE Computer Society.

[11] Naono, K., Yamamoto, Y., Igai, M., Hirayama, H. and Ioki, N. (2000). "A Multi-color Inverse Iteration for a High Performance Real Symmetric Eigensolver", Ludwig, B. and Wismuller, K. (eds.), *Proc. of Euro-Par 2000* (Lecture Notes in Computer Science 1900), pp. 527–531, Springer-Verlag.

[12] Salvini, S.A. and Mulholland, L.S. (1999). "The NAG Fortran SMP Library", *Proceedings of the 9th SIAM Conference on Parallel Processing for Scientific Computing*, Philadelphia, PA: SIAM.

[13] Tamaki, Y., Sukegawa, N., Ito, M., Tanaka, Y., Fukagawa, M., Sumimoto, T. and Ioki, N. (1999). "Node Architecture and Performance Evaluation of the Hitachi Super Technical Server SR8000", *Proceedings of the 12th International Conference on Parallel and Distributed Computing Systems*, pp. 487–493.

[14] Wilkinson, J.H. and Reinsch, C. (eds.)(1971). *Linear Algebra*, Springer-Verlag.

[15] Wilkinson, J.H. (1965). *The Algebraic Eigenvalue Problem*, Oxford: Claredon Press.

[16] Yamamoto, Y, Igai, M. and Naono, K. (2001). "A New Algorithm for Accurate Computation of Eigenvectors on Shared-Memory Parallel Processors and its Evaluation on the SR8000" (in Japanese), *Journal of the Information Processing Society of Japan*, Vol. 42, No. 4, pp. 771–778.

III

LOAD BALANCING

Chapter 7

LOAD BALANCING IN SPMD APPLICATIONS: CONCEPTS AND EXPERIMENTS

A. Plastino*, V. Thomé[†], D. Vianna[‡], R. Costa[§], and O. T. da Silveira Filho
Universidade Federal Fluminense, Department of Computer Science
Niterói, 24210-240, Brazil
plastino@dcc.ic.uff.br, {vthome, dvianna, rcosta}@ic.uff.br, otton@dcc.ic.uff.br

Abstract   The performance of SPMD parallel programs is strongly affected by dynamic load imbalancing factors. The use of a suitable load balancing strategy is essential in overcoming the effects of these imbalancing factors. This chapter deals with concepts and experiments related to load balancing in SPMD applications. Initially, we discuss a set of classification criteria for load balancing algorithms designed for SPMD applications. In addition, we define a load imbalancing index in order to measure the load imbalance of a parallel application execution. In the experimental part of this chapter, we describe the development of an SPMD parallel application which computes the macroscopic thermal dispersion in porous media. Nine versions of this scientific application were developed, each one adopting a different load balancing strategy. We evaluate and compare the performance of these nine versions and show the importance of using an appropriate load balancing strategy for the characteristics of a specific SPMD parallel application.

Keywords: Load balancing, SPMD model, Thermal dispersion in porous media

1.   Introduction

Parallel applications are classically designed based on functional or data parallelism. When associated with MIMD (Multiple Instruction, Multiple Data) architectures, data parallelism corresponds to the SPMD (Single Program, Multiple Data) programming model [15]: the same program is executed on different

*Research of A. Plastino was sponsored by FAPERJ grant 171352/2000 and by CNPq grant 680123/01-6.
[†]Research of V. Thomé was sponsored by CNPq grant 181612/01-1.
[‡]Research of D. Vianna was sponsored by CNPq grant 181611/01-5.
[§]Research of R. Costa was sponsored by FAPERJ grant 152891/2000.

processors, over distinct data sets. Under this model, each task is characterized by the data over which the common code is executed. The SPMD programming model has been widely used in parallel programming. Coding and debugging is usually simpler under this model than in arbitrary MIMD programs. Moreover, data decomposition is a natural approach for the design of parallel algorithms for many problems [7].

The performance of SPMD programs is strongly affected by dynamic load imbalancing factors, which may include: the lack of information about the processing load of each task before its execution, the dynamic creation of new tasks, or the variation of processor load external to the application. The use of suitable load balancing strategies is essential in overcoming these imbalancing factors. Despite the simplicity of the SPMD model, it is often hard to determine the most appropriate load balancing technique for each application, partly because of the large variety of load balancing algorithms that have been proposed in the literature [1, 3, 4, 6, 20, 21].

In this chapter, we deal with concepts and experiments related to load balancing in SPMD applications.

In the conceptual part, we review the set of criteria proposed in [9, 12] to classify load balancing algorithms designed for SPMD applications (Section 2). These criteria provide a basic terminology for describing different algorithms and establish a background for their comparison and classification. We also briefly present the load imbalancing index used in [19] to measure the load imbalance of a parallel application execution (Section 3).

In the experimental part of the chapter, we present the development of an SPMD parallel application which computes the macroscopic thermal dispersion in porous media – the *thermions* application [18] (Section 4). The dynamic imbalancing factor of this parallel application is the different computational load of each task, which is unknown before the task execution. We developed nine versions of this application, each one adopting a different load balancing algorithm. The performance evaluation of these nine different versions aims to identify the most appropriate strategy for the characteristics of this scientific parallel application. The development of the *thermions* parallel application was supported by SAMBA (Single Application, Multiple Load Balancing) [9, 10, 11, 12] – a parallel programming tool. SAMBA is a framework which captures the structure and the characteristics common to different SPMD applications and supports their development.

Concluding remarks are made at the end of the chapter (Section 5).

2.   Classification of Load Balancing Algorithms

In this section, we describe the classification criteria proposed in [9, 12] for load balancing algorithms adopted in SPMD applications. These criteria provide a terminology and background for describing and classifying existing load balancing algorithms, making their understanding easier.

A well established taxonomy for scheduling in distributed systems is described in [2]. However, it deals with the scheduling of jobs in distributed operating systems and with the scheduling of tasks in parallel applications based on functional decomposition. It is not specifically concerned with strategies for load distribution in SPMD applications.

In this work, we use the term task to identify a subset of data which corresponds to a unit of work in an SPMD application. In this sense, a task does not correspond to a process. Accordingly, in the context of classification criteria for load balancing strategies, a task transfer between two machines corresponds to transferring all the data associated with this task and necessary to its execution. This is different from task migration, used in some distributed operating systems, which refers to transferring executing processes from one machine to another.

The described criteria do not establish a rigid hierarchy of load balancing algorithms. Frequently, a given class of algorithms can be subclassified according to more than one criterion. The goal in presenting these criteria is more to develop a common vocabulary to describe different algorithms than to place each algorithm in a predefined slot.

Static versus Dynamic: The first classification criterion is based on the time at which tasks are distributed among processors. *Static* strategies distribute the tasks once and for all at the beginning of the application execution. In contrast, *dynamic* strategies can distribute or transfer tasks among the processors along the execution of the application, so as to compensate dynamic factors which lead to load imbalance.

Transfer-Based versus Demand-Driven: Dynamic strategies can be classified into those that perform an initial task distribution and those that do not. A *transfer-based* strategy distributes all tasks among the processors before the application starts to execute, and then attempts to balance the load by detecting overloaded and underloaded processors and transferring tasks between them. A *demand-driven* strategy postpones the allocation of a large portion of tasks. In this case, each processor initially receives a block of tasks (possibly from a master processor), with a large number of tasks remaining unallocated. The latter compose a pool of tasks. Whenever a processor finishes the execution of its current block of tasks, it requests a new block of tasks. This scheme proceeds until the pool holds no more tasks. Thus, demand-driven strategies implicitly take the performance of each processor into account.

Integrated versus Isolated: Variation and heterogeneity of external load (processor load that is generated by programs other than the SPMD application itself) represent an important load imbalance factor. Dynamic strategies are also classified as either integrated or isolated, according to whether or not they take the external load into account. *Integrated* strategies consider the SPMD application as integrated with a multiprocessing environment. They use an external information policy, which defines an external load index and the method and frequency of its measurement and relay to the processors. In SPMD applications, resource availability at some processor can often be estimated by the time it has taken to execute a certain number of tasks or operations. *Isolated* strategies do not use external load indices in their load balancing decisions.

Global versus Local: Transfer-based strategies may be classified according to the scope of task transfers. In *global* strategies, task transfers may take place between any two processors in the system. *Local* strategies define groups of processors and transfers take place only between two processors in a given group. In global strategies, each processor needs load information from every other processor, whereas in local strategies a processor needs information only about processors in the same group. Global load information reflects in communication costs, since the cost of propagating load information across the entire system is typically high. On the other hand, the use of global information to make decisions about task transfers allows more precision in load balancing decisions.

Partitioned versus Neighborhood-Based: Local strategies may be further classified with respect to the structure of the processor groups. In local *partitioned* algorithms, each processor belongs to exactly one group. If no other scheme is used to exchange load between groups, partitioning schemes may result in permanent unbalance, since transfers occur only inside disjoint sets of processors. In local *neighborhood-based* algorithms, groups are defined by processor neighborhoods associated with the physical topology of the interconnection network or with the logical topology of the application. Load can migrate across the whole system.

Centralized versus Distributed: Another criterion for classifying transfer-based algorithms is the location at which the algorithm itself is executed. In transfer-based *centralized* algorithms, only a single processor performs load balancing. This processor computes the necessary reassignments and informs the others about the transfers. Only this central processor must be informed about the load on other processors. A transfer-based *distributed* algorithm runs locally within each processor, with its code replicated in all processors. Each processor defines and performs by itself the transfers in which it is involved. Distributed strategies require that load information be propagated to all processors, consequently leading to higher communication costs.

Synchronous versus Asynchronous: Distributed strategies may be further classified with respect to their synchronization requirements. The execution of distributed *synchronous* algorithms is characterized by the fact that all processors perform the balancing procedures at the same time. In the case of an *asynchronous* algorithm, each processor runs the balancing procedure independently, without any interprocessor synchronism.

Periodic versus Event-Oriented: A third criterion for classifying transfer-based algorithms is their activation pattern. In the case of *periodic* strategies, load balancing is periodically activated, after intervals which may be defined by elapsed times or by a certain number of executed operations. In the case of *event-*

oriented strategies, a load balancing algorithm is launched by the occurrence of some pre-defined action or condition, such as the reduction of its load to a level below a certain threshold.

Collective versus Individual: The last criterion for classifying transfer-based algorithms is based on their goal. The goal of a transfer-based *collective* algorithm is to balance the load of a group of processors, possibly even all processors in the system. *Individual* algorithms, in contrast, are designed to correct the load at a single processor, at which either an underload or overload condition has been detected.

Receiving versus Sending: The type of condition that an individual algorithm attempts to correct can be used to further classify this class of algorithms. Individual *receiving* strategies try to eliminate an underload condition by identifying overloaded processors from which the underloaded processor can receive tasks. *Sending* strategies focus on an overloaded processor and try to identify underloaded processors to which its tasks can be sent.

Non-Blind versus Blind: Individual *Non-blind* algorithms use load information from recipient or sender candidate processors. *Blind* algorithms, on the contrary, do not take this kind of information into account. In some cases, the processors involved in each load transfer are selected randomly or through some round-robin scheme.

3. Load Imbalancing Index

In this section, we present the load imbalancing index (LII), proposed in [19], to measure the load imbalance of a parallel application execution (E).

The LII of E, on p processors, is defined by $LII = PIT/t_f$, as the ratio between the average of the processors idle time (PIT) and the elapsed time of the processor that at last concluded its tasks (t_f).

The PIT (average of the idle time of the processors) is defined by

$$PIT = \frac{\sum_{i=1}^{p}(t_f - t_i)}{(p-1)}, \tag{7.1}$$

where t_i is the elapsed time of the ith processor ($1 \leq i \leq p$). Note that at most $p-1$ processors become idle and contribute to PIT calculation. We can consider p subtractions (and not $p-1$) in the total sum since one of them is necessarily equal to zero.

4. Load Balancing in a Scientific SPMD Application

In this section, we present the development of an SPMD parallel application which computes the macroscopic thermal dispersion in porous media – the *thermions* application [18]. The thermal dispersion computation method is described in Subsection 4.1. The implementation of the *thermions* application using SAMBA framework is briefly presented In Subsection 4.2. Adopted load balancing algorithms are presented in Subsection 4.3. The computational experiments and the evaluation of the load balancing strategies are reported in Subsection 4.4.

4.1   Thermal dispersion by random walk

In this subsection, we briefly present the method used to evaluate the macro-scopic thermal dispersion in porous media. More details can be found in [18]. This method is applied in an one-equation model [8], which describes the thermal dispersion on a periodic porous media composed of a union of several fundamental cells. Each fundamental cell is composed of solid elements and by fluid.

The thermal dispersion will be evaluated by the movement of hypothetical particles, called *thermions*, which have a fixed quantity of energy. Each *thermion* is represented by its position (x, y) in the space. This position determines in which kind of media the particle is. The movement of a particle is determined by a random component and, when the particle is in the fluid part, also by the flux velocity.

Initially, a large number of *thermions* is released. At each iteration, the position of all *thermions* is updated according to their step length and direction. The direction of a particle movement to the left, right, up or down is chosen randomly. The length of each step depends on the thermal properties of the medium in which the particle is and on the velocity of the fluid flux (if the particle is in the fluid part). Solid and fluid have different thermal properties. In our experiments, there are also distinct solid parts with four different thermal properties.

Whenever a *thermion* reaches a frontier between solid and fluid parts, a probability of passage into the solid (or fluid) is assigned to the particle. This transition probability P depends on the thermal properties of the solid (or fluid) [8, 17]. If a randomly chosen number is less than P, then the particle will cross the boundary. Otherwise, it makes an elastic rebound. This attempt to cross the frontier requires more computational effort than when a particle always goes through the same medium.

Each *thermion* will go through a random way. The evaluation of the total path of each *thermion* may require different computational load. This is due to the different number of times that each particles tries to cross frontiers, and also to the different thermal properties of the distinct solid parts.

After a number of steps, which depends on the thermal properties of the media, the particles reach their final position. From this distribution, we obtain the thermal dispersion.

4.2   The parallel thermions application

An SPMD application can typically be structured into three major components: (a) the single code which is replicated for the execution of a task; (b) the load balancing strategy; and (c) a skeleton (which initializes and terminates the application, manages the tasks, and controls the execution of the other parts). The first component is specific to each application, but the other two usually are not. SPMD applications can thus be modelled by a framework [5, 13, 14, 16].

A framework may be considered as a model of applications which belong to the same domain. A framework acts both as a specification that models applications with common structure and characteristics, and as a partial implementation that can be used as a basis for the development of these applications [5, 13, 14, 16]. This allows the programmer to focus on the specific problem at hand, reducing the programming effort.

Some parts of a framework are purposefully incomplete. These parts, called hot spots, represent the difference among distinct applications of the same domain. The developer must fill in these hot spots to obtain a complete program. This process is known as framework instantiation. The typical user of a framework is an application developer.

The SAMBA framework models the class of SPMD applications [9, 11, 12]. Its three main hot spots are responsible for: generating the tasks, executing a single task, and dealing with the results. SAMBA allows the application designer to "plug-and-play" with different load balancing algorithms. Consequently, SAMBA simplifies the generation of distinct versions of the application for different load balancing strategies.

In order to instantiate the framework to generate the *thermions* parallel application, we implemented SAMBA's hot spots. In this application, a task is represented by its position (x, y) in the space – a pair of reals. So, the first hot spot must generate all the tasks by setting their initial position and deliver them to the task manager of the framework. Each task corresponds to the calculation of the path through which a *thermion* will go. Then, the second hot spot is the single code that will be evaluated over all *thermions*. To process the results, the third hot spot must gather the final position of the set of particles in order to obtain the thermal dispersion.

In the previous subsection, we concluded that the trajectory evaluation of the particles may require different computational efforts. So, in this application, the tasks will have distinct computational loads, which are unknown before their execution. Then, it is not possible to execute beforehand a balanced distribution of the tasks. This issue requires the use of a load balancing algorithm.

4.3 Load balancing algorithms

In this subsection, we describe the nine algorithms used with the *thermions* application, which are available in SAMBA's load balancing library.

1. **Static:** A master processor distributes the set of tasks among all processors, including itself. The same number of tasks is assigned to every processor. Each processor executes the tasks it received, without any dynamic load balancing.

2. Demand-driven (A): A master processor allocates a block of tasks to each other slave processor. Each time a slave finishes the execution of its current block of tasks, it requests and receives a new one.

3. Demand-driven (B): This algorithm is basically the same as algorithm 2, except in that the master processor also executes tasks, concurrently.

4. Distributed, global, collective, event-oriented: A master processor distributes the set of tasks in equal parts to all processors, including itself. Whenever a processor finishes the execution of all tasks it received, it sends a message to all others, asking them to perform a load balancing step. Then, each processor sends to all others its internal load index (the number of tasks still remaining to be executed). Next, a collective load balancing takes place: Each processor defines the necessary task exchanges to achieve exact redistribution and performs the exchanges in which it is involved.

5. Centralized, global, collective, event-oriented: This algorithm is similar to the previous one, except in that decisions are taken by a central processor. Whenever a processor finishes the execution of all tasks it received, it sends a message to all others, asking them to send their internal load indices to a central processor. After receiving this information from all processors, this central processor defines necessary exchanges and informs each processor of the task transfers in which it is involved. Finally, each processor executes the indicated transfers.

6. Distributed, global, receiving, event-oriented: Once again, load balancing is triggered when a processor finishes the execution of all tasks it received. However, in this case the goal consists in correcting an underload condition at this single (individual) processor. Whenever a processor finishes the execution of its tasks, it sends a message to all others and they send back their internal load indices. After receiving load information from all processors, the underloaded processor sends a request for load transfer to the most loaded processor, which then sends back half of its load.

7. Distributed, partitioned, collective, event-oriented: This algorithm is basically the same as algorithm 4, except in that the processors are partitioned into disjoint groups. All load balancing activity takes place inside each group.

8. Distributed, neighborhood-based, receiving, event-oriented (A):
This strategy is similar to algorithm 6, except in that load information and load exchanges occur only between processors in the same ring-based neighborhood (which may reflect physical connections). Each processor interacts with only two neighbors.

9. Distributed, neighborhood-based, receiving, event-oriented (B):
This strategy is basically the same as the previous one, except in that the logical

neighborhood is defined by a hypercube, not by a ring. Each processor interacts with n neighbors in a system of 2^n processors.

4.4 Performance evaluation

The computational experiments reported in this subsection have been carried out on a cluster of 32 IBM Pentium II-400 machines connected by a 10 Mbits IBM switch and running under Linux 2.2.14-5.0. All nodes have a local 6 Gbytes hard disk and 32 Mbytes of RAM, except one which has 64 Mbytes. We have used the Lam 6.3.2 implementation of MPI and the C compiler gcc version egcs-2.91.66. All experiments were carried out in exclusive mode, with no other application running in the cluster.

The nine presented load balancing strategies have been tested and compared. They are numbered according with their description in Subsection 4.3: static (S1), demand-driven-A (S2), demand-driven-B (S3), distributed (S4), centralized (S5), individual (S6), local-partitioned (S7), ring-neighborhood-based (S8), and hypercube-neighborhood-based (S9). Each group of the local-partitioned strategy (S7) was formed by exactly four processors. The main goal of the evaluation of these load balancing algorithms is to identify the appropriate algorithms for the *thermions* application.

The relative behavior of the different load balancing algorithms is assessed in terms of their elapsed times. The most suitable load balancing algorithm for a given application is considered as that leading to smallest elapsed times. We performed two groups of experiments. In the first, the total number of *thermions* (SPMD tasks) was 1 000, and 2 000 in the second.

To illustrate the effect of load imbalance, we consider the static load balancing algorithm (S1) on 4, 8, 16, and 32 processors, with 1 000 and 2 000 *thermions* (tasks). With 1 000 *thermions* (tasks), the load imbalancing indices were 54%, 51%, 51%, and 50%, respectively. With 2 000 *thermions*, the load imbalancing indices were 55%, 50%, 49%, and 46%, respectively. For example, in the execution of S1 on four processors with 1 000 tasks, three $(p - 1)$ processors became idle, on average, 54% of the elapsed time of the slowest processor. This illustrates the need for dynamic load balancing strategies.

4.4.1 Experiments with 1 000 thermions.
Table 7.1 presents elapsed times in seconds for the *thermions* application, executed with 1 000 *thermions*, with different load balancing strategies on 4, 8, 16, and 32 processors. A straightforward comparison between the times observed for the static load balancing (S1) and for the more elaborate algorithms illustrates the effectiveness of dynamic load balancing and the importance of selecting an appropriate algorithm. The reductions in the elapsed time produced by the best algorithm with respect to the strategy S1 were: 49% with 4 processors, 51% with 8 processors, 49% with 16 processors, and 45% with 32 processors.

Table 7.1. Elapsed times in seconds of the different load balancing strategies for the 1 000 thermions application.

Processors	S1	S2	S3	S4	S5	S6	S7	S8	S9
4	3232	2535	2055	1652	1652	1640	1651	1819	1819
8	1692	1092	1041	829	843	847	896	994	904
16	872	518	548	443	443	472	630	703	543
32	462	254	336	281	281	367	368	412	315

Detailed results observed for the strategy S1 clearly show the effect of the imbalancing factor of the *thermions* application. In the run with four processors and 1 000 *thermions*, each of them performed exactly 250 tasks. However, even though they performed the same number of tasks, their running times are quite different: 1061 s, 1359 s, 2086 s, and 3232 s, the latter corresponding to the overall elapsed time given in Table 7.1. We notice that this elapsed time observed for the static strategy (S1) was reduced by 49% when using algorithms S4, S5, S6 or S7 on the same four processors.

The global and collective algorithms (S4 and S5) presented similar and very effective results with 4, 8, and 16 processors. The demand-driven-A (S2), which showed a poor performance with 4 and 8 processors, was the best one with 32 processors. Note that, as the number of processors increases from 4 to 32 (a factor of 8), the elapsed times were reduced by a factor of 10 for the S2 strategy, and by a factor of 6 for strategies S4 and S5. This occurred due to the fact that the communication overhead imposed by the exchange of load indices, in S4 and S5 strategies, increases when the number of processors is larger. On the other hand, in S2 strategy, one processor is entirely dedicated to task distribution and does not contribute to the task computations itself. With only a few processors, this represents a heavy loss in computing power. As the number of processors grows to 32, S2 presents the best result, indicating a tendency for S2 to become the best strategy with a larger number of processors.

The similar results of S4 and S5 strategies indicates that their difference (one is distributed, the other centralized) was not relevant to their performance in the considered application.

The demand-driven strategies (S2 and S3) are very similar. The difference is that in S3 the master processor also executes tasks. S3 is better than S2 with few processors since the master also contributes to the task computation and there is a smaller number of requests from slave processors to attend. But when the number of processors grows, the performance of S3 is very poor. The master processor is not always ready to attend a greater number of requests – the task computing and the requests dealing are concurrent.

The individual strategy (S6) performance showed that a larger number of processors requires a collective load balancing algorithm (S4 and S5). The overhead of S6 is the large number of times in which all processors are interrupted to resolve an individual request.

The bad behavior of the local-partitioned strategy (S7), with 8, 16, and 32 processors, is due to the fact that different processor groups receive initial subsets of tasks with very different computational demands, but are not able to redistribute them to other groups. With 4 processors, S7 is equivalent to S4, since each group has four processors.

The bad performance of the neighborhood-based strategies (S8 and S9) is due to the slow migration of the load among processors in the defined topology. This is more evident in the ring-based strategy (S8), in which each processor may exchange load with only two neighbors.

When running the *thermions* application with distinct load balancing strategies, the total computational effort (and the total elapsed time) required to execute all tasks may be not exactly the same. This is due to the generation of distinct sequences of random numbers which lead the *thermions* to different paths. In the next subsection, we will observe that, despite this random feature of the *thermions* application, the load balancing algorithms, in the two groups of experiments (1 000 and 2 000 *thermions*), presented very similar behavior.

4.4.2   Experiments with 2 000 thermions.   Table 7.2 presents elapsed times in seconds for the *thermions* application, executed with 2 000 *thermions*, with different load balancing strategies on 4, 8, 16, and 32 processors.

Table 7.2.   Elapsed times in seconds of the different load balancing strategies for the 2 000 thermions application.

Processors	S1	S2	S3	S4	S5	S6	S7	S8	S9
4	6405	5060	3977	3205	3205	3197	3203	3514	3514
8	3212	2196	1961	1661	1643	1671	1809	1957	1786
16	1644	1027	1004	841	839	869	1254	1324	1004
32	862	506	550	453	453	542	713	807	557

The reductions in the elapsed time produced by the best algorithm with respect to the strategy S1 were: 50% with 4 processors, 49% with 8 processors, 49% with 16 processors, and 47% with 32 processors. These results are very similar to the 1 000 *thermions* experiments. This shows that the gain with the use of a dynamic load balancing strategies is not affected by the growth on the number of tasks.

It is also interesting to observe that the number of tasks increased by a factor of 2 (from 1 000 to 2 000 *thermions*) and none of the load balancing algorithms had its elapsed time increased by a factor greater than 2. The elapsed times of all strategies increased by a factor ranging from 1.5 to 2. Indicating that some strategies have a better relative performance with a larger number of tasks.

In these experiments, we again observe the tendency for S2 to become the best strategy with the increase of the number of processors. Note that, although the strategy S2 is not any more the best option on 32 processors, the percentage difference between S2 and the best strategy decreases as the number of processors grows. This percentage ranged from 37% to 10% when the number of processors ranged from 4 to 32.

5.   Concluding Remarks

In this chapter, we presented concepts related to load balancing in SPMD applications and also evaluated the performance of nine different load balancing algorithms for a scientific parallel application. In this application, load imbalance was due to different computational requirements for each task. The global and collective strategies (S4 and S5) led to the best results. We observed a tendency for the demand-driven-A strategy (S2) to become the best strategy with a larger number of processors. The performance of S2, S4, and S5 illustrated that the most suitable load balancing strategy may vary with the number of available processors.

Similar work, in which different load balancing strategies are compared when used with SPMD applications, has been described in [3, 6, 9, 10, 11, 12, 20, 21]. Different SPMD applications were considered in order to compute: matrix multiplication [9, 10, 11, 12, 21], numerical integration [9, 10, 11, 12], genetic algorithm [9, 11, 12], recursive database queries [6], N-body simulation [3], and branch-and-bound job scheduling [20]. From the results presented in the above works, we observe that the most suitable load balancing strategy may also vary with the type of the application, more precisely, with the type of load imbalancing factor considered and with the number of tasks of the application. A local-partitioned load balancing strategy, for example, obtained good results for the parallel matrix multiplication and for the parallel genetic algorithm, but had a poor performance for the parallel numerical integration.

All these studies of distinct load balancing algorithms for different SPMD applications clearly illustrate the need for tuning and choosing the best strategy for a given SPMD application.

References

[1] J.N.C. Árabe and C.D. Murta, "Auto-Balanceamento de Carga em Programas Parale-los", *Proceedings of the VIII Brazilian Symposium on Computer Architecture and High Performance Computing*, 1996, pp. 161–171.

[2] T.L. Casavant and J.G. Kuhl, "A Taxonomy of Scheduling in General-Purpose Distributed Computing Systems", *IEEE Transactions on Software Engineering* 14, 1988, pp. 141–154.

[3] M.A. Franklin and V. Govindan, "A General Matrix Iterative Model for Dynamic Load Balancing", *Parallel Computing* 22, 1996, pp. 969–989.

[4] M. Furuichi, K. Taki, and N. Ichiyoshi, "A Multi-Level Load Balancing Scheme for Or-Parallel Exhaustive Search Programs on the Multi-Psi", *Proceedings of the II ACM*

SIGPLAN Symposium on Principles and Practice of Parallel Programming, 1990, pp. 50–59.

[5] E. Gamma, R. Helm, R. Johnson, and J. Vlissides, *Design Pattern – Elements of Reusable Object Oriented Software*, Addison-Wesley, 1994.

[6] S. Lifschitz, A. Plastino, and C.C. Ribeiro, "Exploring Load Balancing in Parallel Processing of Recursive Queries", *Proceedings of the III Euro-Par Conference, Lecture Notes in Computer Science* 1300, 1997, pp. 1125–1129.

[7] T.G. Mattson, "Scientific Computation", em *Parallel and Distributed Computing Handbook* (A.Y. Zomaya, editor), McGraw-Hill, 1996, pp. 981–1002.

[8] C. Moyne, S. Didierjean, H.P.A. Souto, and O.T. da Silveira Filho, "Thermal Dispersion in Porous Media: One-Equation Model", *International Journal of Heat and Mass Transfer* 43, 2000, pp. 3853–3867.

[9] A. Plastino, *Balanceamento de Carga de Aplicações Paralelas SPMD*, Doctorate thesis, Deptartamento de Informática, Pontifícia Universidade Católica do Rio de Janeiro, 2000.

[10] A. Plastino, C.C. Ribeiro, and N. Rodriguez, "A Tool for SPMD Application Development with Support for Load Balancing", *Proceedings of the International Conference ParCo '99*, Imperial College Press, 2000, pp. 639–646.

[11] A. Plastino, C.C. Ribeiro, and N. Rodriguez, "A Framework for SPMD Applications with Load Balancing", *Proceedings of the XII Brazilian Symposium on Computer Architecture and High Performance Computing*, 2000, pp. 245-252.

[12] A. Plastino, C.C. Ribeiro, and N. Rodriguez, "Developing SPMD Applications with Load Balancing", *Parallel Computing* 29, 2003, pp. 743–766.

[13] W. Pree, *Design Patterns for Object-Oriented Software Development*, Addison-Wesley, 1995.

[14] W. Pree, *Framework Patterns*, SIG Books & Multimedia, 1996.

[15] M.J. Quinn, *Parallel Computing: Theory and Practice*, McGraw-Hill, 1994.

[16] J. Rumbaugh, M. Blaha, W. Premerlani, F. Eddy, and W. Lorensen, *Object Oriented Modeling and Design*, Prentice-Hall, 1991.

[17] O.T. da Silveira Filho, *Dispersão Térmica em Meios Porosos Periódicos. Um Estudo Numérico.*, Doctorate thesis, Instituto Politécnico, Universidade Estadual do Rio de Janeiro, 2001.

[18] H.P.A. Souto, O.T. da Silveira Filho, C. Moyne, and S. Didierjean, "Thermal Dispersion in Porous Media: Computations by the Random Walk Method", *Computational and Applied Mathematics* 21(2), 2002, pp. 513–543.

[19] V. Thomé, D. Vianna, R. Costa, A. Plastino, and O.T. da Silveira Filho, "Exploring Load Balancing in a Scientific SPMD Parallel Application", *Proceedings of the IV International Workshop on High Performance Scientific and Engineering Computing with Applications in conjunction with the XXXI International Conference on Parallel Processing*, 2002, pp. 419-426.

[20] M.A. Willebeek-LeMair and A.P. Reeves, "Strategies for Dynamic Load Balancing on Highly Parallel Computers", *IEEE Transactions on Parallel and Distributed Systems* 4, 1993, pp. 979–993.

[21] M.J. Zaki, W. Li, and S. Parthasarathy, "Customized Dynamic Load Balancing for a Network of Workstations", *Journal of Parallel and Distributed Computing* 43, 1997, pp. 156–162.

Chapter 8

DYNAMIC LOAD BALANCE STRATEGY: APPLICATION TO NONLINEAR OPTICS

A. Bourgeade

CEA-CESTA: Commissariat à l'Energie Atomique, BP 2, 33114 le Barp.

bourgeade@cea.fr

B. Nkonga

MAB: Mathématiques Appliquées de Bordeaux,

UMR CNRS 5466, LRC-CEA M03, Univ. Bordeaux 1, 33405 Talence cedex.

nkonga@math.u-bordeaux.fr

Abstract   This chapter present an efficient parallel approach for the numerical computation of pulse propagation in nonlinear dispersive optical media. The numerical approach is based on the Finite Difference Time Domain (FDTD) method, developed in a system of coordinates moving with the group velocity of the main pulse. The parallel strategy, in order to preserves the global load of the optimal sequential computations, is developed in the dynamic load balancing framework. The efficiency of the parallel approaches is investigated with the computation of the second harmonic generation in a KDP type crystal.

Keywords: Interactions matter/laser, Localized pulses, FDTD, Maxwell equations, Nonlinear optics, Message passing strategy, Dynamic load-balance

1.   Introduction

The purpose of this paper is to present an efficient numerical strategy for the simulation of an intense short laser pulse propagating in a nonlinear medium. The numerical scheme is obtained by the Yee's algorithm [18], known as the finite-difference time-domain (FDTD) method [17]. This algorithm combines second-order centered differences in space with second-order leapfrog time marching, both on staggered Cartesian grids. This approach has been preferred for its efficiency and its non-diffusive property [20]. However, the numerical dispersion accumulation is important and we need a fine grid resolution to avoid spurious effects associated to numerical phase error [15]. For high frequency wave propagation, the computer resources requirement becomes excessive and we need to optimize the sequential algorithm and to develop a parallel approach.

The sequential optimization is achieved by the use of an adaptable computational window. At each step , computations are performed only around the localization of the pulse. This adaptation of the computational domain size is an important component of the optimization, it can be compared to the FDTD moving window [10] with dynamic sizes. The challenge is to develop a parallel strategy that is compatible with the adaptive size of the computational domain. For the sake of simplicity, methodologies are presented and analyzed for a one dimensional formulation of the pulse propagation. In the message passing framework, two parallel strategies are proposed. The first one is based on a static load balance associated with window with a length artificially set to the maximum reached in the sequential computations. The advantage of this strategy is the simplicity of the communication structures and the global size of the messages at each step is small. The second strategy is based on a dynamic load balance where a dynamic length window is used. In this case, we will define an estimation of the load balance, a criterion of re-balancing and communications structures for the re-balance. Using the second harmonic generation test case, we have computed and compared the parallel efficiency of the parallel strategies. Provided that the load imbalance is controlled, the dynamic load balance balance strategy is always the most efficient. Extension of the results to the transverse electric (TE) mode is straightforward. The parallel approaches are performed and compared for the one dimensional computation of the second harmonic generation in the KDP crystal. The paper ends with the 2D computation of self-focusing of a laser beams propagating in a Kerr medium.

2.   Nonlinear Maxwell-Lorentz Equations

In order to describe the propagation of light in a crystal with dispersion and nonlinearity effects, we assume that there is no free charges and consider the crystallographic coordinates. In this context, the governing Maxwell's equations are:

$$\begin{cases} \dfrac{d\mathcal{H}}{d\varphi}t \; + \; \dfrac{1}{\mu_0}\nabla \wedge \mathcal{E} = 0, \\[2mm] \dfrac{d\mathcal{D}}{d\varphi}t \; - \; \dfrac{1}{\varepsilon_0}\nabla \wedge \mathcal{H} = 0, \end{cases} \tag{8.1}$$

where $\mathcal{E}$ is the electric field, $\mathcal{H}$ the magnetic field, $\mathcal{D}$ the electric displacement normalized by ε_0, μ_0 and ε_0 are respectively the permeability and the permittivity of vacuum. The electric displacement is related to the electric field and the polarizations through the constitutive equation:

$$\mathcal{D} = \mathcal{E} + \mathcal{P}^{(1)}\left(\mathcal{E}\right) + \mathcal{P}^{(2)}\left(\mathcal{E}\right) + \mathcal{P}^{(3)}\left(\mathcal{E}\right),$$

where $\mathcal{P}^{(1)}$, $\mathcal{P}^{(2)}$ and $\mathcal{P}^{(3)}$ are respectively the linear, quadratic and cubic polarizations (normalized as $\mathcal{D}$).

For the crystal of the $\bar{4}2m$ point group, considered in these investigations, the quadratic and the cubic polarizations are given by:

$$
\mathcal{P}^{(2)}(\mathcal{E}) = \begin{pmatrix} d_{14}\,\mathcal{E}_y\,\mathcal{E}_z \\ d_{14}\,\mathcal{E}_x\,\mathcal{E}_z \\ d_{36}\,\mathcal{E}_x\,\mathcal{E}_y \end{pmatrix} \quad
\mathcal{P}^{(3)}(\mathcal{E}) = \begin{pmatrix} \mathcal{E}_x(\gamma_{x,x}\mathcal{E}_x^2 + \gamma_{x,y}\mathcal{E}_y^2 + \gamma_{x,z}\mathcal{E}_z^2) \\ \mathcal{E}_y(\gamma_{x,y}\mathcal{E}_x^2 + \gamma_{y,y}\mathcal{E}_y^2 + \gamma_{x,z}\mathcal{E}_z^2) \\ \mathcal{E}_z(\gamma_{z,x}\mathcal{E}_x^2 + \gamma_{z,x}\mathcal{E}_y^2 + \gamma_{z,z}\mathcal{E}_z^2) \end{pmatrix}
$$

$$\text{(8.2)}$$

where $d_{14} = 2\mathcal{X}^{(2)}_{xyz} = 2\mathcal{X}^{(2)}_{xzy} = 2\mathcal{X}^{(2)}_{yxz} = 2\mathcal{X}^{(2)}_{yzx}$, $d_{36} = 2\mathcal{X}^{(2)}_{zxy} = 2\mathcal{X}^{(2)}_{zyx}$ and $\mathcal{X}^{(2)}$ is the quadratic tensor. When Kleinmann symmetry applies, we have: $d_{14} = d_{36}$ and $\gamma_{z,x} = \gamma_{x,z}$. Of course for isotropic cubic nonlinearity all $\gamma_{.,.}$ are equals.

The linear polarization can be decomposed as an instantaneous response and a dispersive component:

$$
\mathcal{P}^{(1)}(\mathcal{E}) = \mathcal{P}^{(1)}_\infty(\mathcal{E}) + \mathcal{P}^{(1)}_{disp}(\mathcal{E}), \quad \text{where}, \quad \mathcal{P}^{(1)}_\infty(\mathcal{E}) = \mathcal{X}^{(1)}_\infty\mathcal{E}.
$$

$\mathcal{X}^{(1)}_\infty$ is a diagonal tensor defining the infinite relative frequency permittivity arising from instantaneous polarization response.

According to the Sellmeier relations, the dispersive linear polarization $\mathcal{P}^{(1)}_{disp}$-$(\mathcal{E})$ is characterized by two Lorentz resonances (indexed by a and b). In the space of frequencies, the corresponding permittivity is defined by:

$$
\mathcal{X}^{(1)}_{disp}(\omega) = \alpha_a\mathcal{X}^{(1)}_a(\omega) + \alpha_b\mathcal{X}^{(1)}_b(\omega)
$$

where α_a and α_b are second order tensors satisfying the relation $\alpha_a + \alpha_b = Id$. The tensors $\mathcal{X}^{(1)}_a$ and $\mathcal{X}^{(1)}_b$ are of the form:

$$
\mathcal{X}^{(1)}_a(\omega) = \frac{\mathcal{X}^{(1)}_{disp}(0)}{1 - \frac{\omega^2}{\omega_a^2}} \qquad \mathcal{X}^{(1)}_b(\omega) = \frac{\mathcal{X}^{(1)}_{disp}(0)}{1 - \frac{\omega^2}{\omega_b^2}}
$$

where ω_a and ω_b are angular velocities tensors associated with the Lorentz resonance frequencies. The tensors divisions used here are term to term divisions in the case of diagonal tensors.

Using an inverse Fourier transform, the linear polarization write as:

$$
\mathcal{P}^{(1)}_{disp}(\mathcal{E}) = \alpha_a\mathcal{F} + \alpha_b\mathcal{G}, \tag{8.3}
$$

where the residual linear dispersions $\mathcal{F}$ and $\mathcal{G}$ satisfy the following second order differential equations (Lorentz oscillator for the linear retarded response):

$$
\begin{cases} \partial_t^2\mathcal{F} + \omega_a^2 \cdot \mathcal{F} = \omega_a^2 \cdot \mathcal{X}^{(1)}_{disp}(0) \cdot \mathcal{E} \\ \partial_t^2\mathcal{G} + \omega_b^2 \cdot \mathcal{G} = \omega_b^2 \cdot \mathcal{X}^{(1)}_{disp}(0) \cdot \mathcal{E} \end{cases} \tag{8.4}
$$

The physical properties of the KDP crystal and its invariance groups are such that the tensors defining the linear polarizations are diagonal in the *crystallographic* coordinates:

$$\mathcal{X}^{(1)}(\omega) = \begin{pmatrix} n_o^2(\omega) & 0 & 0 \\ 0 & n_o^2(\omega) & 0 \\ 0 & 0 & n_e^2(\omega) \end{pmatrix}$$

with

$$\begin{cases} n_o^2(\omega) = 1.479715 + \dfrac{0.779560561}{1 - \dfrac{\omega^2}{2.7452372 \times 10^{32}}} + \dfrac{13.00522}{1 - \dfrac{\omega^2}{0.8882644 \times 10^{28}}} \\[4ex] n_e^2(\omega) = 1.42934875 + \dfrac{0.703319254}{1 - \dfrac{\omega^2}{2.8931235 \times 10^{32}}} + \dfrac{3.2279924}{1 - \dfrac{\omega^2}{0.8882644 \times 10^{28}}} \end{cases}$$

The propagation indexes $n(\omega, \theta)$ of a polarized wave is a function of the pulsation ω and the angle between the polarization direction and the extraordinary axes of the medium $\frac{\pi}{2} - \theta$. It is defined by:

$$\frac{1}{n^2(\omega, \theta)} = \frac{\cos^2 \theta}{n_o^2(\omega)} + \frac{\sin^2 \theta}{n_e^2(\omega)}.$$

For a given pulsation ω, the wave number is given by:

$$k(\omega, \theta(\omega)) = \frac{\omega n(\omega, \theta(\omega))}{c_0}.$$

$\theta(\omega) = 0$ for the fundamental wave and $\theta(2\omega) = \theta_*$ is a giving angle for the harmonic wave. The phase mismatch δk is defined by :

$$\delta k = 2k(\omega, 0) - k(2\omega, \theta_*)$$

Phase matching between the fundamental and its second harmonic, is obtained when the angle θ_* satisfy the following relation:

$$\delta k = 0 \quad \Longleftrightarrow \quad n(2\omega, \theta_*) = n(\omega, 0)$$

For pulse with the wave length $\lambda = 1.06 \, \mu m$ polarized in the ordinary direction of the KDP crystal, the phase matching is obtained $\theta = 41.195695^o$.

3.   Numerical Approach

The numerical scheme for the Maxwell-Lorentz equations is developed on a regular spatial and temporal grid. Time integration is performed with the second-order leapfrog scheme where the electric and the magnetic field are staggered in time and in space [18, 12]. Let us denoted by d the space domain dimension. For a given approximated electric field $(\mathcal{E}_m^n)|_{m\in\mathbb{Z}^d})$, the Yee's scheme for Maxwell's components of the system writes as:

$$
\begin{cases}
\dfrac{\mathcal{H}_{m+\frac{1}{2}}^{n+\frac{1}{2}} - \mathcal{H}_{m+\frac{1}{2}}^{n-\frac{1}{2}}}{\Delta t} + \dfrac{1}{\mu_0}\mathcal{M}^h\left(\mathcal{E}_{m+1}^n - \mathcal{E}_m^n\right) &= 0, \\[2mm]
\dfrac{\mathcal{D}_m^{n+1} - \mathcal{D}_m^n}{\Delta t} - \dfrac{1}{\epsilon_0}\mathcal{M}^h\left(\mathcal{H}_{m+\frac{1}{2}}^{n+\frac{1}{2}} - \mathcal{H}_{m-\frac{1}{2}}^{n+\frac{1}{2}}\right) &= 0.
\end{cases} \tag{8.5}
$$

where $\mathcal{M}^h$ is a (3×3) matrix associated to the discrete operator $(\nabla\wedge)$. The definition of the approximations $\mathcal{H}_{m+\frac{1}{2}}^{n+\frac{1}{2}}, \mathcal{D}_j^n, \mathcal{E}_j^n$ and $\mathcal{M}^h$ is recall in the 1D, 2D and 3D cases.

1D case .   For the 1D problems, let us denote by $z_k = k\Delta z$ and $t^n = n\Delta t$ where Δt and Δz are constants. The magnetic field $\mathcal{H}(z,t)$ is approximated at the space-time point $\left(z_{k-\frac{1}{2}}, t^{n+\frac{1}{2}}\right)$ for $k \in \mathbb{Z}$ and $n \in \mathbb{N}$. The other variables are approximated at the space-time point (z_k, t^{n+1}) for $k \in \mathbb{Z}$ and $n \in \mathbb{N}$. We denote $\mathcal{H}_{k-\frac{1}{2}}^{n+\frac{1}{2}}, \mathcal{D}_k^n, \mathcal{E}_k^n, \mathcal{F}_k^n$ and $\mathcal{G}_k^n$ these approximations (see Figure (8.1)) :

$$
\mathcal{H}_{k-\frac{1}{2}}^{n+\frac{1}{2}} = \mathcal{H}\left(z_{k-\frac{1}{2}}, t^{n+\frac{1}{2}}\right), \quad \mathcal{D}_k^{n+1} = \mathcal{D}(z_k, t^{n+1}), \quad \mathcal{E}_k^{n+1} = \mathcal{E}(z_k, t^{n+1})
$$

For a given variable X, the discrete operator $\mathcal{M}^h$ is defined in 1D by:

$$
\mathcal{M}^h = \frac{1}{\Delta z}\mathcal{M}(e_3),
$$

where $e_3 = (0, 0, 1)^T$ and, for a given vector $u = (u_1, u_2, u_3)^T \in \mathbb{R}^3$, the matrix $\mathcal{M}(u)$ is defined as:

$$
\mathcal{M}(u) = \begin{pmatrix} 0 & -u_3 & u_2 \\ u_3 & 0 & -u_1 \\ -u_2 & u_1 & 0 \end{pmatrix}
$$

2D case .   For 2D problems, let us set $m = (i, j)$. The approximated variables are defined by:

$$
\mathcal{H}_{m-\frac{1}{2}} = \begin{pmatrix} (\mathcal{H}_x)_{i,j-\frac{1}{2}} \\ (\mathcal{H}_y)_{i-\frac{1}{2},j} \\ (\mathcal{H}_z)_{i-\frac{1}{2},j-\frac{1}{2}} \end{pmatrix} \quad \mathcal{D}_m = \begin{pmatrix} (\mathcal{D}_x)_{i-\frac{1}{2},j} \\ (\mathcal{D}_y)_{i,j-\frac{1}{2}} \\ (\mathcal{D}_z)_{i,j} \end{pmatrix} \quad \mathcal{E}_m = \begin{pmatrix} (\mathcal{E}_x)_{i-\frac{1}{2},j} \\ (\mathcal{E}_y)_{i,j-\frac{1}{2}} \\ (\mathcal{E}_z)_{i,j} \end{pmatrix}
$$

where $X_{i,j,k} = X(i\Delta x_1, j\Delta x_2)$ with Δx_1 and Δx_2 fixed. The discrete operator $\mathcal{M}^h$ is then defined by:

$$
\mathcal{M}^h = \sum_{l=1}^{2} \frac{1}{\Delta x_l}\mathcal{M}(e_l),
$$

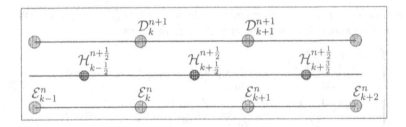

Figure 8.1.   Localization of the discrete approximations variables in the space-time domain: 1D case. In the 1D case, the variables $\mathcal{D}\,\mathcal{E}$, $\mathcal{F}$ and $\mathcal{G}$ have the same localization

where $e_1 = (1, 0, 0)^T$ and $e_2 = (0, 1, 0)^T$. The matrix $\mathcal{M}(e_l)$ is defined as in the 1D case.

The ordinary differential equations for the residual linear polarization are approximated with a three step second-order accurate scheme:

$$\begin{cases} \left(\frac{1}{\omega_a^2} + \frac{\Delta t \delta_a}{2\omega_a^2}\right)\mathcal{F}_m^{n+1} = \left(\frac{2}{\omega_a^2} - \Delta t^2\right)\mathcal{F}_m^n - \frac{1}{\omega_a^2}\mathcal{F}_m^{n-1} + \Delta t^2 \mathcal{X}_d^{(s)}\mathcal{E}_m^n, \\[2mm] \left(\frac{1}{\omega_b^2} + \frac{\Delta t \delta_b}{2\omega_b^2}\right)\mathcal{G}_m^{n+1} = \left(\frac{2}{\omega_b^2} - \Delta t^2\right)\mathcal{G}_m^n - \frac{1}{\omega_b^2}\mathcal{G}_m^{n-1} + \Delta t^2 \mathcal{X}_d^{(s)}\mathcal{E}_m^n, \end{cases}$$
$$(8.6)$$

where $\mathcal{X}_d^{(s)} = \mathcal{X}_{disp}^{(1)}(0)$. Finally, when $\mathcal{D}^{n+1}$, $\mathcal{F}^{n+1}$ and $\mathcal{G}^{n+1}$ have been computed by the previous relations, the electric field $\mathcal{E}^{n+1}$ is obtained by the inversion of the nonlinear system

$$\mathcal{D}_m^{n+1} - \alpha_a \mathcal{F}_m^{n+1} - \alpha_b \mathcal{G}_m^{n+1} = \mathcal{X}_\infty^{(1)}\mathcal{E}_m^{n+1} + \mathcal{P}^{(2)}(\mathcal{E}_m^{n+1}) + \mathcal{P}^{(3)}(\mathcal{E}_m^{n+1}), \quad (8.7)$$

where $\mathcal{E}_m^{n+1}$ is the unknown. This system can be solved using a fixed point procedure. However, we can also compute $\mathcal{E}^{n+1}$ from a linearized constitutive relation:

$$[\mathcal{Q}(\mathcal{E}_m^n)]\,(\mathcal{E}_m^{n+1} - \mathcal{E}_m^n) = \mathcal{D}_m^{n+1} - \alpha_a \mathcal{F}_m^{n+1} - \alpha_b \mathcal{G}_m^{n+1} - \mathcal{X}_\infty^{(1)}\mathcal{E}_m^n \\ - \mathcal{P}^{(2)}(\mathcal{E}_m^n) - \mathcal{P}^{(3)}(\mathcal{E}_m^n) \quad (8.8)$$

where $\mathcal{Q}(\mathcal{E}) = \mathcal{X}_\infty^{(1)} + \partial_\mathcal{E}\mathcal{P}^{(2)} + \partial_\mathcal{E}\mathcal{P}^{(3)}$ is an approximation of the Jacobian matrix $\partial_\mathcal{E}\mathcal{D}$. The system (8.8) is the first iteration of the Newton procedure for the resolution of the nonlinear equation (8.7).

The linear stability analysis of a Yee's like scheme applied to the Maxwell-Lorentz equations has been performed in [11] and give rise to a stability condition of the form $\frac{c\Delta t}{n_o \Delta z} \leq 1$. We refer to [16] for the stability analysis of the basic FDTD method.

3.1   Adaptive computational window

In order to reduce the computer resources required for the simulations, the pulse is tracked and computation is performed only where it is needed. For the clarity of the presentation, let us suppose that we have a global grid for the total computational domain and the grid points are numbered from 0 to $N_s + 1$ (from left to right). This is an artificial grid that will not be used in practice because it can require a large memory space. However it allows a simple presentation of the adaptive widow approach. In this global grid, the computational window, at each step n, is defined by the indices's $I_l(n)$ and $I_u(n)$. These bounds are computed in order to satisfy the inequalities $1 \leq I_l(n) < I_u(n) \leq N_s$, and such that the electric field vanishes for all indexes outside of the computational window:

$$\mathcal{E}_i^n = 0 \quad \text{for} \quad i < I_l(n) \text{ and } i > I_u(n)$$

The tracking procedure is achieved by an estimation of the fastest, v_f, and the slowest, v_s, group velocities associated with the pulse. These velocities are estimated according to the light velocity, the angular velocities ω_a and ω_b and the permittivity tensors ($\mathcal{X}_s^{(1)}$ and $\mathcal{X}_\infty^{(1)}$). In practice, v_f is different from v_s and, therefore, the length of the computational window is dynamic. Using the stability condition of the time marching scheme, it is possible to define the evolution of $I_l(n)$ and $I_u(n)$ so as to satisfy the relations:

$$0 \leq I_l(n+1) - I_l(n) \leq 1, \qquad 0 \leq I_u(n+1) - I_u(n) \leq 1.$$

Let us define the parameters $R(n)$ and $r(n)$ by

$$R(n) = \frac{I_u(n) - I_l(n)}{N_s} \quad \text{and} \quad r(n) = \frac{\min_n R(n)}{\max_n R(n)}.$$

For a short pulse propagating a relatively long distance, the ratio $R(n)$ is small. Moreover, the group velocity of the harmonic wave is in general different from the group velocity of the fundamental wave and, therefore, the ratio $r(n)$ is also small. Consequently, the moving window strategy considerably improves the computational time required. However, the computational time required is still too large and we need to develop a parallel approach. To be effective, the parallel approach must take into account the dynamic load associated to the adaptive moving window strategy.

4.   Message Passing Approach

Despite the adaptive moving window strategy and the optimization efforts deployed with the sequential implementation, the computational time required for these simulations (for 2D and 3D target test cases) is relatively long for realistic configurations. This difficulty is related to the narrowness of the wave beam in comparison with the size of the crystal. A parallel approach by message passing is an effective way to reduce the reaction time of the simulations, but also to make possible computations with large crystals for which memory overloading would be extremely penalizing. Two parallel approaches have been developed: one with static load balancing and the other with adaptive load balancing. Only the strategy based on a dynamic load balance is developed here for the one dimensional case are straightforwardly extendable to the multidimensional case by partitioning the propagating direction. Indeed, in all our applications the number of discrete points in the transverse direction is small compared to those in the propagating direction.

4.1   Dynamic load strategy

The purpose here is to develop a parallel approach keeping the same constraints as in the sequential case for the construction space-time computational domain defined by the boundaries $I_l(n)$ and $I_u(n)$. Efforts must be focused on optimization of the (dynamic) distribution of the loads aimed at ensuring a certain load balance. The sub-domains are numbered from 0 to $N_{pe} - 1$ and we denote by $S(n, p) = I_u(n, p) - I_l(n, p)$ the load associated to the pth processor at the time $t^n = n\Delta t$. The initial distribution is made so as to obtain a perfect balance between the first processors: $0 \leq p \leq N_{pe} - 2$. The dynamic load strategy is performed such that, at each step, the perfect load balance on the first processors is preserved: $S(n, p) = S(n, 0)$ for $0 \leq p \leq N_{pe} - 2$ and for any n. We assume that the solution of the problem is mainly composed by forward waves. Therefore, the "expansion", the "shrinkage", and the "re-balance" processes are added to the "shift" process introduced in the previous section.

The expansion of the computational window occurs when a new point, activated ahead the wave, is not compensated by the cancellation of a point behind the wave. The global load, during an expansion process, increases as: $S(n + 1) = S(n) + 1$. The computation of the new point is assigned to the processor associated with the last sub-domain:

$$\text{"expansion"} \implies \begin{cases} \begin{cases} I_l(n+1,p) &= I_l(n,p) \\ I_u(n+1,p) &= I_u(n,p) + 1 \end{cases} & \text{if } p = N_{pe} - 1 \\[2ex] \begin{cases} I_l(n+1,p) &= I_l(n,p) \\ I_u(n+1,p) &= I_u(n,p) \end{cases} & \text{else if} \end{cases}$$

The shrinkage of the computational window occurs when the pulse is going out of the crystal (out of the global domain). In this situation, a point is cancelled behind the pulse and is not compensated by the activation of a point ahead the pulse. The global load, during a shrinkage process, decrease: $S(n + 1) = S(n) - 1$. The load of the processors p, for $0 \leq p \leq N_{pe} - 2$, is kept constant by a shift process and a computational point is cancelled on the last processor:

$$\text{"shrinkage"} \implies \begin{cases} \begin{cases} I_l(n+1,p) &= I_l(n,p) + 1 \\ I_u(n+1,p) &= I_u(n,p) \end{cases} & \text{if } p = N_{pe} - 1 \\[2ex] \begin{cases} I_l(n+1,p) &= I_l(n,p) + 1 \\ I_u(n+1,p) &= I_u(n,p) + 1 \end{cases} & \text{else if.} \end{cases}$$

The "expansion" and the "shrinkage" processes progressively affect the load balance. Unless these processes are controlled, the parallel approach will be inefficient. Let us quantify the load imbalance by the estimator $\mathcal{C}(n)$:

$$\mathcal{C}(n) = \frac{\delta S}{\max_p \left(S(n,p)\right)} \quad \text{where} \quad \delta S = S(n, N_{pe} - 1) - S(n, 0).$$

By the construction of $S(n,p)$, we have $-1 \leq \mathcal{C}(n) \leq 1$. The maximum of imbalance corresponds to $|\mathcal{C}(n)| = 1$ and the perfect load balance to $\mathcal{C}(n) = 0$. When the effective load of the last processor $(N_{pe} - 1)$ is zero, we have $\mathcal{C}(n) = -1$ (-100% imbalance). At the limit, when $S(n, N_{pe} - 1)$ goes to infinity with a fixed $S(n, 0)$, we have $\mathcal{C}(n) = 1$ (100% imbalance). The perfect load balance is possible only when δS is a multiple of N_{pe}. In order to control the effect of the "expansion" and the "shrinkage" processes on the load balance, the "re-balance" process is achieved only when δS is a multiple of N_{pe} ($\delta S = m N_{pe}$). In other words, after the "re-balance" process a perfect load balance is realized: $\mathcal{C}(n) = 0$. We assume that $\delta S = m N_{pe}$ with m an integer that can be strictly positive or strictly negative. When $m \geq 1$, the balancing is performed by transferring points from the processor $p = N_{pe} - 1$ toward the other processors. The communication structure used in this case is plotted on Figure (8.3). When $m \leq -1$, the balancing is performed by transferring points, collected from the processors $0 \leq p \leq N_{pe} - 2$, toward the processor $p = N_{pe} - 1$. The communication structure used when $m \leq -1$ is plotted on Figure (8.4). For any positive or negative integer $m \neq 0$, we can summarize the "re-balance" process as follows

$$\text{"re-balance"} \implies \begin{cases} \begin{matrix} I_l(n+1,p) &=& I_l(n+1,p) + mp \\ I_u(n+1,p) &=& I_u(n+1,p) \end{matrix} & \text{if} p = N_{pe} - 1 \\ \begin{matrix} I_l(n+1,p) &=& I_l(n+1,p) + mp \\ I_u(n+1,p) &=& I_u(n+1,p) + m(p+1) \end{matrix} & \text{else if} \end{cases}$$

The parallel efficiency depends on the value of the parameter m defining the frequency of the "re-balance" process. For the test cases performed in this paper, re-balancing when $|m| = 1$ gives the best efficiency. Toward the end of the computation, the reduction in the calculation load results in setting a minimal load on each active processor. The number of active processors is thus progressively reduced to complete the calculation with just one active processor.

5.   Applications

We now apply the numerical technique to two test cases. The first is a one dimensional test case of the second harmonic generation. The efficiency of the parallel approach is also studied along with this application. The second application is related to the focusing process. This is a 2-D computation of a pulse propagating in a Kerr medium. The behavior of the focusing process is analyzed by the numerical simulations performed with this last test case.

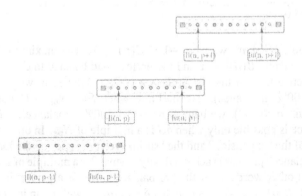

Figure 8.2.   Partitioning and overlapping in the propagating direction. For multidimensional cases, a point of the figure is a set of discrete variables. The local numbering is defined by $I_l(n,p)$ and $I_u(n,p)$: n is the time step and p is the processor number.

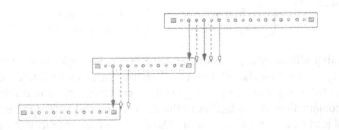

Figure 8.3.   Communication structure for the dynamic load distribution, during a time step with an expansion process. We assume here that that the re-balancing parameter is $m = 1$. The variables sent are: the electric fields $\mathcal{E}_s$ for $s = I_l$ to $s = I_l + mp$, he magnetic fields $\mathcal{H}_s$ for $s = I_l + 1/2$ to $s = I_l + mp + 1/2$ and the other variables $(\mathcal{D}_s, \mathcal{F}_s, \mathcal{G}_s)$ for $s = I_l + 1$ to $s = I_l + mp + 1$. The variables received are: the electric fields $\mathcal{E}_s$ for $s = I_u$ to $s = I_u + 1 + p$, the magnetic fields $\mathcal{H}_s$ for $s = I_u + 1/2$ to $s = I_u + mp + 1/2$ and the other variables $(\mathcal{D}_s, \mathcal{F}_s, \mathcal{G}_s)$ for $s = I_u + 1$ to $I_u + mp + 1$.

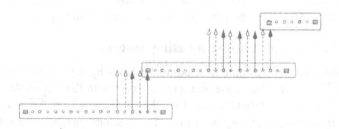

Figure 8.4. Communication structure for the dynamic load distribution, during a time step without a shrinkage process. We assume here that that the re-balancing parameter is $m = -2$. The variables sent are: the electric fields $\mathcal{E}_s$ for $s = I_u + mp + m$ to $s = I_u$, the magnetic fields $\mathcal{H}_s$ for $s = I_u + mp + m + 1/2$ to $s = I_u - 1/2$ and the other variables $(\mathcal{D}_s,\mathcal{F}_s,\mathcal{G}_s)$ for $s = I_u + mp + m + 1$ to $s = I_u$. The variables received are: the electric fields $\mathcal{E}_s$ for $s = I_u$ to $s = I_u + 1 + p$, the magnetic fields $\mathcal{H}_s$ for $s = I_u + 1/2$ to $s = I_u + mp + 1/2$ and the other variables $(\mathcal{D}_s,\mathcal{F}_s,\mathcal{G}_s)$ for $s = I_u + 1$ to $I_u + mp + 1$.

5.1 The second harmonic generation

Consider a brief impulse ($150fs$ i.e. $15 \times 10^{-14}s$) propagating in a KDP type crystal [14] [5]. The angular velocity of the incident wave is $\omega_f = 2.312829144 \times 10^{15}$. The incident wave is agaussian pulse with a wavelength $\lambda_f = \frac{2\pi c}{\omega_f} = 815\,nm$, an amplitude $E_0 = 7.5 \times 10^8 V/m$ and a duration $T_{imp} = 150fs$. In accordance with the experimental study developed in [14], the third order nonlinear effects are overlooked, and the effective coefficient of the quadratic polarization is:

$$\mathcal{X}^{(2)} = 4(4.35 \times 10^{-13})m/V$$

The computations are performed on a structured mesh in space ($\Delta z = 5\,nm$) and time ($\Delta t = 0.003$ femto seconds).. The pulse cross a 2mm crystal (8.5) after about 9×10^5 time steps. The parallel computation are done on a T3E architecture (DEC Alpha EV5: 300MHz, 256 Pe of IDRIS). The computational time obtained with the dynamic load strategy on 16 processors is used as the reference time in the efficiency estimation. The parallel efficiency of the dynamic load balance approach is more than 80% on up to 128 processors and the efficiency of the static load balance is less than 70% with 16 processors (Figure 8.6). The computational time of the parallel algorithm has been reduced to about two hours on 128 processors. The dynamic load distribution enables a substantial improvement in the parallel performances (Figure 8.6). Let us consider a crystal of 50 microns, a mesh size $\Delta z = 1\,nm$ (i.e. 50000 mesh points) and a time step $\Delta t = 0.0015\,fs$ (i.e. 11000 time steps for the computation). For the static load balance approach, the computations performed with 4 processors show that the load is dramatically imbalanced and the perfect load balance is obtained only for few time steps (Figure 8.7). Consequently, the efficiency of the parallel approach is under 75%. For the dynamic load balance approach, the imbalance $|\mathcal{C}(n)|$ is maintained under 15% in the main part of the computation. Therefore, the parallel efficiency is improved (Figure 8.7).

5.2   2D computations: focusing process

We now consider incoming laser beams modelled by the transverse electric mode (TE). The incident wave is a gausian pulse with the amplitude $E_0 = 1.0 \times 10^9 V/m$, the duration $T_{imp} = 10 fs$ the wavelength $\lambda_f = \frac{2\pi c}{\omega_f} = 1.2 \mu m$ and the transverse length $\alpha_y = 10 \mu m$. The quadratic nonlinear effects are overlooked and now the Kerr nonlinearity is taken into account by an effective coefficient:

$$\mathcal{X}^{(3)} = 1.5 \times 10^{-19} m^2/V^2$$

The discretization uses $\Delta z = 20\,nm$, $\Delta y = 200\,nm$ for a spatial computational domain $[0, L_z = 80\mu m] \times [0, L_y = 50\mu m]$ and a time step $\Delta t = 8 \times 10^{-2} fs$. The numerical behavior plotted on Figures 8.9, 8.10 and 8.11) is in accordance with the physical description proposed in [1]. The focusing process always dominates the dispersion and leads to the blow-up of the electric field amplitude (Figure 8.9).

Computations has been performed on the HPC machine of the CEA: HP/CO-MPAQ (Ev68 1GHz ; 8Mbytes Cache; 576 Nodes; 4Go memory/node; 4 processors/node). The parallel strategy is the same as in 1D where points are replaced by sets of points in the transverse direction of the propagation. The number of the points in each set is constant (N_y) and the parallel strategy developed in the 1D case is transposed on the sets of points in 2D case. For the computations of a short pulse duration $(30 fs)$ with $N_y = 121$ points in the transverse direction and $N_{max} \sim 40000$ points, in the computational window, we obtain the following results after 50000 time steps:

Nuber of proc.	CPU time (s)	Comm. Time (s)	Efficiency %	Imbalance %	$\frac{Nl_{max}}{N_{pe}}$
16.	7603	213	100.0	0.3	143.4
32.	3608	262	105.3	1.4	36.2
64.	1742	292	109.1	5.3	9.4
128.	1039	330	91.4	18.3	2.7

where $Nl_{max} = \max\limits_{p} (S(n,p))$. When the pulse duration is large $(960 fs)$ with $N_y = 30$ and $N_{max} \sim 320000$, after 25000 time steps we have:

Nuber of proc.	CPU time (s)	Comm. Time (s)	Efficiency %	Imbalance %	$\frac{Nl_{max}}{N_{pe}}$
64	7988	760	100.0	0.6	78.9
128	3973	533	100.5	2.5	20.1
256	2173	602	91.9	9.2	5.4
512	1422	667	70.2	28.9	1.7
1024	1365	911	36.5	62.0	0.8

This results shows the importance of the dynamic load balance for the parallel efficiency. Indeed, the lost of efficiency is directly related to the grow of the imbalance: Efficiency + imbalance $\simeq 100\%$. Therefore, better efficiency will be obtained when the intrinsic imbalance associated to the parallel strategy is small. For applications using a large number of processors, the previous condition is satisfied when:

$$\frac{\max\limits_{p}\left(S(n,p)\right)}{Npe} \gg 1$$

This is why, despite of the large imbalance (18.3 %) in the first case, the parallel efficiency on 128 processors is still reasonable. However, when $\frac{\max_p\left(S(n,p)\right)}{Npe} \simeq 1$ the parallel strategy need to be improved. To achieved this goal, one can, for example, develop a partial load balance in groups of processors.

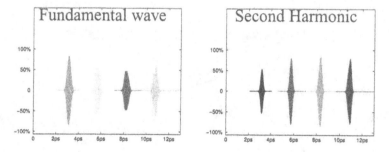

Figure 8.5. Evolution of the normalized electric field of the fundamental and the second harmonic: case of the numerical phase matching.

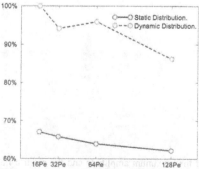

Figure 8.6. Parallel Efficiency of the static and the dynamic load strategies. 4×10^5 global mesh points and 9×10^5 time steps. The the dynamic load computational time with 16 processors is used as the reference time for the estimation of the efficiency.

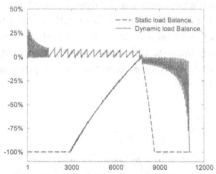

Figure 8.7.   Evolution of the imbalance $\mathcal{C}(n)$, at each step of the computation, for a decomposition with 4 sub-domains ($N_{pe} = 4$): 50000 global mesh points and 11000 time steps.

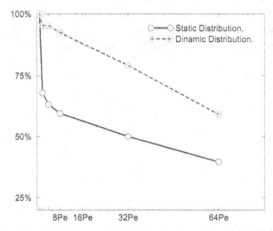

Figure 8.8.   Parallel Efficiency: 50000 global mesh points and 11000 time steps.

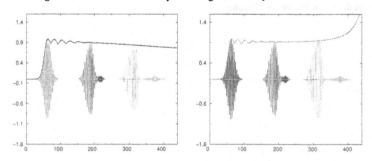

Figure 8.9.   Evolution of the maximum amplitude and the electric field, during time, at the points $z_* = 0$, $z_* = 20\mu m$ and $z_* = 40\mu m$. Nonlinear Keer medium with: $\alpha_y = \infty$ 1D case (left) and $\alpha_y = 10\mu m$ 2D case (right).

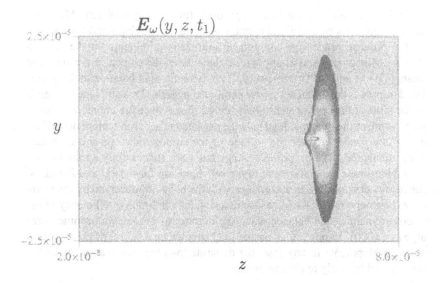

Figure 8.10. Fundamental component of the electric field at the time $t_1 = 440 fs$. Nonlinear Keer medium. The pulse length in the transverse direction $\alpha_y = 10 \mu m$.

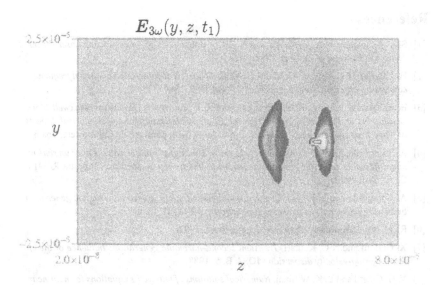

Figure 8.11. Third Harmonic component of the electric field at the time $t_1 = 440 fs$. Nonlinear Keer medium. The pulse length in the transverse direction is $\alpha_y = 10 \mu m$.

6.   Conclusion

We have proposed an efficient approach for solving nonlinear Maxwell-Lorentz equations by an FDTD method. A dynamic moving window has been used in order to reduce the computer resources requirements for the computations. Moreover, parallel approaches have been developed in the message passing (PVM and MPI) framework. The dynamic load balance strategy proposed improves the efficiency of the parallel approach. This efficiency depends on the ratio of the cost or the re-balancing process over the unbalanced tolerance. Some of the dynamic load balance parameters are architecture dependent and can be used to reduce the volume of the communications and introduce more imbalance. The proposed strategy has been successfully applied to the second harmonic generation and to the self-focusing for the 1D and 2D cases. The results obtained are in accordance with the behavior observed by the physical experimentations. We have also investigated the limits of efficiency of the propose dynamic load balance when the number of processors becomes very large (~ 1000). In this limits, partial load balance on a subset of processors is under development. In any case, the dynamic load balance is an unavoidable strategy and has only to be improved.

Acknowledgments

The T3E used for our computations belongs to the French computer resources center (IDRIS). This work was partially supported by the CEA-CESTA.

References

[1]   S. A. Akhmanov, V. A. Vysloukh, and A. S. Chrirkin, *Optics of Femptosecond Laser Pulses*. American Institute of Physics, 1992.

[2]   H. J. Bakker, P.C.M. Planken, and H.G. Muller, *Numerical calculation of optical frequency-conversion processes: a new approach*, JOSA B, 6, 1989.

[3]   B. Bidégaray, A. Bourgeade, D. Reigner, and R. W. Ziolkowski, *Multilevel maxwell-bloch simulations*, in *Proceeding of the Fifth Int. Conf. on Mathematical and Numerical Aspects of Wave Propagation*, pages 221–225, 2000. July 10-14, Santiago de Compostela, Spain.

[4]   A. Bourgeade, *Etude des propriétés de la phase d'un signal optique calculé avec un schéma aux différences finies de Yee pour un matériau linéaire ou quadratique*, Preprint R-5913, CEA, Avril 2000.

[5]   A. Bourgeade and E. Freysz, *Computational modeling of the second harmonic generation by solving full-wave vector maxwell equations*, JOSA, 17, 2000.

[6]   R. W. Boyd. *Nonlinear Optics*, Academic Press, 1992.

[7]   X. Carlotti and N.C. Kothari, *Transient second-harmonic generation: Influence of the effective group-velocity dispersion*, JOSA B, 5, 1988.

[8]   V. H. Cheryl and L. K. William, *Numerical solutions of maxwell's equations for nonlinear-optical pulse propagation*, J. Opt. Soc. Am. B, 13:1135–1145, 1996.

[9]   T. Colin and B. Nkonga, *Computing oscillatory waves of nonlinear hyperbolic sytsems using a phase-amplitude approach*, in Proceeding of the Fifth Int. Conf. on Mathematical

and Numerical Aspects of Wave Propagation, page 954, 2000. July 10-14, Santiago de Compostela, Spain.

[10] B. Fidel, E. Heymann, R. Kastner, and R.W. Ziolkovski, *Hybrid ray-FDTD moving window approach to pulse propagation*, J. Comput. Phys., 138:480–500, 1997.

[11] L. Gilles, S. C. Hagness, and L. Vazquez, *Comparison between staggered and unstaggered finite-difference time-domain grids for few-cycle temporal optical soliton propagation*, J. Comput. Phys., 16n1:379–400, 2000.

[12] R. M. Joseph and A. Taflove. *FDTD maxwell's equations models for nonlinear electrodynamics and optics*, IEEE Trans. Atennas and Propagation, 45, 1997.

[13] A. C. Newell and J. V. Moloney. *Nonlinear Optics*, Addison-Wesley Publiching Compagny, 1991.

[14] R. Maleck Rassoul, A. Ivanov, E. Freysz, A. Ducasse, and F. Hache. *Second harmonic generation under phase and group velocity mismatch. influence of cascading, self and cross phase modulations*, Opt. Letters, 22, 1997.

[15] Petropoulos, Peter G. *Numerical dispersion and absorbing boundary conditions*, Int. J. Numer. Model., 13(5):483-498, 2000.

[16] F. Rob Remis. *On the stability of the finite-difference time-domain method*, J. Comput. Phys., 163(1):249–261, 2000.

[17] A. Taflove. *Computational Electrodynamics: The Finite-Difference Time-Domain Method*, Artech Housse, Norwood, MA, 1995.

[18] K. S. Yee. *Numerical solution of initial boundary value problems involving maxwell's equations in isotropic media*, IEEE Trans. Atennas and Propagation, 14:302-307, 1966.

[19] D. W. Zingg, H. Lomax, and H. M. Jurgens. *High-accuracy finite-difference schemes for linear wave propagation*, SIAM J. Sci. Comput., 17(2):328–346, 1996.

[20] W. D. Zingg. *Comparison of high-accuracy finite-difference methods for linear wave propagation*. SIAM J. Sci. Comput., 22(2):476–502, 2000.

Chapter 9

MESSAGE-PASSING PARALLEL ADAPTIVE QUANTUM TRAJECTORY METHOD

R. L. Cariño, I. Banicescu* and R. K. Vadapalli[†]
ERC Center for Computational Sciences, Mississippi State University
PO Box 9627, Mississippi State MS 39762
{rlc,ioana,raviv}@erc.msstate.edu

C. A. Weatherford
Department of Physics, Florida A&M University, Tallahassee FL 32307
weatherf@cennas.nhmfl.gov

J. Zhu
Department of Theoretical and Applied Mathematics, University of Akron
Akron OH 44325-4002
jzhu@math.uakron.edu

Abstract   Time-dependent wavepackets are widely used to model various phenomena in physics. One approach in simulating the wavepacket dynamics is the quantum trajectory method (QTM). Based on the hydrodynamic formulation of quantum mechanics, the QTM represents the wavepacket by an unstructured set of pseudoparticles whose trajectories are coupled by the quantum potential. The governing equations for the pseudoparticle trajectories are solved using a computationally-intensive moving weighted least squares (MWLS) algorithm, and the trajectories can be computed in parallel. This work contributes a strategy for improving the performance of wavepacket simulations using the QTM on message-passing systems. Specifically, adaptivity is incorporated into the MWLS algorithm, and loop scheduling is employed to dynamically load balance the parallel computation of the trajectories. The adaptive MWLS algorithm reduces the amount of computations without sacrificing accuracy, while adaptive loop scheduling addresses the load imbalance introduced by the algorithm and the runtime system. Results of

* Also with Department of Computer Science, Mississippi State University, PO Box 9637, Mississippi State MS 39762
† Presently at Department of Physics, Oklahoma State University, Stillwater OK 74078

experiments on a Linux cluster are presented to confirm that the adaptive MWLS reduces the trajectory computation time by up to 24%, and adaptive loop scheduling achieves parallel efficiencies of up to 90% when simulating a free particle.

Keywords: Wavepacket simulations, Quantum trajectory method, Adaptive loop scheduling

1.   Introduction

Time-dependent wavepackets are widely used to model various phenomena in physics. Classical approaches for computing the wavepacket dynamics include space-time grids, basis sets, or combinations of these methods. An unstructured grid approach, the quantum trajectory method (QTM), based on the hydrodynamic interpretation of quantum mechanics by Bohm [1], was implemented for a serial computing environment by Lopreore and Wyatt [2]. The QTM solves the quantum hydrodynamic equations using a moving weighted least-squares (MWLS) algorithm to compute needed derivatives.

A simulation code for wavepacket dynamics using the QTM on a shared-memory environment was developed by Brook *et al.* [3]. Starting from a serial code that utilizes an implicit update scheme, OpenMP parallelizing directives were inserted before computationally-intensive loops. The directives defaulted to an equal partitioning of loop iterates among the participating processors. Parallel efficiencies of up to 65% on eight processors were achieved. Modifications were recommended to enhance the performance of the parallel code; specifically, an explicit update scheme to reduce the number of synchronization barriers, and the integration of loop scheduling to correct runtime system-induced load imbalance.

This chapter describes a QTM code for a message-passing environment; the code incorporates the recommendations of Brook *et al.* [3], and other enhancements by Vadapalli *et al.* [5] to further improve the performance of wavepacket simulations. A message-passing environment is targeted in order to be able to utilize more processors for larger problem sizes and smaller time step sizes. Moreover, for large problem sizes, numerical tests indicated that the accuracies achieved by Brook *et al.* [3] can be obtained using smaller sizes of the overdetermined linear systems being solved. Thus, a simple adaptive scheme was also incorporated in the MWLS algorithm to reduce the amount of computations without sacrificing accuracy. Since this adaptive scheme introduces algorithmic load imbalance during the execution of the computationally-intensive loops, adaptive loop scheduling was also integrated into the QTM code.

The remainder of this chapter is organized as follows. Background information on the QTM and the lessons learned from simulating wavepacket dynamics with the QTM on a shared-memory environment are given in Section 2. The issues relevant in migrating the QTM code to a message-passing environment, the incorporation of adaptivity in the MWLS, and the integration of loop scheduling into the QTM are discussed in Section 3. Timing results on a Linux cluster which confirm the performance improvements in the QTM arising from the adaptive MWLS and the loop scheduling are presented in Section 4. The conclusions and short descriptions of ongoing work are given in Section 5.

2.   The Hydrodynamic Formulation of Quantum Mechanics

The study of many problems in quantum mechanics is based on finding the solution to the time-dependent Schrödinger equation (TDSE)

$$i\hbar\frac{\partial}{\partial t}\Psi = \hat{H}\Psi, \quad \hat{H} \equiv -\frac{\hbar^2}{2m}\nabla^2 + V \tag{9.1}$$

which describes the dynamics of quantum-mechanical systems composed of a particle of mass m moving in a potential V. Following Lopreore and Wyatt [2], the hydrodynamic formulation of quantum mechanics is obtained by substituting the polar form of the system wavefunction

$$\Psi(r,t) = R(r,t)e(iS(r,t)/\hbar), \tag{9.2}$$

($R(r,t)$ and $S(r,t)$ are the real-valued amplitude and phase functions of space and time) into the TDSE (Eqn. 9.1), separating into the real and imaginary parts and expressing in atomic units,

$$-\frac{\partial}{\partial t}\rho(r,t) = \nabla \cdot \left[\rho(r,t)\frac{1}{m}\nabla S(r,t)\right], \tag{9.3}$$

$$-\frac{\partial}{\partial t}S(r,t) = \frac{1}{2m}[\nabla S(r,t)]^2 + V(r,t) + Q(\rho;r,t), \tag{9.4}$$

where $\rho(r,t) = R^2(r,t)$ is the probability density, $v(r,t) = \frac{1}{m}\nabla S(r,t)$ is the velocity, $j(r,t) = \rho(r,t)v(r,t)$ is the flux, and

$$Q(\rho;r,t) = -\frac{1}{2m}(\nabla^2 \log \rho^{1/2} + |\nabla \log \rho^{1/2}|^2) \tag{9.5}$$

is the inherently global quantum potential, in logarithmic form. Taking the gradient of Eqn. 9.4 and employing the Lagrangian time derivative $\frac{d}{dt} = \frac{\partial}{\partial t} + v \cdot \nabla$ leads to the equation of motion

$$m\frac{d}{dt}v = -\nabla(V + Q) = f_c + f_q, \tag{9.6}$$

where f_c and f_q are the classical and quantum force terms, respectively. Rewriting Eqn. 9.3 as

$$\left(\frac{\partial}{\partial t} + v \cdot \nabla\right)\rho(r,t) = \frac{d\rho(r,t)}{dt} = \rho(r,t)\nabla \cdot v$$

and integrating yields the density update equation

$$\rho(r, t + dt) = \rho(r, t)e(-dt\nabla \cdot v). \tag{9.7}$$

A set of N pseudoparticles (each of mass m) is deployed to represent the physical particle. Each pseudoparticle executes a "quantum trajectory" governed by the Lagrangian equations of motion (Eqns. 9.6, 9.7), and the quantum potential Q (Eqn. 9.5). Derivatives of ρ, Q, and v, for updating the equations of motion are obtained by curve-fitting the numerical values of these variables using a moving weighted least squares (MWLS) algorithm, and analytically differentiating the least squares curves.

Lopreore and Wyatt introduced a serial algorithm for wavepacket dynamics using the QTM and applied it to barrier tunneling [2]. Brook *et al.* [3] implemented the algorithm for a shared-memory environment and studied its accuracy for a free particle and a harmonic oscillator [4]. Vadapalli *et al.* [5] demonstrated that for a free particle wavepacket, initializing the velocity field using a distribution obtained by a Fourier transform of the initial wavepacket removes the anomalous behavior of the probability density observed by Brook *et al.* [4]. Cariño *et al.* [6, 7] ported the shared-memory code of Brook *et al.* [3] to utilize the Message Passing Interface (MPI) library to enable the simulation of larger numbers of pseudoparticles on message-passing systems with more processors. The present work extends the MPI version by incorporating adaptivity in the MWLS; the adaptivity induces load imbalance, hence, loop scheduling techniques are also integrated into the QTM for load balancing.

3.   Simulation of Wavepacket Dynamics

A code for simulating wavepacket dynamics using the QTM on a shared-memory environment was developed by Brook *et al.* [3]. Starting from a serial Fortran 90 code based on an implicit update scheme, OpenMP parallelizing directives were inserted before computationally-intensive loops. Parallel efficiencies of up to 65% on eight processors were achieved. To improve performance, the modifications including the following were recommended: the utilization of an explicit update scheme to reduce the number synchronization barriers, and the integration of loop scheduling into the code to address runtime system-induced load imbalance.

The code developed by Brook *et al.* was revised to implement a new initialization scheme and an explicit update scheme, to incorporate adaptivity in the MWLS, and to accommodate the integration of loop scheduling. The revised algorithm is outlined in Figure 9.1; it is generic and can be implemented for serial, shared-memory, or message-passing environments. The arrays for values of the positions, velocities, and probability densities of the N pseudoparticles representing the wavepacket are denoted by $r[.]$, $v[.]$, $\rho[.]$, respectively. These arrays are initialized with appropriate values at the beginning of the simulation. During each time step, values for the classical potential $V[.]$, classical force

---

Initialize time, positions $r[.]$, velocities $v[.]$,
   and probability densities $\rho[.]$
for each timestep in turn **do**
   for pseudoparticle $i = 1$ to N **do** (*Loop 1*)
      Call MWLS $(i, r[.], \rho[.], Np_1, Nb)$
      Compute quantum potential $Q[i]$
   end do
   for pseudoparticle $i = 1$ to N **do** (*Loop 2*)
      Call MWLS $(i, r[.], Q[.], Np_2, Nb)$
      Compute quantum force $f_q[i]$
   end do
   for pseudoparticle $i = 1$ to N **do** (*Loop 3*)
      Call MWLS $(i, r[.], v[.], Np_2, Nb)$
      Compute derivative of velocity $dv[i]$
   end do
   for pseudoparticle $i = 1$ to N **do** (*Loop 4*)
      Compute classical potential $V[i]$
      Compute classical force $f_c[i]$
   end do
   Output $t, r[.], v[.], \rho[.], V[.], f_c[.], Q[.], f_q[.], dv[.]$
   for pseudoparticle $i = 1$ to N **do** (*Loop 5*)
      Update density $\rho[i]$
      Update position $r[i]$ and velocity $v[i]$
   end do
end do timestep

Figure 9.1. Simulation of wavepacket dynamics using the QTM

$f_c[.]$, quantum potential $Q[.]$, quantum force $f_q[.]$, and derivative of velocity $dv[.]$ are derived from $r[.]$, $\rho[.]$, and $v[.]$ of the previous time step. The MWLS algorithm is utilized for $Q[.]$, $f_q[.]$, and $dv[.]$. For each pseudoparticle, the algorithm solves an overdetermined linear system of size $Np \times Nb$. The numerical experiments conducted by Brook *et al.* suggested $Nb=6$, $Np=Np_1=N$ when computing $Q[i]$, and $Np=Np_2=N/2$ when computing $f_q[.]$ or $dv[.]$. The values of $r[.]$, $v[.]$, $\rho[.]$ are then updated for use in the next time step. In the algorithm, *Loops 2, 3,* and *4* can be combined into a single loop; however, these are separated to be suitable for loop scheduling.

The execution profile of a straightforward serial implementation of the QTM indicates that the bulk of the total execution time is spent in the MWLS routine called by *Loops 1, 2,* and *3*. Thus, a significant decrease in overall simulation time can be achieved by distributing the iterates of these loops. Each of these is a *parallel loop*, that is, the iterates can be executed in any order without affecting the correctness of the algorithm; hence, loop scheduling is applicable. (*Loops 4* and *5* are also parallel loops, but the scheduling overhead will be more expensive than the computations only very simple formulas are involved). Also, in the implementation of the MWLS by Brook *et al.* [3], the loop iterates in each of *Loops 1, 2*, and *3* perform the same amount of computations; thus, equal distribution of iterates among participating processors (straightforward static scheduling) will result in good load balance assuming the processors are homogeneous, equally-loaded, and start executing the loop at the same time. However, systemic effects like operating system interference and communication latencies, as well as different amounts of computation per iterate due to adaptivity in the MWLS algorithm, may negate these assumptions thereby justifying the use of adaptive loop scheduling techniques.

4.   The Moving Weighted Least Squares Algorithm

The straightforward MWLS algorithm proceeds as in Figure 9.2. The vector

---

Select the Np pseudoparticles closest to the reference
    pseudoparticle
Set up the $Np \times Nb$ least-squares matrix P
Set up the $Nb \times Nb$ matrix $A = P^T \times W \times P$
Set up the $Nb \times 1$ vector $R = P^T \times W \times$ function value
Solve the linear system $A \times x = R$ for x
Compute return values

Figure 9.2.   Moving Weighted Least Squares Algorithm

x stores the coefficients of a degree Nb-1 least squares polynomial. Brook *et al.* [3] suggested Nb=6. The bulk of the arithmetic occurs in setting up the matrices P and A.

Numerical experiments with varying Np indicate that for a large number of pseudoparticles N, setting Np=N yields similar accuracies as that with much lower values of Np. This observation suggested that solving a sequence $x^{(1)}$, $x^{(2)}$, $x^{(3)}$, ..., until convergence, may require less arithmetic than solving a single x with Np=N. For free particle simulations, solving such a sequence using Np=max$(Nb, N/10) + l * Nb$, $l = 1, 2, 3, ...$, and convergence criterion $||x^{(l)} - x^{(l-1)}|| \leq 5 \times 10^{-7}$ achieved comparable accuracies in less time. However, the rate of convergence for the sequence of the x's for one reference pseudoparticle may not be the same as that of another pseudoparticle; hence, the running time for the MWLS routine may vary across pseudoparticles. One consequence is that the iterates of, say *Loop 1* in Figure 9.1, may have nonuniform execution times; in this case, parallelization of the loop requires load balancing.

5.   Loop Scheduling

In Figure 9.1, the loops over pseudoparticles are *parallel loops*. In particular, *Loops 1, 2* and *3* are computationally intensive and utilize the bulk of the CPU time. Also, due to the the adaptivity of the MWLS, these loops may have nonuniform iterate execution times. Thus, the simple strategy of dividing the loop iterates equally among the processors of a parallel machine will result in processor load imbalance and lead to performance degradation. Thus, load balancing through *loop scheduling* is necessary to enhance the overall performance of the QTM.

5.1 Techniques

Loop scheduling attempts to minimize the overall completion time of a parallel loop on a set of cooperating processors. This is accomplished through the dynamic assignment of *chunks* of loop iterates for execution by processors. The sizes of the chunks are determined according to a loop scheduling technique. A loop scheduling technique may be classified as *non-adaptive,* when the chunk sizes are predictable from information that is available or assumed before loop runtime, or *adaptive,* when the chunk sizes depend on information available only during loop execution.

The non-adaptive loop scheduling techniques which generate *equal-size* chunks are *static scheduling* (STAT), where all the chunks are of size N/P, *self scheduling* (SS), where all the chunks are unit size, and *fixed size chunking* [8] (FSC). STAT provides good load balancing only if the iterate execution times are constant and the processors are homogeneous and equally-loaded. SS is suitable for heterogeneous processors or loops with unequal iterate times only when communication overhead is negligible as it requires sending N control messages. FSC determines an optimal chunk size for executing a loop on homogeneous and equally-loaded processors if the mean and standard deviation of the iterate execution times and a constant overhead time are known *a priori.*

Non-adaptive techniques that generate *decreasing-size* chunks have also been developed. The idea underlying these techniques is to initially schedule large chunks, and later use smaller chunks to smoothen the unevenness of the execution times of the initial larger chunks. *Guided self scheduling* [9] (GSS) computes the chunk size for a processor requesting for work as the number of unscheduled iterates divided by P; this technique assumes that the loop iterates have uniform execution times. *Factoring* [10] (FAC) on the other hand, schedules iterates in batches, where the size of a batch is a fixed ratio of the unscheduled iterates, and the batch is divided into P chunks. The ratio is determined such that the resulting chunks have a high probability of finishing before the optimal time. In general, the ratio depends on the mean and standard deviation of the iterate execution times. When these statistics are not known, the ratio 0.5 has been experimentally proven to be practical. In N-body simulations, the combination of factoring and *tiling*, a technique for organizing data to maintain locality, is known as *fractiling* (FRAC) [11]. *Weighted factoring* [12] (WF) incorporates information on processor speeds in computing chunk sizes. In particular, the factoring chunk sizes are multiplied by the relative processor speeds; thus, from a batch, the faster processors get bigger chunks than slower processors. The relative processor speeds are assumed to be fixed throughout the execution of the loop, so the sizes of chunks executed by a given processor are monotonically decreasing.

A number of techniques that generate *adaptive size* chunks have been evolved from factoring and weighted factoring. *Adaptive weighted factoring* [13, 14] (AWF) relaxes the need for user-supplied relative processor weights in WF. Developed in the context of time-stepping applications, AWF assumes equal processor weights at the beginning of the application and modifies the weights at the end of each timestep. The execution times of chunks during a timestep are recorded, and the data is used to adapt the processor weights for the next timestep. AWF *variants* (AWFv) [15, 16] were also developed for applications that do not use time-stepping. At the start of loop execution, the weights are assumed to be equal, and an initial batch of small-size chunks is scheduled. Each processor measures the execution time of a chunk assigned to it; these measurements are used to compute the rate of execution of iterates by each processor, and the rates are normalized into weights according to the formulas in original AWF scheme. *Adaptive factoring* [17, 18] (AF) relaxes the requirement in factoring that the mean and standard deviation of the iterate execution times to be known *a priori* and to be the same on all processors. AF dynamically estimates these statistics for each processor during runtime. First estimates are obtained from the execution times of small-sized chunks from an initial batch; the succeeding chunk sizes are computed based on the mean and standard deviation of iterate execution times of the most recent chunk executed by each processor.

5.2   Overhead

Let T_1 denote the execution time for the serial implementation of, say *Loop 1*, and let T_P denote the execution time for its implementation with loop scheduling on P processors. This parallel implementation will incur overhead T_{LS}. The aggregate processor time (or cost) for the loop scheduling implementation of *Loop 1* can be expressed as: Cost $= P * T_P = T_1 + T_{LS}$. The overhead T_{LS} depends on the number of chunks generated by the loop scheduling method. Table 9.1 gives an approximation to T_{LS} for most of the methods.

Table 9.1.   Loop scheduling overhead.

Method	T_{LS}	Method	T_{LS}
STAT	$O(P)$	FAC	$O(P \log \frac{N}{P})$
SS	$O(N)$	FRAC	$O(P \log \frac{N}{P})$
FSC	$O(\frac{N}{K_{opt}})$	AWF	$O(P \log \frac{N}{P})$
GSS	$O(P \log \frac{N}{P})$	WF	$O(P \log \frac{N}{P})$

Since none of the expressions for the overhead grows asymptotically faster than the problem size N, loop scheduling using the appropriate technique is scalable, except possibly with the SS method.

5.3   Implementation

A general-purpose routine for loop scheduling has been developed by Cariño and Banicescu [19]. The routine is designed for load balancing parallel loops in any application that utilizes the Message-Passing Interface (MPI) library. The routine dynamically schedules the execution of chunks of loop iterates, and directs the transfer of data between processes if needed to achieve load balance. The routine is independent of any application, hence, the code for the computations and communications specific to an application invoking the routine must be supplied as arguments to the routine. The latest version of the routine supports applications in which the data for the loop to be scheduled may be distributed or replicated among the participating processors; in the distributed scheme, each processor stores a segment of the loop data, while in the replicated scheme, each processor has a copy of the entire loop data.

The major consideration for the integration of the loop scheduling routine with the QTM pertains to the location of the pseudoparticle data within the message-passing environment. The replicated scheme was chosen due to its simplicity. The present implementation of the MWLS algorithm requires all pseudoparticle data to be present in each processor. Also, the memory requirements for the expected values of N do not justify the distributed scheme. However, simulations of two- and three-dimensional systems may necessitate using the distributed scheme.

6.   Experiments

Experimental timings for the message-passing QTM code were obtained on 1, 4, 8, and 12 processors of the Linux cluster at the Mississippi State University Engineering Research Center. The cluster has IBM x330 compute nodes with dual Intel Pentium III processors, runs the Red Hat Linux operating system and is connected via fast Ethernet switches with gigabit Ethernet uplinks. The cluster was executing other jobs when the experiments were conducted.

A free particle was simulated for 1000 timesteps using N=501, 1001, and 1501 pseudoparticles. The free particle has a mass of 2000 atomic units (a.u.), width of 2 a.u., and is represented by the Gaussian wavepacket

$$\Psi = \left(\frac{2\beta}{\pi}\right)^{\frac{1}{4}} e(-\beta(x - x_0)^2 + ik_0 x),$$

with center x_0=2, width β=10, and k_0=10.45715361. At t=0, the N pseudoparticles are uniformly distributed around x_0. Each pseudoparticle is initialized with probability density equal to the square of the modulus of the wavefunction at each position and velocity derived from a momentum distribution obtained by Fourier transforming the initial Gaussian wavepacket with group velocity assumption. Output of state information during a timestep was deactivated during the experiments. Figure 9.3 illustrates the trajectories computed by the code for a subset of the pseudoparticles.

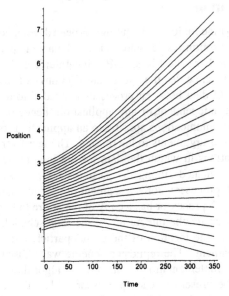

Figure 9.3.   Free particle simulation.

On a single processor, the elapsed time (minimum of three runs) of the $N=501$ simulation with the original MWLS algorithm is 3188.36 seconds, while the corresponding time with the adaptive MWLS algorithm is 2414.87 seconds. This 24% decrease in elapsed time confirms that the adaptive MWLS significantly reduces the amount of arithmetic in the QTM. In a one-processor setup, the code does not invoke the loop scheduling routine or MPI library routines except for the initialization, finalization, and timing routines.

Table 9.2 gives the parallel efficiencies achieved by the QTM with the adaptive MWLS algorithm and loop scheduling on $P=4$, 8 and 12 processors when $N=501$, 1001 and 1501. Each efficiency is computed from the minimum execution time of three simulation runs. From the efficiency data, we observe the following regarding the message-passing parallel QTM code:

- the parallelization is effective, that is, simulation runtime is significantly reduced by using more than one processor;

- the dynamic loop scheduling techniques (GSS, FAC, AWFv and AF) are consistently more effective than straightforward parallelization (STAT);

- the factoring techniques (FAC, AWFv and AF) are consistently more effective than GSS; this is attributed to the fact that the factoring techniques

Table 9.2. Parallel efficiencies for N=501, 1001, 1501 when P=4, 8, 12

N	P	Loop Scheduling Techniques				
		STAT	GSS	FAC	AWFv	AF
501	4	67	76	86	85	86
501	8	59	73	83	78	82
501	12	54	66	78	70	75
1001	4	66	70	86	88	87
1001	8	58	66	85	83	87
1001	12	56	62	82	78	83
1501	4	62	70	87	90	90
1501	8	55	66	87	87	88
1501	12	53	63	84	85	85

were designed for loops with nonuniform iterate execution times, while GSS assumes that the iterate execution times are uniform;

- for a fixed N, the efficiency of each loop scheduling technique decreases with increasing P; this is the expected behavior since overhead increases with the number of processors if the problem size is maintained;

- the similar efficiencies achieved by the combinations N=501/P=4, N=1001/P=8 and N=1501/P=12 for each of the techniques FAC, AWFv and AF indicates the scalability of the QTM with adaptive MWLS and loop scheduling with an appropriate technique.

7. Concluding Remarks

This chapter demonstrates that the performance of the quantum trajectory method (QTM) in simulating wavepacket dynamics is improved by the integration of a combined strategy of an adaptive MWLS algorithm and loop scheduling. Numerical experiments using the QTM code with such enhancement on a Linux cluster confirm the effectiveness of the combined strategy. Results presented in this chapter indicate that for large problem sizes, the adaptive MWLS algorithm reduces by up to 24% the arithmetic performed by the original nonadaptive MWLS algorithm, without sacrificing accuracy. The load imbalance induced by the adaptivity is addressed by dynamic loop scheduling. Parallel efficiencies of up to 90% is achieved by the improved code on a free particle simulation.

Work is under way to to extend the MWLS methodology to two- and three dimensional problems which involve significantly more computations. Also, the Hamiltonian $\hat{H}$ in the TDSE may explicitly depend on time through interaction with the potential V although, the present application assumed that $\hat{H}$ is independent of time. Hence, we are investigating the applicability of our approach for simulating applications, such as electron correlations, that involve time-dependent potentials. Results of these numerical experiments will be reported elsewhere.

Acknowledgments

This work was supported by the National Science Foundation Grants NSF ITR/ACS Award ACI0081303, NSF CAREER Award ACI9984465, and Award EEC-9730381.

References

[1] D. Bohm. 1952. "A Suggested Interpretation of the Quantum Theory In Terms of Hidden Variables." *Physical Review 85*, No. 2, January:166-193.

[2] Lopreore, C. L. and R. W. Wyatt. 1999. "Quantum Wavepacket Dynamics With Trajectories." *Physical Review Letters 82*, No. 26, June:5190-5193.

[3] Brook, R. G.; P. E. Oppenheimer; C. A. Weatherford; I. Banicescu; J. Zhu. 2001. "Solving the Hydrodynamic Formulation of Quantum Mechanics: A Parallel MLS Method." *International Journal of Quantum Chemistry 85*, Nos. 4-5, October: 263-271.

[4] Brook, R. G.; P. E. Oppenheimer; C. A. Weatherford; I. Banicescu; J. Zhu. 2002. "Accuracy Studies of a Parallel Algorithm for Solving the Hydrodynamic Formulation of the Time-dependent Schrödinger Equation." *Journal of Molecular Structure (Theochem) 592*, April: 69-77.

[5] Vadapalli, R. K.; C. A. Weatherford; I. Banicescu; R. L. Cariño; J. Zhu. 2003. "Transient Effect of a Free Particle Wave Packet in the Hydrodynamic Formulation of the Time-dependent Schrödinger Equation." *International Journal of Quantum Chemistry 94*, Issue 1:1-6.

[6] Cariño, R. L.; R. K. Vadapalli; I. Banicescu; C. A. Weatherford; J. Zhu. 2002. "Wavepacket Dynamics Using the Quantum Trajectory Method on Message-Passing Systems." *Proceedings of the ITAMP Workshop on Computational Approaches to Time-Dependent Quantum Dynamics*, (to be published in the Journal of Molecular Science).

[7] Cariño, R. L.; I. Banicescu; R. K. Vadapalli; T. Dubreus; C. A. Weatherford; J. Zhu. 2003. "Wavepacket Simulations Using the Quantum Trajectory Method With Loop Scheduling." *Proceedings of the High Performance Computing Symposium (HPC) 2003*, (Orlando, FL, March 30-April 3). Society for Computer Simulation, 93-99.

[8] Kruskal, C. and A. Weiss. 1985. "Allocating Independent Subtasks on Parallel Processors." *IEEE Trans. Software Eng SE-11*, No. 10, October: 1001–1016.

[9] Polychronopoulos, C. and D. Kuck. 1987. "Guided Self-Scheduling: A Practical Scheduling Scheme for Parallel Supercomputers." *IEEE Trans on Computers C-36*, No. 12, December: 1425–1439.

[10] Flynn Hummel, S., E. Schonberg; L. E. Flynn. 1992. "Factoring: A Method for Scheduling Parallel Loops." *Communications of the ACM 35*, No. 8, August:90-101.

[11] Banicescu, I. and S. F. Hummel. 1995. "Balancing Processor Loads and Exploiting Data Locality in N-Body Simulations." *Proceedings of the 1995 ACM/IEEE Supercomputing Conference*, (San Diego, CA, December 3-8). ACM/IEEE, http://www.supercomp.org/sc95/proceedings/ 594_BHUM/SC95.HTM.

[12] Flynn Hummel, S.; J. Schmidt; R. N. Uma; J. Wein. 1996. "Load-Sharing in Heterogeneous Systems via Weighted Factoring." *SPAA '96: Proceedings of the 8th Annual ACM Symposium on Parallel Algorithms and Architectures*, (Padua, Italy, June 24-26). ACM, 318-328.

[13] Banicescu, I. and V. Velusamy. 2001. "Performance of Scheduling Scientific Applications with Adaptive Weighted Factoring." *Proceedings of the 15th International Parallel and Distributed Processing Symposium (IPDPS-01), 10th Heterogeneous Computing Workshop,* (San Francisco, CA, April 23-27). IEEE Computer Society Press, on CD-ROM.

[14] Banicescu, I., V. Velusamy and J. Devaprasad. 2003. "On the Scalability of Dynamic Scheduling Scientific Applications with Adaptive Weighted Factoring." *Cluster Computing, The Journal of Networks, Software Tools and Applications 6,* July:215-226.

[15] Cariño, R. L. and I. Banicescu. 2002. "Dynamic scheduling parallel loops with variable iterate execution times." *Proceedings of the 16th International Parallel and Distributed Processing Symposium (IPDPS-02) - Workshop on Parallel and Distributed Scientific and Engineering Applications,* (Ft. Lauderdale, FL, April 15-19). IEEE Computer Society Press, on CD-ROM.

[16] Cariño, R. L. and I. Banicescu. 2002. "Load Balancing Parallel Loops on Message-Passing Systems." *Proceedings of the 14th IASTED International Conference on Parallel and Distributed Computing and Systems, S. G. Akl and T. Gonzales (Eds.)* (Cambridge MA, Nov. 4-6). ACTA Press, 362-367.

[17] Banicescu, I. and Z. Liu. 2000. "Adaptive Factoring: A Dynamic Scheduling Method Tuned to the Rate of Weight Changes." *Proceedings of the High Performance Computing Symposium (HPC) 2000,* (Washington DC, April 16-20). Society for Computer Simulation, 122-129.

[18] Banicescu, I. and V. Velusamy. 2002. "Load Balancing Highly Irregular Computations with the Adaptive Factoring." *Proceedings of the 16th International Parallel and Distributed Processing Symposium (IPDPS-02) - Heterogeneous Computing Workshop,* (Ft. Lauderdale, FL, April 15-19). IEEE Computer Society Press, on CD-ROM.

[19] Cariño, R. L. and I. Banicescu. 2003. "A Load Balancing Tool for Distributed Parallel Loops." *Proceedings of the International Workshop on Challenges of Large Applications in Distributed Environments (CLADE) 2003,* (Seattle WA, June 21). IEEE Computer Society Press, 39-46.

IV

PERFORMANCE EVALUATION

Chapter 10

VERIFYING LARGE-SCALE SYSTEM PERFORMANCE DURING INSTALLATION USING MODELLING

Darren J. Kerbyson, Adolfy Hoisie and Harvey J. Wasserman

Los Alamos National Laboratory
Performance and Architectures Laboratory (PAL), CCS-3
P.O. Box 1663, Los Alamos, NM 87545
{djk,hoisie,hjw}@lanl.gov

Abstract   In this paper we describe an important use of predictive application performance modelling - the validation of measured performance during a new large-scale system installation. Using a previously-developed and validated performance model for SAGE, a multidimensional, 3D, multi-material hydrodynamics code with adaptive mesh refinement, we were able to help guide the stabilization of the Los Alamos ASCI Q supercomputer. This system was installed in several stages and has a peak processing rate of 20-Teraflops. We review the salient features of an analytical model for SAGE that has been applied to predict its performance on a large class of Tera-scale parallel systems. We describe the methodology applied during system installation and upgrades to establish a baseline for the achievable "real" performance of the system. We also show the effect on overall application performance of certain key subsystems such as PCI bus speed and processor speed. We show that utilization of predictive performance models can be a powerful system debugging tool.

Keywords: Performance modelling, Terascale systems, Performance validation, High performance computing

1.   Introduction

Performance modelling is a key approach that can provide information on the expected performance of a workload given a certain architectural configuration. It is useful throughout a system's lifecycle: starting with a design when no hardware is available for measurement, in procurement for the comparison of systems, through to implementation / installation, as well as being able to examine the effects of updating a system over time.

We have previously reported the development and validation of an analytical model that captures the performance and scaling characteristics of an important ASCI (Accelerated Strategic Computing Initiative) application [5]. We have also described one interesting use of the model to predict the effect on runtime of a key algorithmic change to the application enabling a different parallel decomposition method.

In this paper we report another interesting use of this same model. Los Alamos National Laboratory (LANL) has recently installed a Tera-scale computing system called ASCI Q that comprises 2048 compute servers with an interconnect fabric composed of federated switches. ASCI Q has a peak performance of 20-Teraflops. The installation of a system with such a large number of components is subject to a variety of both hardware- and software-related issues that effectively result in a "stabilization period" during which the system's performance may be sub-par. The question is: how does one identify sub-par performance in a large-scale parallel system, especially one that is larger than any previously available for testing. Performance observations made on a newly-installed system do not necessarily represent just the cost of processing the workload but often include temporary idiosyncrasies of the hardware and system software, i.e., bugs, faulty or poorly configured hardware components, and so on.

We report here our experiences using a performance model to validate the measured performance during system integration of ASCI Q. Several sets of measurements of the application performance were made on the system during installation over a period of months. Only after several iterations of hardware refinements and software fixes did the performance of the system achieve the performance predicted by the model. The model did not necessarily reveal precisely what hardware and/or software refinements were needed; however, it was ultimately the only way to determine that no such further refinements were necessary. During this process the model and corresponding system measurements exposed several important performance characteristics associated with the system, such as the effect of PCI bus speed and the effect of processor speed on the overall application performance. This work builds on earlier analysis during the initial stages of the installation of ASCI Q [8].

2.   Performance Modelling

Performance modelling is an important tool that can be used by a performance analyst to provide insight into the achievable performance of a system on a given workload. It can be used throughout the life-cycle of a system, or of an application, from first design through to maintenance. For example:

Design: performance modelling can be used to quantify the benefits between alternatives when architectural details are being defined and hence examine trade-offs that arise.

Implementation: when a small system becomes available, perhaps in the form of a prototype, modelling can be used to provide an expected performance for systems of larger size.

Procurement: performance modelling can be used to compare competing systems by a purchaser. Measuring application performance is typically not possible on the systems being proposed due to either the scale of the system required being larger than anything available, or due to the system using next generation components which are not yet available.

Installation: performance modelling can provide an expectation of what level of performance should be achieved and hence verify that the system is correctly installed and configured. As we show in this work, this is an important aspect which to date is not routinely considered.

Upgrade or Maintenance: performance modelling can quantify the impact on possible upgrades prior to the changes being implemented.

Although the examples listed above are considered in terms of a system, most are equally applicable to application codes. For instance from a software perspective in the early development of an application it may be appropriate to compare alternative design strategies and to understand their impact on performance in advance of implementation.

A performance model should also mirror the development of the application and/or system. As details are refined through implementations, the performance model should also be refined. In this way, performance models can be used throughout the life-cycle. At Los Alamos we have used performance models in many of these ways: in the early design of systems, during the procurement of ASCI purple (expected to be a 100-Tflop system to be installed in 2004/5), to explore possible optimizations in code prior to implementation [5], to consider the impact on possible improvements in sub-system performance [6], and to compare large-scale systems (e.g. the Earth Simulator compared to ASCI Q [7]).

In general, there are two main components that contribute to a performance model:

System Characteristics - This includes computational aspects (processor clocks, functional units etc.), the memory hierarchy (cache configuration, memory bus speeds etc.), node configuration (processors per node, shared resources etc.), inter-processor communication (latency, bandwidth, topology), and I/O capabilities.

Workload Characteristics - This includes the application mix, their processing flow, their data structures, their use of and mapping to system resources, their frequency or use, and their potential for resource contention etc.

For modularity and model re-use, the characteristics of the system should ideally be described, and values obtained, independently of any application. Similarly the description of the characteristics of any workload should be described independently of specific systems. Thus, once a model for particular system has been developed, it can be used to examine performance on a multitude of applications. Similarly, application performance can be compared across systems without any alteration to the application model. This modular approach of hardware and software model separation has been taken in a number of modelling activities include the PACE system [11] for high performance computing, and also INDY [12] for E-commerce based applications.

Many of the performance modelling approaches currently being developed can be classified into two categories: those that use a trace of the application (collected from an application run), and those that generate a trace the application activities during its execution. We term these two approaches as *re-play* and *pre-play* respectively.

Replay approaches take an application trace as their input and effectively replay the trace within a modelling environment which combines the trace-events with the characteristics of the system(s) being studied. Since the trace input is usually specific to a certain problem size and processor count, replay approaches cannot be used to fully explore the impact of scalability. Replay approaches include Dimemas [3], the Trace Model Evaluator at Los Alamos, and also the approach taken at San Diego Supercomputing Center [3].

Pre-play approaches use an abstract representation of the application and effectively generate a trace of events that should occur during the application execution. These events are again combined with the characteristics of the system within the modelling environment. Pre-play approaches tend to encapsulate the scaling behavior of the applications with their models parameterized in the same way as the application. Thus allowing a higher degree of performance scenarios to be studied. Pre-play approaches include PACE [11] and INDY [12].

The approach we take is application centric and fits into the pre-play category. It involves the understanding the processing flow in the application, the key data structures, how they use and are mapped to the available resources, and also its scaling behavior. An analytical performance model of the application is constructed from this understanding. The aim is to keep the model of the application as general as possible but parameterized in terms of the application's key characteristics.

Our view is that a model should provide insight into the performance of the application on available as well as future systems with reasonable accuracy. Hardware characteristics should not be part of the application model but rather be specified as a separate component. For instance a model for inter-processor communication may be parameterized in terms of the message size. The actual model may take the form of a simple linear analytical expression in terms of latency and bandwidth, or be more complex. Hardware characteristics may use measurements made by micro-benchmarks, or specified by other means.

An application performance model needs to be validated against measurements made on one or more systems for several configurations (or data sets). Once a model has been validated it can be used to explore performance and to provide insight into new performance scenarios. An overview of a performance model for SAGE and its validation results are given in Section 4.

3. The Alpha-Server ES45 Supercomputing System

ASCI Q consists of 2048 AlphaServer ES45 nodes. Each node contains four 1.25-GHz Alpha EV68 processors internally connected using two 4-GB/s memory buses to 16 GB of main memory. Each processor has an 8-MB unified level-2 cache, and a 64-KB L1 data cache. The Alpha processor has a peak performance of 2 floating point operations per cycle. Thus the Q machine has a peak performance of 20-Tflop.

Nodes are interconnected using the Quadrics QsNet high-performance network. This network boasts high-performance communication with a typical MPI latency of $5\mu s$ and a peak throughput of 340-MB/s in one direction (detailed measured performance data are discussed in Section 5). The Quadrics network contains two components - the Elan network interface card (NIC), and the Elite switch. The Elan/Elite components are used to construct a quaternary fat-tree topology - an example is shown in Figure 10.1. A quaternary fat-tree of dimension n is composed of 4^n processing nodes and $n.4^{n-1}$ switches interconnected as a delta network. Each Elite switch contains an internal 16x8 full crossbar. A detailed description of the Quadrics network can be found in [14].

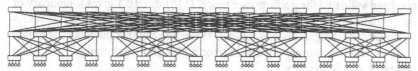

Figure 10.1. Network topology for a dimension 3 quaternary fat-tree network with 64 nodes.

In order to implement a fat-tree network a single NIC is used per node in addition to a number of Elite switch boxes. The Elite switches are packaged in 128-way boxes which by themselves implement a dimension 3 fat-tree. A 1024-node system, as shown in Figure 10.2, requires two rows of 16 switch boxes.

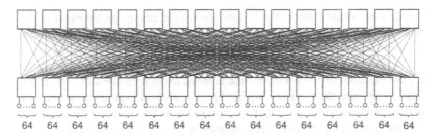

64   64   64   64   64   64   64   64   64   64   64   64   64   64   64   64

Figure 10.2.   Interconnection of a federated Quadrics network for a dimension 5 fat-tree.

Using multiple independent networks, also known as "rails" is an emerging technique to overcome bandwidth limitations and to enhance fault tolerance [2]. The Q machine contains two rails, i.e. two Elan cards on separate PCI interfaces per node, and two complete sets of Elite switches.

4.   The Application and the Model

The application used to analyze the performance of ASCI Q is SAGE (SAIC's Adaptive Grid Eulerian hydrocode). It is a multidimensional (1D, 2D, and 3D), multimaterial, Eulerian hydrodynamics code with adaptive mesh refinement (AMR) consisting of 100,000+ lines of Fortran 90 code using MPI for inter-processor communications. It comes from the LANL Crestone project, whose goal is the investigation of continuous adaptive Eulerian techniques to stockpile stewardship problems. SAGE has also been applied to a variety of problems in many areas of science and engineering including: water shock, energy coupling, cratering and ground shock, stemming and containment, early time front end design, explosively generated air blast, and hydrodynamic instability problems [16]. SAGE represents a large class of production ASCI applications at Los Alamos that routinely run on 1,000's of processors for months at a time.

A detailed description of SAGE, the adaptive mesh processing, and the characteristics of its parallel scaling were described previously in which we developed and validated the performance model [5]. Table 10.1 gives a summary of the validation results in terms of average and maximum prediction errors across all processor configurations measured. It can be seen that the model is highly accurate with an average prediction error of 5% and maximum of 11% being typical across all machines.

5.   Use of the SAGE Model to Validate System Performance

The model is parametric in terms of certain basic system-related features such as the sequential processing time and the communication network performance; these had to be obtained via measurements on a small system and are listed in Table 10.2 and Table 10.3 respectively. The SAGE model is based on weak

Table 10.1. SAGE performance model validation results.

System	Configurations tested	Processors tested (maximum)	Error (maximum)	Error (average)
ASCI Blue (SGI O2K)	13	5040	12.6	4.4
ASCI Red (Intel Tflops)	13	3072	10.5	5.4
ASCI White (IBM SP3)	19	4096	11.1	5.1
Compaq AlphaServer ES40	10	464	11.6	4.7
Cray T3E	17	1450	11.9	4.1

scaling in which the global problem size grows proportionally with the number of processors. The subgrid size remains constant at approximately 13,500 cells per subgrid.

Table 10.2. Measured ES45 Performance Parameters for the SAGE Model.

Parameter	1-GHz Alpha EV68	1.25-GHz Alpha EV68
$T_{comp}(E)(s)$	0.38	0.26
$T_{mem}(P)(\mu s)$	$\begin{cases} 1.8 & P = 2 \\ 4.8 & P > 2 \end{cases}$	$\begin{cases} 1.7 & P = 2 \\ 3.3 & P > 2 \end{cases}$

Table 10.3. Measured Communication Performance Parameters for the SAGE Model.

Parameter	33-MHz PCI bus	66-MHz PCI bus
$L_c(S)(\mu s)$	$\begin{cases} 9.0 & S < 64bytes \\ 9.70 & 64 \leq S \leq 512 \\ 17.4 & S > 512 \end{cases}$	$\begin{cases} 6.11 & S < 64bytes \\ 6.44 & 64 \leq S \leq 512 \\ 13.8 & S > 512 \end{cases}$
$1/B_c(S)(ns)$	$\begin{cases} 0.0 & S < 64bytes \\ 17.8 & 64 \leq S \leq 512 \\ 12.8 & S > 512 \end{cases}$	$\begin{cases} 0.0 & S < 64bytes \\ 12.2 & 64 \leq S \leq 512 \\ 8.30 & S > 512 \end{cases}$

The model is based on a static analysis of the code and includes a summation of the time to process a single cell (multiplied by the number of cells per processor) and the communication of boundary data between processors. The amount of overlap between messaging and computation is negligible. The model is parameterized in terms of dynamic aspects of the code - i.e. those features which are not known through a static analysis. These include: the number of cells, the number of newly adapted cells, and also any load-balancing across processors. These "histories" need to be known on a cycle by cycle basis if the model prediction is to be accurate.

The installation process required that the model predict performance for the first phase of ASCI Q with 2 different PCI bus speeds (initially 33-MHz and later 66-MHz). The PCI bus speed determines the available bandwidth between the Quadrics NIC and processor memory and has a significant impact on performance. In addition, when two NICs are present within the node (in a 2-rail system), the asymptotic bandwidth increases by approximately 180% if simultaneous messages can take advantage of the two rails [14]. Individual messages are not striped across rails.

Later in the installation process, the Alpha processors were upgraded from a clock speed of 1-GHz to 1.25-GHz. The faster processors also had an increased L2 cache capacity of 16MB in comparison to the 8MB cache of the slower processors. Thus during the installation there were actually three configurations of processors and PCI bus speeds: initially a 1-GHz processor with a 33-MHz bus, a 1-GHz processor with a 66-MHz bus, and finally a 1.25-GHz processor with a 66-MHz bus.

5.1 Expected performance

The performance model was used to provide the expected performance of SAGE on the ES45 system with a 33-MHz and 66-MHz PCI bus and a 1-GHz and 1.25-GHz Alpha EV68 processors. These predictions are shown in Figure 10.3.

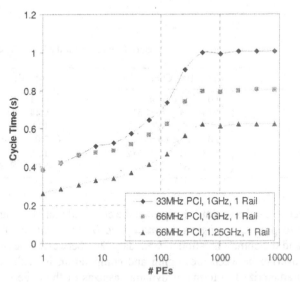

Figure 10.3. Performance predictions of SAGE on an ES45 system with QsNet.

We note the following observations: 1) since the runs of SAGE were performed for weak scaling, the time should ideally be constant across all processor configurations; 2) the model predicts that the two-fold improvement in PCI bus speed results in only a 20% performance improvement in the code overall; 3) the 25% improvement in processor clock speed results in a 22% performance improvement overall; 4) the SAGE cycle time is predicted to plateau above 512 processors - this is the point at which all gather/scatter communications are out-of-node.

5.2 Measured performance

Table 10.4 summarizes the test conditions on each test date and the refinements made from one test to another. There are three distinct phases of the installation representing: initial hardware of 1-GHz processors with a 33-MHz PCI bus (tested between Sept and Oct '01), 1-GHz processors with a 66-MHz bus (tested between Jan and April '02), and the final hardware of 1.25-GHz processors with a 66-MHz bus (tested between Sept '02 and May '03).

Table 10.4. Summary of Test Conditions.

Date	# nodes in system	Performance issues
9-Sept-01	128	Some faulty nodes and communication links resulted in poor communication performance, especially on 2 rails
24-Sept-01	128	Faulty hardware replaced, still poor 2-rail performance
24-Oct-01	128	2-Rail OS patch improved Quadrics Performance
04-Jan-02	512	PCI bus upgraded to 66 MHz; SAGE performance at pre-Oct-24 (not all nodes successfully ran at 66 MHz)
02-Feb-02	512	All nodes at 66 MHz but some configured out causing lower performance in collective communications
20-April-02	512	All nodes configured in, collectives improved
21-Sept-02	1024	Processors upgraded to 1.25-GHz. 1st Phase of ASCI Q. Performance lower than expected on processor counts above 512
25-Nov-02	1024	2nd phase of ASCI Q, performance consistent with 1st phase
27-Jan-03	1024	Impact of operating system events reduced, performance significantly improved
1-May-03	2048	First test of full-system

The performance of SAGE was measured at several points after the installation of the initial hardware had taken place: as soon as the machine was up and running (Sept. 9th), after a O/S upgrade and faulty hardware was replaced (Sept. 24th), and after an O/S patch (Oct. 24th). The upgrades that were most significant in terms of performance included bug fixes to the Quadrics RMS resource scheduling software and O/S patches that affected the priority of a process that determined the allocation of the two rails. Interestingly, this affected both 1- and 2-rail performance. These three sets of measurements, which are based on the 1-GHz processors with a 33-MHz PCI bus, are compared with the model in Figure 10.4.

The corresponding model prediction and measurements based on the 1-GHz processors after the PCI bus was upgraded to 66-MHz are shown in Figure 10.5. Initially (Jan 4th), not all nodes ran at 66-MHz. By Feb 2nd this had been resolved; however, not all nodes were available for testing. The Quadrics QsNet requires contiguous nodes in order to use its hardware-based collective operations. When nodes are configured out then a software component in the collectives is required which reduces overall performance. By April 20th all nodes were configured in and SAGE achieved the performance predicted by the model for all configurations except for the largest count of 512 nodes.

The performance of the system was again measured after upgrading the processors to 1.25-GHz, and the system increasing in size, first to separate two segments of 1024 nodes each and then to a combined 2048 node system. The first measurements made on each of the two segments (Sept. 21st, and Nov. 25th) resulted in performance highly consistent with each other. However, a major performance issue was identified concerning the impact of the operating system within each cluster of 32 nodes. This resulted in very poor performance on applications with synchronization requirements. These effects were minimized by reducing the number of operating system daemons, reducing the frequency of some monitoring activities, and configuring out 2 nodes per 32-node cluster [15]. The performance measured after this (Jan. 27th) showed much improved performance, very close to the model on the highest processor counts. In addition, the first test on the full ASCI Q system (May 1st) resulted in performance consistent with that in Jan. '03. This data has not been included in Figure 10.6 as only a few measurements were taken at this point. The minimization of the impact of the operating system is ongoing.

The differences between the model predictions and the final set of measurements obtained for each of the three installation phases are shown in Figure 10.7. Note that in the difference is small in all but the case of the largest processor counts. We expect the performance on largest configurations to improve after further operating system optimizations. The average difference across all the data shown in Figure 10.7, between the measurements and model predictions, is 3.7%.

Figures 10.4, 10.5 and 10.6 show that only after all the upgrades and system debugging had taken place that the measurements closely matched the expected performance. When the measured data matched the modelled data there was some confidence in the machine performing well. Without the model, it would have been difficult to know conclusively when to stop debugging, or more importantly when not to. When differences did occur between the model and measurements, microkernel benchmarks were run on the computational nodes and the communication network to help identify the source of the problem. This was especially important in the minimization of operating system effects

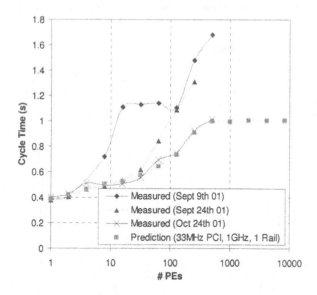

Figure 10.4. Measured performance of SAGE (33-MHz PCI bus, 1-GHz processors) compared with model predictions using a single rail.

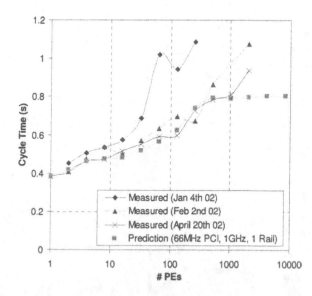

Figure 10.5. Measured performance of SAGE (66-MHz PCI bus, 1-GHz processors) compared with model predictions using a single rail.

that resulted in a significant performance improvement on very large processor counts [15].

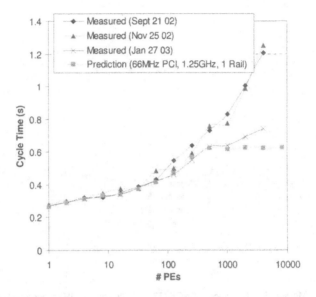

Figure 10.6.   Measured performance of SAGE (66-MHz PCI bus, 1.25-GHz processors) compared with model predictions using a single rail.

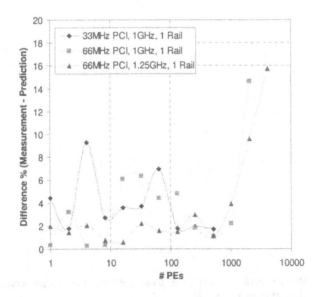

Figure 10.7.   Difference between measurements and predictions for SAGE.

6. Summary

Our team's research over the last few years has focused on the development of analytical performance models for the ASCI workload. It has been said that modelling and predicting the performance of large-scale applications on HPC systems, is one of the great, unsolved challenges for computer science [13]. Clearly, ASCI has a critical need for information on how best to map a given application to a given architecture, and performance modelling is the only means by which such information can be obtained quantitatively. Our approach has been successfully demonstrated for the 100,000-line+ adaptive mesh code reported here, for structured [4], and unstructured mesh transport codes [9], and for a Monte-Carlo particle transport code [10].

The work reported in this paper represents a small but important step in applying our performance models in a very practical way. We expect that ASCI platforms and software will be performance engineered, and that models will provide the means for this. The models can play a role throughout a system's lifecycle: starting at design when no hardware is available for measurement, in procurement for the comparison of systems, through to implementation / installation, and to examine the effects of updating a system over time. At each point the performance model provides an expectation of the achievable performance with a high level of fidelity. The SAGE performance model has been used for procurement purposes but company-sensitive information precludes disclosure of this in the literature. We can report, as here, how the model becomes the tool for assessing machine performance. Implementation milestone tests related to ASCI Q contractual obligations were based partially on comparison of observed data with predictions from the SAGE model, in a manner similar to the process described in this paper.

When installing a new system, refinements to both the software system, and hardware components, are often necessary before the machine operates at the expected level of performance. The performance model for SAGE has been shown to be of great use in this process. The model has effectively provided the performance and scalability baseline for the system performance on a realistic workload. Initial system testing showed that its performance was almost 50% less than expected. After several system refinements and upgrades over a number of months, the achieved performance matched closely the expectation provided by the model. Thus, performance models can be used to validate system performance.

Acknowledgments

Los Alamos National Laboratory is operated by the University of California for the National Nuclear Security Administration for the US Department of Energy.

References

[1] L. Carrington, A. Snavely, N. Wolter, X. Gao, A Performance Prediction Framework for Scientific Applications, in *Proc. Workshop on Performance Modeling and Analysis*, ICCS, Melbourne, Australia, June 2003.

[2] S. Coll, E. Frachtenberg, F. Petrini, A. Hoisie and L. Gurvits, Using Multirail Networks in High-Performance Clusters, in *Proc. of Cluster2001*, Newport Beach, CA, 2001.

[3] S. Girona, J. Labarta and R.M. Badia, Validation of Dimemas communication model for MPI collective operations, in *Proc. EuroPVM/MPI2000*, Balatonfured, Hungary, September 2000.

[4] A. Hoisie, O. Lubeck and H.J. Wasserman, Performance and Scalability Analysis of Teraflop-Scale Parallel Architectures Using Multidimensional Wavefront Applications, *Int. J. of High Performance Computing Applications*, 14 (2000) 330–346.

[5] D.J. Kerbyson, H.J. Alme, A. Hoisie, F. Petrini, H.J. Wasserman and M.L. Gittings, Predictive Performance and Scalability Modeling of a Large-scale Application, in *Proc. SC2001*, Denver, CO, 2001.

[6] D.J. Kerbyson, H.J. Wasserman and A. Hoisie, Exploring Advanced Architectures using Performance Prediction, in *Innovative Architectures for Future Generation High-Performance Processors and Systems* (A. Veidenbaum and K. Joe, Eds), IEEE Computer Society, 2002.

[7] D.J. Kerbyson, A. Hoisie and H.J. Wasserman, A Comparison between the Earth Simulator and AlphaServer Systems using Predictive Application Performance Models, in *Proc. of Int. Parallel and Distributed Processing Symposium (IPDPS)*, Nice, France, April 2003.

[8] D.J. Kerbyson, A. Hoisie and H.J. Wasserman, Use of Predictive Performance Modeling during Large-Scale System Installation, Parallel Processing Letters, World Scientific Publishing Company, 2003.

[9] D.J. Kerbyson, A. Hoisie and S.D. Pautz, Performance Modeling of Deterministic Transport Computations, in *Performance Analysis and Grid Computing*, Kluwer, 2003.

[10] M. Mathis, D.J. Kerbyson, A. Hoisie and H.J. Wasserman, Performance Modeling of MCNP on Large-Scale Systems, in *Proc. Los Alamos Computer Science Institute Symposium*, Santa Fe, NM, Oct. 2002.

[11] G.R. Nudd, D.J. Kerbyson, E. Papaefstathiou, S.C. Perry, J.S. Harper and D.V. Wilcox, PACE: A Toolset for the Performance Prediction of Parallel and Distributed Systems, *Int. J. of High Performance Computing Applications*, 14 (2000) 228–251.

[12] E. Papaefstathiou, Design of Performance Technology Infrastructure to Support the Construction of Responsive Software, in *Proc. 2ns ACM Int. Workshop on Software and Performance (WASP)*, Ottawa, Canada, (2000) 96–104.

[13] See http://perc.nersc.gov/main.htm.

[14] F. Petrini, W.C. Feng, A. Hoisie, S. Coll and E. Frachtenberg, The Quadrics Network, *IEEE Micro*, 22(1) (2002) 46–57.

[15] F. Petrini, D.J. Kerbyson and S. Pakin, The Case of the Missing Supercomputer Performance: Achieving Optimal Performance on the 8,192 Processors of ASCI Q, in *Proc. of SC2003*, Phoenix, AZ, 2003.

[16] R. Weaver, Major 3-D Parallel Simulations, BITS - Computing and communication news, Los Alamos National Laboratory, June/July, (1999) 9–11.

Chapter 11

MIXED LEVEL MODELLING AND SIMULATION OF LARGE SCALE HW/SW SYSTEMS*

Murali K. Nethi and James H. Aylor

University of Virginia, Charlottesville, Virginia, USA

mkn5v@cms.mail.virginia.edu

Abstract   Current large-scale computing systems consist of computation-intensive application software, a huge computational platform, possibly other system components such as sensors and actuators, and other performance instrumentation components. The new system architectures being proposed are huge distributed and parallel systems with thousands of processors distributed widely over space and executing large applications. Significant emphasis has been placed on the evaluation of the performance of these systems. The following paper surveys some of the recent performance evaluation tools that have been developed to evaluate the performance of such large scale parallel and distributed systems. A new methodology of performance evaluation using mixed level modelling techniques is proposed and its advantages over other existing tools is discussed.

Keywords: Parallel HW/SW system design, Mixed level simulation, Hardware/software modelling, Performance modelling, Simulation based performance evaluation

1.   Introduction

Rapid advancements in the area of high performance computing have provided a huge computational resource base for solving very complex scientific and engineering applications. Recent developments in the area of device technologies, architectural structures and parallel algorithms have resulted in enormous improvements in processing, storage and communication in large computer systems. Gradually, the computing platforms and applications are being transformed into large globally distributed, heterogeneous computing platforms consisting of large grid networks, which can support petaflop opera-

*A shorter version of this chapter appeared in the special issue of Hardware/Software Support for High Performance Scientific and Engineering Computing at Parallel Processing Letters, 2004.

tions. Thomas Sterling et. al. [1] describe the field of petaflop computing as new architectures that deliver performance at petaflop levels and applications that can be solved because of the availability of such computer systems. This gives us a perspective of the future systems. Further, it has been realized by the software community that the software for these huge systems cannot be developed in isolation, but has to be developed in coordination with the computing hardware architecture, network structure, processor configuration, and system software involving applications, compilers, runtime support and operating system components. One major concern of the parallel processing community in developing these systems and their applications is the lack of good performance evaluation tools for application software on existing and future architectures. It should be noted that the purpose of this paper is not to deal with all the issues involved with the performance evaluation, workload characterization or various techniques that have evolved over time for performance evaluation of parallel systems. An excellent survey in that area has been done by Lei Hu and Ian Gorton [2]. Instead, this paper surveys currently existing performance evaluation tools developed for these large distributed and parallel systems, and suggests a novel method called "mixed level modelling" to evaluate the performance of these systems with more efficiency and accuracy.

2.   Performance Estimation Techniques

Performance evaluation of computer systems is one of the key research areas for complex system development. Future system require accurate and fast performance evaluation techniques in order to efficiently make design tradeoffs before actually constructing the systems. The main issue involved in developing the performance evaluation techniques for these parallel/distributed systems is the trade-off that has to be achieved between the accuracy and cycle time of evaluation. While the focus of earlier work in performance evaluation of parallel systems has largely been determining execution of workload on some processor models, a recent view of a parallel/distributed system has changed. Rather, now the entire system architecture is viewed as consisting of components of application, runtime infrastructure, operating system and hardware architecture. Therefore, a layered approach is being used to model the system components, and these components are being represented at multiple level of detail and abstraction, and depending on fidelity of evaluation that is required, different components are being integrated to form a complete representation of system. The Wisconsin Wind Tunnel [3] is used to evaluate the performance of interconnection models with different configurations, ranging from a simple, functionally correct model to cycle accurate simulation models to understand detailed interactions within the design. POEMS [4] is another ongoing effort to create an end-to-end performance modelling of complex parallel and distributed systems. This effort spans the domains of application software, runtime and operating system software and hardware architecture. The entire system is designed from the component models designed at different levels of abstraction and detail. Different models range from analytical models such as LogGP [5] to detailed simulation models of instructions executing on an instruction simulator such as Simplescalar [6]. The hardware is modelled using hierarchical dependence graphs and the application is modelled as dynamic and static task graphs in which the node represents the task that has to be executed and the edge represents the communication between the nodes. Associative interfaces are developed to maintain input coherency when components are described at different levels of granularity. This multiple level modelling approach can be used to obtain more accurate performance results without compromising on speed of simulation. The PACE [7] methodology is another approach to performance evaluation of parallel and distributed systems. It is based on the layered approach where the hardware and software are separated through the parallelization template. Initially, the application is specified using the performance specification language, CHIP3S [8]. CHIP3S allows for the specification of the application in the form of parallel subtasks. The parallelization template converts this specification into parallel subtasks in terms of computation/communication interactions between the hardware. These subtasks are then mapped onto the distributed hardware model, which can be specified at multiple levels of detail and analyzed or simulated to obtain the performance specifications. Petasim [9] is a performance analysis tool that can be used in earlier stages of design of large distributed systems. In this approach, a Java Interface description language is used to specify the various components of the system including the processors, applications, communication networks and memories. Parsec [10] is a parallel simulation environment for complex environments in which a process-interaction approach is used for obtaining discrete-event simulations. Logical process models are described in a programming language such as C and events on the entities are modelled by message-passing communications between the processes. The Pablo project for performance evaluation was initiated to provide a performance evaluation environment for applications of massively parallel systems. It is a collection of tools including Autopilot [11], SvPablo [12], Parallel File System (PPFS) [13] and Delphi [14]. The Autopilot tool is being developed to model very large distributed and parallel applications by integrating dynamic performance instrumentation, performance data reduction using resource management algorithms, and real-time adaptive control mechanisms to provide for dynamic task management. SvPablo is a tool developed for visualizing and monitoring software performance for applications. It provides for application capture of software and also allows for studying the hardware/software interactions through usage of performance counters. The Delphi project is aimed at developing measurement, analysis, and performance prediction of applications executing on a variety of machine configurations (both parallel and distributed). A' la Carte [15], which is being developed at Los Alamos National Laboratory (LANL), is a tool being developed for performance evaluation of extremely large systems. It aims to provide simulation-based analysis for performance evaluation of existing and future architectures. The project models processors as simple delays based on direct execution of specific pieces of application code. The primary goal is this effort is focused on understanding the impact of the interconnection strategy on the overall performance. It uses the DaSSF simulation engine [16] for discrete event simulation and uses a domain modelling language to specify the architecture and application workload. SimOS [17] is a computer simulation environment for both uniprocessor and multiprocessor systems providing detailed estimation of the entire performance of hardware and the OS environment. The components are modelled at different levels of detail such that compromise can be made between the speed and accuracy of simulation. Other examples of performance evaluation tools that are being used for efficient performance estimation of the huge distributed systems are tools like RSIM [18], AppleS [19] and COMPASS [20].

3.   Our Modelling Approach

Analyzing previous work dealing with performance evaluation of large scale system modelling has led us to identify ways to improve the performance evaluation environments. Currently, complex systems are modelled in such a way that parallelism is extracted from the application code using compiler techniques and the resultant task graphs are "executed" on simulators such as MPI-SIM (used in POEMS effort) or other simulators. Many times, direct execution might not give accurate performance results because of difference in architectures of host and target architectures. Alternately, if we use a simulator, such as Simplescalar, we would have to encounter a large simulation time overhead along with synchronization problems. An additional problem is the assumption by the existing modelling paradigms that application code is available at the beginning of the system design effort. Many times when building large software systems, application code may not be available during initial stages of software system design. Instead, the entire application might be described as a task graph model, made up of a collection of parallel tasks or in some cases sequential tasks, which can be parallelized by some compiler. Therefore, significant effort is needed to model the components of the application software at higher levels of abstraction and hardware that executes the software, along with other system components so as to estimate the performance of the entire system. Finally, if some parts of the software are described at an abstract level and others described at a detailed level, there must be some a mechanism whereby the entire system can be simulated for performance estimation. Therefore, automatic interfaces have to be generated that allow for interaction of tasks described at multiple levels of abstraction so that more accurate performance estimates can be obtained with lesser simulation time. Our previous work has concentrated on using Hardware Description Languages (HDLs) for performance evaluation of these large systems. The mixed level simulation approach as used in ADEPT [21] is proposed for effective performance estimation of multiprocessor systems. The proposed modelling methodology uses the capability of certain Hardware Description Languages (HDLs) to model the various components (both hardware and software) at multiple levels of abstraction and detail. HDL's have been chosen because provide support for both concurrency and timing during description of system components. The methodology involves the description of software application at multiple levels of abstraction (Figure 1) where taskgraphs have been used to model the software. A detailed modelling of software can be as shown in Figure 1. Therefore, the application can be described at any level ranging from the simple high level high-level functional specification to a detailed code level description. The hardware must have components to process these software modules which are described at any level of granularity.

3.1   Hardware representation

Hierarchical control flow graphs provide an excellent framework for modelling different hardware components. They allow for design of same components at multiple level of granularity and provides for modelling independent, concurrently operating model components where each component has its own thread. Our hardware components include a collection of processor, memory, switch and I/O elements that can be described at any level of detail depending on the type of functionality needed. Along with the hardware components, an extra interface controller component is added as suggested in Culler et. al. [22]. Figure 2 above shows a generic hardware representation. The interface controller provides for tight interaction between the processor and the memory units based on type of architecture that is being represented. In addition, the interface controller resolves the problems that arise due to abstraction differences between the modules.

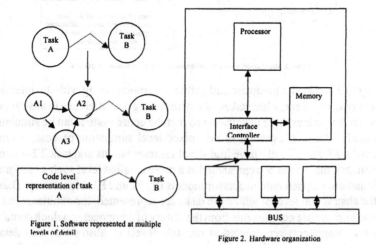

Figure 1. Software represented at multiple levels of detail

Figure 2. Hardware organization

4.   Mixed Level System Simulation Environment

The next issue is providing for mixed level simulation of the entire system. This kind of environment can provide for a more accurate simulation framework without compromising the speed of simulation. The entire system is composed of different components of software, hardware and OS/runtime represented at different levels of detail. These modules are allowed to interact with one another through the mapping provided to map the software onto hardware in order to simulate the system to obtain performance estimates. An additional component is added which is called interface match unit. The interface matching unit resolves the differences in inputs between software represented at different levels of detail to maintain input consistency when mapping to hardware. This allows for mixed level simulation between units at different level of detail and abstraction. The entire mixed model system simulation is shown in Figure 3.

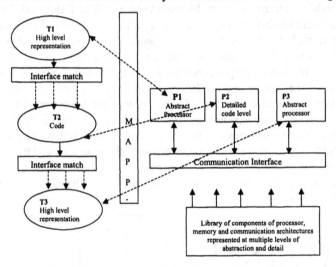

Figure 3. Mixed model simulation environment for various system components

Figure 3 shows the hardware and software mapping along with the interface generator component, which takes care of resolving the difference in abstraction between the various tasks in software so that the entire system can be simulated efficiently. As an illustration of our mixed level simulation process, assume that tasks T1 and T3 only have high-level representations and task T2 is some critical task that has to be represented at a more detailed level such as program code and are mapped onto processor models P1, P2 and P3 respectively. Based on the abstraction level at which the tasks are represented, the simulator has to choose appropriate components from the library of components, which contains various components represented at multiple levels of abstraction and detail. The purpose of the interface component is to accept the output from tasks and give input to the next task in the queue maintaining the input consistency and data abstraction so that mixed level simulation of the entire system is possible. Automatic generation of these interfaces is an active issue that we are currently researching.

5.   Preliminary Results

Early results in our mixed level performance modelling approach have been very encouraging. In our earlier work on developing ADEPT [21], techniques have been developed for simulation of hybrid elements with unknown interpreted inputs by MacDonald [23]. Techniques such as extremum experimentation [24] and sensitivity analysis [25] have been used to obtain interpreted inputs to simulate modules at different levels of abstraction to obtain mixed level simulation. Initially, we used an "uninterpreted," high level, description of system. After we identified system bottlenecks, only critical components were resolved to lower levels which we called as "interpreted" models while remaining system was still kept at high level. The main problem when developing such mixed level modelling technique is based on how to resolve dependencies in components at different levels and how to fill in the unknown inputs to the interpreted element to achieve meaningful results. We solved this by identifying the statistically important inputs to the combinational component (in terms of delay) - Delay Controlling Inputs (DCI) and assigning values to DCIs to produce minimum or maximum delay while ignoring other inputs as "don't cares". Typically, the number of DCIs decrease dramatically as other inputs become known as shown in Figure 4.

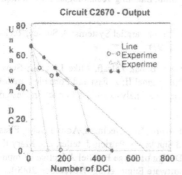

Figure 4. Unknown DCI Vs. No. Of DCI

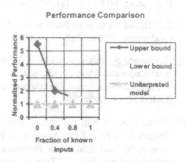

Figure 5. FSMD Interpreted Element Results

Moyassed [26] has developed methods for integrating performance models and sequential interpreted elements thereby creating modular structure of interface and methods used for handling differences in abstraction levels of different domains in the model. Finite state machine based representation was used for modelling the interpreted part of the system and then searching algorithms were used to find the shortest delay path across the sequential elements. We applied our modelling technique to a finite state machine description (FSMD) mixed level model. In this case, it was a performance model of a processor with a fetch unit, an integer unit and a floating-point unit. The floating-point unit was replaced with its interpreted (behavioral) representation. The results in Figure 5 show how the upper and lower bounds (minimum and maximum delay) on performance can be generated for the model at various levels of refinement. As the model is refined, the fraction of inputs for which the actual values are known from the performance model increase, and the bounds get tighter and finally converge.

6.   Conclusions and Future Work

The paper surveys various existing techniques for performance estimation of large parallel/distributed systems and presents a novel of mixed level performance modelling technique for performance evaluation of large parallel/distributed systems. The approach we have proposed in this paper aims to present a new methodology of using HDL based environment to perform mixed level modelling to improve the performance prediction capability of these huge systems. More work is underway in constructing the resource/request model to efficiently map the application task graphs on hardware architecture and generation of automatic interfaces between the components to obtain the mixed mode simulation of these systems.

References

[1] Thomas Sterling, Paul Messina, and Paul H. Smith, Enabling Technologies for Petaflops Computing, MIT Press, ISBN 0-262-69176.

[2] Lei Hu and Ian Gorton, Performance Evaluation for Parallel Systems: A Survey, Technical report, UNSW-CSE-TR-9707, (October 1997).

[3] Shubhendu S. Mukharjee, Steven K. Reinhardt, Babak Falsafi, Mike Litzkow, Steve Huss-Lederman, Mark D. hill, Wisconsin Wind Tunnel II: A Fast and Portable Parallel Archietcture Simulator, Workshop on Performance Analysis and Its Impact on Design (PAID), (June 1997).

[4] Vikram S. Adve, Rajive Bagrodia, James C. Browne, Ewa Deelman, Aditya Dube, Elias Houstis, John Rice, Rizos Sakellariou, David Sundaram, Patricia J. teller, and Mary K. Vernon, POEMS: End to End Performance Design of Large Parallel Adaptive Computational Systems, In IEEE Transactions on software Engineering (November, 2000).

[5] Alexandrov, A., M. Ionescu, K.E.Schauser, and C. Schieman, LogGP:Incorporating Long Messages into the LogP Model, Proc. 7th Annual ACM Symposium on Parallel Algorithms and Architectures (1995).

[6] Doug Burger and Todd M. Austin, The Simplescalar Tool set, Version 2.0, University of Wisconsin-Madison Computer Sciences Department Technical Report No. 1342, (June 1997).

[7] Kerbyson, D.J., J.S.Harper, A.Craig, and G.R.Nudd, PACE: A toolset to investigate and Predict Performance in Parallel Systems, European Parallel Tools Meeting, (October. 1996).

[8] E.Papaefstathiou, D.J.Kerbyson, G.R.Nudd, and T.J.Atherton, An Overview of the CHIP3S Performance Prediction Toolset for Parallel Systems, Proceedings 8th ISCA International Conference on Parallel and Distributed Computing Systems, (1995).

[9] Yohong Wen, Geoffery C. Fox, A performance Estimator for Parallel Hierarchical Memory Systems-Petasim, ISCA 12th International Conference on Parallel and Distributed Systems, (August, 1999).

[10] R. Bagrodia, R. Meyer, M. Takai, Y.A.Chen, X. Zeng, J. Martin, and H.Y.Song, Parsec: a Parallel Simulation Environment for Complex Systems, IEEE Computer, Vol. 31, (October 1998).

[11] R.L. Ribler, J.S. Vetter, H. Simitci, D.A. Reed, Autopilot: Adaptive Control of Distributed Applications, Proceedings of the 7th IEEE Symposium on High-Performance Distributed Computing, Chicago, IL, (July 1998).

[12] L. DeRose, D. Reed, SvPablo: A Multi-Language Architecture-Independent Performance Analysis System, Proceedings of the International Conference on Parallel Processing, Fukushima, Japan, (September 1999).

[13] J.V. Huber Jr., C.L. Elford, D.A. Reed, A.A. Chein, D.S. Blumenthal, PPFS: A High Performance Portable Parallel File System, Proceedings of the International Conference on Supercomputing, Vol. 9 (July 1995), pp. 385-394.

[14] D.A. Reed, D.A. Padua, I.T. Foster, D.B. Gannon, B.P. Miller, Delphi: An Integrated Language-Directed Performance Prediction, Measurement, and Analysis Environment, Frontiers '99: The 7th Symposium on the Frontiers of Massively Parallel Computation, (February 1999).

[15] "A'la carte", Los Alamos National Laboratory, LA-UR-01-5735/LA-LP-01-243.

[16] J. Liu and D.M. Nicol, DaSSF 3.1 User's Manual, (April 2001).

[17] Rosenblum, M., S.A.Herrod, E. Witchel, and A. Gupta, Complete Computer System Simulation: The SIMOS approach, IEEE Parallel and Distributed Technology, (1995).

[18] V.S.Pai, P. Ranganath, and S.V.Adve, RSIM Reference Manual. Version 1.0, In Department of Electrical and Computer Engineering, Rice University, Technical Report 9705, July 1997.

[19] Fran Berman, Rich Wolski, Silvia Figueira, Jennifer Schopf and Gary Shao, Application-level scheduling on distributed heterogeneous networks , Proceedings of the 1996 ACM/IEEE conference on Supercomputing, (November 1996).

[20] Bagrodia, R. E. Deelman, S. Docy, and T. Phan, Performance Prediction of Large parallel Applications Using Parallel Simulation, ACM SIGPLAN Symposium on principles and Practices of Parallel Programming, (May 1999).

[21] Moshe Meyassed, Bob McGraw, Robert Klenke, James Aylor and Barry Johnson, ADEPT: A Unified Environment for System Design, RASSP Digest - Vol. 3, (September 1996).

[22] David E. Culler, Jaswinder Pal Singh, and Anoop Gupta, Parallel computer architecture:a hardware/software approach, 1st edition, MKP publishers Inc. , San Fransisco, CA. 1999.

[23] MacDonald R.A., Hybrid Modelling of Systems with Interpreted Combinational Elements, PhD. Dissertation, Department of Electrical Engineering, University of Virginia, (May 1995).

[24] Dixon J.R., Computer-Based Models of Design Process : The Evolution of Designs for Redesign, Proceedings of NSF Engineering Design Research Conference, Armhest, (June, 1989).

[25] J.C.Helton, R.L.Iman, J.E.Campbell, An Approach to Sensitivity Analysis of Computer Models: Part I - Introduction, Input Variable Selection and Preliminary Assesment, Journal of Quality Technology, Vol. 13, No. 3, (July 1981).

[26] Meyassed Moshe, System Level design : Hybrid Modelling with Sequential Interpreted Elements, Phd. Dissertation, Department of electrical Engineering, University of Virginia, (January 1997).

V

GRID COMPUTING

Chapter 12

ENGINEERING AN AUTONOMIC PARTITIONING FRAMEWORK FOR GRID-BASED SAMR APPLICATIONS

S. Chandra, X. Li, and M. Parashar

The Applied Software Systems Laboratory, Department of Electrical and Computer Engineering
Rutgers University, Piscataway, NJ, USA

Abstract   Dynamic structured adaptive mesh refinement (SAMR) methods for the numerical solution to partial differential equations yield highly advantageous ratios for
cost/accuracy when compared to methods based upon static uniform approximations. However, distributed Grid-based SAMR implementations present significant challenges. This chapter presents ARMaDA, an autonomic partitioning
framework that provides adaptive, system and application sensitive partitioning,
load balancing and configuration support to address these challenges. The overall
goal of ARMaDA is to manage the dynamism and space-time heterogeneity of
SAMR applications and Grid environments, and support the efficient and scalable
execution of Grid-based SAMR implementations.

Keywords: Autonomic partitioning, Grid computing, Structured adaptive mesh refinement,
Dynamic load balancing

1.   Introduction

The Grid [8] is rapidly emerging as the dominant paradigm for wide area
distributed computing [10, 9]. Its goal is to provide a service-oriented infrastructure that leverages standardized protocols and services to enable pervasive
access to, and coordinated sharing of geographically distributed hardware, software, and information resources.

The emergence of computational Grids and the potential for seamless ag-
gregation, integration, and interactions has made it possible to conceive a new
generation of realistic scientific and engineering simulations of complex physical phenomena. These applications will symbiotically and opportunistically
combine computations, experiments, observations, and real-time data, and will
provide important insights into complex systems such as interacting black holes

and neutron stars, formations of galaxies, subsurface flows in oil reservoirs and aquifers, and dynamic response of materials to detonations. However, the phenomenon being modelled by these applications is inherently multi-phased, dynamic and heterogeneous (in time, space, and state) requiring very large numbers of software components and very dynamic compositions and interactions between these components. Furthermore, the underlying Grid infrastructure is similarly heterogeneous and dynamic, globally aggregating large numbers of independent computing and communication resources, data stores, and sensor networks. The combination of the two results in application development, configuration, and management complexities that break current paradigms.

Clearly, there is a need for a fundamental change in how these applications are formulated, composed, and managed so that their heterogeneity and dynamics can match and exploit the heterogeneous and dynamic nature of the Grid. In fact, scientific applications have reached a level of complexity, heterogeneity, and dynamism for which the current programming environments and infrastructure are becoming unmanageable and insecure. This has led researchers to consider alternative programming paradigms and management techniques that are based on strategies used by biological systems to deal with complexity, heterogeneity, and uncertainty. The approach is referred to as autonomic computing [11]. An autonomic computing system is one that has the capabilities of being self-defining, self-healing, self-configuring, self-optimizing, self-protecting, contextually aware, and open.

This chapter presents ARMaDA, an autonomic partitioning framework that provides adaptive (system and application sensitive) partitioning, load balancing and configuration mechanisms for Grid-based Structured Adaptive Mesh Refinement (SAMR) applications. The overall goal of ARMaDA is to manage the dynamism and space-time heterogeneity of SAMR applications and Grid environments, and support the efficient and scalable execution of Grid-based SAMR implementations. Dynamically adaptive techniques such as SAMR [2] can yield highly advantageous ratios for cost/accuracy when compared to methods based upon static uniform approximations. SAMR provides a means for concentrating computational effort to appropriate regions in the computational domain. These techniques can lead to more efficient and cost-effective solutions to time dependent problems exhibiting localized features. Distributed implementations of these methods offer the potential for accurate solutions of physically realistic models of complex physical phenomena. However, the dynamic structure and space-time heterogeneity of the adaptive grid hierarchy underlying SAMR algorithms makes their efficient implementation in Grid environments a significant challenge. This chapter describes the architecture and operation of ARMaDA and outlines its support for application and system sensitive partitioning and load balancing for SAMR applications. An experimental evaluation of ARMaDA is presented.

The rest of the chapter is organized as follows. Section 2 presents the motivations and challenges for autonomic partitioning and runtime management

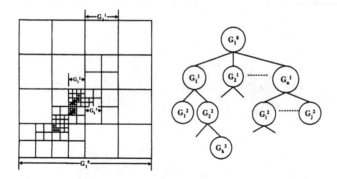

Figure 12.1. 2-D adaptive grid hierarchy (Berger-Oliger AMR scheme)

of SAMR applications. Section 3 presents an architectural overview of the ARMaDA autonomic partitioning framework and describes the design and operation of its components. Section 4 presents an experimental evaluation of the components. Section 5 presents summary and conclusions.

2. Problem Description

SAMR techniques track regions in the domain that requires additional resolution and dynamically overlay finer grids over these regions. These methods start with a base coarse grid with minimum acceptable resolution that covers the entire computational domain. As the solution progresses, regions in the domain requiring additional resolution are tagged and finer grids are overlaid on these tagged regions of the coarse grid. Refinement proceeds recursively so that regions on the finer grid requiring more resolution are similarly tagged and even finer grids are overlaid on these regions. The adaptive grid hierarchy of the SAMR formulation by Berger and Oliger [2] is shown in Figure 12.1.

Figure 12.2 shows a 2-D snapshot of a sample Grid-based SAMR application that investigates the simulation of flames [19]. The figure shows the mass-faction plots of various radicals produced during the ignition of H_2-Air mixture in a non-uniform temperature field with 3 "hot-spots". The application exhibits high dynamism and space-time heterogeneity and is representative of the simulations targeted by this research.

2.1 Computation and communication for parallel SAMR

In the targeted SAMR formulation, the grid hierarchy is refined both in space and in time. Refinements in space create finer level grids which have more grid points/cells than their parents. Refinements in time mean that finer grids take smaller time steps and hence have to be advanced more often. As a result, finer grids not only have greater computational loads, but also have to be integrated and synchronized more often. This results in a space-time heterogeneity in the SAMR adaptive grid hierarchy. Furthermore, regridding occurs at regular

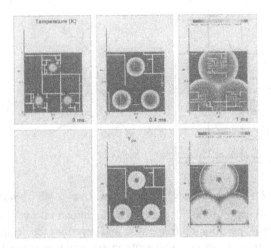

Figure 12.2.   Flames simulation: ignition of H_2-Air mixture in a non-uniform temperature field (Courtesy: J. Ray, et al, Sandia National Labs, Livermore)

intervals at each level and results in refined regions being created, moved, and deleted. Together, these characteristics of SAMR applications makes their efficient distributed implementation a significant challenge.

Parallel implementations of hierarchical SAMR applications typically partition the dynamic heterogeneous grid hierarchy across available processors and each processor operates on its local portions of this domain in parallel. Each processor starts at the coarsest level, integrates the patches at this level, and performs intra-level or ghost communications to update the boundaries of the patches. It then recursively operates on the finer grids using the refined time steps - i.e., for each step on a parent grid, there are multiple steps (equal to the time refinement factor) on a child grid. When the parent and child grids are at the same physical time, inter-level communications are used to inject information from the child to its parent. The solution error at different levels of the SAMR grid hierarchy is evaluated at regular intervals and this error is used to determine the regions where the hierarchy needs to be locally refined or coarsened. Dynamic re-partitioning and re-distribution is typically required after this step.

The overall performance of parallel SAMR applications is limited by the ability to partition the underlying grid hierarchies at runtime to expose all inherent parallelism, minimize communication and synchronization overheads, and balance load. A critical requirement of the load partitioner is to maintain logical locality across partitions at different levels of the hierarchy and at the same level when they are decomposed and mapped across processors. The maintenance of locality minimizes the total communication and synchronization overheads.

The timing diagram (note that this diagram is not to scale) in Figure 12.3 illustrates the operation of the SAMR algorithm described above using a 3-level grid

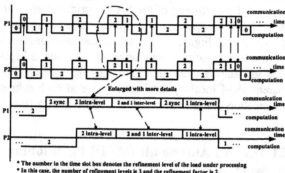

* The number in the time slot box denotes the refinement level of the load under processing
* In this case, the number of refinement levels is 3 and the refinement factor is 2.
* The communication time consists of three types, intra-level, iter-level and synchronization cost

Figure 12.3. Timing diagram for parallel SAMR algorithm

hierarchy. For simplicity, only the computation and communication behaviors of processors $P1$ and $P2$ are shown. The three components of communication overheads (listed in Section 2.2) are illustrated in the enlarged portion of the time line. This figure shows the exact computation and communication patterns for parallel SAMR implementations. Note that the timing diagram shows that there is one time step on the coarsest level (level 0) of the grid hierarchy followed by two time steps on the first refinement level and four time steps on the second level, before the second time step on level 0 can start. Also, note that the computation and communication for each refinement level are interleaved. As mentioned above, the grid hierarchy itself is quite dynamic and the grids at different levels are created and deleted on-the-fly. This behavior makes it quite challenging to partition the dynamic SAMR grid hierarchy to both balance load and minimize communication/synchronization overheads.

2.2 Communication overheads for parallel SAMR applications

As described in Section 2.1 and shown in Figure 12.3, the communication overheads of parallel SAMR applications primarily consist of three components: (1) *Inter-level communications* are defined between component grids at different levels of the grid hierarchy and consist of prolongations (coarse to fine transfer and interpolation) and restrictions (fine to coarse transfer and interpolation). (2) *Intra-level communications* are required to update the grid-elements along the boundaries of local portions of a distributed grid and consist of near-neighbor exchanges. These communications can be scheduled so as to be overlapped with computations on the interior region. (3) *Synchronization costs* occur when the load is not well balanced among all processors. These costs may occur at any time step and at any refinement level due to the hierarchical refinement of space and time in SAMR applications. Note that there are additional communication costs due to the data movement required during dynamic load balancing and redistribution.

Clearly, an optimal partitioning of the SAMR grid hierarchy and scalable implementations of SAMR applications requires careful consideration of the timing pattern as shown in Figure 12.3 and the three communication overhead components. Critical observations from the timing diagram in Figure 12.3 are that, in addition to balancing the total load assigned to each processor and maintaining parent child locality, the load balance at each refinement level and the communication and synchronization costs within a level need to be addressed.

3.   ARMaDA: An Autonomic SAMR Partitioning Framework

The overall behavior and performance of SAMR applications depends on a large number of system and application parameters. Consequently, optimizing the execution of SAMR applications requires identifying an optimal set and configuration of these parameters. Furthermore, the relationships between the contributing factors might be highly intricate and depend on current application and system state. ARMaDA is an autonomic partitioning framework that reactively and proactively manages and optimizes the execution of SAMR applications in Grid environments using current system and application state, online predictive models for system behavior and application performance, and an agent based control network. It defines a hierarchical partitioning scheme with autonomic partitioner management and application-aware and system-sensitive adaptations and optimizations at each level of the hierarchy.

ARMaDA is based on the concept of the *vGrid autonomic runtime* proposed by M. Parashar and S. Hariri [12, 1]. It is currently under development at The Applied Software Systems Laboratory (TASSL) at Rutgers University. This chapter focuses on the design, prototype implementation, and evaluation of the core building blocks of the framework, i.e. the hierarchical partitioning scheme and application and system aware partitioning and mapping. These components are described in the following sections.

3.1   Hierarchical autonomic partitioning and mapping

In the ARMaDA framework, an autonomic runtime manager (ARM) resides within each computational resource and ARMs are hierarchically organized as shown in Figure 12.4 (a). Each ARM makes local partitioning decisions at runtime based on application and system state, and communicates with other managers at various levels of the hierarchy. The autonomic partitioning component within each ARM is organized into a three layer partitioner stack as shown in Figure 12.4 (b). The partitioning strategies within this stack are based on Space Filling Curves (SFC) [20] and use these curves to decompose the SAMR application domain.

The foundation of the autonomic SAMR partitioner in ARMaDA (using the partitioner stack in Figure 12.4 (b)) is a set of domain-based SFC partitioners,

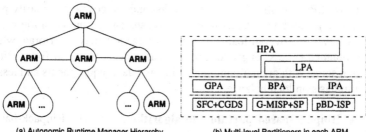

(a) Autonomic Runtime Manager Hierarchy   (b) Multi-level Partitioners in each ARM

Figure 12.4. Hierarchical autonomic partitioning and mapping

namely, SFC+CGDS (space filling curve partitioner with composite grid distribution strategy), G-MISP+SP (geometric multilevel inverse space-filling curve partitioner with sequence partitioning), and pBD-ISP (p-way binary dissection inverse space-filling curve partitioner) [18, 22, 3, 5]. On top of these basic partitioners, there are three partitioners categorized based on their load-balancing schemes as Greedy Partitioning Algorithm (GPA), Binpack-based Partitioning Algorithm (BPA), and Iterative Partitioning Algorithm (IPA) [13]. Compared to the simple GPA scheme, BPA and IPA provide better load balance with additional overheads. At the top of the partitioner stack are high-level partitioners, namely, the Hierarchical Partitioning Algorithm (HPA) and the Level-based Partitioning Algorithm (LPA). These two partitioners further refine the partitioning quality to reduce the communication and synchronization overheads. The components of the partitioner stack are described below.

3.1.1 Domain-based SFC partitioners. The bottom layer of the partitioner stack is a set of domain-based SFC partitioners that partition the entire SAMR domain into sub-domains that can be mapped by the ARM onto application computational units, which are then partitioned and balanced among available processors. The partitioners within the ARMaDA framework include SFC+CGDS from GrACE distributed AMR infrastructure [15, 17, 16] and G-MISP+SP and pBD-ISP that belong to the Vampire SAMR partitioning library [22]. Their characteristics [4] are as follows:

- **SFC+CGDS:** The SFC+CGDS scheme is fast, has average load balance, and generates low overhead, low communication and average data migration costs. This scheme is suited for application states associated with low-to-moderate activity dynamics and more computation than communication.

- **G-MISP+SP:** The G-MISP+SP scheme is aimed towards speed and simplicity, and favors simple communication patterns and partitioning speed over amount of data migration. Sequence partitioning used by G-MISP+SP significantly improves the load balance but can be computationally expensive.

- **pBD-ISP:** The pBD-ISP scheme is fast and the coarse granularity partitioning generated results in low overheads and communication costs. However, the overall load balance is average and may deteriorate when refinements are strongly localized. This scheme is suited for application states with greater communication and data requirements and lesser emphasis on load balance.

3.1.2   Binpack-based partitioning algorithm.   The Binpack-based partitioning algorithm (BPA) attempts to improve the load balance during the SAMR partitioning phase, where the computational workload associated with patches at different levels of the SAMR hierarchy is distributed among available processors. The distribution is performed under constraints such as the minimum patch size and the aspect ratio. BPA distributes the workload among processors as long as the processor work threshold is not exceeded. Patches with a workload larger than the threshold limit are split into smaller patches. Unallocated work is first distributed using a "best-fit" approach. If this fails, the "most-free" approach is adopted. BPA technique improves the load balance between partitions and, hence, the execution time for a SAMR application. However, as a result of multiple patch divisions, a large number of patches may be created.

3.1.3   Level-based partitioning algorithm.   The computational workload for a certain patch of the SAMR application is tightly coupled to the refinement level at which the patch exists. The computational workload at a finer level is considerably greater than that at coarser levels. The level-based partitioning algorithm (LPA) [13] attempts to simultaneously balance load and minimize synchronization cost. LPA essentially preprocesses the global application computational units represented by a global grid unit list (GUL), disassembles them according to refinement levels of the grid hierarchy, and feeds the resulting homogeneous units at each refinement level to GPA. The GPA scheme then partitions this list to balance the workload. Due to preprocessing, the load on each refinement level is also balanced. LPA benefits from the SFC+CGDS technique by maintaining parent-children relationship throughout the composite grid and localizing inter-level communications, while simultaneously balancing the load at each refinement level.

3.1.4   Hierarchical partitioning algorithm.   In the hierarchical partitioning algorithm (HPA), the partitioning phase is divided into two sub-phases: local partitioning phase and global partitioning phase. In the local partitioning phase, the processors within a group partition the group workload based on a local load threshold and assign a portion to each processor within the group. Parent groups iteratively partition among their children groups in a hierarchical manner. In the global partitioning phase, the root group coordinator decides if a global re-partitioning has to be performed among its children groups according to the group threshold.

The HPA scheme attempts to exploit the fact that, given a group with adequate number of processors and an appropriately defined number of groups, the number of global partitioning phases can be greatly reduced, thereby eliminating unnecessary communication and synchronization overheads. The prototype implementation has two variants of the HPA scheme, namely, Static HPA (SHPA) and Adaptive HPA (AHPA) [14].

In SHPA scheme, the group size and group topology are defined at startup based on available processors and size of the problem domain. The group topology then remains fixed for the entire execution session. In order to account for application runtime dynamics, the AHPA scheme proposes an adaptive strategy. AHPA dynamically partitions the computational domain into sub-domains to match the current adaptations. The sub-domains created may have unequal workloads. The algorithm then assigns the sub-domains to corresponding non-uniform hierarchical processor groups which are constructed at runtime.

3.2   Application aware partitioning and mapping

The application aware partitioning and mapping mechanism is an adaptive strategy within the ARMaDA framework. It uses the state of the application and its current requirements to select and tune partitioning algorithms and parameters. It is composed of three components: application state characterization component, partitioner selection component and policy engine, and runtime adaptation (meta-partitioner) component. The state characterization component implements mechanisms that abstract and characterize the current application state in terms of the computation/communication requirements, application dynamics, and the nature of the adaptation. The policy engine defines the associations between application state and partitioner behavior. Based on the state characterization and defined policies, the appropriate partitioning algorithm and associated partitioning parameters (such as granularity) are selected at runtime from the available repository of partitioners. The partitioners include a selection from broadly used software tools such as GrACE [15, 17, 16] and Vampire [22]. The runtime adaptation component dynamically configures partitioning granularity and invokes the appropriate partitioner, thus adapting and optimizing application performance. Experimental studies of the ARMaDA application aware adaptive partitioning [5] framework have shown that it can significantly improve the efficiency and performance of parallel/distributed SAMR applications.

3.2.1   Mechanism for characterizing application runtime state.   The application runtime state is characterized in terms of the computation/communication requirements ("CCratio"), application dynamics ("Dynamics"), and the

nature of the adaptation ("Adapt"), i.e.

$$CCratio = \frac{\sum (\text{Volume of patches})}{\sum (\text{Surface area of patches})}$$

$$Dynamics = Size\ of(\text{Current state} \cap \text{Previous state})$$

$$Adapt = \frac{\text{Coarse volume}}{\text{Domain volume}} * \text{No. of coarse patches}$$

Using normalization and scaling techniques, the ARMaDA framework computes three ratios, namely, computation/communication ratio ("Cratio"), application dynamics ratio ("Dratio") , and the adaptation ratio ("Aratio"), to represent the current state of the SAMR application.

3.2.2   Policies for mapping application state and partitioners.   The octant approach [23] is used to classify the state of the SAMR application and identify its partitioning requirements. According to the octant approach, application runtime state is classified with respect to (a) the adaptation pattern (scattered or localized), (b) whether runtime is dominated by computations or communications, and (c) the activity dynamics in the solution (for example, a rapidly changing adaptation pattern). Policies are then defined, using experiments and heuristics, to assign partitioner(s) to application-state octants based on their ability to meet the requirements of that octant [24, 4]. The associations of application state octants to partitioning techniques are summarized in Figure 12.5.

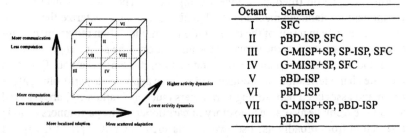

Octant	Scheme
I	SFC
II	pBD-ISP, SFC
III	G-MISP+SP, SP-ISP, SFC
IV	G-MISP+SP, SFC
V	pBD-ISP
VI	pBD-ISP
VII	G-MISP+SP, pBD-ISP
VIII	pBD-ISP

Figure 12.5.   The octant approach for mapping application state and partitioners

3.2.3   Runtime adaptation.   The combination of the three ratios (Cratio, Dratio, and Aratio), computed by the state characterization component, maps the application state to a specific octant position. Using the octant-partitioner mapping policies described above, the application-aware framework selects the appropriate partitioner from the available repository of partitioners. The adaptation component configures the selected partitioner with the appropriate partitioning parameters (e.g., partitioning granularity) and uses it to partition the SAMR grid hierarchy.

One concern during runtime adaptation using the application aware scheme is the possibility of thrashing due to very frequent state changes which, in turn, can result in increased overheads due to rapid switching of partitioners. To avoid thrashing, the framework uses a dynamic history of application characteristics based on the current state and two preceding application states. This "3-step sliding history window" approach for computing application ratios helps to avoid the ill-effects of transient changes and oscillations in application state.

Furthermore, care must be taken that the overheads of characterizing application state and adapting runtime behavior do not offset the benefits of the adaptation. As a result, efficient algorithms and mechanisms must be employed. The application aware scheme within ARMaDA uses efficient algorithms based on union and interaction operations on the grid/patch geometry to characterize application state (computation/communication requirements and activity dynamics) and compute the required metric ratios. ARMaDA also provides a number of control parameters that can be used to customize the sensitivity, quality, and overheads of the adaptation. User/system defined thresholds are used to quickly determine when a change in partitioner and/or partitioning parameters is required. Application-dependent weights fine-tune the sensitivity of the quality metric to closely match the needs of the dynamic application. For example, in a computationally-intensive SAMR application, the weight of Cratio (computation/communication ratio) can be set higher than the weights for other metric ratios, making the partitioner selection strategy more sensitive to changes in the computational requirements of the application.

3.3   System sensitive partitioning and mapping

The adaptive system sensitive partitioner uses system capabilities and current system state to select and tune distribution parameters by dynamically partitioning and load balancing the SAMR grid hierarchy. Current system state is obtained at runtime using the NWS [25] resource monitoring tool. NWS periodically monitors and dynamically forecasts the performance delivered by the various network and computational resources over a given time interval. Measurements include the fraction of CPU time available for new processes, the fraction of CPU available to a process that is already running, end-to-end TCP network latency, end-to-end TCP network bandwidth, free memory, and the amount of space unused on a disk.

System state information provided by NWS is used to compute a relative capacity metric [21] for each processor. Assume that there are K processors in the system among which the partitioner distributes the workload. For node k, let $\mathcal{P}_k$ be the percentage of CPU available, $\mathcal{M}_k$ the available memory, and $\mathcal{B}_k$ the link bandwidth. The available resource at k is first converted to a fraction of total available resources, i.e.

$$P_k = \mathcal{P}_k / \sum_{i=1}^{K} \mathcal{P}_i, \qquad M_k = \mathcal{M}_k / \sum_{i=1}^{K} \mathcal{M}_i, \qquad B_k = \mathcal{B}_k / \sum_{i=1}^{K} \mathcal{B}_i$$

The relative capacity C_k of a processor is then defined as the weighted sum of these normalized quantities, i.e.

$$C_k = w_p P_k + w_m M_k + w_b B_k$$

where w_p, w_m, and w_b are the weights associated with the relative CPU, memory, and link bandwidth availabilities, respectively, such that

$$w_p + w_m + w_b = 1$$

The weights are application dependent and reflect its computational, memory, and communication requirements. Note that

$$\sum_{k=1}^{K} C_k = 1$$

If the total work to be assigned to all the processors is denoted by L, then the work L_k assigned to the kth processor can be computed as $L_k = C_k L$. In contrast to the system sensitive partitioner, the default partitioning scheme provided by GrACE (data management infrastructure for parallel/distributed SAMR) [15, 17, 16] assumes homogeneous processors and performs an equal distribution of the workload on the processors.

Performance functions can be used in conjunction with system-sensitive partitioning [6] to predict the application execution time based on current loads, available communication bandwidth, current latencies, and available memory. These performance estimates are then used to adjust the relative capacity associated with each processor.

4.   An Experimental Evaluation of Autonomic Partitioning Policies

This section presents an experimental evaluation of the hierarchical autonomic partitioning, application-aware partitioning, and system-sensitive partitioning techniques within the ARMaDA framework, described in the previous section. The performance improvement due to the adaptation in each scheme is evaluated by comparing the execution time and other runtime parameters for SAMR application runs with and without the adaptive strategy.

4.1   Evaluation of static HPA

The Static HPA scheme is implemented as part of the GrACE toolkit [15, 17, 16]. The groups are created using communicators provided by the MPI library. Communication within groups is through intra-communicators while communication between processors belonging to different groups is through inter-communicators.

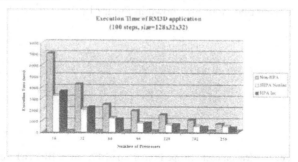

Figure 12.6. Execution time: Static HPA vs. Non-HPA scheme

The Static HPA scheme is evaluated on the "Blue Horizon" IBM SP2 cluster at the San Diego Supercomputing Center. The application used in these experiments is the 3-D Richtmyer-Meshkov instability solver (RM3D) encountered in compressible fluid dynamics. RM3D has been developed by Ravi Samtaney as part of the virtual test facility at the Caltech ASCI/ASAP Center [7]. The experiments measure the total execution time of RM3D using Static HPA and Non-HPA schemes. To evaluate the benefits of incremental load balancing, two experiments for the Static HPA scheme are performed: SHPA without incremental balancing (labeled as SHPA NonInc in the figure) and SHPA with incremental load balancing (labeled as SHPA Inc in the figure). As illustrated in Figure 12.6, the SHPA schemes significantly improve the overall execution time. The maximum performance gain is obtained for 192 processors using SHPA Inc scheme and results in 59% reduction in the overall execution time as compared to Non-HPA scheme. For relatively small number of processors, the SHPA NonInc scheme outperforms the SHPA Inc scheme due to better load balancing, since it globally re-distributes the load more frequently. However, for larger number of processors, the SHPA Inc scheme outperforms the SHPA NonInc scheme in the long run due to a reduction in the synchronization and global communication overheads as a result of incremental load balancing. As shown by the evaluation, the benefits of SHPA depends on the appropriate setup of processor group hierarchies, which in turn depends on the system and the application. The adaptive HPA scheme attempts to address this limitation by dynamically managing processor groups.

4.2   Evaluation of adaptive HPA

The AHPA scheme is evaluated using trace-driven simulations. First, the refinement trace for an SAMR application is obtained by running the application on a single processor. Then, the trace file is fed into HPA partitioners to partition and produce a new trace file for multiple processors. Finally, the new trace file is input into the SAMR simulator to obtain the runtime performance measurements on multiple processors. The simulation results for the 2D Transport Equation and the Wave3D applications are shown in Figure 12.7.

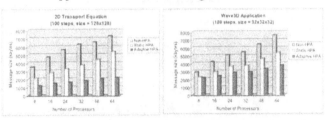

Figure 12.7.   Communication cost: comparison of Non-HPA, Static HPA and Adaptive HPA schemes

As shown in Figure 12.7, the communication cost (measured as the total message size for intra-level and inter-level communication) is greatly reduced using HPA schemes as compared to the Non-HPA scheme. This is primarily due to reduced global communication and concurrent communications in hierarchical processor groups. Compared to the SHPA scheme, the AHPA scheme further reduces communication costs. In the figure, the communication cost increases with increasing number of processors due to higher inter-processor communication traffic. An important observation is that the rate of increase for the Non-HPA and SHPA schemes are greater than that for the AHPA scheme. This indicates that the AHPA scheme has a better scalability. The reduction in communication cost is significant, up to 70%, for the AHPA scheme as compared to the Non-HPA scheme. These simulations validate that the Adaptive HPA scheme is potentially an efficient solution to gain better system performance. Further experimental evaluation of the AHPA scheme is currently in progress.

4.3   Evaluation of application aware partitioning

The application aware scheme within the ARMaDA framework [3] performs application sensitive adaptations at runtime and autonomically selects and configures the appropriate partitioning strategy to match the current application state. The different partitioners in the ARMaDA framework include SFC or ISP, G-MISP+SP, pBD-ISP, and adaptive combinations of these partitioners based on runtime state. The benefits of autonomic partitioning in comparison to pre-defined partitioners is experimentally evaluated for the RM2D application running on 64 processors on "Blue Horizon". The RM2D application has a base grid of size 128*32 and executes for 60 iterations with 3 levels of factor 2 space-time refinements with regridding performed every 4 time-steps at each level. The application execution times for RM2D on 64 processors for different partitioning configurations in the application aware scheme are shown in Figure 12.8.

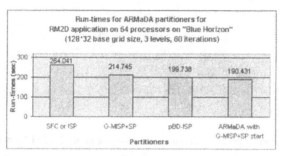

Figure 12.8. RM2D execution times for ARMaDA partitioners on 64 processors on "Blue Horizon"

The application starts out with greater computation requirements, low activity dynamics, and more scattered adaptation, placing it in octant IV. Consequently, the application aware adaptive partitioner starts out with the G-MISP+SP or SFC partitioner, as these partitioners are better suited for the initial stages of the application. Due to the efficient application state sensing and characterization algorithms, the application aware scheme has an overhead of only 0.415 seconds for the RM2D experiment, which is small as compared to the overall application execution times. The execution speedup provided by the application aware scheme for the RM2D application is 4.66%, 11.32%, and 27.88% over pBD-ISP, G-MISP+SP, and SFC partitioners respectively.

4.4 Evaluation of system sensitive adaptation

This evaluation experimentally demonstrates the system-sensitive performance of the autonomic framework which enables the application to adapt to system load dynamics. Current load is obtained using the on-line monitoring approach as discussed in Section 3.3. This experiment compares the SAMR application runtime performance using the system-sensitive "ACEHeterogeneous" partitioner against the default "ACEComposite" partitioner within the GrACE infrastructure. The evaluation is performed on 64 processors of the "Frea" Beowulf cluster at TASSL for the RM3D application with a 128*32*32 base grid size and 3 levels of factor 2 space-time refinements. The results are averaged over 3 runs and various execution times are measured (Ttotal = total execution time, Tcp = total computation time, and Tcm = total communication time). Figure 12.9 illustrates the performance comparison for the two partitioning schemes.

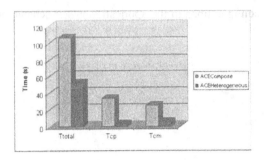

Figure 12.9.   Performance of system-sensitive partitioning for RM3D on 64 processors

4.5   Evaluation of adaptations for memory availability

Memory availability for each processor is captured using the NWS system monitoring tool and is used by the autonomic framework to adapt and optimize partitioning parameters, i.e. the upper bound on the size of SAMR patches is tuned so that it conforms to the available memory. In the case of processors with higher memory availability, the framework attempts to maximize the size of SAMR patches at each level so as to increase cache locality and reduce overall communication. However, when the available memory is limited, the framework constrains the size of the patches to conform to the available memory by assigning smaller refined patches to the processors with limited memory before breaking the larger patches.

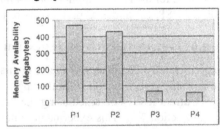

Figure 12.10.   Memory availability of 4 processors

The capability of the framework to autonomically adapt to variation in memory availability is evaluated using RM3D on 4 processors of the "Frea" Beowulf cluster at TASSL. A "rogue" program that randomly utilizes memory is executed on each of the processors and simulates the variability in available memory. In our experiment, two processors ($P1$ and $P2$) have higher memory availability and the other two ($P3$ and $P4$) have limited memory availability. Figure 12.10 shows the memory availability for the 4 processors. As the application executes, processors $P3$ and $P4$ are assigned smaller patches to match their limited available memory while $P1$ and $P2$ are assigned relatively large patches. Figure 12.11 illustrates the variance of maximum patch size allocated to the processors, which indicates that the partitioning scheme with memory adaptation changes the patch size according to the memory availability for each processor.

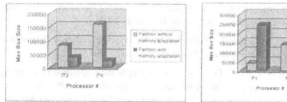 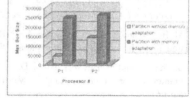

Figure 12.11. Maximum patch size (grid points) variance for 4 processors with and without memory adaptations

5. Summary and Conclusions

Distributed Grid-based implementations of dynamic structured adaptive mesh refinement (SAMR) applications present significant challenges due to the heterogeneity and dynamics of the application and the Grid execution environment. This chapter presented the ARMaDA autonomic partitioning framework that provides adaptive, system and application sensitive partitioning, load balancing, and configuration support to address these challenges. ARMaDA reactively and proactively manages and optimizes the execution of SAMR applications in Grid environments using current system and application state, online predictive models for system behavior and application performance, and an agent based control network. It defines a hierarchical partitioning scheme with autonomic partitioner management and application-aware and system-sensitive adaptations and optimizations at each level of the hierarchy. The design, prototype implementation, and evaluation of the core building blocks of ARMaDA were presented in this chapter. Current efforts are focused on integrating the components along with a deductive Grid middleware to support highly flexible, self-configuring, self-adapting, and self-optimizing Grid-based implementations of SAMR applications.

Acknowledgments

The authors acknowledge the contributions of S. Sinha and H. Zhu (system sensitive partitioning and mapping) and J. Steensland (application state characterization and Vampire partitioning library) to the research presented in this paper. The authors would also like to thank R. Samtaney and J. Ray for making their applications available. This research was supported in part by NSF via grants numbers ACI 9984357 (CAREERS), EIA-0103674 (NGS) and EIA-0120934 (ITR), and by DOE ASCI/ASAP (Caltech) via grant numbers PC295251 and 1052856.

References

[1] M. Agarwal, V. Bhat, Z. Li, H. Liu, B. Khargharia, V. Matossian, V. Putty, C. Schmidt, G. Zhang, S. Hariri, and M. Parashar. Automate: Enabling Autonomic Applications on the Grid. To appear in *Proceedings of the Autonomic Computing Workshop, 5th Annual International Active Middleware Services (AMS) Workshop*, 2003.

[2] M. Berger and J. Oliger. Adaptive Mesh Refinement for Hyperbolic Partial Differential Equations. In *Journal of Computational Physics*, 53:484–512, 1984.

[3] S. Chandra and M. Parashar. ARMaDA: An Adaptive Application-sensitive Partitioning Framework for Structured Adaptive Mesh Refinement Applications. In *Proceedings of the IASTED International Conference on Parallel and Distributed Computing Systems (PDCS)*, pages 446 – 451, Cambridge, MA, 2002.

[4] S. Chandra and M. Parashar. An Evaluation of Partitioners for Parallel SAMR Applications. In *Proceedings of the 7th International European Conference on Parallel Computing (Euro-Par)*, editors: R. Sakellariou, J. Keane, J. Gurd, and L. Freeman, Springer-Verlag, volume 2150, pages 171–174, August 2001.

[5] S. Chandra, J. Steensland, M. Parashar, and J. Cummings. An Experimental Study of Adaptive Application Sensitive Partitioning Strategies for SAMR Applications. In *Proceedings of the 2nd Los Alamos Computer Science Institute Symposium (also Best Research Poster at Supercomputing Conference 2001)*, October 2001.

[6] S. Chandra, Y. Zhang, S. Sinha, J. Yang, M. Parashar, and S. Hariri. Adaptive Runtime Management of SAMR Applications. In *Proceedings of the 9th International Conference on High Performance Computing (HiPC)*, Lecture Notes in Computer Science, editors: S. Sahni, V. K. Prasanna, U. Shukla, Springer-Verlag, volume 2552, Bangalore, India, December 2002.

[7] J. Cummings, M. Aivazis, R. Samtaney, R. Radovitzky, S. Mauch, and D. Meiron. A Virtual Test Facility for the Simulation of Dynamic Response in Materials. In *Journal of Supercomputing*, 23:39–50, 2002.

[8] I. Foster and C. Kesselman. Computational Grids. In *The Grid: Blueprint for a New Computing Infrastructure*, editors: I. Foster and C. Kesselman, Morgan Kaufmann Publishers, 1998.

[9] I. Foster, C. Kesselman, J. Nick, and S. Tuecke. The Physiology of the Grid: An Open Grid Services Architecture for Distributed Systems Integration. Open Grid Service Infrastructure Working Group, Global Grid Forum, June 2002.

[10] I. Foster, C. Kesselman, and S. Tuecke. The Anatomy of the Grid: Enabling Scalable Virtual Organizations. In *International Journal of High Performance Computing Applications*, 15:200–222, 2001.

[11] P. Horn. Autonomic Computing: IBM's Perspective on the State of Information Technology. Technical Report, IBM Corporation, October 2001.

[12] B. Khargharia, S. Hariri, and M. Parashar. vGrid: A Framework for Building Autonomic Applications. To appear in *Proceedings of the 1st International Workshop on Heterogeneous and Adaptive Computing - Challenges of Large Applications in Distributed Environments (CLADE)*, 2003.

[13] X. Li and M. Parashar. Dynamic Load Partitioning Strategies for Managing Data of Space and Time Heterogeneity in Parallel SAMR Applications. To appear in *Proceedings of the 9th International European Conference on Parallel Computing (Euro-Par)*, Klagenfurt, Austria, 2003.

[14] X. Li and M. Parashar. Hierarchical Partitioning Techniques for Structured Adaptive Mesh Refinement Applications. To appear in *Journal of Supercomputing*, Kluwer Academic Publishers, 2003.

[15] M. Parashar. GrACE: Grid Adaptive Computational Engine. URL: http://www.caip. rutgers.edu/~parashar/TASSL/Projects/GrACE.

[16] M. Parashar and J. Browne. A Common Data Management Infrastructure for Adaptive Algorithms for PDE Solutions. In *Proceedings of the Supercomputing Conference*, 1997.

[17] M. Parashar and J. Browne. Distributed Dynamic Data-Structures for Parallel Adaptive Mesh Refinement. In *Proceedings of the International Conference for High Performance Computing*, pages 22–27, December 1996.

[18] M. Parashar and J. Browne. On Partitioning Dynamic Adaptive Grid Hierarchies. In *Proceedings of the 29th Annual Hawaii International Conference on System Sciences*, pages 604–613, January 1996.

[19] J. Ray, H. N. Najm, R. B. Milne, K. D. Devine, and S. Kempka. Triple Flame Structure and Dynamics at the Stabilization Point of an Unsteady Lifted Jet Diffusion Flame. To appear in *Proceedings of Combust. Inst.*

[20] H. Sagan. Space Filling Curves. Springer-Verlag, 1994.

[21] S. Sinha and M. Parashar. Adaptive Runtime Partitioning of AMR Applications on Heterogeneous Clusters. In *Proceedings of the 3rd IEEE International Conference on Cluster Computing*, 2001.

[22] J. Steensland. Vampire. URL: http://www.tdb.uu.se/~johans/research/ vampire/vampire1.html.

[23] J. Steensland, S. Chandra, and M. Parashar. An Application-centric Characterization of Domain-based SFC Partitioners for Parallel SAMR. In *IEEE Transactions on Parallel and Distributed Systems*, 13(12):1275–1289, 2002.

[24] J. Steensland, S. Chandra, M. Thune, and M. Parashar. Characterization of Domain-based Partitioners for Parallel SAMR Applications. In *Proceedings of the IASTED International Conference on Parallel and Distributed Computing and Systems (PDCS)*, pages 425–430, Las Vegas, NV, November 2000.

[25] R. Wolski, N. T. Spring, and J. Hayes. The Network Weather Service: A Distributed Resource Performance Forecasting Service for Metacomputing. In *Future Generation Computer Systems*, 15(5-6):757–768, 1999.

Chapter 13

A RESOURCE DISCOVERY SERVICE FOR A MOBILE AGENTS BASED GRID INFRASTRUCTURE

R. Aversa, B. Di Martino, N. Mazzocca and S. Venticinque

Dipartimento di Ingegneria dell' Informazione - Second University of Naples - Italy
{rocco.aversa, beniamino.dimartino, nicola.mazzocca, salvatore.venticinque}@unina2.it

Abstract   Mobile agents can provide a suitable framework for supporting resource and service discovery in computational grids. In this paper we deal with the utilization of Web services technology to discover Mobile Grid resources and services, within a Mobile Agent based GriD Architecture (MAGDA) we have designed and have been implementing. Web services paradigm and SIP and UDDI technologies are utilized to realize a resource discovery service that allow users and mobile agents to look for and access distributed resources and applications.

Keywords: Mobile agents, Web services, Resource discovery, Grid, OGSA

1.   Introduction

Grid technologies are emerging as a standardized middleware aimed at enabling sharing and coordinated usage of diverse variety of resources scattered around the world within dynamic, heterogeneous and distributed computing systems [7]. An important component of resource sharing is resource description, discovery and interoperability. Among the many operational or under development Grid platforms and infrastructures, the *Globus Toolkit* [8] is certainly the most widespread. The project [4] aims to build a substrate of low-level services such as communication, resource location and scheduling, authentication, and data access on which higher-level metacomputing software can be built.

Web services are rapidly imposing, over equivalent technologies such as CORBA, DCOM, RMI, as a de-facto standard for describing software components and methods for discovering and accessing them, based on standardised ASCII based protocols and languages such as XML and HTTP. SOAP, WSDL and Ws-Inspection. They are able to support interoperability and independence from transport protocols, programming languages and models and system software.

The alignment - and augmentation - of Grid and Web services technologies is the aim of the *Open Grid Services Architecture* (OGSA) effort [12]. This architecture uses the Web Services Description Language (WSDL) to achieve self-describing, discoverable services and interoperable protocols, with extensions to support multiple coordinated interfaces and change management. The result is a standards-based distributed service system that supports the creation of the sophisticated distributed services required in modern enterprise and interorganizational computing environments.

In this paper we focus on the utilization of Web services technology to discover Mobile Grid resources and services, within a Mobile Agent based GriD Architecture (MAGDA) [20] we have designed and have been implementing.

Mobile agents [19] in fact can provide a suitable programming and execution paradigm for supporting resource and service discovery in computational grids. MAGDA platform offers to developers a set of mobile agent based services and a mobile agent SDK.

Within MAGDA framework, resources and services are characterized by mobility features. In fact in our architecture a resource is defined as a node able to host a mobile agent. A service is an application server or a mobile agent. The user is able to discover available services or to start its own services downloading the agent code or asking for agent's creations.

In the discovery service design we have to deal with the added issue of mobility. We have addressed the issue of localization of the discovered service or resource in a mobile setting. In order to make the localization process transparent to the user we bind the discovered service to a unique identifier. The identifier is used as a key in a SIP compliant protocol in order to retrieve the effective address and protocol and to start the session between the involved resources.

The paper proceeds as follows. In the following section we provide with an overview of Grid and Web services aims and technology. In the third section we introduce the MAGDA (Mobile Agents based GriD Architecture), with a description of the different layers of the architecture in accordance to the layered grid model. In section 4 we focus on a resource discovery service we are designing and implementing that allow users and agents to look for and access distributed resources and applications. Web services, and in particular UDDI technology are utilized to provide the architecture with this functionality. In section 5 and 6 related work and concluding remarks are presented.

2.   The Grid And Web Services Models

A widely accepted model for a Grid architecture is the layered model [7] shown in Figure 13.1. The *Application* collects user applications and SDK frameworks, software API and libraries for developers. The *Collective* layer provide the protocols which are involved in coordination of multiple Grid resources. Typical services are data replication, workload management and resource discovery. The *Resource* layer provide protocols for the monitoring and management of the individual resource. The layer ignore the global Grid state and the distribution. The *Connectivity* layer defines communication and authentication protocols required for the interaction among the Grid resource managed at fabric layer. The *Fabric* layer provides the access to the physical resources, such as storage, network, CPU, Operative System and peripherals. In order to grant the access to this resources the layer implementation may involve platform dependent protocols which do not deal with the Grid architecture. In the following section we describe the architecture model of our platform highlighting the relationship with the layered model described above.

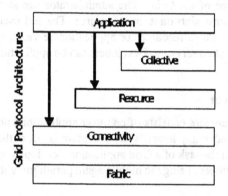

Figure 13.1. The layered model of the Grid

Web services [14] are an emerging distributed computing paradigm which focus on Internet-based standards technology such as XML and HTTP, SOAP, WSDL and Ws-Inspection. They have been designed to support interoperability, i.e. independence of the transport protocols, programming language, programming model and system software. For our purpose the web services support the dynamic registering and discovery of services in heterogeneous environments. WS-Inspection [5] defines a simple XML language and related conventions for locating service descriptions published by a server provider. The service is usually a URL to a WSDL document. WSDL [22] is an XML document for describing Web services. It can be referenced in a Universal Description, Discovery and Integration (UDDI) register [18]. In our architecture usually a resource is a node able to host a mobile agent. A service is an application server or an agent codebase. The user is able to discover available services or to start its own services downloading the agent code or asking for agent's creations.

3.   A Magda Overview

In this section we present, using the terms of the layered Grid model, a brief description of the most significant protocols, services and application programming interfaces provided by Magda. First of all we define the expected users of the Grid according to the following profiles:

- administrator

- developer

- end-user

Each profile can be owned by an human user or an application. We have an administrator for each resource of the Grid. The administrator can state sharing policies and application constraints on its own resource. The end-users of the Grid can be vendors who publish resources or application services, or consumers which invoke the published services. Developers can be application programmers or Grid developers.

3.1   The application layer

The higher layer in Grid architecture consists of end-user applications developed relying on services defined at any lower layer. The main issue, at this level, is to make ease and efficient the task of a Grid application developer. At present, we support only the developers using the mobile agent paradigm, with a set of Java packages that:

- help the building oh distributed applications through the use of different predefined parallel skeletons

- allow an effective utilization of the available Grid resources by means of dynamic load balancing mechanisms customized to the specific application

3.2   The collective layer

At this layer of the Grid architecture we implement different sharing behaviours of collective resources:

Services discovery through UDDI technology:
In section 5 we show in detail the use of the web Services technology for services discovery in the Grid.

Resource allocation:
In the Grid the user is just the owner of its application. The user requests the allocation of resources for its application and can ask for a desired performance profile. The provided resource allocation system, calling upon services offered by the underlying levels, such as a monitor system, an information collector and

a local resource manager, assigns to the application those available resources that best suit the required performance profile.

Reliability:
In a distributed system we have to deal with the management of unexpected events such as a fault or a degraded behaviour of the system. In order to manage this kind of occurrences we introduce different protocols to ensure both the reliability to the applications and a dynamic reconfiguration of the available resources in the Grid platform.

3.3   The resource layer

In order to support the services realized at the upper levels each resource in the Grid needs to be administrated and monitored.

Access control and authorization policies:
The administrator is able to fix a policy according to which its resource is shared. The same policy must be published in order to allow any application and user to know what are the constraints on the utilization of the discovered resource. Further when a resource is shared it is exposed to undesired attacks. The administrator should be able to define access and authorization policies.

System Monitoring:
In order to support the upper layers in the resource allocation each Grid resource is provided with a parameterized system monitor engine.

3.4   The Connectivity layer

Here we introduce the protocols which allow the low-level interaction among the components of our Grid architecture.

Agent's protocols
The basic services of the Grid are provided through the different mobile agent methods: Dispatch, Retract, Fetch and Message. All this methods are based on the RMI and the *ATP* (Agent Transfer Protocol) [15].

Localization protocol
We provide the Grid with a Session Protocol, SIP compliant. This service allows the applications to register and update their address, so that the developers and users are able to localize the resource by its identifier.

Information Protocols
In order to collect information in the Grid, for example the current performance figures of the system, we have an information agent that reside on each host. The agent is deactivated until he receives a request through the aglet messaging

protocol. When it is activated he looks for the required information in a specific database and replies to the sender.

Authorization protocols:
The end-user, in order to access the Grid platform, is authenticated through a standard console. Once the user was authenticated each invocated application inherits the user's profile. On the other side the developer must describe the security profile of its application in an XML file according to a standard XML DTD. Finally, if the application successfully matches the user's profile the resources are allocated.

3.5   The fabric layer

The Java Virtual Machine and the support of the standard Internet protocols are to be considered the Fabric layer of our Grid architecture.

4.   The Discovery And Invocation Service

We are designing and partially implementing a services discovery functionality for the MAGDA platform 13.2, mainly exploiting web services technology. Within MAGDA framework, resources and services are characterized by mobility features. In fact in our architecture a resource is defined as a node able to host a mobile agent. A service is an application server or a mobile agent. The user is able to discover available services or to start its own services downloading the agent code or asking for agent's creations. The agents are able to discover new hosting node in order to explore the network or to move to less busy machines, to look for required resources or application.

The user must be able to search in the Grid for the desired service. He needs to request a service to the Grid, to submit its input data and to collect its results.

An user or an application must be able to get the visibility of the Grid in order to ask for its resources. He has to be provided with a discovery service that allows to know what are the available resource, their exported services and access policies.

Our design follows the web services approach and reuses its technology. Each server is a services provider and must publish its address and services in a UDDI register. These references are bind to specific applications or data.

As shown in Figure 13.3 the platform is able to access an UDDI register by a set of APIs which implement an UDDI interface. Either the platform and any agent running on it are able to use the UDDI interface in order to publish or search a service.

At least the publication should provide the following items:

- the features of the shared resource: amount of memory, CPU power, number of nodes, bandwidth of the network, operative system, available compilers ...

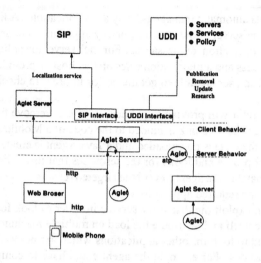

Figure 13.2. The interaction among Grid Agent Platforms

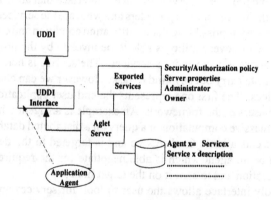

Figure 13.3. Each server publish its property and services in UDDI register. Users and application agents are able to look for active server and for the provided services.

- access and authorization policies

- owner and administrator's reference

- system services: system monitoring, code base repository, application and data hosting

- application services: running application listening for service requests, application client (binary or source code)

In our prototypal implementation the published services are references to mobile agents. An XML description for each service has to be published to allow to allow its automatic management by any application . A link binded to the address of the server allows the user or any applications to ask for mobile agent's download, creation, or messaging. For each server the policy file, which describes the access and authorization rules on that host, is provided. Either an application and an user are able to get the policy in order to check their rights on that resource.

The administrator will provide to publish, update or remove the references in the UDDI. Each service link is binded to the code of a Mobile agent. When the agent starts the code is downloaded and a Java Agent is created. The agent inherits the user profile and looks for the resources that its application needs. The system dispatches the agent toward the targeted resource, where, on arrival, the agent starts the required application.

An agent can exploit the discovery service in order to look for a less busy node or to clone itself and distribute the load on multiple machines. The agent itself could need to look for other applications which are not available on the host where it resides. For example the agent could have to compile a source code for a target platform, so it need to look for a platform provided with an available compiler in order to carry out its task.

The local console provides a service discovery interface that allows the user to know what are the active services providers and what are the services they export. For each service it is possible to define utilization condition and constraints when it needs. The discovery utility is able to be invoked by the programmer in its own applications to use vendor's services. The service is here intended as an agent which can carry out any kind of task. However we can characterize two kind of services. The first one represents the end-user applications and it is invoked by the users of the framework. An example is an agent which starts and carries out a massive computation or a query on a distributed database. The second one represents a basic Grid service and is targeted to the developers. An example can be an agent which is able negotiate for the requirements of developer's application and to start it on the target node.

An user friendly interface allows the user to look for services and to start them. In Figure 13.4 we can see how the user is able to explore the available services provider and to chose the offered services.

Following the same approach, if the local console is not available on the user's machine any UDDI client, which may be accessed by a standard browser, is able to exploit the discovery service introduced above.

After we have discovered the shared resources we have to interact with them. In a distributed environment the location of resources and applications can often change, above all when we deal with mobile stations, users or agents. An example is an host that gets a different IP address by DHCP after the reset and a restart. Another feasible example is a server that starts and gets a different port because the default one is busy. About mobile users or agents, while they travel across the network, they always get new addresses and are forced to use different communication protocols.

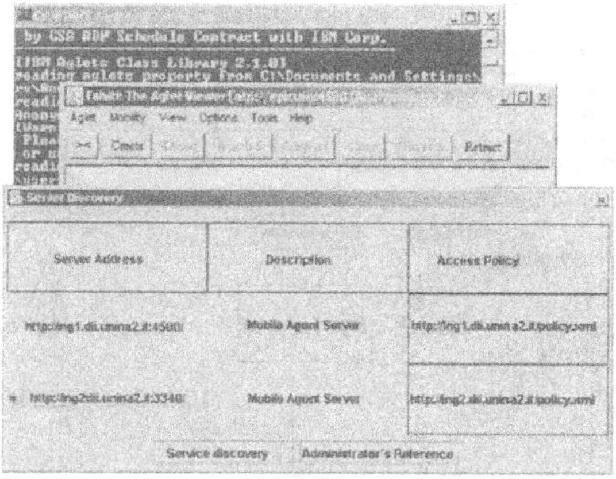

Figure 13.4.   Service discovery Console

We need a session protocol which allows the connection between two end-point nodes and is transparent as regards the effective address and the application protocol. To achieve this goal we extended the agent server with a connection manager that implements a SIP compliant protocol. Each server is identified by a unique tag (the SIP identifier) and a correspondent URL. Each time the server gets a new address it updates its address on a SIP register. When another server attempts to establish a connection with it and the previous address is not valid, the effective address can be retrieved accessing the SIP register with the SIP identifier as a key. Some implementations of the SIP register are able to redirect automatically the connection to the effective address. An agent too is able to register its new location after he has been dispatched from an host to another. As shown in Figure 13.5 the connection manager implements a SIP interface which is accessed by the server and the agents in order to:

- update the agent server effective address

- retrieve the effective address of the active servers

- update the new effective address of the agent after a dispatch

- retrieve the reference to a dispatched agent of an not more valid proxy

5.   Related Work

Different approaches are introduced in order to provide, to share or access distributed resources. For example many applications of file sharing such as Napster and Gnutella, which are based on peer to peer protocols, are actually widespread in Internet, but they are not compliant with standard protocols and are not multipurpose applications for metacomputing..

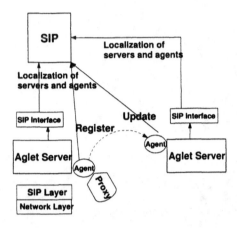

Figure 13.5.   A SIP compliant protocol is used to localize agents and servers

Among the several Grid platforms currently operational or under development we limit to cite Globus [8] and Legion [11]. Globus philosophy and purposes have been described above. The goal of the Legion research project is to provide secure shared object and name spaces, application-controlled fault-tolerance, improved response time, and greater throughput. Multiple language support is another of its goals.

Many works address some basic services which are relevant in a Grid environment. A management tool for performance analysis, parameter studies on Grid architectures is described in [23]. Some examples of interface to a Grid system for access and configuration are introduced in [21]. A Grid portal that allows trusted users to create and handle computational grids on the fly exploiting a simple and friendly gui is described in [2].

The similarities of Grid systems with Multi-Agent Systems (MAS) are much higher, since entities in a MAS and the grid have autonomous behavior (i.e. distributed control). Autonomy is one of the key abstraction features of agents. Other features of agents relevant for grid entities include social ability, as well as reactive and pro-active intelligence [27].

Many works consider mobile code, applets and mobile agents in order to exploit distributed resources through an on-demand pull execution model, see for instance Javelin [4], Charlotte [1],[25]. Many works about the employment of mobile agents in Agent Based High Performance Distributed Computing can be found in literature [17] [9] [10]. They represent a kind of agent based applications in distributed or parallel computing which involve a typically master-slave computations in wide-area distributed environments [9]. In these systems, large computations are initiated under control of a coordinating agent that distributes the computation over the available re-sources by sending mobile agents to these resources. All these projects are designed explicitly to run parallel applications and provide a specific programming model. They often lack a defined infrastructure that provides interoperability and allows all internet users to share their resources.

In order to support a standard, easy, and available mechanism that satisfies these requirements Web based volunteer computing has been proposed in [25] [4].Web based volunteer computing allows people to cooperate in solving large parallel problems by using web browsers to volunteer their computers' processing power.

No one of the proposals above aims to define a full featured Grid infrastructure. Multiple languages and standard protocols are other goals often lacking in the these works. A number of initiatives to apply agents in computational grids have been initiated in recent years [3].

[16] present an overview of different perspectives to grid environments and describe DARPA Control of Agent-Based Systems (CoABS) agent grid [26]. A good example of an agent grid is presented by [24]. They identify the need to combine problem-specific problem solving environments (PSEs), facilitating interoperability between various tools and specialized algorithm each PSE supports.

Many works on design of agent based grid platforms focus on the implementation of basic services such as routing and handling of FIPA ACL messages [27], load balancing [26], fault masking [1] and service discovery [13]. A Grid-based architecture for Multimedia services management is presented in [6]. Especially [13] defines an architecture of a services discovery functionality implemented through mobile agent technology.

References

[1] Z. Kedem A. Baratloo, M. Karaul and P. Wycko. Charlotte: Metacomputing on the web. In *9th International Conference on Parallel and Distributed Computing systems*, Dijon, France, September 1996.

[2] Giovanni Aloisio, Massimo Cafaro, Paolo Falabella, Carl Kesselman, and Roy Williams. Grid computing on the web using the globus toolkit. In *HPCN Europe*, pages 32–40, 2000.

[3] M. van Steen B. J. Overeinder, N. J. E. Wijngaards and F. M. T. BrazierOvereinder. Multi-agent support for internet-scale grid management. In *AISB '02 Symposium on AI and Grid Computing*, pages 18–22, London, UK, April 2002.

[4] Peter Cappello Bernd O. Christiansen and Al. Javelin: Internet-based parallel computing using java. *Concurrency: Practice and Experience*, 9(11):1139 – 1160, Nov 1997.

[5] P. Brittenham. P. an overview of the web services inspectin language, June 2002.

[6] Angelo Zaia Dario Bruneo, Mirko Guarnera and Antonio Puliafito. A grid-based architecture for multimedia services management. In *Annual Crossgrid Project Workshop, 1st European Across Grids Conference*, 2003.

[7] Ian Foster. The anatomy of the Grid: Enabling scalable virtual organizations. *Lecture Notes in Computer Science*, 2150:1–??, 2001.

[8] Ian Foster and Carl Kesselman. Globus: A metacomputing infrastructure toolkit. *The International Journal of Supercomputer Applications and High Performance Computing*, 11(2):115–128, Summer 1997.

[9]   J. C. Collis Ghanea-Hercock and D. T. Ndumu. Co-operating mobile agents for distributed parallel processing. In ACM Press, editor, *Third International Conference on Autonomous Agents AA99*, Mineapolis, USA, May 1999.

[10] Jacek Gomoluch and Michael Schroeder. Information agents on the move: A survey on load-balancing with mobile agents. *Software Focus*, 2(2):31–36, 2001.

[11] A. S. Grimshaw and Wm. A. Wulf. The legion vision of a worldwide virtual computer. *Communications of the ACM*, 40(1), January 1997.

[12] J. M. Nick I. Foster, C. Kesselman and S. Tuecke. The physiology of the grid: An open grid services architecture for distributed systems integration. Technical report, http://www.globus.org/research/papers/ogsa.pdf, 2002.

[13] Darren j. Kerbyson Junwei Cao and R. Nudd Graham. High performance services discovery in large-scale multi-agent an mobile-agent systems. *International Journal of Software Engineering and Knowledge Engineering*, 2(5):621–641, 2001.

[14] Heather Kreger. Web services conceptual architecture(wsca 1.0), May 2001.

[15] D. Lange and M. Oshima. *Programming and Deploying Java Mobile Agents with Aglets*. Addison-Wesley, 1998.

[16] Manola and Thompson. Characterizing the agent grid. Technical report, Object Services and Consulting, Inc., June 1999.

[17] C. Muthukrishnan and T. B. Suresh. A multi-agent approach to distributed computing. In ACM Press, editor, *Third International Conference on Autonomous Agents AA99*, Mineapolis, Washington, USA, May 1999.

[18] OASIS. Uddi technical white paper. Technical report, www.uddi.org, September 2000.

[19] V. A. Pham and A. Karmouch. Mobile software agents: an overview. *IEEE Communications Magazine*, 36(7):26–37, July 1998.

[20] N. Mazzocca R. Aversa, B. Di Martino and S. Venticinque. Magda: A software environment for mobile agent based distributed applications. In *11th Euromicro Conference on Parallel Distributed and Network Based Processing (PDP03)*, 2003.

[21] D. Laforenz R. Baraglia, M. Danelutto and Al. A grid configuration tool for the assist parallel programming environment. In *11th Euromicro Conference on Parallel Distributed and Network Based Processing (PDP03)*, 2003.

[22] J. Moreau R. Chinnici, M. Gudgin and S. Weerawarana. Web services description language (wsdl) version 1.2, March 2003.

[23] F. Franchetti R. Prodan, T. Fahringer and Al. On using zenturio for performance and parameter studies on cluster and grid architectures. In *11th Euromicro Conference on Parallel Distributed and Network Based Processing (PDP03)*, 2003.

[24] O. F. Rana and D. W. Walker. The agent grid: Agent-based resource integration in pses. In *16th IMACS World Congress on Scientific Computing, Applied Mathematics and Simulation*, Lausanne, Switzerland, August 2000.

[25] Sarmenta and L.F.G. Bayanihan. Web-based volunteer computing using java. In Springer, editor, *WWCA'98 LNCS*, volume 1368, pages 444–461, Berlin, 1998.

[26] Paul T. Groth Suri Niranyan and Jeffrey M. Bradshaw. While you're away: A system for load-balancing and resource based on mobile agents. In Rajkumar Buyya, editor, *1st IEEE International Conference on Cluster Computing and the Grid*, Brisbane, Australia, 2001. IEEE Computer Society Press.

[27] Amund Tveit. jfipa - an architecture for agent-based grid computing. In *AISB'02 Convention, Symposium on AI and Grid Computing*, London, United Kingdom, April 2001.

Chapter 14

XDGDL: TOWARDS AN XML-BASED DATAGRID DESCRIPTION LANGUAGE

Erich Schikuta

Institute of Computer Science and Business Informatics, University of Vienna
Rathausstr. 19/9, A-1010, Vienna, Austria
erich.schikuta@univie.ac.at

Abstract   We present xDGDL, an approach towards a concise but comprehensive Datagrid description language. Our framework is based on XML and makes it possible to store syntactical and semantical information together with arbitrary files. This information can be used to administer, locate, search and process data stored on the Grid.

Keywords: Parallel and distributed I/O, Meta information, Datagrid, Distributed file systems

1.   Introduction

File I/O in parallel or distributed applications remains a problematic issue until now. This situation did not change even of a strong research focus in the last few years [13]. Very often we face the situation that in specific high performance applications the program code is changed on purpose to omit physical I/O. This is not only due to the I/O bottleneck and the missing I/O bandwidth to the external storage media but also to the fact that *persistence* is not an objective valued by this type of applications. File I/O in this context is mainly a necessity to extend the limited main memory of the physical hardware.

In typical supercomputing applications six types of I/O can be identified [10]: (1) input, (2) debugging, (3) scratch files, (4) checkpoint/restart, (5) output, and (6) accessing out-of-core structures.

All these types of I/O handle the stored data, in one way or the other, as volatile information. Data is only a sequence of bytes, which has a meaning only in the context of the program reading and/or writing the data. After the execution of the program this information is practically lost and the stored data is just garbage on the disk. Until now no standardized functional mechanism for technical and/or scientific data produced by high performance programs exist to maintain this information beyond the lifespan of the program.

Today new and stimulating data-intensive problems in biology, physics, astronomy, space exploration, human genom research arise, which bring new high-performance applications with the need to store, administer and search intelligently gigantic data set spread over globally distributed storage resources [16].

We face a similar situation as in the well-known area of database systems [1], where data represents a model of the reality. Thus data has to be attributed with meta information describing the specific semantics of the information in a standardized and processable way. This meta information allows applications to search the stored information intelligently.

However meta information in the context of Grid computing has to describe not only the logical part of the data (semantical information) but also specific structural information on the physical distribution of the data (syntactical information). Thus we propose xDGDL, an XML based language to act as a notational tool to describe meta information for any data stored on the Grid.

At the moment only few similar approaches exist, but these are in an early state, e.g. [9], or target mostly very specific application domains, e.g. [4].

The layout of the paper is as follows. In the next section we present a novel file architecture defining the different level of file views. The XML-based xDGDL language is introduced in section 3. This is followed by a comprehensive example of the application of the xDGDL language. Finally we describe briefly our mechanism as a central part of a novel distributed file system and give an outlook on using our approach for information stored on the Datagrid.

2.   A Novel File Hierarchy

The goal of a database system is to simplify and facilitate access to data [1]. This goal also holds adequately for data produced in high performance applications. We can learn from database systems to follow a similar approach to free the user from the burden of physical details. In database systems the above objective is achieved by the well-known three layered approach separating levels of different abstraction.

By keeping this model in mind we can define a similar approach for high performance data. To allow full flexibility for the programmer and the administration methods, we propose an architecture with three independent layers in the parallel I/O architecture (similar to the three-level-architecture of database systems):

Problem layer. Defines the problem specific data distribution among the co-operating parallel processes.

File layer. Provides a composed (canonical) view of the persistently stored data in the system.

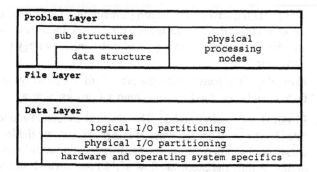

Figure 14.1. File hierarchy

Data layer. Defines the physical data distribution among the available disks.

These layers are separated conceptually from each other with mapping functions between these layers. *Logical data independence* exists between the problem and the file layer, and *physical data independence* exists between the file and data layer, which is analogous to the notation in database systems.

An even finer granularity of these layers is necessary to identify the different conceptual views for a typical parallel solution. These sub layers reach from pure logical information on the problem to physical representation of the data and comprise data representation, structured file information, physical distributed data layout, problem specific data partitioning, and general information semantics and so forth.

We will have a closer look on these layers (also depicted in Figure 14.1) and sub layers and will show the instantiation by a running example (which is used in the remainder of the paper). We assume a typical, very simple, parallel HPF (High Performance Fortran) program writing high performance physics data (an array with 1000 real values representing energy levels) to disk, which is administered by a parallel file system.

1 **Problem layer:** The problem layer represents the user's view on the problem specific data, which is expressed by the code of an HPF program.

   (a) **Data structure:** The first focus of interest is the data structure to write, which is only derived from the problem specification without any anticipation of the parallel execution flow. This data structure is basically a container type provided by the programming language. In practice (e.g. HPF) this is mostly a multi-dimensional array of an integral data type (e.g. *real*).

   Example: In our example this is a 1 dimensional array of 1000 real values.

   (b) **Sub structures (SPMD derived):** The HPF language makes it possible to specify a problem specific partitioning of the data within the SPMD framework, by defining a mapping of data structure elements to a logical processor array. This defines sub arrays, which are distributed accordingly to a defined distribution strategy (blocked, cyclic, etc.).

Example: This phase splits the array into 4 sub arrays in cyclic fashion and maps the fragments onto a 4 processor array.

(c) **Physical processing nodes:** The physical execution mode is defined by the numbers and types of real processors available for execution on the high performance hardware. This execution mapping defines mainly the execution flow of the program and consequently the data stream written/read to/from the underlying I/O environment.

Example: When the program is loaded only 2 physical processing nodes are available where 2 logical processors each are mapped respectively.

2 **File layer:** The file layer resembles the conceptual (logical) view of the data, which represents a "model of the real world". Basically it defines a sequential and structural (record information) form of the distributed data in a canonical normal form. This is the general view onto the stored information from any application, sequential or parallel.

Example: In our example it gives the pure logical semantics of the data, e.g. it describes a sequence of real values representing energy levels of a HEP (high energy physics) experiment. From the programmers point of view it is the persistent mapping of the 1 dimensional FORTRAN array in column-major order onto a sequential file.

3 **Data layer:** The data layer is the lowest level of abstraction and describes how the data is actually stored. On this level the low-level data fragments are described.

(a) **Logical I/O partitioning:** This level defines the partitioning of data supported by the underlying I/O subsystem mechanism. Basically it defines the mapping of main memory locations to storage locations (buckets) on the I/O media (buffer management).

Example: Defines a I/O system specific view onto the data, e.g. striding. This could be done by the MPI-I/O view mechanism.

(b) **Physical I/O partitioning:** The physical layout of the data (file fragments) onto the available storage media is defined by this level. It maps the information to store onto physical files on disks according to a specified fragmentation and layout which results into a set of files. This is system specific and dependent on the underlying software (file system) and hardware (storage media) architecture.

Example: Delivers a set of physical files identified by unique file names, which can be accessed by the mechanism of the underlying file system.

(c) **Hardware and operating system specifics:** Finally on the lowest level in our hierarchy this level defines the physical representation of the integral data information, which is dependent on the underlying software and hardware architecture.

Example: This level defines how the real values of our data set are stored, e.g. big endian or little endian.

Consequently it is our goal to propose a framework, which can express the information on all layers of the presented file hierarchy. This led to the design of the xDGDL language.

3. xDGDL - the XML Data Grid Description Language

As basic framework for the goal to add semantic information to data files we chose XML (eXtensible Markup Language), which is a language to describe languages. XML is simple, but still a powerful language. It has all the virtues of HTML (Hypertext Markup Language), but without HTML's limitations. As a direct consequence XML is well suited for annotating data with structural and semantic information. XML also enjoys a great popularity, which grows day by day, and due to its proliferation it can serve as a common interface between different applications.

We propose the XML Data Grid Description Language (xDGDL) as a convenient tool for the specification of meta information of data stored on the Grid. We derived xDGDL from PARSTORAGE [3], which was specifically designed as meta language for parallel IO data.

The xDGDL descriptor consists of a logical and a physical view to the file. The logical view describes the semantical information and the physical view the syntactical information (the physical layout) of the file.

Focusing the Grid we have to specify a very general Grid architecture hosting our framework. From our point of view the Grid consists of an arbitrary number of *collaborations*, which are defined by organizational domains [7], interconnected by WAN technology. In practice such a collaboration will be usually (but must not be) a coherent IT infrastructure represented by a cluster like system, which consists of a number of execution nodes. These *nodes* are *processing nodes* and/or *data (server) nodes*. The latter type provides data storage resources by a number of storage *devices* (e.g. disks, tapes, etc.). It is to note that a single data node can host an arbitrary number of devices.

3.1 The goals of xDGDL

The basic idea of the XML based approach is quite simple: Together with any "chunk" of data an xDGDL description of the meta information of the data is stored, in other words, any arbitrary number of bytes stored within our framework is attributed with its describing information, delivering the following properties:

3.1.1   Semantics of data.

Applications create files, which represent the output of a specific problem solution approach. Thus applications do not write simply bytes into a file; they write integers, real numbers, characters, records of arbitrary types etc., basically a sequence of typed elements. Without knowledge on the application we have no clue about the data's contents. Today we have the urge for analyzing and processing data found on the Grid (as in typical OLAP applications), thus there is an undeniable need for semantic description. Simply said, data without semantics is dead, data with semantics lives. This statement leads naturally to the next issue, persistency of data.

3.1.2   Persistency of data.

Data stored without the context of the semantics of the creating process is just a sequence of bytes without any meaning. For other applications this data is useless. With a description of its semantics by the xDGDL other application have now the possibility to interpret, understand and conclusively reuse the data. Specifically in the context of the Grid with novel application harnessing unknown resources this framework makes it possible to "revive" data, which is otherwise lost.

A practical Java-based example of interpreting stored data is given in [2].

3.1.3   Portability.

In a distributed environment parts of data can migrate from one system to another. On different hosting environments the data formats can change. However when moving data from one system to another, applications must still be able to read the data. By the description of the format the data can be interpreted and can be easily transformed into any proprietary format of the target machine [9].

3.1.4   Performance and efficiency.

To enhance the bandwidth of the IO media (to fight the famous IO bottleneck) it is the most common technique to distribute data among different nodes and/or devices and perform accesses in parallel. If the user has knowledge about the available nodes or the application behavior he/she can describe the distribution of the file by the xDGDL to his/her needs. This can lead to performance improvements specifically if the user is aware of node's performance, the given network latency, the network bandwidth to each server, etc.

3.2   The xDGDL specification

The Extensible Markup Language (XML) is the universal format for structured documents and data on the Web. XML documents are made up of storage units called entities, which contain either parsed or unparsed data. Parsed data is made up of characters, some of which form character data, and some of which form markups. A markup encodes a description of the document's storage layout and logical structure. XML provides a mechanism to impose constraints on the storage layout and logical structure.

The structure of XML is fundamentally tree oriented. Therefore a document can be modelled as an ordered, labelled tree, with a document vertex serving as the *root* vertex and several *child* vertices. Without the document vertex, an XML document may be modelled as an ordered, labelled forest, containing only one root element, but also containing the XML declaration, the doctype declaration, and perhaps comments or processing instructions at the root level.

To define the legal building blocks of an XML document, a DTD (Document Type Definition) can be used. It defines the document structure with a list of legal elements.

A DTD can be declared inline in an XML document, or as an external reference.

It was a clear decision to choose XML as the basis for our framework due to its undeniable success within the Internet community and its acceptance as basis for beneath any standard movement in the Grid community, e.g. WSDL [5].

3.3 The xDGDL document type definition

Basically we distinguish between pure semantic information, which comprises the problem and file layer and distribution information describing the data layer.

Thus in our framework typical xDGDL descriptions (can) consist of the following modules:

- Document Root. The root of the document specifies the version and timestamp of the file of the XML description.

- Semantic Information. It contains processor, data type and alignment information describing the data set from a logical point of view.

- Distribution information. It describes the physical data layout onto the Grid by defining islands, servers, devices and views.

3.3.1 Document root.
The root of the document is described by the element PARSTORAGE. It has the attribute VERSION that contains the version of the document and the attribute TIMESTAMP that identifies the external name together with the logical file. Both attributes are mandatory.

3.3.2 Semantic information.
The root element can contain several child elements. The PROCESSORS and the ALIGN children are optional.

- PROCESSORS describes the named processor arrays. A document may contain zero or more processor array definition, which are normally derived from the HPF definition.

- TYPE describes the data types and variables stored in the logical file. Types enhance the quality of stored data. They define the meaning of the information stored. This leads to the fact that not only the program that stored the data can use them. Every program that understands the type information of the data can use the stored bytes. Because of these meta information it is also possible to migrate data from one machine to another. There must be at least one TYPE element in the document. For more information on types see [3].

- ALIGN describes the alignments of the variables.

Example:

```
<PARSTORAGE VERSION="1.0"
            TIMESTAMP="testfile_regular">
   <PROCESSORS NAME="proc4">
      <PROC_DIMENSION UPPER="4"/>
   </PROCESSORS>
   <TYPE>
      <ARRAY NAME="a" DISTRIBUTE_ONTO="proc4">
      ...
      </ARRAY>
   </TYPE>
   <ISLAND NAME="vidgrid.pri.univie.ac.at">
   ...
   </ISLAND>
</PARSTORAGE>
```

3.3.3   Distribution information.   The ISLAND describes several server interconnected together. These servers can be distributed across the Grid. The island is identified by an island name. The ISLAND consists of one or more servers. At least one server is needed to write the file sequentially to that server. The number of servers are received from the number of children present.
Example:

```
<ISLAND NAME="vidgrid.pri.univie.ac.at">
   <SERVER HOST="vidgrid0.pri.univie.ac.at">
   </SERVER>
</ISLAND>
```

The SERVER identifies uniquely a node. It has an attribute called HOST which mirrors the name of the server.

The SERVER element consists of one or more DEVICE elements. At least one must be present for each server to know how the file should be distributed on the several disks. For this purpose the number of available devices on a specific server should be known.
Example:

```
<ISLAND NAME="vidgrid.pri.univie.ac.at">
   <SERVER HOST="vidgrid0.pri.univie.ac.at">
      <DEVICE DEVICE_ID="/dev/vda1">
      </DEVICE>
   </SERVER>
```

```
</ISLAND>
```

Devices are the disks holding the data on the specific server. On one SERVER there could be more than one physical device. The server can have a RAID system for example with several disks connected onto it. The devices need not to be physical, even a mounted NFS device on another server could be a device which could be accessed from a processing node. Although there can be many devices on a specific server, in most cases there will be only one device available.

The DEVICE element consists of the attribute DEVICE_ID only, which specifies the physical device on the system. To describe the structure of the parts of the file to be written to disk, one or more BLOCK elements is used. The BLOCK element can have two types of children. It can have a BYTEBLOCK element, which means, that either there are no more BYTE elements or it can consist of one or more BLOCK elements themselves. Theoretically there can be an infinite number of BLOCK elements, but at least one is needed. The BLOCK itself can have another BLOCK element within itself. This leads to a recursive structure which allows for arbitrary distributions.
Example:

```
<DEVICE DEVICE_ID="/dev/vda1">
    <BLOCK OFFSET="0" REPEAT="3" COUNT="5" STRIDE="7" SKIP="0">
        <BYTEBLOCK/>
    </BLOCK></DEVICE>
```

The BLOCK element consists of the following attributes (see Figure 14.2):

- OFFSET describes how many bytes should be skipped from the starting point of the current BLOCK.

- REPEAT defines how often the BLOCK should be read/written.

- COUNT gives the number of bytes to be read/written at each BLOCK operation.

- STRIDE is the number of bytes to skip at each BLOCK operation.

- SKIP is the number of bytes to find the end of the respective block (it can also be a negative number).

The contents of an arbitrary physical file can be described as a block. With the BLOCK element we can specify any mapping of a logical file portion to a physical file.

4.   A Practical xDGDL Example

In the following we take the running example from section 2 and will present (only a few of) the possibilities that the xDGDL description provides.

We assume a file is created by a distributed application (e.g. an MPI or HPF program) on a Grid resource (in this example "vidgrid.pri.univie.ac.at"),

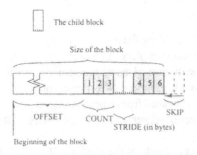

Figure 14.2.   Semantic of the BLOCK attributes

which contains an real*1 array with 1000 elements. The array is distributed onto 4 nodes in a cyclic(2) way. A physical file is assigned to each node, and each physical file contains the portion of the array stored by its assigned node. Each of the 4 physical files is attributed by an xDGDL description. This information can be part of the physical file – for example MPI-IO supports header information in physical files – , or can be stored separately either next to the physical file location or in a database.

Fore simplicity we present the full description for the first file only (which, to keep the example simple, is assumed to be mapped onto the first node called "vidgrid0.pri.univie.ac.at"). At the location denoted by "..." similar descriptions for the other 3 nodes have to be added.

For simplicity we present the xDGDL description for the first file only. The other 3 xDGDL files look similar, just the device name and the block parameters are different defining the specific distribution layout.
Example:

```
<?xml version="1.0" encoding="ISO-8859-1"?> <!DOCTYPE PARSTORAGE
SYSTEM "XDGDL.dtd"> <PARSTORAGE VERSION="1.0"
TIMESTAMP="testfile_regular">
  <PROCESSORS NAME="proc4">
    <PROC_DIMENSION UPPER="4"/>
  </PROCESSORS>
  <TYPE>
    <ARRAY NAME="a" DISTRIBUTE_ONTO="proc4">
      <TYPE> <ETYPE TYPE="REAL" LENGTH="4"/> </TYPE>
      <DIMENSION UPPER="1000" DISTRIBUTE="CYCLIC" DIST_SCALAR="2"/>
    </ARRAY>
  </TYPE>
  <ISLAND NAME="vidgrid.pri.univie.ac.at">
    <SERVER HOST="vidgrid0.pri.univie.ac.at">
      <DEVICE DEVICE_ID="/dev/vda1">
        <BLOCK OFFSET="0" REPEAT="125" COUNT="2" STRIDE="24" SKIP="0">
          <BYTEBLOCK/>
        </BLOCK>
      </DEVICE>
    </SERVER>
  </ISLAND>
</PARSTORAGE>
```

5.   An Application of xDGDL

ViPIOS - the Vienna Parallel Input Output System - is an I/O system that tries to solve the well-known I/O bottleneck of high-performance computing [15]. ViPIOS was originally designed as a client-server system satisfying parallel I/O needs of high performance applications. Due to the requirements of the Datagrid initiative ViPIOS was extended to Meta-ViPIOS, which harnesses distributed I/O resources [8].

5.1   ViPIOS islands

A *ViPIOS island* (resembling roughly a collaboration within our Grid architecture) can be seen as a logically independent system, residing on a defined set of processing nodes. Conventionally this is a typical cluster system, but it can also be an arbitrary set of world-wide distributed machines. An island comprises an arbitrary number of ViPIOS servers processing the I/O requests of connected applications. To reach such an island the client needs to know the hostname (or IP-address) of a dedicated connection server responsible for that island (for more information see [14]).

An island provides several interfaces; beside the native interface, an MPI-IO interface (ViMPIOS), a HPF/VFC (Vienna Fortran Compiler) interface as well as a Unix file access interface (ViPFS) are supported.

The system defines two modes to describe the distribution of a file. By default the automatic modes allows ViPIOS to decide how to distribute the given file among the available servers. The user guided modus in contrast let the user decide how to distribute the file. In this modus a xDGDL file describes the distribution of a given file.

5.2   ViPFS

Basically ViPFS is a library which overloads the standard file calls in UNIX. This methods allows users easily and efficiently for the transparent employment of services provided by ViPIOS. Thus all Unix tools for file accesses can be used without recompiling. The idea is to redirect the calls with "conventional" data files to the standard I/O library and to redirect the calls with ViPFS data files to the ViPIOS system. This approach is similar to PVFS [12].

Beside the overloaded Unix interface ViPFS also provides a C-Interface, which can be linked with C-programs. This interface provides nearly the same functionality as the standard I/O interface.

For users it is very easy to define the meta information for the data file in focus. A respective xDGDL file has to be created and stored in the same directory as the data file, which has the same name as the data file, but with the prefix ".vd." (The prefix stands for *ViPIOS description*). With an open statement the ViPFS library checks if there is a corresponding xDGDL file for the given file. The prefixed dot is used because these files are not visible with the common ls command. When it is parsed, its is checked against the given data type definition (DTD). If the file is erroneous or does not exist the respective data file will be distributed with the standard distribution of ViPFS which is a cyclic distribution among the available ViPIOS servers. This approach makes it possible easily to distribute arbitrary files onto ViPFS transparently by any application, which uses the standard I/O library, simply by creating a .vd.-description in the same directory as the file in focus.

6.   Conclusions and Future Work

We presented xDGDL, an XML based language for storing meta information for distributed files on the Grid. The proposed XML approach acts in the system in two ways; on one the hand it provides a user interface to specify the contents (semantical information) and the layout (physical information) of the file, on the other hand it is the expressive mechanism within the system to administer the distribution information of the files stored in the file system across several sites on the Grid.

The xDGDL language can be a starting point for a new way of defining data access paths on the Grid. We are working on an approach to use Grid I/O patterns for defining I/O data streams on the Grid easily. A stream can be seen as a graph where the vertices are modules, which are instantiated from Grid I/O patterns, and the edges are the data streams. Data is moved along such streams and carries along from vertex to vertex its self-describing information based on the xDGDL language. This enables the modules, which in fact are active I/O resources (Grid fabrics), as distributed file systems, database systems, etc., to interpret and to process the data. This approach allows for automatic generation of such Grid I/O graphs based on heuristic methods.

Acknowledgement

Special thank goes to András Belokosztolszki and Rene Felder for their work on PARSTORAGE and xDGDL [6] respectively. The work described in this paper was financially supported by the Special Research Program SFB F011 AURORA of the Austrian Science Fund.

References

[1] A. Silberschatz, H. F. Korth, S. S. (1996). *Database System Concepts*. McGraw-Hill.

[2] Belokosztolszki, A. (2000). An XML based language for meta information in distributed file systems. Master's thesis, University of Vienna / ELTE University Budapest.

[3] Belokosztolszki, A. and Schikuta, E. (2003). An XML based framework for self-describing parallel i/o data. In *11-th Euromicro Conference on Parallel, Distributed and Network based Processing*, Genoa, Italy. IEEE Computer Society.

[4] Bhatti, N., Goff, J.-M. L., Waseem, H., Kovacs, Z., Martin, R., McClatchey, P., Stockinger, H., and Willers, I. (2000). Object serialisation and deserialisation using XML. In *10th International Conference on Management of Data (COMAD 2000)*, Pune, India.

[5] Christensen, E., Curbera, F., Meredith, G., and Weerawarana, S. (2001). Web services description language (wsdl) 1.1. http://www.w3.org/TR/wsdl.

[6] Felder, R. (2001). ViPFS: An XML based distributed file system for cluster architecture. Master's thesis, University of Vienna.

[7] Foster, I., Kesselman, C., Nick, J. M., and Tuecke, S. (2002). The physiology of the grid.

[8] Fuerle, T., Jorns, O., Schikuta, E., and Wanek, H. (2000). Meta-vipios: Harness distributed i/o ressources with vipios. *Iberoamerican Journal of Research "Computing and Systems", Special Issue on Parallel Computing,* 4(2):124–142.

[9] G., F. D. and Tomer, K. (2001). *High Performance Mass Storage and Parallel I/O: Technologies and Applications,* chapter XML, Hyper-media, and Fortran I/O. John Wiley and Sons.

[10] Galbreath, N., Gropp, W., and Levine, D. (1993). Applications-driven parallel I/O. In *Proceedings of Supercomputing '93,* pages 462–471. Reprinted in the book "High Performance Storage and Parallel I/O" (http://www.buyya.com/superstorage/, 2001, pages 539–547).

[11] hdf. The NCSA HDF home page. http://hdf.ncsa.uiuc.edu/.

[12] Ligon, W. B. and Ross, R. B. (1996). Implementation and performance of a parallel file system for high performance distributed applications. In *Proceedings of the Fifth IEEE International Symposium on High Performance Distributed Computing,* pages 471–480.

[13] Rajkumar, B., Hai, J., and Toni, C. (2001). *High Performance Mass Storage and Parallel I/O: Technologies and Applications.* John Wiley and Sons.

[14] Schikuta, E. and Fuerle, T. (2002). Vipios islands: Utilizing i/o resources on distributed clusters. In *15th International Conference on Parallel and Distributed Computing Systems.*

[15] Schikuta, E., Fuerle, T., and Wanek, H. (1998). ViPIOS: The Vienna Parallel Input/Output System. In *Proc. of the Euro-Par'98,* Lecture Notes in Computer Science, Southampton, England. Springer-Verlag.

[16] Segal, B. (2000). Grid computing: The european data project. In *IEEE Nuclear Science Symposium and Medical Imaging Conference,* Lyon.

Appendix: xDGDL DTD

```
<?xml version="1.0" encoding="ISO-8859-1"?>
<!ELEMENT PARSTORAGE (PROCESSORS*, TYPE*, ALIGN*, ISLAND)>
<!ATTLIST PARSTORAGE
  VERSION CDATA #REQUIRED
  TIMESTAMP ID #REQUIRED
>
<!ELEMENT PROCESSORS (PROC_DIMENSION)+>
<!ATTLIST PROCESSORS
  NAME CDATA #REQUIRED
>
<!ELEMENT PROC_DIMENSION EMPTY>
<!ATTLIST PROC_DIMENSION
  LOWER CDATA "1"
  UPPER CDATA #REQUIRED
>
<!-- Problem layer description -->
<!ELEMENT TYPE (ETYPE | ARRAY | TYPE)+>
<!ATTLIST TYPE
  TYPENAME CDATA #IMPLIED
```

```
  NAME CDATA #IMPLIED
>
<!ELEMENT ETYPE EMPTY>
<!ATTLIST ETYPE
  TYPE CDATA #REQUIRED
  LENGTH CDATA #REQUIRED
  NAME CDATA #IMPLIED
>
<!ELEMENT ARRAY (TYPE, DIMENSION+)>
<!ATTLIST ARRAY
  NAME CDATA #IMPLIED
  MAJOR (ROW | COLUMN) "ROW"
  DISTRIBUTE_ONTO CDATA #IMPLIED
>
<!ELEMENT DIMENSION EMPTY>
<!ATTLIST DIMENSION
  LOWER CDATA "1"
  UPPER CDATA #REQUIRED
  DISTRIBUTE (BLOCK | CYCLIC | NO) #IMPLIED
  DIST_SCALAR CDATA "1"
>
<!ELEMENT ALIGN EMPTY>
<!ATTLIST ALIGN
  WHAT CDATA #REQUIRED
  WITH CDATA #REQUIRED
>
<!-- Data layer description -->
<!ELEMENT ISLAND (SERVER*)>
<!ATTLIST ISLAND
  NAME CDATA #REQUIRED
>
<!ELEMENT SERVER (DEVICE*)>
<!ATTLIST SERVER
  HOST CDATA #REQUIRED
>
<!ELEMENT DEVICE (BLOCK*)>
<!ATTLIST DEVICE
  DEVICE_ID CDATA #REQUIRED
>
<!ELEMENT BLOCK (BLOCK | BYTEBLOCK)>
<!ATTLIST BLOCK
  OFFSET CDATA #REQUIRED
  REPEAT CDATA #REQUIRED
  COUNT CDATA #REQUIRED
  STRIDE CDATA #REQUIRED
  SKIP CDATA #REQUIRED
>
<!ELEMENT BYTEBLOCK EMPTY>
```

VI

SCIENTIFIC AND ENGINEERING APPLICATIONS

Chapter 15

A LARGE-SCALE MD SIMULATION FOR FORMATION PROCESS OF CARBON CLUSTER ON A PARALLEL COMPUTER

A Parallelization Case-Study of MD Simulation of a Low Density Physical System

Ryoko Hayashi

School of Information Science, Japan Advanced Institute of Science and Technology
ryoko@jaist.ac.jp

Kenji Tanaka

Department of Computational Science, Faculty of Science, Kanazawa University

Susumu Horiguchi

School of Information Science, Japan Advanced Institute of Science and Technology

Yasuaki Hiwatari

Department of Computational Science, Faculty of Science, Kanazawa University

Abstract   A case study on the parallelization of a classical molecular dynamics code for simulating the formation of carbon clusters is presented. Parallelization is based on the domain decomposition method, as the Tersoff potentials used are short-range. However, at low particle densities, high-performance parallel execution of MD simulations is quite difficult. Methods for improving the performance achieved by parallelization of low-density MD simulations are discussed and initial results for a low-density system are presented.

Keywords: Molecular dynamics simulation, Tersoff potential, Parallelization method, Domain decomposition method, Performance analysis, T3E, MPI

1.   Introduction

The formation of fullerenes has been studied via Molecular Dynamics (MD) simulations. In the present paper, we deal with the initial stage of fullerene formation, the growth of fullerene-like carbon clusters in a dilute gas-phase. Classical MD simulations seem well suited to this kind of investigation, because neither experimental nor theoretical explanations exist. Carbon atom potential functions are taken from Tersoff [1]. These potentials were successfully used in the relaxation process creating C_{60} by Maruyama and Yamaguchi [2]. A cluster temperature control was used in the MD simulations to simulate the annealing process, with a perfect C_{60} molecule obtained [3]. However, the formation of fullerene-like clusters remains unknown, and this is the main objective of our MD simulations. As the details of simulation results have already been presented [4], the present study concentrate on the parallelization process.

In order to deal with C_n clusters for $n \sim 100$, MD simulations are required to deal with millions of particles. For such large-scale simulations, we parallelized the MD simulation code and executed MD simulations on a parallel computer, T3E [5] with MPI [6]. Since the spatial decomposition parallelization domain decomposition method (DDM) is superior to short-range $O(N)$ potential in large-scale MD simulations [7], DDM is used in our parallelization. However, high computational performance cannot be obtained by a simple implementation at the very-low-particle densities of interest. Based on a discussion of suitable domain shape [8] [9], better MD simulation performance is achieved, even in very-low-density systems.

The present paper is organized as follows: Section 2 describes basic information such as the physical characteristics of the simulation, parallelization methods and the parallel computer used. Section 2 also discusses the optimum distribution of simulation space among PEs. Section 3 describes the process of parallelization. The primary subject of section 3 is the determination of suitable parameters. The result of parallelization is shown in section 4. Section 5 discusses the results and outstanding problems. Section 6 presents concluding remarks.

2.   Basic information

2.1   Physical properties

Carbon atom potential functions and parameter values are the same as those of references [2] and [3], the Tersoff potential is given by:

$$E_b = \frac{1}{2} \sum_{i}^{N} \sum_{j(\neq i)}^{N} \left[V_R(r_{ij}) - B_{ij}^* V_A(r_{ij}) \right], \qquad (15.1)$$

$$V_R(r_{ij}) = f_{ij}(r_{ij}) \frac{D^{(e)}}{S-1} exp(-\sqrt{2S}\beta(r_{ij} - R^{(e)})), \qquad (15.2)$$

$$V_A(r_{ij}) = f_{ij}(r_{ij}) \frac{D^{(e)} S}{S-1} exp(-\sqrt{2/S}\beta(r_{ij} - R^{(e)})), \qquad (15.3)$$

$$f_{ij}(r_{ij}) = \begin{cases} 1, & \text{for } r_{ij} < R^{(1)} \\ \frac{1}{2}\left(1 + cos\frac{\pi(r_{ij}-R^{(1)})}{R^{(2)}-R^{(1)}}\right), & \text{for } R^{(1)} < r_{ij} < R^{(2)} \\ 0, & \text{for } R^{(2)} < r_{ij} \end{cases} \qquad (15.4)$$

$$B_{ij}^* = \frac{B_{ij} + B_{ji}}{2}, B_{ij} = \left(1 + \sum_{k(\neq i,j)} [G_c(\theta_{ijk})f(r_{ik})]\right)^{-\delta}, \qquad (15.5)$$

$$G_c(\theta) = a_0\left(1 + \frac{c_0^2}{d_0^2} - \frac{c_0^2}{d_0^2 + (1 + cos\theta)^2}\right). \qquad (15.6)$$

Although the Tersoff potential contains three-body interactions, it is short-range and essentially has a computational complexity of $O(N)$ because only interactions within $R^{(2)}$ are considered. Table 15.1 shows the parameters used in the potential. These values were used by Maruyama and Yamaguchi [3] to completely anneal C_{60}.

Table 15.1. Tersoff potential parameters.

Parameter	Value	Denomination	Parameter	Value	Denomination
$D^{(e)}$	6.325	eV	$R^{(2)}$	2.0	$\mathring{A}$
S	1.29		δ	0.80469	
β	1.5	$1/\mathring{A}$	a_0	0.011304	
$R^{(e)}$	1.315	$\mathring{A}$	c_0	19	
$R^{(1)}$	1.7	$\mathring{A}$	d_0	2.5	

Experimentally, carbon clusters form into fullerenes in a helium-gas atmosphere. In order to effectively simulate these physical conditions in MD simulations that treat only carbon atoms, a cluster-temperature control mechanism is preferable [2]. Cluster-temperature control was applied after each 100 timesteps in the MD simulations. Temperature control was applied to each atom and to three types of freedoms: translational, rotational and vibrational modes.

2.2   Parallelization method

Parallelization of MD simulations has been discussed by several researchers, and DDM is thought to be one of the superior parallelization methods for short-range interactions. Since the potential in this MD simulation is short-range, DDM is used in the parallelization. DDM allocates domains of the simulation space to processing elements (PE). Figure 15.1 illustrates DDM in (a) two-dimensional simulation space and (b) three-dimensional MD simulation space. The entire space containing all particles is divided into small squares referred to as "cells" as shown in Figure 15.1(a). Each row of cells is allocated to each PE as a "domain". In this case, PEs are virtually interconnected in ring by periodic boundary conditions. If cell sizes are greater than $R^{(2)}$, forces between particles are obtained by computing the interactions between particles within eight neighboring cells in the two-dimensional space. Since interactions between particles are restricted to neighboring cells only, the computational complexity of DDM is $O(N/P)$. DDM greatly reduces computation time and inter-processor communication overhead.

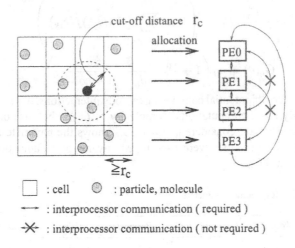

(a) An example of DDM in a two-dimensional MD simulation.

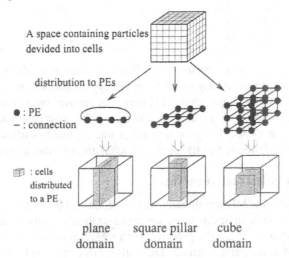

(b) The three domain shapes in three-dimensional MD simulations.

Figure 15.1.   Domain decomposition method.

In three-dimensional MD simulations, DDM cells are cubic, with forces between particles thus obtained by computing interactions between particles within a cell and in the 26 neighboring cells. DDM in three-dimensional simulation space has several domain shapes closely related to interprocessor communication overhead. Figure 15.1(b) shows the three domain shapes in three-dimensional MD simulations. Next, based on the discussion in [8], the procedure used to estimate optimum domain shape is described.

2.3   Optimum domain shape

Here we estimate optimum domain shape for our MD simulation on a MIMD parallel computer using message passing. Each time step of simulation requires inter-processor communications between PEs to exchange simulation data. There are two types of communications: local communication and global communication. In order to compute interactions between particles, PEs exchange simulation data by local communications via message passing. On the other hand, global communication is generally used to obtain a total value such as a summation, a maximum value, or a minimum value. Since global communication has well-designed architecture and is much faster than local communication on most of parallel computers, we concentrate herein on local communication overhead.

Based on the actual communication overhead, we will modelize communication time and estimate the communication time of MD simulations. Figure 15.2 shows the result of a test run for local communication overhead. Roughly speaking, the communication overhead in Figure 15.2 is linear. Thus, the local communication time between two PEs, T_c, is approximately given by

$$T_c = T_s + W \times T_t, \tag{15.7}$$

where T_s is the communication set-up time, T_t is the data transfer time per word, and W is the number of words to be transferred. Using equation (15.7), the entire communication time T_w is expressed as follows:

$$T_w = P_t T_s + C_t W_{cell} T_t, \tag{15.8}$$

where P_t is the number of neighboring PEs to set up local communications, C_t is the total number of surrounding cells for a domain, and W_{cell} is the number of transferred words per cell. In Equation 15.8, W_{cell} is decided by the simulation condition, and T_s and T_t are estimated by simple test execution on a parallel computer, as shown in Figure 15.2. P_t and C_t depend on domain shape and remain unknown. Let us next approximate P_t and C_t.

Figure 15.3 shows the data transfer model on the plane domain. As shown in Figure 15.3(a), the entire simulation space has C cells and each edge has $C^{1/3}$ cells. In the plane domain, each PE has two neighboring PEs, as shown in Figure 15.3(b), and a domain having the shape shown in Figure 15.3(c). Since each PE exchanges one layer of cells with a neighboring PE, as shown in Figure

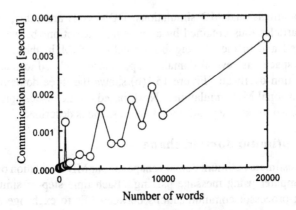

Figure 15.2.   Maximum local communication time on a parallel computer T3E among 128 PEs.

15.3(d), we have $C_t = 2 \times C^{1/3} \times C^{1/3} = 2C^{2/3}$. The relationships between surrounding PEs and C_t for the square pillar domain and the cube domain are shown in Figures 15.4 and 15.5, respectively. Then, the communication time T_w of the three domains are given by

plane domain

$$T_w = 2T_s + 2C^{2/3}W_{cell}T_t, \qquad (15.9)$$

square pillar domain

$$T_w = 8T_s + 4\left(\frac{C^{2/3}}{\sqrt{P}} + C^{1/3}\right)W_{cell}T_t, \qquad (15.10)$$

cube domain

$$T_w = 26T_s + \left(6\left(\frac{C}{P}\right)^{2/3} + 12\left(\frac{C}{P}\right)^{1/3} + 8\right)W_{cell}T_t.(15.11)$$

Let us compare these equations in order to estimate optimum domain shape. $f_1(C, P)$ represents the difference between Equations (15.9) and (15.10). Since we can regard $f_1(C, P)$ as a second-order equation of $C^{1/3}$, we can factorize $f_1(C, P)$ as the following:

$$f_1(C, P) = (15.9) - (15.10),$$
$$= a_1(C^{1/3} - \alpha_1)(C^{1/3} - \beta_1), \qquad (15.12)$$

where $\beta_1 \leq \alpha_1$. Table 15.2 shows a_1, α_1 and β_1. When $f_1(C, P) < 0$, the plane domain can reduce communication time to a greater degree than

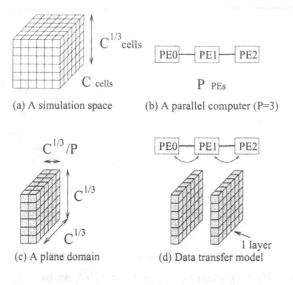

(a) A simulation space

(b) A parallel computer (P=3)

(c) A plane domain

(d) Data transfer model

Figure 15.3. Data exchange on plane domain.

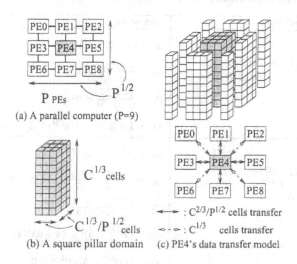

(a) A parallel computer (P=9)

(b) A square pillar domain

(c) PE4's data transfer model

←──→ : $C^{2/3}/P^{1/2}$ cells transfer

←-→ : $C^{1/3}$ cells transfer

Figure 15.4. Data exchange on square pillar domain.

can the square pillar domain. Although the range $\beta_1 < C^{1/3} < \alpha_1$ results in $f_1(C, P) < 0$, the situation β_1 is negative in Table 15.2, and when $0 < C^{1/3}$, we have $0 < C^{1/3} < \alpha_1$ for $f_1(C, P) < 0$. On the other hand, when $f_1(C, P) > 0$, the square pillar domain can reduce the communication time to a greater degree than can the plane domain. Although the ranges $C^{1/3} < \beta_1$ or $\alpha_1 < C^{1/3}$

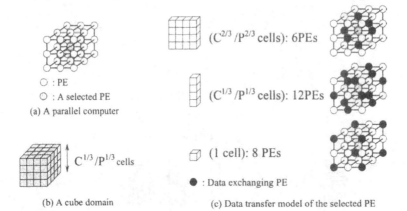

O : PE
O : A selected PE
(a) A parallel computer

$(C^{2/3}/P^{2/3}$ cells): 6PEs

$(C^{1/3}/P^{1/3}$ cells): 12PEs

$C^{1/3}/P^{1/3}$ cells

(1 cell): 8 PEs

● : Data exchanging PE

(b) A cube domain

(c) Data transfer model of the selected PE

Figure 15.5.   Data exchange in the cube domain.

result in $f_1(C, P) > 0$, when $\beta_1 < 0$ and $0 < C^{1/3}$, we have $\alpha_1 < C^{1/3}$ for $f_1(C, P) > 0$.

Table 15.2.   Factorization results ($\lambda = T_s/(W_{cell}T_t) > 0$).

Theoretical difference	Parameters
$f_1(C, P) = (15.9) - (15.10)$ $= a_1(C^{1/3} - \alpha_1)(C^{1/3} - \beta_1)$ $P \geq 9$	$a_1 = \left(1 - 2/\sqrt{P}\right) > 0$ $\alpha_1 = \dfrac{1+\sqrt{D_1}}{1-2/\sqrt{P}} > 0$ $\beta_1 = \dfrac{1-\sqrt{D_1}}{1-2/\sqrt{P}} < 0$ $D_1 = 1 + 3\lambda(1 - 2/\sqrt{P}) > 1$
$f_2(C, P) = (15.10) - (15.11)$ $= a_2(C^{1/3} - \alpha_2)(C^{1/3} - \beta_2)$ $P \geq 27$	$a_2 = (2P^{1/6} - 3)/P^{2/3} > 0$ $\alpha_2 = \dfrac{-(P^{1/3}-3)+\sqrt{D_2}}{2P^{1/6}-3} P^{1/3} > 0$ $\beta_2 = \dfrac{-(P^{1/3}-3)-\sqrt{D_2}}{2P^{1/6}-3} P^{1/3} < 0$ $D_2 = (P^{1/3} - 3)^2 + (4 + 9\lambda)(2P^{1/6} - 3) > 0$
$f_3(C, P) = (15.11) - (15.9)$ $= a_3(C^{1/3} - \alpha_3)(C^{1/3} - \beta_3)$ $P \geq 27$	$a_3 = -(P^{2/3} - 3)/P^{2/3} < 0$ $\alpha_3 = \dfrac{3+\sqrt{D_3}}{P^{2/3}-3} P^{1/3} > 0$ $\beta_3 = \dfrac{3-\sqrt{D_3}}{P^{2/3}-3} P^{1/3} < 0$ $D_3 = 9 + 4(1 + 3\lambda)(P^{2/3} - 3) > 9$

Using the same procedure, the difference between Equations (15.10) and (15.11), $f_2(C, P)$ and the difference between Equations (15.11) and (15.9), $f_3(C, P)$ are factorized as shown in Table 15.2. As discussed for $f_1(C, P)$ with regard to positivity and negativity, we can compare the communication time of each domain by discussing $f_2(C, P)$ and $f_3(C, P)$. From the factorization result of $f_1(C, P)$, $f_2(C, P)$ and $f_3(C, P)$, we can estimate each domain's optimum range as follows:

Plane domain:

$$0 < C^{1/3} < \alpha_1 \text{ and } 0 < C^{1/3} < \alpha_3 \text{ and } P \geq 3 \qquad (15.13)$$

Square pillar domain:

$$\alpha_1 < C^{1/3} \text{ and } 0 < C^{1/3} < \alpha_2 \text{ and } P \geq 9 \qquad (15.14)$$

Cube domain:

$$\alpha_2 < C^{1/3} \text{ and } \alpha_3 < C^{1/3} \text{ and } P \geq 27 \qquad (15.15)$$

A graph of the optimum ranges for the domains is shown in Section 3.

2.4 Parallel computer T3E

The parallel computer T3E consisted of 128 PEs, with each PE containing a DECchip 21164 (300 MHz, 600 MFLOPS, 1200 MIPS). The DECchip 21164 has an 8 KB data cache, a 8 KB instruction cache, And a 96 KB secondary cache. PEs are connected by a three-dimensional torus interconnection, yielding a communication performance of 2.8 GB/second per PE. The T3E supports the message-passing interface (MPI)[6] and FORTRAN90. DDM was implemented on the T3E using a SPMD type algorithm. Execution times are measured using the MPI function MPI_Wtime.

3. Parallelization Process

3.1 Cell size determination

Figure 15.6 shows the relationship between cell size and execution time, with Figure 15.6(a) showing the results for a single PE for various particle densities, and Figure 15.6(b) comparing the results from a single PE with results from eight PEs. The MD program involves loops repeated over a number of cells. A trade-off therefore exists between the number of loops executed and the number of forces calculated. Thus, most of the curves in Figures 15.6(a) and (b) have minima which correspond to optimum cell sizes. In Figure 15.6(a), the optimum cell size for lower particle density is greater than for a higher particle density. In Figure 15.6(b) the parallel execution's optimum cell size is approximately same as the serial execution's. Table 15.3 shows the number of particles per cell

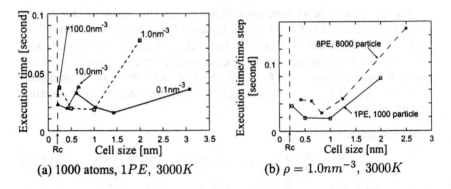

(a) 1000 atoms, $1PE$, $3000K$ (b) $\rho = 1.0nm^{-3}$, $3000K$

Figure 15.6.   Relationships between cell size and execution time.

at optimum cell sizes for different particle densities. The number of particles at each optimum cell size is estimated by

$$(\, number \ of \ particle) = (\ optimum \ cell \ size)^3 \times \rho. \qquad (15.16)$$

For $\rho = 0.1nm^{-3}$, the number of particles per cell is $(7 \times 0.2)^3 \times 0.1 \sim 0.27$. This means that the number of cells is much larger than the number of particles.

Table 15.3.   Number of particles per cell for optimum cell sizes.

Density	Optimum cell size	The number of particles per cell
$0.1nm^{-3}$	1.4	0.27
$1.0nm^{-3}$	0.5	0.125
$10.0nm^{-3}$	0.4	0.64
$100.0nm^{-3}$	0.2	0.8

3.2   Domain shape determination

Figure 15.7 shows the range of simulation parameters for which each of the three domain shapes are most suitable, as determined from an argument for the relationship between interprocessor communication latency and optimum domain shape. Estimates of T_s and T_w for a parallel computer T3E are:

$$T_s = 5.8 \times 10^{-5} second, \qquad (15.17)$$
$$T_w = 1.7 \times 10^{-7} second/word, \qquad (15.18)$$

where one word is four bytes. Since our MD simulation is three-dimensional and $N_{cell} = 0.27$, $W_{cell} = 3N_{cell} = 3 \times 0.27 = 0.81$ in Equation (15.8). In Figure 15.7, the plane domain can be seen to be suitable for many MD simulations, with $N \sim 10000$ and $P \sim 100$. Simulations are first performed

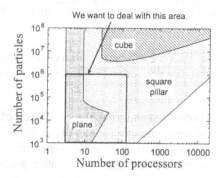

Figure 15.7. Relationship between the most suitable domain shape and simulation conditions on T3E, when the number of particles in a cell is 0.27, cell size is $1.4nm$ and $\rho = 0.1nm^{-3}$.

up to $N \sim 10000$ and $P \sim 20$, and so the plane domain is used in the present MD simulations.

4. Parallelization Results

The main procedures of the MD simulation are:

Redistribution of particles As particles move with each timestep, particles cross cell borders, moving into different cells. Moreover, particles cross domain boundaries, moving into new domains. Thus DDM reallocates particles to cells by position and redistributes particles to PEs by cell.

Communication of position To calculate interactions between particles, PEs need to exchange the positions of particles situated close to the domain boundaries.

Distance computations In order to compute interactions between particles, DDM calculates the distances between particles in each cell, and in the neighboring 26 cells in general. In order to prevent double counting of interactions, inter-particle distance calculations are only performed for 13 of the neighboring cells.

Force computation DDM then calculates forces from the Tersoff potential for each particle. Only particles within the cut-off distance $R^{(2)}$ are needed for this process.

Communication of forces Since the MD simulation uses the law of action and reaction, PEs need to exchange forces after computations.

Cluster processing After computing distances, DDM has a list of interacting pairs of particles. Cluster processing determines the clusters from this list and executes temperature control based on these clusters. Two schemes were used to parallelize cluster processing:

Serial cluster All atom data is gathered onto a single PE and cluster processing is executed serially.

Parallel cluster Each PE estimates partial cluster information, then exchanges this data with other PEs to complete cluster processing.

Figure 15.8 shows both serial and parallel execution times of the MD simulations. Comparing the serial execution to parallel execution using serial clustering reveals that the execution time of serial cluster processing is increased by parallelization, whereas the execution time of other processing is reduced. In contrast, parallel execution using parallel clustering results in a remarkable reduction in cluster processing time, so the total execution time is much less than for serial execution.

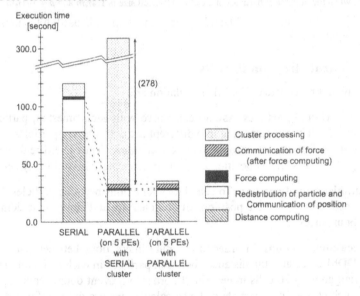

Figure 15.8.   Execution times for (4913 atoms, 2000 timesteps and 5 PE for $\rho = 0.1nm^{-3}$ at $3000K$).

Table 15.4 lists the serial execution time, parallel execution time and improvements in each procedure in the MD program. Because the time complexity of each procedure in Table 15.4 is $O(N/P)$, the execution time of large-scale MD simulation can be reduced by parallel execution. Table 15.4 shows that parallel execution time on five PEs is approximately $1/4$ of the serial execution time. This trend is thought to be due to interprocessor communication overhead on parallel computers. Therefore, the parallelized code appears to be very scalable, making the execution of larger simulations more practical on parallel computers than on serial computers.

Table 15.4. Execution time of each process in the parallel MD simulation and improvement over serial processing for 4913 particles and 2000 timesteps.

Process	Serial execution time [second]	Parallel execution time on 5 PEs [second]	Improvement (Serial time)/ (Parallel time)
Redistribution of particles and communication of positions	28.0	10.5	2.7
Distance computation	77.1	17.0	4.5
Force computation	1.7	0.9	1.9
Communication of forces	–	1.6	–
Cluster processing	10.6	1.8	5.9
Total	117.4	31.8	3.7

5. Approximation of Execution Times and Outstanding Problems

Table 15.5 shows predicted execution times on serial and parallel computers. The predicted execution time depends on computational complexity and real execution times. The number of particles is scaled as $4913/5 \simeq 126000/128$, and the execution time is scaled as $O(N/P)$. Thus, these predictions indicate that parallelization techniques are quite useful for large-scale MD simulations.

Table 15.5. Predicted execution time for 10^6 timestep MD simulations.

	Serial computer	Parallel computer
126000 particle simulation	17 days	11 hours

Although the parallel performance was improved, the following problems remain:

Robust implementation method: The optimum cell size presented is only applicable to the initial conditions of $\rho = 0.1nm^{-3}$. When carbon clusters form, local density increases, and larger cells increase execution times. Execution time is highly dependent on implementation. A direct-cell-base implementation using loops over the number of cells is used in the proposed system. A number of disadvantages exist in this implementation at very low densities. Future studies will attempt to develop an implementation that is robust to changes in density.

Flexible timestep: In very-low-density systems, flexible timestep methods, in which timesteps vary according to collisions between particles, greatly reduce execution times. However, temperature control is currently required for every 100 timesteps in order to form clusters, the flexible timestep method must be confirmed not to cause any problems in the cluster formation processes.

Load balancing: In the MD simulation of the carbon cluster formation processes, local density varies when carbon clusters are created. DDM then produces overhead by an unbalanced load between PEs. A dynamic load balancing method has been discussed[9], and after examining a robust implementation method, the use of a dynamic load balancing will be considered.

6. Conclusion

The performance of molecular dynamics simulation of carbon cluster growth on a parallel computer T3E was examined. The main parameters of the parallelization were cell size optimization and domain shape selection. Serial clustering was found to cause enormous overheads in this parallel system, and thus clustering was also parallelized, greatly reducing the execution time. As a result, parallel execution time on five PEs reduced the execution time by $1/4$ compared to that for serial execution. Although a sufficient improvement was achieved in this first step, a number of important problems still need to be solved before actual execution of large-scale simulations. Future studies will examine implementations that are robust to varying particle densities.

References

[1] J. Tersoff, Modeling solid-state chemistry: Interatomic potentials for multicomponent systems, *Physical Review B*, Vol. 39, No. 8, (1989), 5566-5568.

[2] Y. Yamaguchi, S. Maruyama, A molecular dynamics simulation of the fullerene formation process, *Chemical Physics Letters* **286**, (1998), 336-342.

[3] Y. Yamaguchi, S. Maruyama, A molecular dynamics demonstration of annealing to a perfect C_{60} structure, *Chemical Physics Letters* **286**, (1998), 343-349.

[4] Ryoko Hayashi, Kenji Tanaka, Susumu Horiguchi, Yasuaki Hiwatari, A Classical Molecular Dynamics Simulation of the Carbon Cluster Formation Process on a Parallel Computer, *Diamond and Related Materials*, (2001), 1224-1227.

[5] Cray Research, Inc., *CRAY T3E Fortran Optimization Guide*, 1996.

[6] W. Gropp, E. Lusk, A. Skjellum, *Using MPI*, (The MIT Press, Massachusetts, 1996).

[7] D. M. Beazley, P. S. Lomdahl, N. Grønbech-Jensen, R. Giles, P. Tamayo, Parallel Algorithms for Short-range Molecular Dynamics, in *Annual Reviews in Computational Physics*, eds. D. Stauffer, (World Scientific, 1995) Vol. 3, 119-175.

[8] R. Hayashi, S. Horiguchi, Domain Decomposition Scheme for Parallel Molecular Dynamics Simulation, in *Proc. HPC Asia '97*, (1997), 595-600.

[9] R. Hayashi, S. Horiguchi, Efficiency of Dynamic Load Balancing Based on Permanent Cells for Parallel Molecular Dynamics Simulation, in *Proc. of International Parallel and Distributed Processing Symposium (IPDPS 2000)*, (2000), 85-92.

Chapter 16

COMPARING VARIOUS PARALLELIZING APPROACHES FOR TRIBOLOGY SIMULATIONS*

V. Chaudhary, W. L. Hase, H. Jiang, L. Sun, and D. Thaker

Institute for Scientific Computing, Wayne State University, Detroit, MI 48202

Abstract

Different parallelization methods vary in their system requirements, programming styles, efficiency of exploring parallelism, and the application characteristics they can handle. For different situations, they can exhibit totally different performance gains. This chapter compares OpenMP, MPI, and *Strings* for parallelizing a complicated tribology problem. The problem size and computing infrastructure is changed to assess the impact of this on various parallelization methods. All of them exhibit good performance improvements and it exhibits the necessity and importance of applying parallelization in this field.

Keywords: Molecular dynamics, OpenMP, MPI, Distributed shared memory(DSM)

1. Introduction

Traditionally supercomputers are the essential tools to solve these so-called "Grand challenge" problems. Recent improvements in commodity processors and networks have provided an opportunity to conduct these kind of task within an everyday computing infrastructure, such as symmetrical multiprocessors (SMPs) or even networks of workstations (NOWs).

Friction, the resistance to relative motion between contact sliding surfaces, happens everywhere in human life and is a costly problem facing industry. Understanding the origin of friction force [13] and the energy dissipation during the friction process [14], therefore, has both theoretical and practical importance and it has attracted considerable interest in tribology study. A complete

*This research was supported in part by NSF IGERT grant 9987598, NSF MRI grant 9977815, NSF ITR grant 0081696, NSF grant 0078558, ONR grant N00014-96-1-0866, Institute for Manufacturing Research, and Institute for Scientific Computing. A version of this paper appeared in the HPSECA 2002 Workshop held with ICPP 2002.

understanding of these friction processes requires detailed information at the atomic level. With recent development of experimental techniques [15] and the theories [13], physicists and chemists have been able not only to probe the atomic-level friction process but also to "see" what really takes place at the sliding interface via computer simulation. Because computer simulation which utilizes the molecular dynamics(MD) method can follow and analyze the dynamics of all atoms, it is has become a powerful tool to investigate various tribology phenomena.With molecular dynamics simulation, detailed information such as possible pathways of the frictional energy dissipation, temperature gradients, effect of surface properties on friction force can be investigated at the microscopic level. In the pioneering work of McClelland and Glosli [25] MD simulations were employed to study the friction between two monolayers of alkane molecules with the temperature ranges from 0 K to 300 K. Both the interactions of the alkane chains and the temperatures are important for the friction. Harrison *et al.* [26] simulated the H- and alkyl-terminated diamond surface sliding systems and have identified mechanisms account for the friction of these surfaces and the energy dissipation paths. The agreement between the MD simulations by Robbins *et al.* [27] and the experimental work by Simizu *et al.* [28] demonstrates the validity of using MD simulation technique in the study of tribology.

In an MD simulation, the motion of each atom is governed by the Newton's equation of motion and their positions are determined by the time evolution of the Newton's equation. At each time integration step the force between atoms, the potential energies and kinetic energies are evaluated. The computational effort grows linearly with the number of Newton's equations, so it is an ideal method to treat mid-sized systems (e.g. 10^2 atoms). However, there are generally two factors limiting the application of MD to large scale simulation (e.g. 10^6 atoms). First, the time step of integration in an MD simulation is usually about a femtosecond (10^{-15} s) due to the numerical and physical consideration. In contrast to simulation, the time scale for tribology experiments is at least in nanoseconds (10^{-9} s). The time step in simulation is so small compared with experiment that it generally requires a large number of integration steps to reach a desired total evolution time. Second, when the number of atoms in the simulation system increases, the computation time for force evaluation increases rapidly.

Parallel and distributed processing is a promising solution for these computational requirements discussed above [16]. Significant advances in parallel algorithms and architecture have demonstrated the potential for applying current computation techniques into the simulation of the friction process. Among the different approaches of parallel processing, there are numerous implementation cases for MD simulation using MPI, the parallelization with "thread" method so far is limited.

There is particular interest in the friction of alumina surfaces since alumina is an important technological material. In this chapter, we report a practical implementation of parallel computing techniques for performing MD simulations of friction forces of sliding hydroxylated α-aluminum oxide surfaces. There are many systems and tools exploring parallelism for different types of programs. Besides system requirements, different parallelization approaches vary in programming style and performance gain. Some methods enable programmers to write code easily, or even provide parallelization service completely transparent to programmers. But normally this kind of method cannot provide expected performance improvement all the time. Other methods might require programmers to put reasonable effort in order to achieve substantial gain.

The tribology code is written using OpenMP, MPI, and DSM *Strings* [12] (a software distributed shared memory). OpenMP can be used only for shared memory systems whereas MPI and strings can be used for both shared memory systems and network of workstations. The programming paradigms in each of these are very different with the labor requirements ranging from "little" for OpenMP to "large" for MPI. The programming effort for *Strings* is considerably less than MPI. Therefore, to evaluate an approach's ability to exploit parallelism for a particular application domain, many factors need to be considered, including system requirement, programming style, time to program, performance gain, etc.

The remainder of this chapter is organized as follows: Section 2 describes various parallelization approaches in high-performance computing. In Section 3 we discuss molecular dynamics program in detail and how we plan to parallelize it. Section 4 presents some experiment results and discuss the performance. We wrap up with conclusions and continuing work in Section 5.

2.   Parallelization Approaches

There are several approaches suitable for transforming sequential Tribology programs into parallel ones. These approaches impose different requirements on compilers, libraries, and runtime support systems. Some of them can execute only on shared memory multiprocessors whereas others can achieve speedups on networks of workstations.

2.1   Parallelization with vendors' support

Some vendors, such as Sun Microsystems, provide compiler or library options for parallel processing. Sun MP C is an extended ANSI C compiler that can compile code to run on SPARC shared memory multiprocessor machines. The compiled code, may run in parallel using the multiple processors on the system [4].

The MP C compiler generates parallel code for those loops that it determines are safe to parallelize. Typically, these loops have iterations that are independent of each other. For such loops, it does not matter in what order the iterations are executed or if they are executed in parallel. This compiler is also able to perform extensive automatic restructuring of user code. These automatic transformations expose higher degrees of loop level parallelization. They include: loop interchange, loop fusion, loop distribution and software pipelining. This C compiler provides explicit and automatic capabilities for parallelizing loops.

Sun Performance Library can be used with the shared or dedicated modes of parallelization (as defined by Sun Microsystems, Inc.), that are user selectable at link time. The dedicated multiprocessor model of parallelism has the following features: specifying the parallelization mode improves application performance by using the parallelization enhancements made to Sun Performance Library routines [5].

The shared multiprocessor model of parallelism has the following features:

- Delivers peak performance to applications that do not use compiler parallelization and that run on a platform shared with other applications.

- Parallelization is implemented with threads library synchronization primitives.

The dedicated multiprocessor model of parallelism has the following features:

- Delivers peak performance to applications using automatic compiler parallelization and running on an multiprocessor platform dedicated to a single processor-intensive application.

- Parallelization is implemented with spin locks.

On a dedicated system, the dedicated model can be faster than the shared model due to lower synchronization overhead. On a system running many different tasks, the shared model can make better use of available resources.

To specify the parallelization mode:

- Shared model - Use -mt on the link line without one of the compiler parallelization options.

- Dedicated model - Use one of the compiler parallelization options [-xparallel | -xexplicitpar | -xautopar] on the compile and link lines.

- Single processor - Do not specify any of the compiler parallelization options or -mt on the link line.

Due to the potential of aliasing in programming languages, it is especially hard to determine the safety of parallelization. Normally vendors' compilers and libraries do not offer any capabilities to automatically parallelize arbitrary regions of code. Therefore, this loop parallelization strategy can achieve good performance only when many big loops exist and their iterations are independent or with regular dependency patterns.

2.2   OpenMP

As an emerging industry standard, OpenMP is an Application Program Interface (API) that may be used to explicitly direct multi-threaded, shared memory parallelism in C/C++ and Fortran on all architectures, including Unix platforms and Windows NT platforms. It is comprised of three primary API components: compiler directives, runtime library routines, and environment variables. Jointly defined by a group of major computer hardware and software vendors, OpenMP is a portable, scalable model that gives shared-memory parallel programmers a simple and flexible interface for developing parallel applications for platforms ranging from the desktop to the supercomputer [6].

The OpenMP API defines a set of program directives that enable the user to annotate a sequential program to indicate how it should be executed in parallel. In C/C++, the directives are implemented as #*pragma* statements, and in Fortran 77/90 they are implemented as comments. A program that is written using OpenMP directives begins execution as a single process, called the *master thread* of execution. The *master thread* executes sequentially until the first parallel construct is encountered. The PARALLEL / END PARALLEL directive pair constitutes the parallel construct. When a parallel construct is encountered, the *master thread* creates a team of threads, and the master thread becomes the master of the team. The program statements that are enclosed in a parallel construct, including routines called from within the construct, are executed in parallel by each thread in the team.

Upon completion of the parallel construct, the threads in the team synchronize and only the *master thread* continues execution. Any number of parallel constructs can be specified in a single program. As a result, a program may fork and join many times during execution (see Figure 16.1).

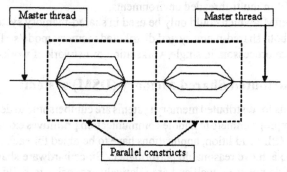

Figure 16.1.   OpenMP execution model

The degree of parallelism in an OpenMP code is dependent on the code, the platform, the hardware configuration, the compiler, and the operating system. In no case are you guaranteed to have each thread running on a separate processor [7].

2.3   MPI

MPI is a message-passing application programmer interface, together with protocol and semantic specifications for how its features must behave in any implementation (as a message buffering and message delivery progress requirement) [9]. The main advantages of establishing a message-passing standard are portability and ease-of-use. In a distributed memory communication environment in which the higher level routines and/or abstractions are build upon lower level message passing routines the benefits of standardization are particularly apparent. Furthermore, the definition of a message passing standard provides vendors with a clearly defined base set of routines that they can implement efficiently, or in some cases provide hardware support for, thereby enhancing scalability [8].

MPI includes point-to-point message passing and collective operations, all scoped to a user-specified group of processes. MPI provides process abstraction at two levels. First, processes are named according to the rank of the group in which the communication is being performed. Second, virtual topologies allow for graph or Cartesian naming of processes that help relate the application semantics to the message passing semantics in a convenient, efficient way.

MPI also provides some additional services: environmental inquiry, basic timing information for application performance measurement, and a profiling interface for external performance monitoring. To support data conversion in heterogeneous environments, MPI requires datatype specification for communication operations. Both built-in and user-defined datatypes are provided.

MPI supports both SPMD and MPMD modes of parallel programming. Furthermore, MPI supports communication between groups and within a single group. MPI provides a thread-safe application programming interface (API), which is useful in multi-threaded environments.

Unlike OpenMP which could only be used in shared-memory systems, MPI can work for both shared-memory and distributed memory models. Therefore, MPI can utilize processors in single workstation or network of workstations.

2.4   Distributed Shared Memory (DSM) systems

Applications for distributed memory systems are cumbersome to develop due to the need for programmers to handle communication primitives explicitly, just as coding in MPI. In addition, applications have to be tuned for each individual architecture to achieve reasonable performance. Since hardware shared memory machines do not scale well and are relatively expensive to build, software distributed shared memory (DSM) systems are gaining popularity for providing a logically shared memory over physically distributed memory. These software DSM systems combine programming advantages of shared memory and the cost advantages of distributed memory. The programmer is given the illusion of a large global address space encompassing all available memory, thereby eliminating the task of explicitly moving data between processes located on separate machines.

Research projects with DSMs have shown good performance, for example *TreadMarks* [11], *Millipede* [10] and *Strings* [12]. This model has also been shown to give good results for programs that have irregular data access patterns which cannot be analyzed at compile time, or indirect data accesses that are dependent on the input data-set.

DSMs share data at the relatively large granularity of a virtual memory page and can suffer from a phenomenon known as "false sharing", wherein two processes simultaneously attempt to write to different data items that reside on the same page. If only a single writer is permitted, the page may ping-pong between the nodes. One solution to this problem is to "hold" a freshly arrived page for some time before releasing it to another requester. Relaxed memory consistency models that allow multiple concurrent writers have also been proposed to alleviate this symptom. The systems ensure that all nodes see the same data at well defined points in the program, usually when synchronization occurs. Extra effort is required to ensure program correctness in this case. One technique that has been investigated to improve DSM performance is the use of multiple threads of control in the system. Up to now, the third generation DSM systems utilize relaxed consistency models and multithreading technologies.

We parallelize the tribology program by using a multi-threaded DSM, *Strings*, designed for clusters of Symmetrical Multiprocessors (SMPs). *Strings* was developed at Wayne State University and consists of a library that is linked with a shared memory parallel program. The program thus uses calls to the distributed shared memory allocator to create globally shared memory regions.

Strings is built using POSIX threads, which can be multiplexed on kernel lightweight processes. The kernel can schedule these lightweight processes across multiple processors on symmetrical multiprocessors (SMPs) for better performance. Therefore, in *Strings*, each thread could be assigned to any processor on the SMP if there is no special request, and all local threads could run in parallel if there are enough processors. *Strings* is designed to exploit data parallelism by allowing multiple application threads to share the same address space on a node. Additionally, the protocol handler is multi-threaded. The overhead of interrupt driven network I/O is avoided by using a dedicated communication thread. *Strings* is designed to exploit data parallelism at the application level and task parallelism at the run-time level.

Strings starts a master process that forks child processes on remote nodes using rsh(). Each of these processes creates a dsm_server thread and a communication thread. The forked processes then register their listening ports with the master. The master process enters the application proper and creates shared memory regions. It then creates application threads on remote nodes by sending requests to the dsm_server threads on the respective nodes. Shared memory identifiers and global synchronization primitives are sent as part of the thread create call. The virtual memory subsystem is used to enforce coherent access to the globally shared regions.

2.4.1   Kernel threads.   Thread implementations can be either user-level, usually implemented as a library, or kernel-level in terms of light-weight processes. Kernel level threads are more expensive to create, since the kernel is involved in managing them. User level threads suffer from some limitations, since they are implemented as a user-level library, they cannot be scheduled by the kernel. If any thread issues a blocking system call, all associated threads will also be blocked. Also on a multi-processor system, user-level threads bound to a light-weight process can only on one processor at a time. User level threads do not allow the programmer to control their scheduling within the process, on the other hand kernel level threads can be scheduled by the operating system across multiple processors.

2.4.2   Shared memory.   *Strings* implements shared memory by using the mmap() call to map a file to the bottom of the stack segment. With dynamically linked programs, it was found that mmap() would map the same page to different addresses on different processors. Allowing multiple application threads on the same node leads to a peculiar problem. Once a page has been fetched from a remote node, its contents must be written to the corresponding memory region, so the protection has to be changed to writable. At this time no other thread should be able to access this page. Suspending all kernel level threads can lead to a deadlock and also reduce concurrency. In *Strings*, every page is mapped to two different addresses. It is then possible to write to the shadow address without changing the protection of the primary memory region.

A release consistency model using an update protocol has been implemented. When a thread tries to write to a page, a twin copy of the page is created. When either a lock is released or a barrier is reached, the difference (diff) between the current contents and its twin are sent to threads that share the page. Multiple diffs are aggregated to decrease the number of messages sent.

3.   Molecular Dynamics

3.1   Model system

The sequential code has been used to study the friction process by sliding hydroxylated a-aluminum surfaces [29, 30, 31]. The model consists of a smaller hydroxylated α-aluminum surface (top surface) moving on a much bigger aluminum surface (bottom surface). The bulk α-Al_2O_3 has a rhombohedral structure with the crystal unit cell parameter of $a = b = 4.74$ Å and $c = 12.95$ Å in x-,y- and z-plane [32] The top and bottom surfaces are built by repeating the unit cell structure. At the interfaces of top and bottom layer, H atom is added and bonded with an oxygen atom to produce the hydroxyl surface. In this chapter, for example, the small top surface initially used has the size of 25

Å x 25 Å x 12 Å in x, y and z direction which contains about 943 atoms and corresponds to approximately 36 unit cells. To simulate the experiments, force (load) is applied on top of the small top surface and the driving force that moves the top surface with respect to the bottom surface is also added to the system in the direction parallel to the contacting surfaces. The distance between the two surfaces is thus subjected to the magnitude of the load applied on the top surface. By selecting "iop" options as described in the code (see Appendix A), different pressure and driving forces, i.e. different energy dissipative systems, are selected. Besides the driving force that moves the upper sliding surface, each atom in the system is exposed to the interaction with other atoms. The potential energy functions which define the interaction between atoms are given as analytical functions (see Section 3.2.1 and 3.2.2). These functions were derived from the available experimental and electronic structure calculation data [17, 33, 34]. The functions for α-alumina were first derived from the *ab initio* calculations of an Al_4O_6 cluster model [17]. Parameters in the functions are obtained by fitting to the vibrational frequencies of either the experiment or electronic structure calculations. With these function, the interaction energy of the system at any time can be determined. The force on a particular atom can be determined by taking the first order partial derivatives of the potential energy functions. The general types of interaction can be divided into two categories: intramolecular bonded and inter-molecular nonbonded forces. The bonded forces are represented by internal coordinate bond distance, bond angles, and constants determined by the interacting atoms. The inter-molecular forces are Van der Waals interaction. The simulation are carried out with a constant number of atoms, constant volume and constant temperature (NVT). Temperature control is achieved by Berenden's method [18]. The integration of Newton's equation of motion is done by using Velocity Verlet algorithm [19].

3.2   Simulation procedure

The simulation is carried out by solving the classical equations of motion. Initial velocities are either set to zero or calculated by the program according to the user's demand. Newton's equation is numerically integrated to predict the position of all atoms in the next short period of time. The atomic forces are evaluated during each of the integration step. In the hydroxylated α-alumina systems, the type of forces are bonded and non-bonded. The sequential code used in the tribology study here has the structure depicted in Figure 16.2 (see Appendix A for more details).

3.2.1   Bonded forces calculation.   The interactions between adjacent atoms connected by chemical bonds are described by bonded forces. The bonded forces are two-centered harmonic stretches with three centered harmonic bends. Their interaction potential functions are modelled by harmonic potential energy functions

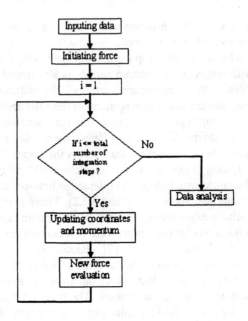

Figure 16.2. Flow chart of MP simulation

$$V_{str} = \frac{1}{2}k_{str}(r - r_0)^2 \qquad (16.1)$$

where k_{str}, r and r_0 are bond stretching force constant, bond length, and equilibrium bond distance and

$$V_\theta = \frac{1}{2}k_\theta(\theta - \theta_0)^2 \qquad (16.2)$$

where k_θ, θ and θ_0 are the bond angle bending force constant, bond angle, and equilibrium bond angle, respectively.

The forces are assigned to each involved atom by taking the first derivatives of the potential.

There are two types of stretching interactions, i.e., O-H, Al-O. For example, the r_0 and k_{str} for O-H stretching are $r_0 = 0.9482$ Å and $k_{str} = 7.98$ mdyn/Å, respectively. Since all the parameters are listed in [34], parameters for the potential energy functions are not listed in this and the following section. The H-O-Al, Al-O-Al and O-Al-O bending interactions are considered in the simulation.

3.2.2   The nonbonded calculation.   The nonbonded interactions here contain only Lennard-Jones type of potentials

$$V_{L-J}(r_{ij}) = 4\varepsilon[\frac{\sigma}{r_{ij}^6} - \frac{\sigma}{r_{ij}^{12}}] \qquad (16.3)$$

where r_{ij} is the distance between atom i and atom j. ε and σ represent the nonbonded iteraction parameters. The types of non-bonded interactions are H—H, H—O, H—Al, O—O, O—Al, Al—Al.

Although the computation effort for bonded interactions grows linearly with the size of the system, the nonbonded interaction exhibits a quadratic dependence on the number of atoms. Hence, the evaluation of the nonbonded Lennard-Jones terms are generally the most computationally intensive constituent in the MD code.

Lennard-Jones type of interaction is long range interaction that vanishes slowly at large distance. To reduce the computation effort for calculating the small forces on atoms at large distance, a cut-off radius is generally introduced. Lennard-Jones interaction beyond the cut-off distance is then treated as zero. Therefore, a neighbor search is carried out to find the atoms within the cut off radius. By introducing the cut off radius the computational effort scales linearly with the number of atoms. However, the nonbonded force is still the most time consuming part in the each iteration of the force evaluation.

3.3 Implementation

There are various data partition schemes in parallel molecular dynamics simulation [8-12]. In general three parallel algorithms are often used to decompose and distribute the computational load.

First, the number of atoms in the simulation system is equally divided and assigned to each processor; Second, the forces of interaction are equally divided and assigned to each processor; Third, the spatial region is equally divided and assigned to each processor. Each algorithm has its advantages and therefore they are often implemented according to the specific problem under study, i.e., system size and evolution time. For example, when using MPI to implement the third method, the molecular system is divided into subspaces, each processor calculates the forces on the atoms within the subspace and update the corresponding positions and velocities. However, the extent of forces always cover the neighboring subspaces or even the whole space, the updating of forces on atoms requires communication at least among neighboring subspaces at each integration step. The cost increases with number of processors and increase in size of integration steps. Therefore, this algorithm is often used for large molecular system with relatively fewer integration steps.

In the tribology application considered here, the evaluation of forces (98-99% execution time) is the most time consuming. So the parallelization is focused on evaluation of forces. To compare the performance between OpenMP, MPI, and DSM *Strings* methods, the basic parallel algorithm is maintained. Forces on atoms are evenly assigned to each processor. For bonded forces, the computational load on each processor/threads equals the number of harmonic stretch forces divided by the number of processors/threads in MPI, OpenMP, and *Strings*. For the nonbonded force terms, there are two situations. The nonbonded interaction with the same surfaces are distributed to each processor/thread in the same way as for bonded forces. The Lennard-Jones interactions between different surface atoms are calculated by searching the neighbor list and therefore the atom dividing scheme is employed. There are obvious shortcomings for this simple algorithm for both MPI and DSM Stings implementation. Even though the force calculation is divided into small parts, the communication between all processors to update the coordinates has to be done at each integration step. Therefore, it is necessary for comparison to be done for different size of system and different time integration step.

4.   Experiments and Analysis

The computing environment used and the analysis of data from the experiments is described in this section.

4.1   Experiment infrastructure

The experiments were carried out using a cluster of SMPs. The SMPs used were a SUN Enterprise E6500 with 14 processors (4Gbytes of RAM) , and four SUN Enterprise E3500s with 4 processors (and 1Gbytes of RAM) each. Each of these processors were 330 MHz UltraSparcIIs. The operating system on the machines was Sun Solaris 5.7. The interconnect was fast ethernet using a NetGear switch.

The application was run sequentially, using OpenMP (on the large SMP), using MPI (the MPICH implementation was used) on the cluster of SMPs, and using *Strings* on the same cluster. The OpenMP code was compiled using the SUN High Performance Compiler. Both the MPI and the *Strings* version of the application were also run on the large SMP in order to compare their performance with OpenMP. Two data sizes, one small and another large were used. The comparisons were done for the application on one node using one, two, four and eight processors each, on two nodes with one, two and four processors each and finally on four nodes with one, two and four processors each.

4.2   Results and analysis

This section describes the results that were obtained from the experiments described earlier. In case of one large SMP, it can be seen from Figures 16.3 and 16.4, that immaterial of the problem size, the results are consistent. OpenMP outperforms the others on the large SMP. For OpenMP, the SUN High Performance Compiler was used, which was able to optimize it for the SUN Enterprise machines. For MPI, we used the MPICH implementation, which being portable loses out on performance compared to OpenMP. The performance for MPI and *Strings* is very similar on one SMP.

When considering multiple SMPs, we could only use the MPI version and the *Strings* version of the application. We used up to four SMPs each with four processors. Again for both program sizes, the results are consistent. For MPI, it was observed that performance degraded when we used 4 processes per nodes, for both 2 nodes and 4 nodes. This can be directly attributed to the substantial increase in communication as seen from Figures 16.7 and 16.8. Another observation was that for MPI, increasing the number of processes per machine increases the total communication time. This is because the MPI code uses MPI_Reduce and MPI_Broadcast calls at the end of each computation cycle. This is an area where performance could be improved by using other MPI primitives.

For the distributed shared memory (*Strings*) version of the application, it can be seen that increasing the number of compute threads always results in an increase in performance. As we increase the number of nodes that the application uses, the performance degrades as this increases communication. For example, the application on 1 machine and 4 compute threads performs better than on 2 machines with 2 compute threads, which in turn is better than 4 machines with 1 compute thread. This shows that within an SMP, *Strings* is able to effectively use shared memory to communicate. Another interesting observation was that the total execution time when using 4 compute threads on 4 machines, is very close to the execution time when using 2 compute threads on 4 machines. It can be seen from Figure 16.10, that increasing the number of nodes increases the number of page faults, both read and write.

In the final analysis, it can be seen that *Strings* outperforms MPI for this application by a big margin when running on a cluster of SMPs. The fraction of time spent in communication for *Strings* is much less than that of MPI (see Figures 16.7, 16.8, and 16.9). Also using the SUN High Performance Compiler and OpenMP provides the best results for a single SMP.

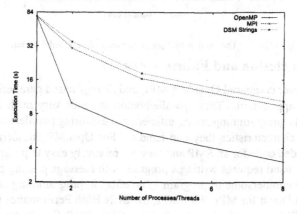

Figure 16.3.   The smaller MD program executed on 1 node.

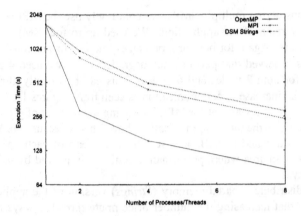

Figure 16.4.   The bigger MD program executed on 1 node.

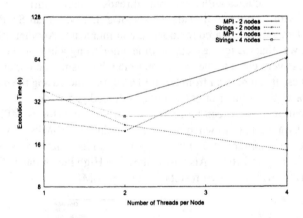

Figure 16.5.   The smaller MD program executed on 2 and 4 nodes.

5.   Conclusion and Future Work

This chapter compared OpenMP, MPI, and *Strings* based parallelization of a tribology application. These parallelization methods vary in their system requirements, programming styles, efficiency of exploring parallelism, and the application characteristics they can handle. For OpenMP and *Strings*, one writes threaded code for an SMP and they are relatively easy to program. MPI on the other hand requires writing a program with message passing primitives and is more cumbersome to program. The effort in programming is least for OpenMP and most for MPI. For SMPs, the SUN High Performance Compiler and OpenMP provides the best results for a single SMP. For cluster of SMPs, *Strings* outperforms MPI for this application by a big margin when running on a cluster of SMPs.

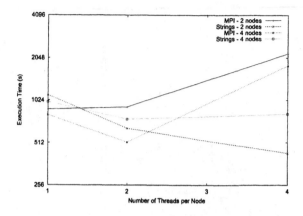

Figure 16.6. The bigger MD program executed on 2 and 4 nodes.

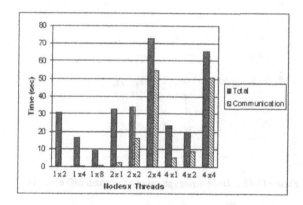

Figure 16.7. MPI communication time in the smaller MD execution.

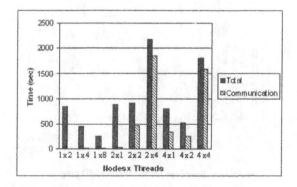

Figure 16.8. MPI communication time in the bigger MD execution.

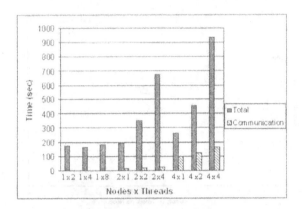

Figure 16.9.   DSM communication time in a certain MD execution.

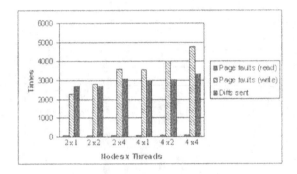

Figure 16.10.   DSM Strings statistics in a certain MD execution.

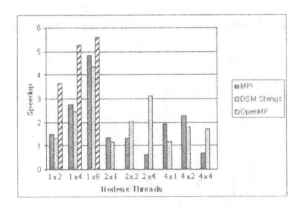

Figure 16.11.   Speedups for the smaller MD program.

It appears that combining OpenMP and *Strings* would yield best results for a cluster of SMPs. We are currently implementing OpenMP and *Strings*

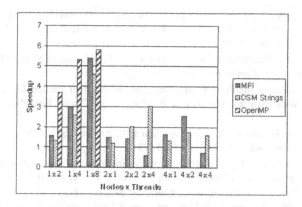

Figure 16.12.   Speedups for the bigger MD program.

together. Also, we are looking into different types of parallelization of the tribology code. One method would divide the atoms in the simulations equally among the processors. Another method would divide the spatial region equally among the processors.

References

[1] Sumit Roy, Ryan Yong Jin, Vipin Chaudhary, and William L. Hase, Parallel Molecular Dynamics Simulations of Alkane/Hydroxylated α-Aluminum Oxide Interfaces, *Computer Physics Communications*, pp. 210-218, 128 (2000).

[2] D. Cociorva, G. Baumgartner, C. Lam, P. Sadayappan, J. Ramanujam, M. Nooijen, D. Bernholdt and R. Harrison, Space-Time Trade-Off Optimization for a Class of Electronic Structure Calculations, *Proceedings of ACM SIGPLAN 2002 Conference on Programming Language Design and Implementation (PLDI)*, June 2002, To Appear.

[3] G. Baumgartner, D. Bernholdt, D. Cociorva, R. Harrison, M. Nooijen, J. Ramanujam and P. Sadayappan, A Performance Optimization Framework for Compilation of Tensor Contraction Expressions into Parallel Programs, *7th International Workshop on High-Level Parallel Programming Models and Supportive Environments (held in conjunction with IPDPS '02)*, April 2002.

[4] Vinod Grover and Douglas Walls, Sun MP C Compiler, http://docs.sun.com/.

[5] Sun Microsystems, Sun Performance Library User's Guide, http://docs.sun.com/.

[6] The OpenMP Forum, OpenMP: Simple, Portable, Scalable SMP Programming, http://www.openmp.org/.

[7] National Energy Research Scientific Computing Center, NERSC OpenMP Tutorial, http://hpcf.nersc.gov/training/tutorials/openmp/

[8] Message Passing Interface (MPI) Forum, MPI: A message-passing interface standard, *International Journal of Supercomputing Applications*, 8(3/4), 1994.

[9] William Gropp and Ewing Lusk and Nathan Doss and Anthony Skjellum, High-performance, portable implementation of the MPI Message Passing Interface Standard, *Parallel Computing*, Vol. 22, 6, 1996.

[10] A. Itzkovitz, A. Schuster, and L. Wolfovich, Thread Migration and its Applications in Distributed Shared Memory Systems, *Journal of Systems and Software*, vol. 42, no. 1, pp. 71–87, 1998.

[11] P. Keleher, A. Cox, S. Dwarkadas and W. Zwaenepoel, TreadMarks: Distributed Shared Memory on Standard Workstations and Operating Systems, *Proc. of the Winter 1994 USENIX Conference*, 1994.

[12] S. Roy and V. Chaudhary, Design Issues for a High-Performance DSM on SMP Clusters, *Journal of Cluster Computing*, 2(1999) 3, 1999, pp. 177–186.

[13] Mark O. Robbins, Martin H. Müser, Computer Simulation of Friction, Lubrication, and Wear, *Modern Tribology Handbook*, B. Bhushan, Ed. (CRC press, Boca Raton, 2001) pp. 717.

[14] I. L. Singer, Friction and Energy Dissipation at the Atomic Scale: A Review, *Journal of Vacuum Science and Technology*, A. 12, 5 1994.

[15] Robert W. Carpick, Miquel Salmeron, Scratching the Surface: Fundamental Investigations of Tribology with atomic Force Microscopy, *Chemical Review*, pp. 1163-1194, 97, 1997.

[16] Parallel Computing in Computational Chemistry: developed from a symposium sponsored by the Division of Computers in Chemistry at the 207th National Meeting of the American Chemical Society, San Diego, California, March 13-17, 1994, Timthy G. Mattson, Ed., Washington, DC, American Chemical Society.

[17] J. M. Wittbrodt, W. L. Hase, H. B. Schlegel, Ab Initio Study of the Interaction of Water with Cluster Models of the Aluminum Terminated (0001) α-Aluminum Oxide Surface, *Journal of Physical Chemistry B*, pp. 6539-6548,102 1998.

[18] H. J. C. Berendsen, J. P. M. Postma, W. F. van Gunsteren, A. Di-Nola, J. R. Haak, Molecular-Dynamics With Coupling to an External Bath, *Journal of Chemical Physics*, pp. 3684-3690, 81, 1984.

[19] W. C. Swope, H. C. Andersen, P. H. Berens, K. R. Wilson, A Computer-Simulation Method for the Calculation of Equilibrium-Constants for the Formation of Physical Clusters of Molecules- Application to Small Water Clusters, *Journal of Chemical Physics*, pp. 637-649, 76, 1982.

[20] S. Y. Liem, D. Brown, J. H. R. Clarke, A Loose-Coupling, Constant Pressure, Molecular Dynamics Algorithm for Use in the Modeling of Polymer Materials, *Computer Physics Communication*, pp. 360-369, 62, 1991.

[21] D. Brown, J. H. R. Clarke, M. Okuda, T. Yamazaki, A Domain Decomposition Parallel-Processing Algorithm for Molecular Dynamics Simulations of Polymers, *Computer Physics Communication*, pp. 1-13, 83 1994.

[22] D. Brown, J. H. R. Clarke, M. Okuda, T. Yamazaki, A Domain Decomposition Parallelization Strategy for Molecular Dynamics Simulations on Distributed Memory Machines, *Computer Physics Communication*, pp. 67-80, 74, 1993.

[23] S. Plimpton, Fast Parallel Algorithms for Short Range Molecular Dynamics, *Journal of Computational Physics*, pp. 1-19, 117, 1995.

[24] R. Murty, D. Okunbor, Efficient Parallel Algorithms for Molecular Dynamics Simulation, *Parallel Computing*, pp. 217-230, 25, 1999.

[25] J. N. Glosli and G. M. McClelland, Molecular Dynamics Study of Sliding Friction of Ordered Organic Monolayers, *Phys. Rev. Letter*, pp.1960-1963, 70, 1993.

[26] J. A. Harrison, C. T. White, R. J. Colton and D. W. Brenner, Effects of chemically bound, flexible hydrocarbon species on the frictional properties of diamond surfaces, *Journal of Physical Chemistry*, pp 6573 - 6576, 97, 1993.

[27] A. R. C. Baljon and M. O. Robbins, Energy Dissipation During Rupture of Adhesive Bonds, *Science*, pp.482-484, 271, 1996.

[28] J. Simizu, H. Eda, M. Yoritsune and E. Ohmura, Molecular Dynamics Simulation of Friction on Atomic Scale, *Nanotechnology*, pp. 118-123, 9, 1998.

[29] H. Xie, K. Song, D. J. Mann and W. L. Hase, Temperature Gradients and Frictional En-
      ergy Dissipation in the Sliding of Hydroxylated α-Alumina Surfaces, *Physical Chemistry
      Chemical Physics*, pp. 5377-5385, 4, 2002.

[30] D. J. Mann, L. Zhong and W. L. Hase, Effect of Surface Stiffness on the Friction of Sliding
      Model Hydroxylated α-Alumina Surfaces, *Journal of Physical Chemistry B*, pp. 12032-
      12045, 2001.

[31] D. J. Mann and W. L. Hase, Computer Simulation of Sliding Hydroxylated Alumina Sur-
      face, *Tribology Letter*, pp. 153-159, 7, 1999.

[32] de Sainte Claire, P, K. C. Hass, W. F. Schneider and W. L. Hase, Comparison Between
      United and Explicit Atom Models for Simulating Alkane Chains Physisorbed on an Alu-
      minum Terminated (0001) α-Aluminum Oxide Surface, *Journal of Physical Chemistry B*,
      pp.3885-3895, 103, 1999.

[33] K. Bolton, S. B. M. Bosio, W. L. Hase, W. F. Schneider, K. C. Hass, Comparison Between
      United and Explicit Atom Models for Simulating Alkane Chains Physisorbed on an Alu-
      minum Terminated (0001) α-Aluminum Oxide Surface, *Journal of Physical Chemistry B*,
      pp.3885-3895, 103, 1999.

[34] E. F. Sawilowsky, O. Meroueh, H. B. Schlegel, W. L. Hase, Structures and Energies for
      Methane Complexed with Alumina Clusters, *Journal of Physical Chemistry A*, pp.4920-
      4927, 104, 2000.

Appendix: A. Sequential Code

```
program tribology

program main()
read in information required for computation
when time=0      -----> initial condition
call force  -----> calculate forces
call energy -----> calculate energies
write initial results
if iop*= 1,2...            ----->select surface sliding conditions
   do i=1, i<= total number of integration steps
     call verlet ----->velocity verlet algorithm to update
            ----->coordinates and momenta
     if print data=true
        call energy
        write intermediate results
     endif
   enddo
else
write "input iop error"
endif
end program main

subroutine verlet()
if iop=1,2...
   adjust velocities for different iops
endif
```

```
do i=1, number of atoms
    update the velocity of each atom
    except thermal bath ----->velocity verlet algorithm
enddo
call force                -----> force evaluation
do i=1, number of atoms
    update momenta of each atom
    except thermal bath ----->velocity verlet algorithm
enddo
if iop=1,2...
    adjust momenta
    apply Berendsen methods
endif
end verlet subroutine

subroutine forces()
do i=1, number of stretches ----->harmonic strech forces
    r[i]=...        ----->bond length calculation
    f[i]=constant1*(r[i]-constant2)^2 ----->force evaluation
enddo
do i=1, number of bending terms ----->harmonic bending forces
    angle[i]=...        ----->bond angle calculation
    f[i]=constant1*(angle[i]-constant2) ----->force evaluation
enddo
call itralj        ----->intra-molecular Lennar_Jones forces
do i=1, number of lj forces
    lj evaluation
enddo
call interlj            ----->inter-molecular Lennard-Jones forces
do i=1, number of atoms
    build neighbor count list of lj terms
    calculate lj forces
enddo
end force subroutine

subroutine energy()
    total energy = potential energy + kinetic energy
end energy subroutine
```

*iop is the option to select different model systems

iop = 1: constant load, pull center of mass of upper surface
iop = 2: constant load, pull outer layer atoms in the upper surface
iop = 3: constant distance, pull center of mass of the upper surface
iop = 4: constant distance, pull outer layer atoms in the upper surface

where load is the force applied to the upper surface that brings
two surfaces together and the pull force is the lateral force that
moves the upper surface with respect to the bottom surface so that
upper surface can slide on the bottom surface.

Appendix: B. OpenMP Code

```
parallel for loops in force subroutine, master thread takes care
of the rest.
#pragma omp parallel for default(shared) private(local variable)
          reduction(+:inter)

do i=1, number of forces terms(strech, bend, Lennard-Jones)
    local variable= local variable evaluation
    r[i]=...
    angle[i]=...
    f[i]= function of (local variables, r[i], angle[i], etc)
    inter=  + calculated intermediate physical quantities
enddo
```

Appendix: C. MPI Code

```
MPI initialization
if processor id=0
        call readin()        -----> read in data
    write initial information
endif
do i=1, total number of integration steps
    if processor id=0
        MPI_Bcast initial coordinates
    endif
    localload = calculate work load for each processor
    do i=1,localload      -----> for each processor
        local_r[i]=...
        local_angle[i]=...
        .....
        local[i]=....
    enddo
    localload = distribute evenly the atoms in neighborlist
              to each processor
    do i=1, localload
        f[i]=Lennard-Jones terms on each processor
    enddo
    if processor id=0
        MPI_Reduce  ----->force summation on to processor 0
        MPI_Gather  ----->gather bond length, angle and
                  ----->other variables
        update coordinates and momenta using
        velocity verlet algorithm
        call energy to calculate energy
        write intermediate results
    endif
enddo
MPI_Finalize
```

Appendix: D. *Strings* DSM Code

```
DSM initialization
Create DSM global regions for shared data
fork threads on local and remote machines
for all threads
   if current thread is the first one on current node
        call readin()        -----> read in data
     write initial information
   endif
   do i=1, total number of integration steps
    reach a barrier to wait for all threads' arrival
    localload = calculate work load for each processor
    do i=1,localload      -----> for each processor
           local_r[i]=...
           local_angle[i]=...
           .....
           local[i]=....
    enddo
    localload = distribute evenly the atoms in neighborlist
                to each processor
    do i=1, localload
        f[i]=Lennard-Jones terms on each processor
    enddo
    acquire critical section lock
          update coordinates and momenta using
          velocity verlet algorithm
          call energy to calculate energy
          write intermediate results
     release critical section lock
   enddo
   DSM terminates
endfor
```

Chapter 17

HIGH PERFORMANCE AIR POLLUTION
SIMULATION ON SHARED MEMORY SYSTEMS

María J. Martín, Marta Parada and Ramón Doallo

Computer Architecture Group, University of A Coruña, 15071 A Coruña, Spain

{mariam,doallo}@udc.es

Abstract   The aim of this work is to provide a high performance air quality simulation using the STEM-II (Sulphur Transport Eulerian Model 2) program, a large pollution modelling application. The execution of the sequential program on a workstation requires significant CPU time and memory resources. Thus, in order to reduce the computational cost, we have applied parallelization techniques to the most costly parts of the original source code. Experimental results on a 32-processor SGI Origin 2000 show that the parallel program achieves important reductions in the execution times. This will allow us to obtain results in valid response times and with the adequate reliability for the industrial environment where it is intended to be applied.

Keywords: Air pollution model, STEM-II, Shared-memory systems, OpenMP

1.   Introduction

Air pollution chemistry models need to solve tens to hundreds of gas-phase chemical reactions, coupled to the air pollution transport. Gas-phase chemistry is a heavy task for uniprocessor workstations. Aqueous chemistry and scavenging processes add more complexity to the problem; thus, parallel systems should be applied to achieved a reasonable response time.

The STEM-II [1] is an air quality model used for simulating the behavior of pollutants in the air. It includes different pollutant emissions, transport by advection, convection and turbulence, with dynamic meteorological conditions; chemical transformation by gas-phase and aqueous-phase, and pollutants removal by dry and wet deposition. This model is being applied together with a meteorological prediction model to verify the environmental impact caused by As Pontes Power Plant. This plant is located in the NW of Spain, Galicia, an Atlantic climate region with intermediate terrain. As a result of that, the meteorological conditions are very changeable, and the terrain influence in the plume transport is significant. Air pollution prediction can provide a pre-alert to the power plant staff, in order to decide the coal mixing to burn along the following day, depending on the meteorological prediction and the energy production planned.

In this work, we present a parallel version of the STEM–II code on a distributed shared memory (DSM) machine, specifically we have tested our parallel version on a SGI O2000 multiprocessor. First, a sequential optimization of the program is carried out mainly focusing on the optimization of memory accesses. A 16.87% reduction of the execution time of the sequential program has been obtained. Then, we tried an automatic parallelization of the code using the automatic parallelizer available on the SGI platforms, PFA [5]. Unfortunately, the automatic parallelizer does not obtain speedup since it is only able to detect trivially-parallel innermost loops. Then, we focus on the manual parallelization of the most time consuming stages of the program using OpenMP shared memory directives. OpenMP is nowadays a standard 'de facto' for shared memory parallel programming. Using OpenMP the shared memory parallel programs can be made portable across a wide range of platforms. The standard defines a set of directives and library routines for both Fortran and C/C++ [2, 4]. A parallel version of the code on a distributed memory machine using the MPI message-passing library can also be found in [3].

This paper is organized as follows. Section 2 describes air quality modelling focusing mainly on the STEM-II model. Section 3 presents a detailed analysis of the sequential STEM-II program. In this section the most time-consuming parts of the program are identified. Section 4 explains the different optimization techniques applied to the sequential code and shows the results obtained. In Section 5 the parallelization of the program using OpenMP directives is discussed. This section includes the experimental results obtained with automatic parallelizer PFA. We end with a summary and the conclusions reached in this work.

2.   Air Pollution Modelling

The study of pollution in the air requires the development of models which are able to describe and to predict the behavior of atmospheric pollutants. In this way, it is possible to design actions for the maintenance of a healthy environment. Air quality models are computer-based models which calculate the distribution of the pollutants in the atmosphere from specified emission sources and meteorological scenarios.

In the literature there are a large number of alternatives for the representation of the pollutants flow in the atmosphere. These approaches do not represent exactly the behavior of the real atmosphere. Its deviation depends on the meteorological conditions, the size of the considered region, the type of considered emissions, the time scales of prediction, and the average time demanded for that prediction. All these factors determine the selection of one model for each particular case.

Due to the wet environment in As Pontes and the noticeable SO_2 concentrations of emissions of the power plant, a complete study will be feasible only by means of the modelling and the simulation of the gas-phase and aqueous-phase chemistry. We decided to use the Sulphur Transport Eulerian Model 2 (STEM–II).

2.1 The STEM-II model

STEM-II is an Eulerian air quality model which simulates transport, chemical transformations, emissions and depositions processes in an integrated framework. It depends on weather forecast data and it includes many chemical reactions and transport simulation for both dry and wet conditions. The program is modular in structure and this permits us to split the simulation of the dispersion of pollutants. It is not scale-specific nor region specific except as the input data depend on particular locations and as the physical, chemical and meteorological modules relate to certain time and length scales. It can be driven by observed or modelled meteorological data.

The basic component parts of the STEM–II model are shown schematically in Figure 17.1. The program requires as input data the initial chemical concentrations, topological data, and meteorological data as temperature, cloud bottom height, surface precipitation rates, etc. The output consists of spatially and temporally resolved gaseous and aqueous concentrations fields of each modelled species, as well as reaction rates, fluxes out of or into the modelling domain, amount deposited, and ionic concentrations of hydrometeors. In addition the model also calculates mass inventories of selected species, and total sulphur, nitrogen and carbon balances. The model is described in deep in [1], which can be referred to for more details on its mathematical, computational, physical and chemical structure.

The STEM-II code has been used for simulating the environment of the Power plant of As Pontes, estimating the depositions of oxidized S and N generated by emissions of this power station. The meteorological data are provided by a meteorological prediction model. The simulated environment covers an area of $61 \times 61 \ km^2$ centered in the power plant; vertically it goes up to 4200m. The application is computationally intensive and therefore an excellent candidate to be parallelized.

3. Sequential Profile of the STEM-II Program

The pseudocode of the STEM-II model is shown in Figure 17.2. The nested loop structure is similar to any simulation based on a finite difference method. The sequential program consists of 4 main nested loops: a temporal loop (loop_t), and a loop for each dimension of the simulated space (loop_x, loop_y and loop_z). The temporal loop specifies the duration of the simulation process and the time

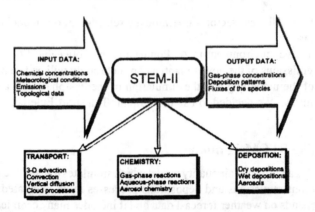

Figure 17.1. Simplified block diagram of STEM–II program

simulated in each iteration. Usually meteorological prediction data are used to evaluate the pollutants behavior of next day, therefore we will need to simulate at least 24 real hours. In our experiments each iteration of the temporal loop corresponds to a minute of real time. Besides, there exists a fifth loop, loop_trfl, corresponding to the reaction time of the aqueous-phase.

The basic modules and routines of the program are shown (in lower case and bold letter) in the figure. The main modules in the program are: horizontal transport module (hor), vertlq module and I/O module. Inside the vertlq module, the vertical transport and the chemical reactions are calculated. The horizontal transport and the chemical simulation processes are independent. Regarding the I/O module, before starting the temporal loop the time independent data are read. These data are: longitude and latitude of the domain, topography of the environment and initial concentration of the pollutants. In each iteration of the temporal loop the time-dependent data are read. These data are: density of the air, relative humidity, the temperature in each point of the grid, the components of wind, velocity of deposition, etc. Most of these input data are supplied by a meteorological simulation model. Finally, the output of the program provides the pollutant concentrations in all the points of the grid.

3.1   Computational cost

All the experiments were executed on a SGI O2000 multiprocessor. The Origin 2000 is a DSM (*Distributed Shared Memory*) with cache coherence maintained via a directory-based protocol (Cache-Coherent Non-Uniform Memory Access system, CC-NUMA). The system includes architectural features to address the NUMA aspects of the machine. The processors have a pair of counters implemented on the chip processor which allow the occurrence of several events in the system to be evaluated (cache memory misses, floating point operations, load and store operations ...). These hardware counters make it possible to profile the behavior of a program in many ways without modifying

```
input1: Input time independent data
DO loop_t
    input2: Input time dependent data
    hor: Horizontal transport


                        Begin vertlq Module

    DO loop_x
      DO loop_y
        IF (∃ gas_phase and ∃ aqueous_phase) THEN
            asmm : cloud parameters model (includes loop_z)
            vertcl: vertical transport for gas species (includes loop_z)
            DO loop_trfl
                vertcl: vertical transport for aqueous species (includes loop_z)
                rxn: chemical reaction (includes loop_z)
            END DO
        ELSE
            vertcl: vertical transport for gas species (includes loop_z)
            rxn: chemical reaction (includes loop_z)
        END IF
      END DO
    END DO

                        End vertlq Module

    output: Compute totals accumulated in the time and print result files
END DO
```

Figure 17.2. Pseudocode of the STEM-II program

the code. Cache memory has a two-level hierarchy (L1 and L2 caches). The replacement policy used in both levels is LRU (*Least Recently Used*).

The O2000 used in this work consists of 32 R10000 processors at 250 MHZ and IRIX 6.5 operating system, a 64-bit operating system. All the programs were compiled using the Fortran 77 compiler version 7.3.1 and compiler flags -64 -O3; using the -64 flag, pointers and long integers are 64 bits in length (then full advantage may be taken of the 64-bit operating system); the -O3 flag specifies the optimization level applied by the compiler (-O3 flag enables software pipelining and loop nest optimizations).

Figure 17.3 shows the execution time and percentages of the most important modules in the program for a sequential execution (using only one processor) of 300 iterations of the temporal loop, that is, a simulation of 5 real hours. We concluded that the vertlq module was the most costly part of the program.

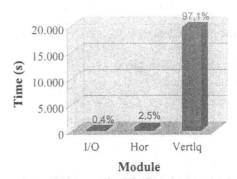

Figure 17.3.   Computational cost of the main modules in the STEM-II program

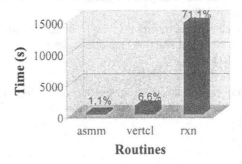

Figure 17.4.   Computational cost of the main routines in the vertlq module

In order to evaluate the importance of each process in greater detail, we have carried out an analysis of the computational cost of each routine inside the vertlq module. Figure 17.4 shows the results. As can be seen, the rxn routine is the most time-consuming stage in the program. This routine computes the chemical reactions, both in gas and aqueous phases, and it represents 71,1% of the execution time of the vertlq module.

4.   Optimization of the Sequential Code

The STEM-II code has large requirements of memory. A large number of variables are used (as physical information for each point of the mesh, concentration of species, temperatures, etc.) and must be stored using large arrays (for the simulated environment a total of 172 Mb of data memory is used). Thus, memory use and its access method greatly influences the efficiency of this code. This section analyzes the optimization of the sequential STEM-II program mainly focusing on memory accesses with the aim of increasing data locality. There exists in the bibliography well-known techniques to improve the performance of memory hierarchy [6]. Specifically we applied loop interchange for optimal data locality, loop fusion to reduce unnecessary memory references, loop distribution to increase register reuse, and loop unrolling to increase register, data cache and TLB locality. All these techniques have been applied, in different proportion, to the code inside the `vertlq` module, the most costly part inside the program. In some loops these techniques are automatically applied by the compiler when the optimization level 3 is used.

Additionally, we applied an array reordering technique with the aim of improving, even more, spatial data locality. This technique obtained the best results in terms of execution time reduction of the sequential program. It is explained in detail in next section.

4.1   Array reordering

The array reordering strategy is a two-phase technique. First, an analysis of the access order of arrays with 2 or more dimensions is carried out. Then, the storage order of these arrays is changed at the same time these data are accessed for the first time (when they are read from a file or generated for the first time in the program). Thus, consecutively accessed elements are stored in contiguous memory locations.

For instance, the array KV is generated inside the `input1` routine as shown in Figure 17.5(a). In Fortran the arrays are stored by columns, thus array KV is stored following the sequence:

$KV(0,0,0)$, $KV(1,0,0)$, $KV(2,0,0)$, ..., $KV(IX,0,0)$, $KV(0,1,0)$, $KV(1,1,0)$, $KV(2,1,0)$, ..., $KV(IX,1,0)$, ...

However, this array is used inside the `vertlq` module and accessed by rows in the way shown in Figure 17.5(b), which degrades the behavior of memory hierarchy. This problem could be solved by interchanging the loops, but in this case it is not possible due to dependences in other points of the program. Our proposal solution consists in changing the storage order of the array KV when this array is generated inside the `input1` routine as shown in Figure 17.5(c).

The array reordering technique is adequate for all the arrays accessed always in the same order through the program. Its overhead is worthless as the arrays are reordered at the same time they are stored in memory for the first time. The effect of this technique is exactly the same as a loop interchange technique, but loop interchange is not always possible due to dependences inside the loop. However, the reordering of arrays in memory does not present that problem.

4.2   Experimental results

Tables 17.1 and 17.2 shows a summary of the results obtained by applying all the optimization techniques. We are considering only one iteration of the temporal loop in all the measures. The execution times are expressed in seconds. Note that an improvement of 22.45% is obtained in the `vertlq` module. This is translated into an improvement of 16.87% in the execution time of the whole program; 96.18% of this improvement corresponds to the array reordering strategy.

```
DO i = 1, IX
    DO j = 1, IY
        DO k = 1, IZ
            KV(i, j, k) = (SIGMA * W(i, j, k) * 2)/0.324
        END DO
    END DO
END DO
```

(a) KV array generation

```
DO i = 1, IX
    DO j = 1, IY
    . . .
        DO k = 1, IZ
        . . .
            WT = (ABS(SUM * W) * DH(i, j) * DZ(k))/KV(i, j, k)
                 +KV(i, j, k + 1)
        . . .
        END DO
    . . .
    END DO
END DO
```

(b) KV array access

```
DO i = 1, IX
    DO j = 1, IY
        DO k = 1, IZ
            KV(k, j, i) = (SIGMA * W(i, j, k) * 2)/0.324
        END DO
    END DO
END DO
```

(c) KV array reordering

Figure 17.5.   Array reordering example

Table 17.1. Execution time for the original and the optimized program

	Original	Optim.
vertlq	60.77s	47.13s
TOTAL	77.59s	64.50s

Table 17.2. Improvement (in seconds and percentage) of the sequential program

	Time	%
vertlq	13.64s	22.45%
TOTAL	13.09s	16.87%

Table 17.3. L1 Cache misses in the original and optimized programs

	Original	Optim.
vertlq	80.88×10^6	43.23×10^6
TOTAL	94.90×10^6	59.60×10^6

Table 17.4. L2 Cache misses in the original and optimized programs

	Original	Optim.
vertlq	18.66×10^6	3.44×10^6
TOTAL	19.75×10^6	5.37×10^6

The reduction in the execution times illustrated in Tables 17.1 and 17.2 is a direct consequence of the improvement in data locality introduced by our optimizations. We have used the R10K event counters to measure L1 and L2 cache misses. Tables 17.3 and 17.4 show the results. Note that L2 cache misses are reduced by factor 4 in the optimized program.

5. Parallel Code Using OpenMP

After sequential optimization, the program was compiled using the PFA (Power Fortran Analyzer) automatic parallelizer [5]. We used this tool to parallelize our program and analyze the generated output. PFA was able to detect parallelism in some small loops inside the vertlq module, but it was not able to parallelize the outer loops (*loop_x* or *loop_y*) of this module because of the presence of a very complex structure of subroutine calls. In fact, the automatic parallelizer is too conservative with complex loops and too zealous with simple loops. In our case it did not help in the parallelization of our program because it was not able to determine if the iterations of the outer loops (*loop_x* or *loop_y*) were independent. Therefore, the programmer must study the feasibility of a more ambitious parallelization and include the appropriate directives.

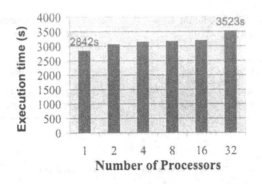

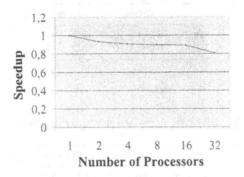

Figure 17.6.   Parallel performance of the STEM-II program provided by the PFA tool

Figure 17.6 shows the results obtained using PFA. We considered 60 iterations of the temporal loop (a simulation of 1 real hour) in all the measures. Note that the automatic parallelizer does not obtain any speedup. This is due to the fact that the parallelization of a loop implies some overhead caused by the creation and destruction of the corresponding threads. This overhead is greater as the number of processors increases. The execution time consumed by only one processor is even less than the time consumed by 32 processors, as can be seen in the figure. As only small loops are parallelized, the overhead overcomes the benefits obtained by the parallelization.

At the sight of the obtained results, it was necessary to carry out a manual parallelization to obtain a good performance in the program. We have focused again on the vertlq module. The outer loops of this module were not parallelized by the PFA compiler. The next step is to check if these loops can be parallelized, and insert the appropriate OpenMP directives.

The lack of dependences among different loop iterations will determine the chances of code parallelization. The vertlq module can be parallelized both in *loop_x* and in *loop_y*. The compiler does not allow nested parallelism, and therefore only *loop_x* or *loop_y* can be parallelized. In order to reduce the overhead of the parallelization the outer loop (*loop_x*) has been parallelized

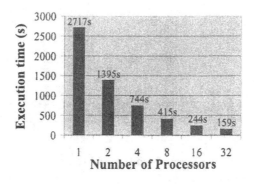

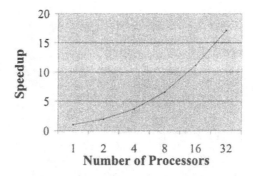

Figure 17.7.   Parallel performance of the **vertlq** module

We used the PARALLEL DO directive to carry out its parallelization specifying the *shared* and the *private* variables. The classification of all the variables inside its corresponding class (private or shared) was the most time consuming task of the parallelization process. It must be taken into account that all the private variables modified inside *loop_x* and used outside must be declared as *lastprivate* in order to keep their values outside the parallel region. In the same way, all the private variables modified before *loop_x* and used inside must be declared as *firstprivate* in order to keep their values inside the parallel region (by default, all the private variables are initialized to zero).

5.1   Results

We have executed the parallel code on the SGI O2000 in single-user mode. The implemented parallel code is independent of the number of processors, and it is portable to any type of shared memory multiprocessor system. We considered 60 iterations of the temporal loop (*loop_t*) in all these measures. Figure 17.7 shows the parallel performance of the **vertlq** module. As can be seen a reasonable scalability has been obtained.

Figure 17.8 shows the performance results of the parallel code for the whole program. Note that only the **vertlq** module has been parallelized; therefore,

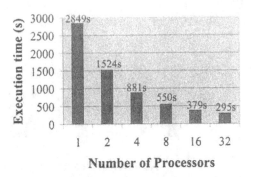

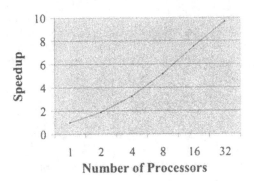

Figure 17.8.   Parallel performance of the STEM-II program

according to Amdahl's law, the speed up is limited by the sequential portion of the program. This sequential portion is proportionally more important as the number of processors increases and, thus, the performance of the parallelization degrades for a large number of processors.

Finally, we have evaluated the different scheduling strategies provided by OpenMP using the SCHEDULE directive. This directive admits three types of iteration distribution: static, dynamic and guided. The static is the strategy applied by default by our compiler (the default scheduling is implementation dependent), and it corresponds with a block cyclic distribution of the iterations. The dynamic is also a block cyclic distribution but in this case each thread obtains a new set of iterations as it finishes the previously assigned set. In the guided type the size of each block is reduced in an exponentially decreasing way. Figure 17.9 shows the results. As can be observed the scheduling strategy does not affect significantly to the parallel execution. This is due to the fact that a good load balance is obtained in all the cases. In our program there are not important differences in the workload between different iterations of $loop\_x$.

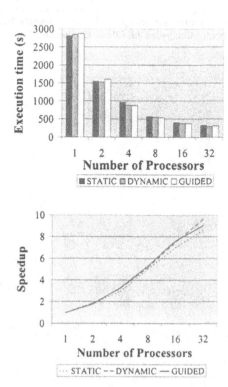

Figure 17.9. Parallel performance of the STEM-II program using different scheduling strategies

Acknowledgments

This work was funded by the European Union under the FEDER project (Ref: 1FD97-0118) and the CrossGrid project (Ref:IST-2001-32243). We gratefully thank CSC (Complutense Supercomputing Center, Madrid) for providing access to the SGI Origin 2000 multiprocessor.

References

[1] Carmichael, G.R., Peters, L.K., and Saylor, R.D. (1991). The STEM-II regional scale acid deposition and photochemical oxidant model - I. an overview of model development and applications. *Atmospheric Environment*, 25A:2077–2090.

[2] Chandra, Rohit, Menon, Ramesh, Dagum, Leo, David Kohr, Dror Maydan, and McDonald, Jeff (2000). *Parallel Programming in OpenMP*. Morgan Kaufmann Publishers.

[3] Mouriño, J.C., Martín, M.J., Doallo, R., and D.E. Singh, F.F. Rivera, J.D. Bruguera (2001). The STEM-II Air Quality Model on a Distributed Memory System. In *Workshop on High Performance Scientific and Engineering Computing with Applications, Proceedings of the 2001 ICPP Workshops*, pages 85–92.

[4] OpenMP (1997-2003). OpenMP, Simple, Portable, Scalable SMP Programming. http://www.openmp.org.

[5] PFA (1996). MIPSpro Power Fortran 77 Programmer's Guide. Silicon Graphics Inc.

[6] Wolfe, M.J. (1989). Optimizing supercompilers for supercomputers. Research Monographs in Parallel and Distributed Computing. MIT Press, Cambridge.

Chapter 18

AN ANT COLONY OPTIMIZATION BASED ROUTING ALGORITHM IN MOBILE AD HOC NETWORKS AND ITS PARALLEL IMPLEMENTATION

Parimala Thulasiraman*, Ruppa K. Thulasiram[†], and Mohammad T. Islam[‡]

Department of Computer Science, University of Manitoba, Winnipeg, MB, R3T 2N2, Canada
{thulasir,tulsi,towhid}@cs.umanitoba.ca

Abstract

A mobile ad hoc network (MANET) consists of mobile wireless nodes that communicate in a distributed fashion without any centralized administration. The nodes instantaneously and dynamically form a network on the fly when it is needed. We define an irregular application as one that changes the network dynamically during runtime, exhibits chaotic load balancing among the processors and unpredictable communication behavior among the nodes during runtime. An ad hoc network has all these characteristics and hence could be considered as an irregular application from the parallel computing perspective.

In this chapter, we describe the design of an on-demand routing algorithm called *source update* for MANETs using a metaheuristic based on the ant colony optimization (ACO) search technique. We develop a mechanism to detect cycles, parallelize this algorithm on a distributed memory machine using MPI, and study the performance of the parallel algorithm. We report the performance of this algorithm on a distributed network of workstations.

Keywords: Ant colony optimization, Parallel computing, Mobile ad hoc networks

*The author acknowledges the partial support from Natural Sciences and Engineering Research Council (NSERC) of Canada.
†The author acknowledges the partial support from Natural Sciences and Engineering Research Council (NSERC) of Canada.
‡The author is thankful for the graduate fellowship award from Faculty of Science, University of Manitoba, Graduate scholarship from department of computer science, and for the award of University of Manitoba Graduate Fellowship (UMGF).

1.   Introduction

In recent years there has been a growing interest in "ad hoc" networks. A mobile ad hoc network (MANET) consists of mobile wireless nodes that communicate in a distributed fashion without any centralized administration. Due to the node's mobility, it is difficult to determine a network topology that the nodes can utilize at any given instance of time to route the data. The nodes instantaneously and dynamically form a network on the fly when they are needed. Therefore, ad hoc networks are also called as "infrastructureless" networks. These nodes are operated by low power batteries which limits their transmission range to nodes that are closest to them. Nodes that are out of range communicate through intermediate nodes. A node, therefore, serves as both a host and also as a router transmitting data to other mobile nodes that may not be within the transmission range. In an ad hoc routing protocol, each node can discover multihop paths through the dynamic network to any other node. Ad hoc networks have applications in areas such as military, health or any situation where the geographical nature of the system cannot be determined and therefore requires a totally distributed network topology.

We define an irregular application as one that changes the network dynamically during runtime, exhibits chaotic load balancing among the processors and unpredictable communication behaviour among the nodes during runtime. An ad hoc network has all these characteristics and hence could be considered as an irregular application [31] from the parallel computing perspective. Also, note that the computation per node is fine-grained in the sense that the task of each mobile node is limited due to its low powered batteries. In this chapter, we focus on all-pair routing between the nodes (that is, determine the best path from any node to any other node in the network). To our knowledge, the parallel implementation of an all-pair routing algorithm for ad hoc networks has not been reported in the literature.

In this chapter, we describe the design of an on-demand routing algorithm for MANET's using a metaheuristic search technique based on *swarm intelligence* [4, 6, 30]. In particular, we employ the ant colony optimization (ACO) search technique [14, 13], which is a subset of swarm intelligence. The ACO techniques have been used in many combinatorial optimization and scheduling problems. This technique is inspired by real ants in nature that are capable of finding the shortest path from the source to the nest [1]. The ants communicate their designated selection of paths by depositing a substance called *pheromone* on the ground, thereby establishing a trail. The amount of pheromone deposited varies in quantities. An ant chooses a trail depending on the amount of pheromone deposited on the ground. The larger the concentration of pheromone in a particular trail, the greater is the probability of the trail being selected by an ant. The ant then reinforces the trail with its own pheromone. The idea behind this technique is that the more the ants follow a particular trail, the more attractive is that trail for being followed by other ants. These ants use the notion of *stigmergy* to communicate indirectly among the ants and dynamically find a path when needed.

The focus of this work, is to design, develop a routing algorithm for MANETs using the ACO technique and implement on a distributed memory multiprocessor using MPI. Parallelization has been considered for many static applications using ACO [8, 12, 19, 26, 29] in the literature. We consider a dynamic application (MANET) and apply the parallel ACO algorithm.

The rest of the chapter is organized as follows. In the next section, we briefly outline the related work on ad hoc networks and ACO. In section 3, we present our routing algorithm called *source update*. In section 4, we discuss the results of our experiments conducted on the distributed memory architecture. In section 5 we derive some conclusions.

2. Background

In this section, we briefly discuss the background and related work for ad hoc networks and ant colony optimization metaheuristic.

2.1 Ad hoc networks

An ad hoc network is a collection of mobile nodes that route packets without any central administration or standard support services like those available on wired networks. These nodes are operated by low powered batteries which limits their transmission range to nodes that are closest to them. For example, consider Figure 18.1 with three wireless mobile hosts. The circles around the nodes indicate that these nodes are within transmission range. Nodes 1 and 2 are reachable from one another as nodes 2 and 3 are also reachable. However, node 3 in this case is not in the transmission range of node 1. If node 1 and 3 wish to communicate (route packets), they need to get the aid of the intermediate node, node 2, to route or forward the packets since node 2 is within the transmission range of both node 1 and node 3. A node, therefore, acts as both a host and a router transmitting data to other mobile nodes that may not be within the transmission range. Suppose another node is added to the above network (Figure 18.2). The situation changes considerably, since there are now multiple paths between nodes 1 and 3. We can route packets from 1-2-3 or 1-4-3 or 1-2-4-3. The situation becomes more complicated when more nodes are involved in the network. An ad hoc routing protocol must, therefore, determine the "best" path to route the packets between the nodes.

Another problem that may be unique to wireless networks is when we assume uni-directional links between the nodes. Consider Figure 18.3. Node 1 in this figure has a large enough transmission range to route a packet to node 3. However, node 3 has a short transmission range and requires the help of node 2 to route the packets. If we redesign this as a graph, there is an edge from 1 to 3, from 3 to 2 and not from 3 to 1. However, the ad hoc routing protocols assume that the links are bidirectional (undirected graph).

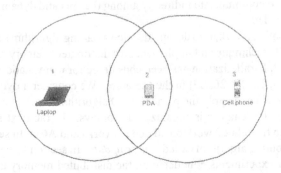

Figure 18.1.   An Adhoc Network with 3 nodes

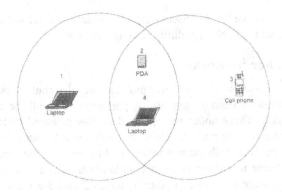

Figure 18.2.   An Adhoc Network with one additional node

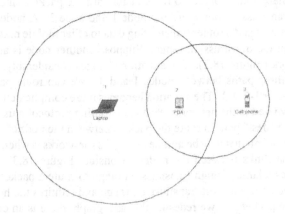

Figure 18.3.   An ad hoc network with varying transmission range

The nodes in the network are dynamic in nature due to their mobility. There is no fixed network topology that the nodes can use at any given instance of time. New nodes may unexpectedly enter the network and the existing nodes may shut down or move away from the network. Thus, the nodes instantaneously form a network on the fly when they are needed. Also, the bandwidth of the links between the nodes is very limited. They operate at significantly lower bit rates than wired networks. Ad hoc networking protocols must ensure that there is not too much flooding of packets which may consume large amount of bandwidth. The routing protocols must also ensure that the packets are not routed in a cycle which consume valuable bandwidth. Therefore, a fast convergence rate is very critical for ad hoc networks in finding the shortest path.

The ad hoc routing protocols maybe classified as proactive (table driven) or reactive (demand driven) routing protocols.

In table driven protocols, all nodes keep one or more tables that keep up to date information about all other nodes in the network. When a node joins or leaves the network, update messages are relayed to all the nodes. Destination-Sequenced Distance-Vector (DSDV) routing protocol [25] is a table driven and one of the earliest routing protocol developed. It applies the Bellman-Ford [2] routing algorithm with certain improvements. In DSDV protocol packets are routed between nodes using a routing table. Global State Routing (GSR) [9] is similar to DSDV but improves upon DSDV protocol by avoiding flooding of packets relying on the link state routing protocols. However, the drawback of GSR is the large update messages (each update message contains information about all nodes) that are necessary to keep the routing table up to date, which wastes network bandwidth. To solve this problem, the Fisheye State Routing (FSR) [23] protocol exchanges information between nodes that are closer than nodes that are farther. Wireless routing protocol [21] is based on path-finding algorithms that are attractive for wireless networks, solving some of the drawbacks of other protocols which are based on distributed shortest path algorithm.

On-demand routing protocols create routing tables when they require. Not all updates are preserved at every node. Cluster Based Routing Protocol (CBRP) [20], Dynamic Source Routing (DSR) [18], Temporally-Ordered Routing Algorithm (TORA) [22] and Ad hoc On Demand Distance Vector (AODV) [24] are all on-demand routing protocols. In CBRP the nodes are divided into clusters with the nodes that are closer belonging to one cluster. Each cluster has a leader or cluster head that has complete knowledge of the nodes within its cluster. DSR uses the source routing technique where the sender of a packet determines the sequence of nodes through which this packet needs to be forwarded. TORA is a distributed algorithm that is very scalable. It is a source-initiated on-demand routing protocol. AODV allows both unicast and multicast routing.

Core-Extraction Distributed Ad hoc Routing (CEDAR) [28] algorithm focuses on QoS routing in ad hoc networks. Zone Routing Protocol (ZRP) [17] is a hybrid algorithm that addresses the problem of proactive and reactive routing schemes by combining both of these schemes. Optimized Link State Routing protocol [10], is a proactive link state routing protocol. It involves periodic message exchanges for topological information in each node in the network. For more information on routing protocols, please refer to [32].

2.2   Ant colony optimization metaheuristic

Swarm of bees, swarm of ants or schools of fish provide an useful intuition to solve many hard problems in combinatorial optimization, distributed networks and now distributed wireless networks. Swarm intelligence [1, 4, 5, 27, 33] is an area inspired by observing the behavior of insects such as wasps, ants or honeybees. In particular, the ants, for example, have very little intelligence and live in a hostile and dynamic environment. However, with the aid of other ants they cooperate to survive and learn about their environment, thereby performing tasks such as finding food easier.

Dorigo et. al [14] first applied the ACO metaheuristic to the classical traveling salesperson problem (TSP) and compared it to other methods such as tabu search and simulated annealing. Bullnheimer et.al. [7] considered the vehicle routing problem using ACO. Bland [3] addressed the space planning problem together with tabu search. ACO has also been studied in quadratic assignment problem [4], graph coloring [16] and scheduling problems [12].

One of the critical parameters to consider is the amount of pheromone that evaporates at a given time and the interval of time for which the pheromone scent is stronger. We can assume ants to be mobile agents that collectively cooperate to perform a task. These ants are dynamic and move randomly. Ants may join a group or leave the group when they desire. This analogy falls directly for ad hoc networks which are also dynamic and communicate from point to point.

The ACO technique is quite amenable to ad hoc networks due to their similar characteristics. An artificial ant acts like a mobile agent or a node in an ad hoc network. An ant creates a path dynamically on the fly as the routing protocols in MANETs. Though the communication between ants is very minimal as in MANETs, the communication links may change dynamically and hence a node routes packets depending on the link conditions. Similarly, an ant can also exploit the link conditions in the amount of pheromone it deposits on a trail. A recent paper [15] introduces a new on-demand routing algorithm for ad hoc networks called ARA (Ant-Colony-Based Routing Algorithm) using the ant colony technique. Their algorithm is implemented on the ns-2 simulator. The algorithm, however, is not scalable and does not detect cycles in the network.

2.3   Parallelization techniques for ACO

The ACO is an inherently parallelizable technique, but little research has been conducted in this aspect. An initial investigation of the parallelization techniques for ACO was studied by Bullnheimer et.al. [8], however, was not implemented. Stützle [29] applied a master slave approach to parallelize the

ACO searches. The algorithm is easily applicable to multiple instruction multiple data architectures. Michel et.al. [19], developed an island model where separate ant colonies exchange trail information. Different parallel decomposition strategies is explained in Randall [26], which is specifically applied to the TSP. The work studies an empirical evaluation of one particular scheme, called *parallel ants* by implementing the technique on a message passing environment using MPI. Another ACO parallelization technique by Delisle et.al. [12] for industrial scheduling problem is examined using the OpenMP language on a shared memory multiprocessor.

3. Parallel ACO Routing Algorithm

An ad hoc network is composed of nodes and links associated with a weight on each link. The weight on the links may represent the distance, transmission range, time during which the nodes may interact and so on. In our case, we consider the weight as the time parameter. The network can be represented as a graph $G = (V, E)$ where V is the number of vertices (nodes) and E is the number of edges (links).

We apply the ACO metaheuristic search algorithm to find the shortest or best path from a given source to the destination. Each link $e = (v_i, v_j)$ is associated with two variables. $\varphi(v_i, v_j)$, represents the pheromone value on each link and $w(v_i, v_j)$ represents the time (a period for which the links may be in connection). The pheromone value gets updated by the ants as they traverse the links. The ants change the concentration of the pheromone value on their journey to the destination and on their way back to the source.

In our algorithm, an ant chooses a node that produces the best path from the node to the destination. To do so, an ant first selects a node that has not yet been visited by other ants. The reason behind this is as follows: Assume an ant randomly chooses a node v_j from v_i to traverse and adjusts the pheromone concentration. Let us assume that another ant also follows the same trail. Since the pheromone value on the trail considered is higher (due to its recent traversal) than the other neighboring trails it may select this node again. However, the ant does not know if this path leads to the best path. Ants maybe following a trail that may lead to a longer path. To avoid this situation, we *explore* all nodes not yet considered (visited) before we rely on the pheromone value. Our algorithm can be considered as an *exploration* technique rather than an exploitation mechanism.

If there exists no such unvisited node, the ant searches for the next hop by considering the pheromone concentration. Each node contains a routing table (RT). The size of RT is the degree of the node times all the nodes in the network. That is, if we assume the number of nodes in the network is N and degree of node v_i is d_i, then the size of the table is Nd_i. The rows indicate the neighbors of node v_i and the column represents all the nodes in the network. Since the number of nodes in an ad hoc network is small, this routing table is feasible.

When an ant arrives at a node v_i from a source S to travel to destination D, it considers the node's RT to select its path or the next hop neighbor. It considers node v_i's neighbors, v_j, by looking at each row in the routing table and column D. By considering column D, the ant selects the *best path* from a neighboring node v_j to D rather the best link from $w(v_i, v_j)$. Therefore, it is possible that an ant may take several hops to reach the destination. This is indicated in the pheromone concentration in each of the rows in column D. The greater the pheromone concentration for a particular neighbor v_j, the greater is the probability that this node will lead to the best path.

There are two entries in the routing table for a particular (row, column) pair: a bit indicating whether the node has been visited by other ants and the pheromone content. If there exists at least one neighbor that is not visited by any previous ants in column D, the ant chooses this node as the next hop node; otherwise, it considers to check the pheromone concentration. The value of the pheromone that is the largest is regarded as the next hop neighbor. However, before selecting this node, the ant determines if it has already visited the node before. This is to ensure that the ant does not travel in a cycle. For example, an ant at node v_m may travel to node v_n; v_n in turn may choose to move to node v_p; at this point v_p may choose to go node v_m again. However, v_m is already visited. Therefore, to circumvent this situation, each ant holds a list (called *VisitedHop*) of all the nodes that have been visited by the ant on its current journey to D. An entry of 1 in the list indicates that the ant has visited the node before. An ant also keeps a stack data structure, which contains all the nodes that may give a promising path to D. The maximum size of the stack is $|V|$. If due to obstruction in the environment, it returns to the same node that has already been visited, indicating a cycle, the ant immediately backtracks to the previous node from where it came by using the stack data structure. The list allows the ant to detect cycles. Also note that there may be a situation where there is no path from the current node. In this case it uses the stack to backtrack. An ant keeps in its memory the total time (T) it has travelled thus far.

If a node v_j is selected as the next hop of node v_i, the ant moves to the next node v_j and the pheromone update is as follows for entry (v_i,S) in v_j's RT:

$$\varphi(v_i, v_S) = \varphi(v_i, v_S) + \frac{\epsilon}{T(v_S, v_i) + w(v_i, v_j)} \tag{18.1}$$

where ϵ is a runtime parameter provided by the user. On all other nodes in column S the pheromone value is decremented by

$$\varphi(v_l, v_S) = (1 - E)\varphi(v_l, v_S), \forall\, l \neq i \tag{18.2}$$

where E is the evaporation rate of the pheromone. E is a variable parameter also provided by the user. Since we are updating the source column in the RT we call this as *source update* technique. Each ant also records the total time of the path just traversed as $T(v_S, v_i) + w(v_i, v_j)$.

On its way back to the source, an ant again updates the pheromone concentration. However, it updates it for the *destination* column. It uses the stack to backtrack to the source. For example, an ant at node v_k travelling backwards from node v_b looks at the rows of v_b's neighboring nodes and column D. The pheromone concentration update for entry (v_b, v_D) is :

$$\varphi(v_b, v_D) = \varphi(v_b, v_D) + \frac{\epsilon}{T'} \qquad (18.3)$$

where T' is $T(v_S, v_D) - T(v_S, v_k)$. This emphasizes more pheromone concentration on the path that is closest to the destination. All other neighboring node's pheromone concentration in column D are decremented as above (equation (2)).

Note that by allowing an ant to always perform the source update, it allows another ant which considers the source as the destination to find the path easily. That is, if node v_i is the source for an ant travelling to destination v_d, then the ant updates the pheromone content of the source column in the RT of the node (v_k) that it has just visited and selects the next hop by considering the entries in the destination column for the neighboring nodes of v_k. By doing so, the ant selects the next node based on the best path that one of its neighboring nodes can provide. Also, updating the source column indicates the best available path that is reachable from the source to v_k. When another ant considers v_i as its destination, it always considers the destination column (v_i) to find the best path. The pheromone concentration in the entries in v_i indicates the best path from its current node's neighbors to v_i. This is already updated by the arrival of previous ants that considered it as the source resulting in determining the overall best path to the destination. The step by step algorithm for an ant moving from source S to destination D is as follows:

Forward ant algorithm:

1 Initialize the edges with initial pheromone concentration (a small constant).

2 Push S and the total time traversed thus far, $Total\_Time$ onto the stack.

3 Enlist S into the $VisitedHop$ table of the ant. Let $N_{Current}$ represent the set of neighboring nodes of $Current$.

4 Let $Current = S$.

5 While ($Current$ not equal to destination D) do

   ■ Select the next hop node ($NextHop$) using the $Current$ hop node information

      – Look at all the unvisited neighboring nodes of $NextHop$ using the routing table. That is, look at column D and determine the next node of $Current$ that produces the best path.

- If all nodes have been visited then look at the pheromone concentration (PH) in column D for all neighbors. Select the node with most pheromone concentration. $NextHop = \max_{v_j \in N_{Current}}(PH(v_j, D))$. The greater pheromone value is considered as the next hop node only if the next hop node ($NextHop$) is not visited by the ant already. This information can be obtained from the ant's $VistedHop$ table. (Detects cycles).

- If $NextHop$ is found
  - Let the previous hop parameter $PreHop = Current$.
  - $Current = NextHop$.
  - The ant keeps a record of the total time traversed : Total_Time = Total_Time + $w(PreHop, Current)$.
  - Source Update: Update the routing table for $NextHop$ using the $PreHop$ and source information. Increase the pheromone value in entry $(PreHop, S)$ by equation (1) and decrease pheromone value on all other entries in column S by equation (2).
  - Push the $Current$ node and Total_Time on to the stack.
  - Set the entry in the $Current$ node in the $VisitedHop$ list of the ant to 1.

- else (there is no way to move from this $Current$ node)
  - Pop the $Current$ node from the stack.
  - Set $Current$ and the time to the previous node ($PreHop$) and time at the top of the stack respectively.
  - If $Current = S$ (happens if there is an isolated node in the network)
    * It considers other paths from source (Step 5). If none is found, the ant dies.

Backward ant algorithm:

1 Pop the stack. (Remove the last information which contains the destination node)

2 While ($Current \neq S$)

- Set $PreHop = Current$.
- Pop the $Current$ node and *time* from the stack.
- Set $T' = T(v_S, v_D) - T(v_S, v_k)$.
- Update the routing table of the $Current$ node for destination D column. Increase the pheromone concentration on $(Prehop, D)$ by equation (3) and decrease all other entries in column D by equation (2).

We illustrate our algorithm with an example. Figure 18.4 shows the network of an eight node graph. Each link is associated with a delay parameter. In the table, PH denotes the pheromone concentration and Visit denotes the total number of times the ant has visited this node. Note that, the values in the entries are the actual values obtained by executing the parallel algorithm on the network.

We assume the ant is moving from the source $S = 3$ to destination, $D = 6$. We assume here that the ant has selected node 4 as its next hop ($NextHop = 4$) link. Therefore, the current node $Current$ is 4. At this point, node 4 performs the source update. The RT for node 4 before this update is shown in the Figure 18.5. The ant has memory of the source and the previous hop ($PreHop = 3$) node. It performs the source update by modifying entry (3,3) by increasing the pheromone value on (3,3) from 32.8 to 57.8 and the Visit entry from 4 to 5. For all other entries ((2,3),(5,3)) it decrements the pheromone value. The RT after the update is also shown for node 4 in Figure 18.6.

At node 4, the ant selects the next hop node to traverse. The ant needs to reach destination 6. So, it looks at the destination column, 6. The pheromone value in column 6, indicates the best path to choose. We don't consider the next hop node by looking at the individual links from the current node to its neighbor. Instead, we consider the best path that will reach the destination from a particular node. This path maybe a few hops away from the node.

Since all nodes have been visited by previous ants, it considers the pheromone concentration and selects node 5 as the next hop ($NextHop = 5$) node. It updates the number of visits from 10 to 11. The ant then moves to node 5. The RT before source update is shown in the Figure 18.7. Since the previous hop was 4, the ant updates the entry (4,3) (source update technique) by increasing the pheromone concentration (45 to 54) and increasing the Visit entry (6 to 7). It decrements the pheromone values on links (6,3) and (7,3). However, since the value was already 0, there is no update on these entries. The RT after source update for node 5 is shown in Figure 18.8.

Now, note that it is very easy from the table to realize the next node selected by the ant at node 5. We look at the destination column, 6. Since the neighboring node, 6, produces greater value (166.4), this node is selected. When the ant moves to node 6, it realizes it has reached the destination. After the source update at node 6, the backward ant resumes execution.

The same situation as indicated above happens when the ant traverses backward, with the exception that the destination column is updated.

4.   Experimental Results

In this section, we present the performance results of our parallel ACO routing algorithm on a 10 node network of workstations running MPI. All networks were generated by the NETGEN random graph generator [11].

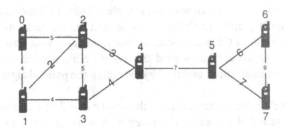

Figure 18.4.   An Example

Source = 3 Destination = 6 Current Node = 4

Routing Table of Node 4 (Before Source Update)

Network Node	0		1		2		3		4		5		6		7		Total	
Neighbor	PH	Visit																	
2	1	1	97.6	8	111.7	5	**38.7**	**5**	0	0	0	1	*0*	*2*	0	1	249	23
3	42	7	1	1	11.7	4	**32.8**	**4**	0	0	0	0	*0*	*1*	0	1	87.5	18
5	0	2	0	1	0	0	**0**	**1**	0	0	140	10	*67*	*10*	64	10	271	34

Figure 18.5.   Routing table of 4 before source update

Source = 3 Destination = 6 Current Node = 4

Routing Table of Node 4(After Source Update)

Network Node	0		1		2		3		4		5		6		7		Total	
Neighbor																			
2	1	1	97.6	8	111.7	5	**27.1**	**5**	0	0	0	1	*0*	*2*	0	1	237.4	23
3	42	7	1	1	11.7	4	**57.8**	**5**	0	0	0	0	*0*	*1*	0	1	112.5	19
5	0	2	0	1	0	0	**0**	**1**	0	0	140	10	*67*	*11*	64	10	271.0	35

Next Hop = 5

Figure 18.6.   Routing table of 4 after source update

Source = 3 Destination = 6 Current Node = 5

Routing Table of Node 5(Before Source Update)

Network Node	0		1		2		3		4		5		6		7		Total	
Neighbor																			
4	24	6	45	7	55	7	45	6	84	6	0	0	*0*	*1*	0	1	253	34
6	0	2	0	2	0	1	0	1	0	1	0	0	*166.4*	*11*	6	3	172.4	21
7	0	1	0	1	0	1	0	1	0	0	0	0	*0.2*	*1*	82.9	10	83.1	14

Figure 18.7.   Routing table of 5 before source update

Source = 3 Destination = 6 Current Node = 5

Routing Table of Node 5(After Source U pdate)

Network Node / Neighbor	0		1		2		3		4		5		6		7		Total	
4	24	6	45	7	55	7	54	7	84	6	0	0	0	1	0	1	262.0	35
6	0	2	0	2	0	1	0	1	0	1	0	0	182.4	12	6	3	188.4	22
7	0	1	0	1	0	1	0	1	0	0	0	0	0.2	1	82.9	10	83.0	14

Figure 18.8. Routing table of 5 after source and destination update

Figure 18.9 shows the scalability results as we increase the number of processors with and without source update for a network of 500 nodes. In the non-source update algorithm, the forward ant does not update the routing table. As can be seen from the figure, we achieve better performance with source update. In the source update algorithm, since we always select a node depending on the best path produced by a node to reach the destination, we obtain faster convergence and this indicated through the figure.

Figure 18.10 illustrates the scalability results with varying number of processors. As the figure indicates, the execution time decreases as we increase the number of processors. We assume here that the number of ants is equal to the number of processors, with one ant per processor. Given N, the number of nodes, and P, the number of processors, $\frac{N}{P}$ amount of data is distributed to the processors. Each ant, residing within a processor, determines the best route for its subgraph. It computes the all-pairs best route for each of its nodes in the subgraph. For example, with 500 nodes and 10 processors, each processor is allocated 50 nodes per processor. An ant executing on a processor communicates at least 50x450 times to compute the best route for all the pairwise nodes. However, as we notice from the figure, this does not degrade the performance of the algorithm. The percentage of communication time versus the number of processors is shown in Figure 18.11. We notice that there is faster convergence for larger nodes, thereby decreasing the percentage of communication as we increase the number of nodes in the network. Also, note that as we increase the data size, the amount of data per processor also increases, thereby increasing the computation overhead. However, the amount of computation per node is very fine-grained. That is, there is very minimal task per node. Therefore, the amount of computation is substantially lower than the communication overhead. As can be seen from Figure 18.12 for 500 nodes, the percentage of computation is only 3.5% on 10 processors. For ad hoc networks, the communication time is the bottleneck. However, our results indicate that our algorithm converges faster with increasing number of ants with varying number of processors.

Finally in Figure 18.13, we show the execution time by varying the number of ants with fixed number of nodes (200 and 300) and fixed number of processors (10). The figure clearly illustrates a decreasing execution time demonstrating the scalability of our parallel algorithm. The best result is obtained when we associate an ant with each processor. This obviously distributes the workload among the ants obtaining a good load balance. With just one ant, the ant is overloaded with work in finding the routes for all pairs of nodes in the network.

The relative speedup of the algorithm is little over 7 for 10 ants (10 processors) in Figure 18.14. Relative speedup is calculated as $\frac{Execution\_time\_of\_1\_ant}{Execution\_time\_of\_10\_ants}$. This speedup again illustrates the scalability of our algorithm.

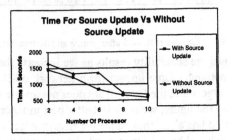

Figure 18.9.   Performance results with and without source update

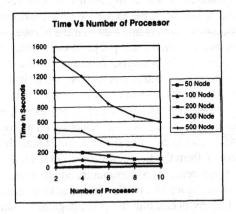

Figure 18.10.   Scalability results with varying number of processors and nodes

5.   Conclusions

In this chapter, we presented development of a parallel all-pair routing algorithm for MANETs using the Ant Colony Optimization (ACO) metaheuristic search technique. The algorithm was implemented on a network of workstations running MPI. We also developed a technique to detect cycles. The parallel algorithm based on source update scales well for varying node and machine sizes. We fixed the number of processors and nodes while varying the number of ants in the algorithm. We produced a gradual decrease in execution time and the best result was obtained when the number of ants was equal to the number of proces-

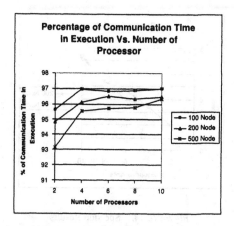

Figure 18.11. Number of processors versus percentage of communication time

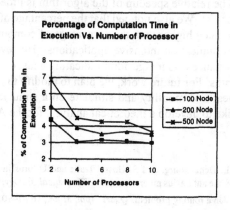

Figure 18.12. Number of processors versus percentage of computation time

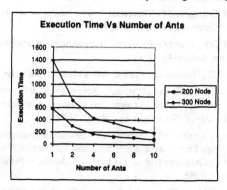

Figure 18.13. Number of ants versus Execution time with fixed number of processors and nodes

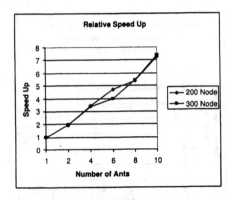

Figure 18.14.   Speedup Results

sors. This resulted in a good load balance due to the even distribution of work among the ants. The relative speedup of the algorithm is little more than 7 for 10 ants (10 processors). We also noticed that the percentage of communication among the ants is much higher than the percentage of computation by an ant. MANETs are communication intensive applications. However, this does not degrade the performance of our algorithm indicating a fast convergence rate in finding the best paths. For future work, we plan to modify the algorithm based on power awareness and mobility and simulate on a simulator such as ns-2. Also, we would like to develop a theoretical analysis for the ACO algorithm.

References

[1] R. Beckers, J.L. Deneubourg, and S. Goss. Trails and U-turns in the selection of the shortest path by the ant Lasius niger. *Journal of Theoretical Biology*, 159:397–415, 1992.

[2] R.E. Bellman. On a routing problem. *Quart. Appl. Math.*, 16:87–90, 1958.

[3] J.A. Bland. Space planning by any colony optimisation. *International Journal of computer applications in technology*, 12(6), June 1999.

[4] E. Bonabeau, M. Dorigo, and G. Theraulaz. *Swarm Intelligence: from natural to artificial systems*. Oxford University Press, Oxford, 1999.

[5] E. Bonabeau, M. Dorigo, and G. Theraulaz. Inspiration for optimization from social insect behaviour. *Nature*, 406:39–42, 2000.

[6] E. Bonabeau and G. Theraulaz. Swarm smarts. *Scientific American*, pages 72–79, 2000.

[7] B. Bullnheimer, R.F. Hartl, and C. Strauss. An improved ant system algorithm for the vehicle routing poblem. *Annals of Operations research: nonlinear economic dynamics and control (Eds. Dawid, Feichtinger and Hartl)*, 1999.

[8] B. Bullnheimer, G. Kostis, and C. Strauss. *Parallelization strategies for the ant systems*, volume 24. In High Performance Algorithms and Software in Nonlinear Optimization Series: Applied Optimization (Ed. R. De Leone, A. Murli, P. Pardalos and G. Toraldo), Kluwer, Dordrecht, 1998.

[9] Tsu-Wei Chen and Mario Gerla. Global state routing: A new routing scheme for ad-hoc wireless networks. In *Proceedings of the IEEE international conference on communications (ICC)*, pages 171–175, Atlanta, GA, June 1998.

[10] T.H. Clausen, P. Jacqet, A. Laouitu, and L. Viennot. Optimized link state routing protocol. In *IEEE international multi topic conference (INMIC)*, Karachi, Pakistan, 2001.

[11] A. Napier D. Klingman and J. Stutz. A program for generalizing large-scale (Un) capacitated assignment, transportation, and minimum cost flow network problems. In *Management Science*, volume 20, pages 814–822, 1974.

[12] P. Delisle, M. Krakecki, M. Gravel, and C. Gagné. Parallel implementation of an ant colony optimization metaheuristic with OpenMP. In *International conference of parallel architectures and complication techniques (PACT), Proceedings of the third European workshop on OpenMP*, pages 8–12, Barcelona, Spain, September 2001.

[13] M. Dorigo and G. Di Caro. Ant colony optimization: a new metaheuristic. In *Proceedings of the 1999 Congress on Evolutionary Computation*, pages 1470–1477, July 1999.

[14] Marco Dorigo. The ant system: Optimization by a colony of cooperating agents. *IEEE transactions on Systems, Man, and Cybernetics-Part B*, 26(1):1–13, 1996.

[15] M. Günes, U. Sorges, and I. Bouazzi. ARA-the ant colony based routing algorithm for MANETs. In *Proceedings of the international conference on parallel processing workshops*, pages 79–85, Vancouver, B.C., August 2002.

[16] Walter J. Gutjahr. A graph-based ant system and its convergence. *Future generation computer systems (FGCS)*, 16(2):873–888, 2000.

[17] Zygmunt J. Hass. A new routing protocol for the reconfigurable wireless networks. In *Proceedings of the IEEE international conference on universal personal communications (ICUPC)*, San Diego, CA, Oct 1997.

[18] David B. Johnson and David A. Maltz. Dynamic source routing in ad hoc wireless networks. *Mobile computing (Ed. Tomasz Imielinski and Hank Korth)*, pages 153–181, 1996.

[19] R. Michel and M. Middendorf. An island based Ant system with lookahead for the shortest common subsequence problem. In *Proceedings of the fifth international conference on parallel problem sloving from nature*, volume 1498, pages 692–708, Springer-Verlag, Berlin, 1998.

[20] Jiang Mingliang, Li Jinyang, and Y.C. Tay. Cluster based routing protocol. Technical Report Internet draft, draft-ietf-manet-cbrp-spec-00.txt, Mobile Computing Group, National University of Singapore, 2000.

[21] Shree Murthy and J.J. Garcia-Luna-Aceves. An efficient routing protocol for wireless networks. *ACM mobile networks and applications journal, special issue on routing in mobile communication networks (MONET)*, 1(2):183–197, 1996.

[22] Vincent D. Park and M. Scott Corson. A highly adaptive distributed routing algorithm for mobile wireless networks. In *Proceedings of the 17th annual joint conference of the IEEE computer and communications societies (INFOCOM)*, Kobe, Japan, April 1997.

[23] Guangyu Pei, Mario Gerla, and Tsu-Wei Chen. Fisheye state routing in mobile ad hoc networks. In *Proceedings of the 20th IEEE international conference on distributed computing systems (ICDCS) workshop on wireless networks and mobile Computing*, Taipei,Taiwan, April 2000.

[24] Charles Perkins and Elizabeth Royer. Ad hoc on-demand distance vector routing. In *Proceedings of the second IEEE workshop on mobile computing systems and applications*, pages 90–100, New Orleans, LA, Feb. 1999.

[25] Charles E. Perkins and Pravin Bhagwat. Highly dynamic destination-sequenced distance-vector routing for mobile networks. In *Proceedings of the SIGCOMM 1994 conference on communications, architectures, protocols and applications*, pages 234–244, London, England, UK, August 1994.

[26] Marcus Randall. A parallel implementation of ant colony optimization. *Journal of Parallel and Distributed Computing (JPDC)*, 62:1421–1432, Jan. 2002.

[27] M. Resnick. *Turtles, termites and traffic jams*. MIT Press, 1997.

[28] Raghupathy Sivakumar, Prasun Sinha, and Vaduvur Bharghavan. CEDAR = Core-Extraction Distributed Ad hoc Routing Algorithm. *IEEE journal of selected areas in communications*, 17(8), August 1999.

[29] T. Stützle. *Parallelization strategies for ant colony optimization*, volume 1498. In Proceedings of Parallel Problem Solving from Nature (Eds. A. Eileen, T. Bäck, M. Schoenauer and H. Schwefel), Lecture Notes in Computer Science, Springer-Verlag, 1998.

[30] Peter Tarasewich and Patrick R. McMullen. Swarm intelligence: Powers in numbers. *Communications of the ACM*, 45(8), August 2002.

[31] Parimala Thulasiraman. *Irregular computations on fine-grain multithreaded architecture*. PhD thesis, University of Delaware, August 2000.

[32] C.-K. Toh. *Ad Hoc Mobile Wireless Networks: Protocols and Systems*. Prentice Hall, 2001.

[33] T. White. Swarm intelligence and problem solving in telecommunications. *Canadian Artificial Intelligence Magazine*, 1997.

Chapter 19

PARALLELIZING SERIALIZABLE TRANSACTIONS BASED ON TRANSACTION CLASSIFICATION IN REAL-TIME DATABASE SYSTEMS

Subhash Bhalla and Masaki Hasegawa

Database Systems Laboratory

University of Aizu, Aizu-Wakamatsu, Fukushima, 965-8580, Japan

{bhalla,d8041201}@u-aizu.ac.jp

Abstract   A real-time database system supports a mix of transactions. These include the real-time transactions that require completion by a given deadline. The present study makes an effort to introduce a higher level of parallelism for execution of real-time transactions. It considers extensions within a transaction processing system. These permit a real-time transaction to avoid delays due to ordinary transactions. In effect, it is a model of transaction execution that permits execution of real-time transactions without interference from other executing transactions, and by reducing other probabilistic delays associated the with competing real-time transactions.

Keywords: Distributed algorithms, Non-blocking protocols, Serializability, Synchronization, Transaction processing

1.   Introduction

The use of real-time database systems is growing in many application areas such as, industrial process control systems, multi-media systems and many critical data access applications. In such a system, a critical transaction (computational task) is characterized by its computation time and a completion deadline. These systems are characterized by stringent deadlines, and high reliability requirements. Many approaches for implementation of Real-Time systems are being studied [7, 1]. In most cases, the designers tend to extend the available approaches for concurrency control for the new environments. However, we propose to eliminate the elements that cause delays and consider introduction of parallelism based on alternative procedures.

The main problem in processing transactions in a real-time database (RT-DBS) management system is that data resources needed to execute a transaction are not known *a priori*. Hence, it impossible to reserve data items for a guaranteed completion within a worst case execution time (WCET) [4]. Therefore, the non-deterministic delays associated with data acquisition pose a challenge for integration of scheduling and concurrency control techniques. Due to the above difficulty, most research efforts do not deal with hard deadlines within RTDBSs. In a real-time system, the consequences of a missed deadline, can be disastrous, as in the case of any large process control application. To deal with such a system, the traditional approaches restrict the set of acceptable transactions to a finite set (with known execution requirements). This reduces the concurrency control problem to simple resource management exercise. Recent studies propose admission control and restriction of transactions that may miss the deadline [4].

Our research is aimed at isolation of real-time transactions (RTTs). Such transactions are proposed to be executed in parallel with no interference from other transactions. Earlier research efforts within concurrency control also try to isolate transaction classes. For example, isolation of read-only transactions [5], multi-class queries [6], and class for restricting admission [4]. Briefly, our goal is -

1 Isolate a RTT and permit it to execute freely in parallel; and

2 Execute two conflicting RTTs with better completion guarantee for both transactions.

For our purpose, we examine the process of data allocation. The characteristics of the 2 Phase Locking based Concurrency Control scheme has been studied. The rest of this paper is organized in the following manner. Section 2. describes the problem with background. Section 3 proposes a validation based selective concurrency control mechanisms that can eliminate delays for the RTTs and reduce interference among other transactions. Section 4 presents a system model of transaction execution. Section 5 examines a criterion for serializability based on the notions of local access graphs (LAGs). Section 6 presents an algorithm for constructing the LAGs. The proof of correctness has been studied in section 7. Section 8 presents a study of performance evaluation.

2.   Nature of Delays

The present study aims at exploring,

- **Transaction Classification** - possibility of executing RTTs (time-critical transactions) with no interference from ordinary transactions;

- **Conflicts Among Remaining RTTs** - possibility of switching precedence in favor of a more urgent transaction; and - eliminate computational losses due to deadlocks, aborts, repeated roll-backs, and excessive overheads associated with access of frequently sought data items.

2.1 Real-time system environment

A requirement often imposed on transaction processing systems is that the schedule formed by the transactions, be Serializable [2]. A common method of enforcing serializability is based on two-phase locking. In a real-time environment, preceding ordinary transactions render a substantial portion of database inaccessible to an arriving real-time transaction. The RTDBS environment has the following type of transactions:

1 Real-Time Transactions (RTTs); These transactions are characterized by a known computation time estimate (Ct), and a execution time deadline (Dt), as -

$$Ct + delays \ll Dt$$

2 Status queries : the read only transactions; and

3 Ordinary Transactions (OTs) : the non-critical transactions that have no execution deadline associated with them.

Table 19.1.   Allocation of data to incoming transactions

Transactions	Data Item x1	Data Item x2	Data Item x3	Data Item x4	Data Item x5	Data Item x6
T1		+		+		
T2	+	+				
T3	+	+		+		
T4	W					
T5			X		X	X
T6			w			

2.1.1 Transaction processing.

All transactions on their arrival, request resources, and data objects. The transactions within the system are further classified as executing scheduled transactions and unscheduled transaction. On its arrival, a real-time transaction can be instantly scheduled, on priority among the unscheduled transactions. Considering the scheduled transactions holding various data resources requested by an RTT, the allocation process poses considerable delays due non-availability of data items [7].

Consider a database system that uses two-phase locking. Assume that it has data items x1, x2,...x6, and transactions T1 to T6. Transactions T1, T2, T3 and T6 are read only transactions and use shared locks for items requested, as T1(x2,x4), T2(x1,x2), T3(x1,x2,x4), and T6(x3). Transactions T4 and T5 are update transactions and require exclusive access to data items requested as T4(x1,x2) and T5(x3,x5,x6). The transaction execution in accordance with the above requests is shown in table 1.1. The allocation of data items is shown by '+' for read only transactions ('w' indicates wait state). Similarly, 'X' denotes allocation of data items in the case of update transactions ('W' indicates wait state). The prominent delays on account of scheduled transactions are -

1 **Preceding Ordinary Transactions** - The transaction T4 fails to get data items requested (with exclusive access). Also, the transaction T6 fails to get data items requested (with shared access). Thus, an incoming RTT may need to wait until the executing transactions, release the data item [1].

2 **Delays and Conflicts Among RTTs** - The problem is further aggravated in case of RTTs that do not have predeclared read-set and write-set items. These seek locks for data items as these proceed with the computation. Consider a transaction T that reads data item x and writes on data item y. After a delay of d1 units, on receiving a lock for data item x, it computes the update values and seeks an exclusive lock for data item y, which becomes available after a delay of d2 units of time. Hence, the worst time estimate for computation time T is given by :

$$Ct + (d1 + d2) \ll Dt$$

3 **Deadlocks Among RTTs** The situation is further complicated by the occurrence of deadlocks, that can introduce more delays.

Thus, RTTs can have worst case estimates depending on the number of transactions executing in the system and the number of items sought by the transactions. This possibility can lead to a failure of an RTT.

3.   The Proposed Model

3.1   Interference from ordinary transactions

In many of cases, a large component of the data resources are held by the scheduled (executing) ordinary transactions. The existing approaches are primitive in nature. These make a transaction manager (TM) dependent on multiple data managers (DMs) for priority based executions and aborts [1].

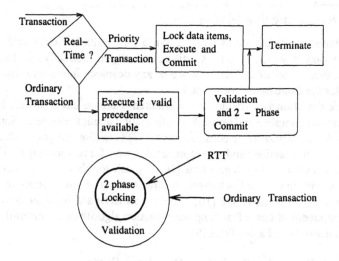

Figure 19.1. Execution of real-time transactions in isolation

A conceptual model of transaction processing is shown in Figure 19.1. As per the idea, only the RTTs are permitted to lock data items. The ordinary transactions can execute by performing an additional validation based check [3]. It ensures that, there is no overlap among items in the RTT lock table, and the items read by ordinary transactions. In case of an overlap, the ordinary transactions roll-back. The resulting transaction processing system can perform all RTTs by ignoring existence of ordinary transactions.

For sake of implementation, in case of conflict between a RTT and an OT, the locks granted to ordinary transactions are ignored. The ordinary transaction is informed about possibility of failure during validation. The transaction commitment by the data manager is denied success, in case of a failure (of validation). Such an implementation reduces the data conflicts. These remain to exist among the few executing RTTs.

3.2 Delays and conflicts among RTTs

In case of blocking, transactions begin to prepare Transaction-Wait-For graphs (TWFGs). Alternatively, probe messages are sent in order to detect the cause of blocking [12]. Consider an example, a frequently sought after item 'X'. Transactions T4, T3, T5, and T1 arrive in the same order. Other than T4, the three transactions detect that they need to wait for T4. Depending on there relative priority of execution, T3 may abort T4. Subsequently, T3 is aborted by T1, due to a higher priority. Similar aborts in the case of multiple frequently sought data items (**hot-spots** [2]), can cause delays due to deadlocks and frequent aborts. The proposed technique transforms the lock table at the DM level into a local access graph. It aligns the incoming transactions as T4 - T1, T3, T5 (if T4 is completing 2nd phase of '2-phase commit'), or as, T1 - T3, T4, T5.

3.3   Delays due dead-locks

A distributed deadlock occurs when a transaction waits for locks held by another transaction, which in turn, is waiting (directly or indirectly) for locks held by the first transaction. The presence of any deadlock introduces delays and degrades the database performance [2].

Deadlock detection is difficult in a distributed database environment, because no site has complete and up-to-date information about the system. Some algorithms detect deadlocks by constructing a TWFG (a directed graph whose nodes represent transactions and arcs represent the wait-for relationships). The proposed deadlock detection algorithms [10, 13], call for abortion (restart) of some transactions in the deadlock cycle. A large amount of information needs to be propagated from site to site [10]. The performance studies indicate that a major component of cost of running the detection algorithms is wasteful. It occurs in the absence of a deadlock [9].

4.   Definitions for Real-time Database System

Based on strict 2-phase locking discipline a set of common assumptions have been assumed [2]. The distributed database system (DDBS) consists of a set of data items (say set 'D'). The DDBS is assumed to be based on a collection of (fixed) servers that are occasionally accessed by real-time hosts. A data item is the smallest accessible unit of data. It may be a file, a record, an array, or an object. Each data item is stored at a site (one only). However, this assumption does not restrict the algorithm in any way and can be relaxed in a generalized case. Transactions are identified as $T_i, T_j, \ldots$; and sites are represented by $S_k, S_l \ldots$; where, $i, j, k, l \ldots$ are integer values. The data items are stored at database sites connected by a computer network.

Each site supports a transaction manager (TM) and a data manager (DM). The TM supervises the execution of the transactions. The DMs manage individual databases. The network is assumed to detect failures, as and when these occur. When a site fails, it simply stops running and other sites detect this fact. The communication medium is assumed to provide the facility of message transfer between sites. A site always hands over a message to the communication medium, which delivers it to the destination site in finite time. For any pair of sites S_i and S_j , the communication medium always delivers the messages to S_j in the same order in which they were handed to the medium by S_i.

4.1   Soft real-time transactions

The system always declares a distinct identity for each real-time transaction. The system possesses knowledge of a time out period, until which the transaction stays active (not aborted). The server is capable of a switch over to a **change of priority** mode for execution of a real-time transactions with changed priorities, at any time during execution. Hosting server is capable of aborting a real-time transaction, or taking corrective action concerning its completion.

4.2 Serializability in a distributed database

This section, describes the correctness criteria for transaction execution in a distributed database. Let $T = T_1, \ldots, T_n$ be a set of active transactions in a DDBS. The notion of correctness of transaction execution is that of serializability [2]. When a set of transactions execute concurrently, the operations may be interleaved. We model such an execution by a structure called a history.

4.2.1 Transaction number (TN).
A global time-stamp is used for generating a distinct identity for each transaction. Few additional assumptions, concerning the time-stamp ordering are as follows.

- Each global time-stamp contains site identity (site of origin) and a local (site) time value, and an indication of transaction type (real-time / ordinary).

- Real-time transactions are accorded such time stamps that provide these with a higher precedence order within the global time-stamps.

- High priority real-time transactions are accorded such time stamps that provide these with a higher precedence order within the group of executing real-time transactions.

Hence, a transaction number (TN) assigned to a transaction for its identity has a 5 element value, as (site-id,local-clock,type,priority,global-identity).

5. Ordering of Transactions in a Distributed System

In the proposed approach, the transactions are ordered by constructing local access graphs (LAGs) for access requests. In this section, we define a LAG.

Definition 3 : A directed graph G consists of a set of vertices $V = V_1, V_2, \ldots$, a set of edges $E = E_1, E_2, \ldots$, and a mapping function Ψ that maps every edge on to some ordered pair of vertices $< V_i, V_j >$. A pair is ordered, if $< V_i, V_j >$ is different from $< V_j, V_i >$. A vertex is represented by a point, and an edge is represented by a line segment between V_i and V_j with an arrow directed from V_i to V_j.

Insertion of an edge $< V_i, V_j >$ into the graph G =(V,E) results in graph G' =(V',E'), where $V' = V \cup \{V_i, V_j\}$ and $E' = E \cup \{< V_i, V_j >\}$. The union of two graphs $G_1 = (V_1, E_1)$ and $G_2 = (V_2, E_2)$ is another graph G_3 (written as $G_3 = G_1 \cup G_2$), whose vertex set is $V_3 = V_1 \cup V_2$ and the edge set is $E_3 = E_1 \cup E_3$.

Let, there be a partial ordering relation $\ll_T$ defined over T (the collection of executing transactions $T_1, \ldots, T_n$), to indicate a precedence order among transactions, based on criteria of serializability.

Definition 4 : An access graph of T_i (AG_i) is a graph $AG_i(V, E)$, where $V \subseteq T$, and $E = \{< T_j, T_i > | LV_j \cap LV_i \neq \phi \text{ and } T_j \ll_T T_i\}$.

Definition 5: A local access graph (LAG) of T_i at S_k, is a graph $LAG_{ik}(V, E)$, where, $V \subseteq T$, and $E = \{< T_j, T_i > | LV_{jk} \cap LV_{ik} \neq \phi \text{ and } T_j \ll_T T_i\}$. In this expression, T_j has previously visited site S_k, and LV_{ik} denotes the part of LV_i, resident at S_k.

When a locking request LR_i (for RT_i) is sent to S_j, a LAG_{ij} is constructed at S_j.

Observation 1 : Let LV_i be stored at sites $S_1, \ldots, S_m$. And, LAG_{ij} be the LAG of T_i at S_j. Then, $AG_i = \cup_{j=1}^{m} LAG_{ij}$. Please refer to [9] for formal discussions and examples.

6.   An Algorithm to Construct LAG

In this section, we describe some of the terms used in the algorithm. The algorithm is presented in the following section.

6.1   Terms used to describe the algorithm

- Home site (**SH$_i$**) :
  The site of origin of T_i is referred to as the home site.

- Transaction number (**TN$_i$**) :
  A unique number (TN_i), is assigned to the transaction T_i on its arrival at the home site. In this paper, both notations TN_i and T_i are used interchangeably and represent individual transactions. A real-time transaction is allotted a distinct identity indicating its type and priority.

- Locking variables (**LV$_i$/LV$_{ik}$**) :
  The items read or to be written by a T_i, constitute the LV_i. The locking variables at S_k constitute LV_{ik}.

- Lock request (**LR$_{ik}$**) :
  It consists of TN_i and LV_{ik}. It is prepared by SH_i on arrival of T_i, and is sent to each concerned site S_k.

- **Odd edge, Even edge** :
  As per access ordering based on dataflow graphs, an edge $< T_j, T_i >$, such that $TN_j > TN_i$, is called as odd edge. It is treated as a negative priority edge as it needs to be interchanged (verified), upon its occurrence.

  The even edges are also called priority edges. A real-time transaction always forms a priority edge (or even edge) with other transactions, due to its real-time priority.

- Access grant status (**AGS$_{ik}$**) :
  It has values 0 or 1. After granting of all the requested locks of data items

at S_k to LR_{ik}, the AGS_{ik} is changed to 1 at site S_k. Otherwise, AGS_{ik} is 0 for waiting transactions.

- Active list :
  The Active list is maintained by each S_k. The Active list of S_k is divided into two tables: active list of lock requests at S_k ($\mathbf{ALT_k}$), and active list of LAGs at S_k ($\mathbf{ALG_k}$). These tables are:

  - $ALT_k = \{(LV_i, AGS_{ik}) \mid T_i \text{ requested data items at } S_k \}$.
  - $ALGk = \{ LAG_{ik} \mid T_i \text{ requested data items at } S_k \}$.

  A transaction T_i is inserted into the ALT_{ik}, after initializing AGS_{ik}. On getting the access grants for LV_{ik}, AGS_{ik} is changed to 1. As a next step, these access grants are sent to SH_i.

- Data table ($\mathbf{DT_i}$) :
  This table is maintained at the SH_i for each T_i. The DT_i contains the lock grants (with values) of T_i. Whenever S_k receives any lock grant from another site, it stores it in a corresponding DT_i.

- Status of a transaction ($\mathbf{ST_i}$) :
  For a T_i, ST_i is maintained at the SH_i. It has values 0 or 1. Initially, ST_i is 0. After receiving all commitment messages in phase 1 of '2-phase commit', ST_i is changed to 1. After this, the final phase of commitment of T_i begins.

- Conflict-set of LAG ($\mathbf{LAG_{ik}}$.conflict – set) :
  Set of transactions in LAG_{ik} which are in conflict with T_i. That is, $LAG_{ik}.conflict - set = \{vertex - set[LAG_{ik}] - [T_i]\}$.

6.2   Informal description of the algorithm

If a transaction needs to access data items, its LR_{ik} are sent to each (concerned) site S_k. The LAG_{ik} is updated at these sites. At any site S_k, if LAG_{ik} contains odd edge $< T_j, T_i >$, then it is an indication of possible blocking or delay. It is proposed that the real-time transactions exchange the precedence with the lock holding transaction, to generate a normal precedence (even edge). In all cases, the odd edge is nullified by exchange of precedence to revoke the grant. This is called the confirmation of the edge.

An **edge is confirmed** by checking the existing AGS_{jk} **locally**, or by sending an "abort the edge" message to the SH_j. That is, if the AGS_{jk} is 0, then an even edge $< T_i, T_j >$ is inserted into the LAG_{jk} and odd edge $< T_j, T_i >$ is deleted from LAG_{ik}. Otherwise, at the SH_j, if T_j is under execution, then a **reverse** grant message is sent to SH_j, and the odd edge $< T_j, T_i >$ is substituted at the LAG_{ik}. The executing transaction T_j performs a partial roll-back.

If T_i is a **real-time transaction**, but the local site is participating in a '2-phase commit' for T_j, the SH_j is sent a message $'T_j.STATE'$. In response, its home site terminates T_j, or communicates the updated values, within a time-out period. Else, the site is treated as a failed site.

If T_i is an **ordinary transaction**, but the local site is executing the 2nd phase of 2 phase locking for T_j, the SH_j is sent a message $'T_j.STATE'$. In response, its home site completes T_j, and communicates the updated values (within a larger time frame). Else, the site is treated as a failed site.

Thus, a time-critical transaction is permitted to execute a revoke grant (if necessary) for the conflicting item, in order to cancel an odd edge.

7.   Performance Evaluation

Distributed deadlocks cause many delays [7]. These do not occur in a distributed system by adoption of the DAG approach. The proposed design permits dynamic allocation and reallocation of data resources. Each DM, on detecting an incorrect precedence, eliminates odd edges. Thus, RTTs do not get blocked for longer durations. It is also a fully distributed system approach.

7.1   Elimination of interference from OTs

The present proposal eliminates the data contention between RTTs and OTs. It reduces the data conflicts faced by RTTs to a low level. In an application, the proportion of RTTs may be as low as 1 % to 10 %. The earlier approaches [1] resort to aborts of lower priority transactions. These do not distinguish between the transaction classes. These incur many overheads. In the present proposal, executing RTTs have conflicts for data resources among themselves (few executing RTTs, level B in Figure 19.2). The ordinary transactions face conflicts with RTTs and among the other OTs (level A). The qualitative performance improvements are depicted in Figure 19.2. The proportion of the RTTs within a system may vary from application to application. The technique successfully separates the resource contention between the RTTs and OTs, by using transaction classification.

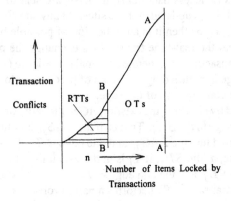

Figure 19.2.   Relative Improvement in Parallel Execution of RTTs

7.2   Delays among RTTs

All odd edges do not introduce blockings or deadlocks. Many odd edges get eliminated by local computations. In contrast, the earlier proposals for scheduling real-time transactions, use priority and aborts [1]. These introduce restart delays and aborts for the low precedence transactions including RTTs. Such an approach is a costly approach. It suffers from "priority inversion" and indiscriminate "aborts" of transactions, within a RTDBS.

As an example, consider the case of two transactions which conflict over some data item X at a site. Based on a test for checking the LAGs, if any one of the transactions has no other data conflict, the odd edge need not be eliminated. Thus, the algorithm can still proceed in accordance with the LAG with an odd edge.

In the case of a real-time transaction, each incorrect precedence requires a message to revoke the grant from the DM. The improved interaction between the TMs and DMs helps to completely avoid deadlocks, excessive delays, priority inversion, and many preventable aborts. This is the result of the process of confirming odd edges. This process needs two messages for each odd edge that may exist. In contrast, most of the earlier deadlock detection algorithms require a large amount of total number of messages to be exchanged, for the deadlock detection process that is initiated periodically by the waiting transactions [12].

7.2.1   Performance and applicability of DAGs .   On analyzing the number of odd edges formed, it can be seen that, for a transaction that seeks 100 items (assuming $5 - 7\%$ conflict rate), up to 6 items may be in conflict. This may result in 3 odd edges being formed on an average. This is so, by considering an equal chance of an odd or even, edge formation. In reality, an incremental clock does not favor equal chances for formation of as many odd edges.

As an example, consider a system that has many 'hot spots' (items that are sought by many executing transactions at the same time, [2]). Also, consider that a large number of conflicting transactions enter the system. In the proposed method, all the transactions that wait for a 'hot spot' item - will sort the order for access while waiting (with $AGS_{ik} = 0$). If necessary, data items held by executing transactions are revoked by higher priority transactions with a single message to home site.

7.2.2   Performance study: simulation of edge formation activity.
The model uses routine programming and random number generation algorithms. This model aims at counting number of different types of edges that occur within a sample system (Figure 19.3). In the simulation model, the number of data items in the database system is chosen as 1000. For a larger value, the conflicts tend to become infrequent.

Table 19.2.   Simulation parameters

Database Size	1000 data items
Number of Sites (M)	5
Transaction Size	8 - 12 data items, uniform distribution
Access Request Pattern	40 % data from other global sites
Concurrent Transactions	Variable (10, 20, . . . , 80)

Within the experiment, clocks are maintained at the sites. After arrival of a transaction, the lock requests are sent to other sites. To consider a generalized situation, the data access sites are traversed one by one. Messages are stored in First-Come-First-Served site queues.

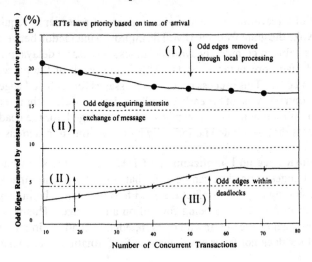

Figure 19.3.   Proportion of odd edges eliminated through local computations

The simulation experiments have been run for 5000 transactions, for a given multiprogramming level. An average of these runs has been taken for evaluation of the following items.

- the total number of edges, versus the number of odd edges formed (Figure 19.3);

- numbers of odd edges removed with local computation (with no intersite communication), and odd edges removed through message exchanges (Figure 19.3);

Figure 19.3 shows the variation in formation of even edges versus odd edges. The chances of occurrence of an odd edge are fewer and not near 50%. As multiprogramming level increases, the number of edges formed increases (total number of edges) due to increase in resource conflict. However, the percentage share of odd edges becomes less.

7.3   Deadlock elimination among RTTs

Distributed deadlocks detection and elimination techniques impose high overheads for making TWFGs or supporting probe messages [12]. From the simulation results, shyu and Li have concluded that, more than 90% of deadlock cycles are of length two [10, 11]. Recent studies [9] show the proportion of deadlocks removed by exchange of precedence (message exchanged for elimination of odd edges). The cost of elimination of odd edges is reduced on account of local processing. The local processing based, odd edge elimination behavior of the algorithm for two level deadlocks is analyzed as per the proposed method [9], [8].

8.   Summary and Conclusions

In the distributed locking based approaches, if transactions from different sites, are in serializability conflict, then some of the submitted transactions are rejected. Transaction rejects and delays are two of the main problems that concern real-time transaction processing activity. In this study, a procedure has been identified that shows a possibility of execution of critical transactions under serializability conditions. As a result, the real-time transactions do not undergo blocking and roll-back due to ordinary transactions. The technique avoids deadlocks, priority inversion and also prevents many avoidable aborts of real-time transactions. A higher level of concurrency is achieved, as a result of removal of excessive blocking, and roll-backs for critical transactions.

References

[1] Abbott R., and H. Garcia-Molina, "Scheduling Real-Time Transactions : A performance Evaluation", *ACM Transactions on Database Systems*, Vol. 17, No. 3, September 1992.

[2] P.A.Bernstein, V.hadzilacos and N.Goodman, "Two Phase Locking", Chapter 3, *Concurrency control and recovery in database systems*, Addison-Wesley,1987.

[3] Bhalla, S., "Executing Serializable Transactions within a Hard Real-time Database System", *5th International Conference on High Performance Computing* (HiPC98), December 1998, Chennai, India.

[4] Bestavros, A., and S. Nagy, "Value-cognizant Admission Control for RTDB Systems", *Proceedings of Real-time Systems Symposium, Washington*, December 1996, pp. 230-239.

[5] Lam Kwok-wa, S.H. Son, V.C.S. Lee, and Sheung-Lun Hung, "Using Separate Algorithms to Process Read-Only Transactions in Real-Time Systems", *Proceedings of IEEE Real Time Systems Symposium*, Dec. 1998, pp. 50-59.

[6] Pang, H., M.J. Carey, and M. Linvy, "Multiclass Query Scheduling in Real-time Database Systems", *IEEE Transactions on Knowledge and Data Engineering*, Vol. 7, No. 4, 1995.

[7] Ramamritham K., "Real-Time Databases", *Distributed and Parallel Databases*, Kluwer Academic Publishers, Boston, USA, Vol. 1, No. 1, 1993.

[8] P.K. Reddy, and S. Bhalla, "A Non-Blocking Transaction Data Flow Graph Based Protocol for Replicated Databases", *IEEE Transactions on Knowledge and Data Engineering*, vol. 7, No. 5, pp. 829-834, October 1995.

[9] P.K. Reddy, and S. Bhalla, "Asynchronous Operations in Distributed Concurrency Control", IEEE Transactions on Knowledge and Data Engineering, vol. 15, No. 3, May 2003.

[10] S.C.Shyu, V.O.K.Li, and C.P.Weng, "An abortion free distributed deadlock detection/resolution algorithm", *Proc. IEEE 10th International Conference on Distributed Computing Systems*, pp.1-8, June 1990.

[11] S.C.Shyu, V.O.K.Li, and C.P.Weng, "Performance Analysis of Static Locking in a Distributed Database System", *IEEE Transaction on Computers*, Vol. 39, No. 6, pp. 741-751, June 1990.

[12] Singhal, M., "Deadlock Detection in Distributed Systems", *IEEE Computer*, pp. 37-47, November 1989.

[13] M.K.Sinha, and N.Natarajan, "A priority based distributed deadlock detection algorithm", *IEEE Transactions on Software Engineering*, vol.SE-11, pp.67-80, January 1985.

Chapter 20

ADAPTIVE SELECTION OF MATERIALIZED QUERIES IN A MEDIATOR FOR THE INTEGRATION OF DISTRIBUTED INFORMATION RESOURCES

Kil Hong Joo and Won Suk Lee

Department of Computer Science, Yonsei University
134 Sedaemoongu Shinchondong, Seoul, Korea
{faholo,leewo}@amadeus.yonsei.ac.kr

Abstract   A global query in a mediator system to integrate distributed information is transformed into a set of its sub-queries and each sub-query is the unit of evaluation in a remote server. Therefore, it is possible to speed up the execution of a global query if the previous results of frequently evaluated sub-queries are materialized in a mediator. Since the integration schema of a mediator can be incrementally modified and the evaluation frequency of a global query can also be continuously varied, query usage should be carefully monitored to determine the optimized set of materialized sub-queries. Furthermore, as the number of sub-queries increases, the optimization process itself may take too long, so that the optimized set identified by a long optimization process may become obsolete due to the recent change of query usage. This paper proposes the adaptive selection of materialized sub-queries such that available storage in a mediator can be highly utilized at any time. In order to differentiate the recent usage of a query from the past, the accumulated usage frequency of a query decays as time goes by. As a result, it is possible to change the set of materialized sub-queries adaptively according to the recent variation of query usage.

Keywords: Mediator, Heterogeneous information systems, Data materialization, Distributed query processing, Decay rate

1.   Introduction

In today's information system environment, related information can be distributed over different systems. However, since they are developed independently, it is difficult to achieve interactions among them in an effective way.

Furthermore, heterogeneous data models in different operating systems cannot keep up with the complicated needs of users for the tight integration of distributed information. For this reason, the study of a mediator system has been actively carried out as an integration method for heterogeneous information resources in distributed environment [1, 4, 5].

A *mediator* is middleware that can provide a user with the effect of accessing a single system by concealing them from the actual heterogeneity of computing environment such as hardware, software, and databases in distributed information systems. A *wrapper* in a remote server is used to support a mediator to access the functions of the server. By wrapping its necessary inner functions, it can service the wrapped functions to a mediator [2]. By using this wrapping technique, an existing system can be expressed into a new form without transforming the existing system. This means that the autonomy of a remote server can be preserved to the highest degree. To design a distributed database in general, local schemata are analyzed and integrated to a unique global schema. However, local schemata in autonomous servers are likely to be varied due to the change of their own requirements. On the contrary, a mediator integrates its necessary information in the local schemata relevant to its function. Consequently, a new view in a mediator can be defined over either local schemata in remote servers or the views of other mediators whenever new requirements for a global user are imposed. When any of them is changed, only the view mappings of a mediator need to be modified since there is no global schema [2]. Therefore, the definition of a view in a mediator can be changed or a new view can be defined incrementally.

To evaluate a global query on a view that integrates several distributed databases, a set of transformed queries is generated by rewriting the query based on the definition of the view to be evaluated in their corresponding remote server respectively. A sub-query is the unit of evaluation in a remote server as well as the unit of data transfer between a remote server and a mediator. To evaluate a sub-query in a mediator, two relational methods: *query modification* and *view materialization* can be considered. The query modification method evaluates every transformed query in its remote server. On the other hand, the materialization method maintains the result of a frequently evaluated transformed query temporarily in a mediator and the materialized result is used instead of evaluating the query. When the same sub-query is associated with different global queries, its materialized result can be shared. Therefore, the up-to-date result of a materialized query can be used instantly as long as an immediate update is made on the spot of an alteration in any base table of the query [3, 15]. In this paper, a transformed query is denoted by a sub-query. In addition, a sub-query evaluated by the modification method is called as a *modified sub-query* while a sub-query evaluated by the materialization method is called as a *materialized sub-query*.

In a mediator system, global views are basically defined by a set of local schemata related to the specific role of the mediator. Therefore, it is possible to improve the performance of query evaluation when the materialization method is considered as an alternative query evaluation method, which has not been recognized by most of the existing mediator systems [4, 5]. In order to evaluate a sub-query by the materialization method efficiently, it is necessary to model the usage patterns of a sub-query precisely. Since the usage patterns of a sub-query in a mediator can be varied as time goes by, they should be monitored continuously, so that the appropriate evaluation method of each sub-query can be determined adaptively. In this paper, a term *'implementation plan (IP)'* is used to describe how the sub-queries of global queries are evaluated. It is denoted by a set of pairs (s_i, I_i). Each pair represents that a sub-query s_i is evaluated by a method $I_i \in \{materialization \ or \ modification\}$. The algorithm presented in this paper is composed of the following three components:

- Modelling the recent variation of usage patterns for the sub-queries of global queries in a mediator.
- Generating an optimized implementation plan for the sub-queries such that the overall evaluation cost of global queries can be minimized for their current usage patterns as well as the available storage space of a mediator.
- Detecting the moment to find a new implementation plan due to the significant change of recent usage patterns.

This paper consists of six parts. Section 2 describes related works and Section 3 introduces an adaptive method of modelling the usage patterns of sub-queries. Section 4 presents how to generate the optimized implementation plan of sub-queries based on their usage patterns. In Section 5, the results of various experiments are presented to analyze the characteristics of the proposed algorithm. In addition, its performance is compared with those of general optimization algorithms. Finally, Section 6 draws overall conclusions.

2.   Related Work

TSIMMIS [4] supports heterogeneous databases in distributed environment by constructing a mediator system. The schema of a mediator is defined by its own Mediator Specification Language (MSL) while the information of each remote server in a wrapper is defined by its own Wrapper Specification Language (WSL). This requires a mapping process between MSL and WSL, so that it is possible to access distributed databases only through its own toolkit and languages. HERMES [5] is another system for semantically integrating heterogeneous information resources. In this framework, a set of domains is abstracted from external information resources and they provide certain functions with pre-specified input and output types. These domains are accessed by a mediator with a logic-based declarative language. As a result, new external sources can be added easily. HERMES also provides a "yellow pages" facility to assist the schema designer of a mediator for locating appropriate data sources. However, it is only applicable to homogeneous computing environment. In both TSIMMIS and HERMES, only the query modification method is used to evaluate the global queries of a mediator.

In [6], a view materialization method in a distributed database is proposed. It shows that the materialization of a view can cut down the evaluation of a global query. In this approach, the evaluation frequencies of frequently requested queries and the update frequencies of their base tables are statically modelled. Based on these usage patterns, the evaluation costs of the two evaluation methods for each view are calculated to find out their differences. Subsequently, a view with the largest difference is chosen one by one to be materialized until available storage space is exhausted. On the other hand, a *least recently used* (LRU) replacement algorithm [16] used in most operation systems is a simple method of buffering recently referenced data units efficiently if the size of a data unit is identical and a data unit is usually referenced consecutively once it is referenced. However, in a mediator, the result size of a sub-query is different and the same sub-query is not requested consecutively, so that the LRU algorithm can not to reflect the differences of evaluation costs among sub-queries.

Materialized views are proven to be useful in new applications such as data warehousing [7, 9, 12, 14]. Materialized view selection is finding a set of materialized views among the sources of a data warehouse such that the selected views can minimize the overall query evaluation cost for the statically analyzed frequency of commonly used queries. In [9], a materialized view selection algorithm based on the data cube of a lattice structure is proposed. For a set of base tables, all possible combinations of materializing plans are identified to a lattice structure and their gross gains are calculated by the difference of two evaluation methods respectively. A plan with the largest gross gain is chosen to materialize the contents of base tables. In [12], a branch-and-bound algorithm is used to select a set of materialized views in order to define the schema of a data warehouse.

The materialized view selection algorithms proposed in data warehouse systems cannot be used in a mediator due to the following reasons. First, the usage patterns of views i.e. the invocation frequencies of commonly used queries and update operations in a data warehouse are modelled statically when a warehouse is designed [10]. As a result, they are assumed to be fixed. Second, in order to select the set of materialized views, potentially all possible combinations of the two evaluation methods for each view should be examined in terms of their gross gains. However, this approach is impractical if the search space becomes large. It has been shown that materialized view selection is NP-hard [11]. Accordingly, as the number of views increases, this search process becomes slow exponentially, which can cause a critical problem in a mediator. This is because the evaluation methods of sub-queries should be changed whenever they become no longer optimum. If the search process takes too long, it may be too late to apply the newly optimized implementation plan since the usage patterns of sub-queries may not be the same as before.

There are several general optimization algorithms such as greedy strategy, dynamic programming and branch-and-bound [12, 16]. The greedy strategy finds a solution by making a sequence of choices, each of which simply looks the best at the moment. The dynamic programming uses a divide-and-conquer approach to divide a large instance of a problem into a set of smaller instances, so that a small instance is solved first. The branch-and-bound algorithm is very similar to backtracking in a state space tree. Although it requires exponential-time complexity in the worst case, it is proven to be effective in many applications for finding an optimum solution.

3.   Decayed Usage Patterns

The usage patterns of a sub-query in a mediator are modelled by both an *access frequency (AF)* and an *update frequency (UF)*. The AF of a sub-query indicates how many times its result is evaluated while the UF of a sub-query indicates how many times the tuples of its information resources in a remote server are updated. For a materialized sub-query, the difference between these two frequencies is the number of sub-query evaluation which utilizes its materialized result in a mediator. Since the evaluation method of a sub-query should be determined by its usage patterns, it is very important to monitor the variation of the recent usage patterns of each sub-query. This can be achieved by decaying its previous usage patterns. A *half-life* [13] of a frequency means a point in time when a new occurrence of an access or update gets its half effect. When the weight of a new occurrence is set to one, a half-life is defined as the number of time units that makes its weight be half. For a given half-life h, the decaying rate of a weight is denoted by a *decay rate d* and defined by Equation (20.1).

$$d = 2^{-\frac{1}{h}} \qquad (20.1)$$

For a user-defined time interval δ, let the previous values of both the AF and UF of a sub-query be decayed respectively as follows.

$$f^a_{i.new} = f^a_{i.old} \cdot d^t + 1 \quad (t = \frac{|R|}{\delta}) \qquad (20.2)$$

$$f^u_{i.new} = f^u_{i.old} \cdot d^t + 1 \quad (t = \frac{|R|}{\delta}) \qquad (20.3)$$

$f^a_{i.new}$ is the newly updated AF of a sub-query s_i at present while $f^a_{i.old}$ is its old AF that was calculated for the latest access of the sub-query occurred at R time units ago. In other words, upon receiving a new access for a sub-query s_i, $f^a_{i.new}$ is evaluated by Equation (20.2) where $f^a_{i.old}$ obtained by its latest access in R time units ago is decayed $|\frac{R}{\delta}|$ times. The decayed frequency is the weighted accumulation of previous accesses relatively to the present. If the time gap R between these two accesses is larger than the predefined interval δ, the previous value is decayed by the multiples of δ. Otherwise, it is not decayed. Similarly, the UF can be modelled in the same manner. For example, the sub-queries s_1 and s_2 in Figure 20.1 are modelled by the same access frequency i.e. 5 if the decaying mechanism is not used. This does not reflect the fact that the sub-query s_1 was used more recently than the sub-query s_2. With the decaying mechanism, the current AF of the sub-query s_1 becomes $f^a_{s_1.tc} = 1 + 2 \cdot (2^{-1}) + (2^{-2}) + (2^{-5}) = 2.28$ while that of the sub-query s_2 becomes $f^a_{s_2.tc} = 1 + 2 \cdot (2^{-3}) + (2^{-4}) + (2^{-5}) = 1.34$ when the half-life is one. By the predefined interval δ, it is possible to control the modelling precision of usage patterns. As it is set to be smaller, the usage patterns can be more precisely monitored.

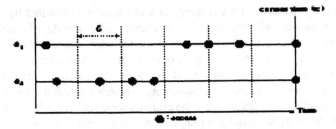

Figure 20.1.   Decaying usage patterns

Figure 20.2 illustrates the overall process of query evaluation in a mediator. When a user issues a global query, the AFs of its corresponding sub-queries are updated by Equation (20.2). Subsequently, according to the current evaluation method of each sub-query, the following operations are performed. For a modified sub-query, it asks its remote server to evaluate the sub-query and send its result. On the other hand, a materialized sub-query uses its materialized result in a mediator if the result is valid. In this case, there is no need to request its remote server to execute the sub-query. However, if the currently materialized result is invalid due to the prior update of any of its information resources in a remote server, the sub-query is executed by the modification method and the newly received result is materialized again in the mediator. In addition, the UF of the sub-query is updated by Equation (20.3). When the results of all the sub-queries are available in a mediator, the result of the global query can be found.

For a materialized sub-query, there are three possible solutions for preserving the consistency between its materialized result in a mediator and the corresponding information resources in its remote server. The first method is that all the local updates of its information resources are performed via a mediator. In other words, any local update should be requested to a mediator first. Upon receiving the request, the mediator asks a remote server to process it. This method can ensure the consistency automatically but the autonomy of a remote server cannot be guaranteed. The second method is that a wrapper notifies the local

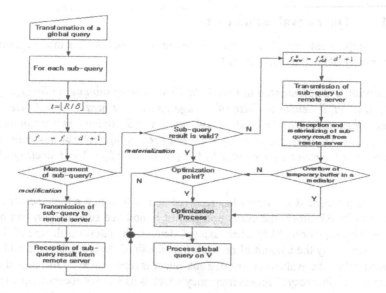

Figure 20.2. The overall query evaluation of a mediator

update of its information resource to every mediator that is affected before the local transaction of the update is completed. Subsequently, the mediator can make the previously materialized result of the corresponding sub-query invalid. This method guarantees not only the consistency but also the autonomy of remote servers. However, every update transaction in a remote server should be carefully designed in order to ensure the correct notification of a remote server. The third method is that a mediator confirms the validity of the currently materialized result of a sub-query to its remote server whenever the sub-query is evaluated. This confirmation process can be easily implemented in a wrapper with a set of status flags for information resources in a remote server.

4.   Implementation Plans

Since the storage space of a mediator is restrictive and the usage patterns of queries can be changed, it is very important to ensure the efficiency of the current implementation plan for the present usage patterns of sub-queries. Upon concluding it is not efficient any longer, a new implementation plan optimized for changed usage patterns should be generated as fast as possible, so that the new implementation plan can be applied quickly. This section presents the generation of the optimized plan based on the cost-based analysis of sub-query evaluation. Furthermore, in order to invoke a new optimization process timely, the monitoring process of the current plan is described.

4.1   Query evaluation cost

An implementation plan for the sub-queries of global queries in a mediator is formally defined by Definition 1.

Definition 2 *Implementation Plan (IP): Given a set of sub-queries S={s_1, s_2, ..., s_n}, let T denote the size of storage space in a mediator and Size(S) denote the total size of the results of sub-queries in S. An implementation plan $IP(L_1, L_2)$ is represented by a set of materialized sub-queries L_1 and a set of modified sub-queries L_2 such that $L_1 \cup L_2 = S, L_1 \cap L_2 = \emptyset$ and Size(L_1)$\leq$T.* ∎

Since a modified sub-query has received its result from a remote server as many as its AF times, the evaluation cost of a modified sub-query s_i can be defined by Equation (20.4) where $size(s_i)$ denotes the latest result size of the sub-query s_i by the amount of network transmission. As it can be noticed by this equation, the evaluation cost of a sub-query is represented by its latest size weighted by its decayed access frequency which is its relative access frequency at the execution time of an optimization process. Although the local evaluation cost of a sub-query in a remote server should also be considered, it is ignored since the cost of network transmission is dominant. Similarly, the evaluation cost of a materialized sub-query s_j can be defined by Equation (20.5) since a materialized sub-query has received its results as many as its UF times. For an $IP(L_1, L_2)$, its *materialized cost* $C(L_1, mat)$ is defined by the sum of the evaluation costs of all materialized sub-queries as in Equation (20.6). Likewise, its *modification cost* $C(L_2, mod)$ is defined by the sum of the evaluation costs of all modified sub-queries as in Equation (20.7). Accordingly, the *gross evaluation cost* of an $IP(L_1, L_2)$ is defined by the sum of these two costs as in Equation (20.8).

$$c(s_i, mod) = size(s_i) \cdot f_i^a \tag{20.4}$$

$$c(s_j, mat) = size(s_j) \cdot f_j^u \tag{20.5}$$

$$C(L_1, mat) = \sum_{i=1}^{k} c(s_i, mat) \quad (L_1 = \{s_1, s_2, ..., s_k\}) \tag{20.6}$$

$$C(L_2, mod) = \sum_{i=k+1}^{n} c(s_i, mod) \quad (L_2 = \{s_{k+1}, s_{k+2}, ..., s_n\}) \tag{20.7}$$

$$Cost(IP(L_1, L_2)) = C(L_1, mat) + C(L_2, mod) \tag{20.8}$$

Theorem 1 *Given two sets W_3 and W_4 of sub-queries, the total evaluation cost of $W_3 \cup W_4$ is the sum of the evaluation costs of W_3 and W_4 respectively i.e., $C(W_3 \cup W_4, I_i) = C(W_3, I_i) + C(W_4, I_i)(I_i \in \{mat, mod\})$.* ∎

Proof: Let $W_3 = \{a_1, a_2, \ldots, a_k\}$, $W_4 = \{a_{k+1}, a_{k+2}, \ldots, a_n\}$

$$C(W_3 \cup W_4, I_i) = \sum_{h=1}^{k} c(a_h, I_i) + \sum_{j=k+1}^{n} c(a_j, I_i) = C(W_3, I_i) + C(W_4, I_i)$$

∎

Given a set of sub-queries with their usage patterns, the objective of an opti-mization process is finding an implementation plan which has the lowest total evaluation cost for the given storage space of a mediator. When a mediator needs to adjust the current plan, the costs of the two evaluation methods for each sub-query are calculated by Equation (20.4) and Equation (20.5) respectively. The difference of the two costs is regarded as the possible gain when the corresponding sub-query is evaluated by the materialization method. As the difference becomes larger, the corresponding sub-query is more likely to be a materialized sub-query. Formally the gain $g(s_i)$ of a sub-query s_i is defined by the difference as follows:

$$g(s_i) = c(s_i, \text{mod}) - c(s_i, mat) \tag{20.9}$$

Since the total gain $G(S)$ of all sub-queries S can be defined by Equation (20.10), the gross gain of a specific $IP(L_1, L_2)$ is equal to the total gain of its materialized sub-queries L_1 as in Equation (20.11).

$$G(S) = \sum_{i=1}^{n} g(s_i) \tag{20.10}$$

$$Gain(IP(L_1, L_2)) = G(L_1) \tag{20.11}$$

Hence, the gross evaluation cost of an $IP(L_1, L_2)$ can be re-expressed by Equation (20.12). Therefore, the gross evaluation cost of an $IP(L_1, L_2)$ is minimized when its gross gain is maximized.

$$Cost(IP(L_1, L_2)) = C(L_1 \cup L_2, \text{mod}) - G(L_1) \tag{20.12}$$

Theorem 2 *Given two sets W_1 and W_2 of materialized sub-queries with their total gains $G(W_1)$ and $G(W_2)$ respectively, the total gain $G(W_1 \cup W_2)$ is the sum of two total gains $G(W_1)$ and $G(W_2)$ i.e., $G(W_1 \cup W_2) = G(W_1) + G(W_2)$* ∎.

Proof: Let $W_1 = \{a_1, a_2, \ldots, a_k\}$ and $W_2 = \{a_{k+1}, a_{k+2}, \ldots, a_n\}$.

$$G(W_1 \cup W_2) = \sum_{i=1}^{n} g(a_i) = \sum_{i=1}^{k} g(a_i) + \sum_{j=k+1}^{n} g(a_j) = G(W_1) + G(W_2)$$

∎

The gain of a sub-query does not indicate how efficiently the limited storage space of a mediator is utilized. This is because it does not consider the difference among the result sizes of sub-queries. Due to this reason, a normalized gain is used to represent the relative efficiency of a sub-query as a materialized sub-query. The normalized gain of a sub-query s_i is defined by Equation (20.13).

$$ng(s_i) = g(s_i)/size(s_i) \qquad (20.13)$$

4.2   Practical implementation plan

Once a mediator is in operation, it is not a good idea to suspend its normal operation for a long period whenever the current implementation plan is not efficient any longer. Therefore, a new implementation plan should be generated as fast as possible. In addition, the generation process should not require large computing resources which are capable of disturbing the normal operation of a mediator. However, in order to ensure whether the newly generated plan is optimum or not, it is necessary to examine all possible implementation plans that are every combination of the two evaluation methods for each of given sub-queries. The search space of this examination grows exponentially as the number of sub-queries increases. Consequently, it could require considerable computing resources in a mediator. If the generation of a new implementation plan takes too long, a newly generated plan may become obsolete to be applied since it may not be optimum any longer. In other words, when it is ready to be applied, the usage patterns of sub-queries may not be the same as before. To generate an optimized implementation plan in linear time complexity, a *practical implementation plan* defined in Definition 2 can be considered.

Definition 3 *A Practical Implementation Plan (PIP): Given a set of sub-queries S and the size of storage space T in a mediator, let $ngl(S) = (s_1, s_2-,..., s_i, ..., s_n)$ denote an ordered list of all sub-queries in S such that $ng(s_i) \geq ng-(s_{i+1})$, $s_i, s_{i+1} \in S$. If two or more sub-queries have the same normalized gain, they are arranged by their sizes in decreasing order. A practical implementation plan $PIP(L_1^*, L_2^*)$ is an implementation plan that is obtained by the following procedure. Let the list ngl(S) be denoted by an array NGL[1..n] where NGL[i] denotes the sub-query s_i with the ith highest normalized gain.*

> Step 1 $L_1^* = \emptyset$
> Step 2   For i=1 to n do
> > if $size(NGL[i]) \leq T - Size(L_1^*)$ then
> > $L_1^* \leftarrow L_1^* \cup \{s_i\}$
> Step 3 $L_2^* \leftarrow S - L_1^*$ ∎

Among the materialized sub-queries of a practical implementation plan, those sub-queries that satisfy Definition 3 are defined by a set of *definitely materialized sub-queries DS*.

Definition 4 *Definitely materialized sub-queries (DS) Given a* $PIP(L_1^*, L_2^*)$ *for a set of sub-queries S.A set of definitely materialized sub-queries DS is a subset of materialized sub-queries* L_1 *and it consists of the common prefix sub-queries of two lists* $ngl(L_1^*)$ *and* $ngl(S)$ *defined in Definition 2.* ∎

Theorem 3 *A practical implementation plan* $PIP(L_1^*, L_2^*)$*for a set of sub-queries S is optimum when all the materialized sub-queries are definitely materialized sub-queries and their total size is equal to the available storage space T of a mediator, i.e.* $L_1^* = DS$ *and* $Size(L_1^*) = T.$ ∎

Proof: Given a set of sub-queries S, suppose a $PIP(L_1^*, L_2^*)$ satisfies the above conditions. Let *max_ng(S)* and *min_ng(S)* denote the maximum normalized gain and the minimum normalized gain respectively among the normalized gains of the sub-queries in S. Consider any implementation plan $IP(L_1, L_2)$ such that $L_1 = L_1^* - a \cup b$ and $L_2 = L_2^* - b \cup a$ where a and b are any member of the power set of $L_1^*$and L_2^* respectively i.e. $a \in 2^{L_1^*}$ and $b \in 2^{L_2^*}$ $(a \neq \emptyset, b \neq \emptyset)$.
min_ng(a) > max_ng(b) since $L_1^* = DS$ —— ①
By Definition 2 and $Size(L_1^*) = T$, $Size(a) \geq Size(b)$ —— ②
From Equation ① and ②, $G(a) > G(b)$ —— ③
By Equation ③, Theorem 2 and Equation (20.11),
$Gain(PIP(L_1^*, L_2^*)) - Gain(IP(L_1, L_2))$
$= G(L_1^*) - G(L_1^* - a \cup b) = G(L_1^*) - G(L_1^*) + G(a) - G(b) > 0.$
Therefore, $PIP(L_1^*, L_2^*)$is optimum

∎

Consequently, the efficiency of a practical implementation plan $PIP(L_1^*, L_2^*)$ can be determined by the ratio of the size of its definitely materialized sub-queries DS over that of all materialized sub-queries L_1^*. This is because the DS portion of the available storage space in a mediator is utilized at best according to Theorem 3. As the ratio becomes larger, the efficiency of a practical implementation plan $PIP(L_1^*, L_2^*)$ is enhanced.

4.3   Invocation of optimization

In order to invoke a new implementation plan timely, it is important to monitor the variation of the total evaluation cost of the current plan for the present usage patterns of sub-queries periodically. The efficiency of the current plan is degraded when the usage patterns of sub-queries are changed as follows. For a modified sub-query, the likelihood to change its evaluation method is increased by one of the following two reasons. One is that the increasing rate of its AF is larger than that of its UF when its size remains the same. The other is that its result size becomes smaller if its usage patterns are not changed. It is vice versa for a materialized sub-query. If the total evaluation cost of the current plan is not efficient any longer, a new optimized plan should be generated as fast as possible. Given the current plan $IP(L_1, L_2)$, let $Cost^{latest}(IP(L_1, L_2))$ denote the total evaluation cost which was calculated at the latest optimization process i.e. when the current $IP(L_1, L_2)$ was generated. On the other hand, let $Cost^{monitoring}(IP(L_1, L_2))$ denote the total evaluation cost that is obtained by the latest monitoring process. A new implementation plan should be searched when Equation (20.14) is satisfied.

$$\left| \frac{Cost^{latest}(IP(L_1, L_2)) - Cost^{monitoring}(IP(L_1, L_2))}{Cost^{latest}(IP(L_1, L_2))} \right| \geq \mu \qquad (20.14)$$

A *cost allowable ratio* μ is a user-defined parameter that denotes the allowable ratio of the monitoring cost relatively to the latest optimized cost. Based on the predefined value of μ, the invocation frequency of a new optimization process can be controlled. As it is smaller, a new optimization process is invoked more frequently. This is because a new optimization process is initiated only when the difference between the two costs exceeds the μ portion of the latest optimized cost.

On the other hand, there are other situations that a new optimization process is invoked. When any base table of a materialized sub-query is updated and its new result is too large to fit in its previous space of the available storage in a mediator, a new optimization process should be initiated to adjust the current plan regardless of the monitoring cost described above. Due to this reason, unnecessary optimization processes may take place frequently even though a little overflow of storage space has only a minor effect on the total evaluation cost. In order to avoid this, temporary storage space can be allocated additionally in a mediator. It is used to hold the overflowed result of a sub-query temporarily until the next optimization process is invoked. Therefore, a new optimization process caused by the lack of storage space is invoked only when the temporary storage space becomes full. On the other hand, when the new result of a sub-query requires less storage space than its previous one, the freed storage space can be utilized by materializing some of modified sub-queries if possible.

5.   Experiments and Analysis of Results

To illustrate the various aspects of the proposed algorithm, this section presents several experiment results. In most of the experiments, the number of sub-queries is set to 300 and the size of temporary storage space is set to the 20 percent of the total storage space 3GB of a mediator unless they are specified differently. Furthermore, the initial result size of each sub-query is randomly chosen from 10MB to 200MB. In order to examine different request ratios between access and update operations, two different request logs are generated. Each log contains a sequence of about 3000 access or update operations each of which is applied to a randomly chosen sub-query. One is denoted by RATIO1 whose ratio between access and update operations is 80:20 and the operations are uniformly distributed over the log. Similarly, that in the other request log RATIO2 is 50:50. In these logs, the updated result size of each sub-query is also randomly chosen from the 10 percent of its previous size to 10 times of its previous size for each update operation. Each experiment in this section is performed on 10 different instances of each log and their average value is presented.

In order to illustrate the efficiency of a practical implementation plan proposed in this paper, the proposed algorithm is compared with three general optimization methods: branch-and-bound, greedy strategy and dynamic programming [12]. Among these methods, the branch-and-bound method finds the optimum plan. Figure 20.3 represents the average difference ratios of the total evaluation costs of these optimization methods relatively to the cost of the optimum plan. In order to eliminate the effect of consecutive optimization processes by a request log, only the result of the first optimization process in each instance of the *RATIO1* log is considered for each method. The modification-only cost MOD denotes the total evaluation cost of a plan that evaluates all sub-queries by the modification method. In average, the proposed algorithm PIP reduces the evaluation cost down to the 54 percent of the modification-only cost and the cost difference between the proposed algorithm and the optimum plan is about 18 percent. Although the result for the *RATIO2* log is not shown, it reduces the cost down to the 40 percent of the modification-only cost and the cost difference between the proposed algorithm and the optimum plan is about 20 percent. This is because the materialization method becomes inefficient as the rate of update operations increases. In average, the ratio of definitely materialized sub-queries over all materialized sub-queries in the PIP of the proposed algorithm is about 90 percent on the *RATIO1* log and 84 percent on the *RATIO2* log respectively. Figure 20.4 shows the execution times of the optimization methods in this experiment. As it can be noticed, there exists significant difference in execution time among the methods as the number of sub-queries is increased. Although the plan generated by the dynamic programming method is the closest to the cost of the optimum plan in Figure 20.3, its execution time takes much longer than that of PIP and the time difference becomes enlarged exponentially as the number of sub-queries increases. On the other hand, the greedy strategy takes almost the same time as PIP in Figure 20.4 but its cost is much larger than that of PIP in Figure 20.3.

Figure 20.5 shows the trace of the evaluation costs based on the proposed algorithm over a series of consecutive optimization processes invoked by the continuous change of sub-query usage patterns in the RATIO1 log. As the cost allowable ratio μ becomes smaller, a new optimization process is invoked more frequently. In other words, the number of optimization processes increases for the same sequence of requests in the *RATIO1* log, so that the recent change of usage patterns can be precisely applied. On the other hand, the proposed algorithm invokes an optimization process whenever the capacity of a temporary buffer in a mediator is exceeded. Figure 20.6 illustrates the number of optimization processes due to the lack of temporary buffer space as the size of the temporary buffer is varied. The size of the temporary buffer is represented

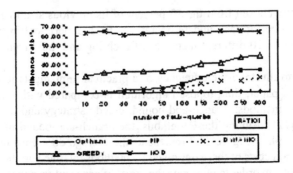

Figure 20.3.   Evaluation costs difference

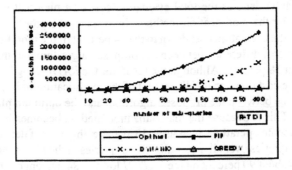

Figure 20.4.   Comparison of optimization time

by its ratio over the total size of available storage space in a mediator. When no temporary buffer is available, the ratio of the temporary buffer is indicated by a 0 percent. The excess rate is defined by the ratio of the number of optimization processes caused by this reason over the total number of optimization processes invoked in the *RATIO1* or *RATIO2* logs. As the size of temporary buffer space increases, the number of optimization processes caused by the lack of storage space is reduced. When the temporary buffer space is about the 20 percent of the total storage space, a new optimization process is rarely invoked.

The effect of a decay rate in the proposed algorithm is shown in Figure 20.7. For the continuous variation of the usage patterns of sub-queries in the *RATIO1* log, a series of consecutive optimization processes is indicated for the different values of a half-life. As the value of a half-life is decreased, a new optimization process is invoked frequently. This is because the recent change of usage patterns is weighted more as the half-life becomes smaller.

6.   Conclusion

In a mediator system, it is possible to improve the performance of query evaluation when the materialization method is utilized to evaluate global queries.

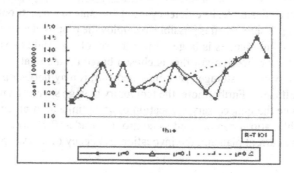

Figure 20.5. Effect of cost allowable ratio

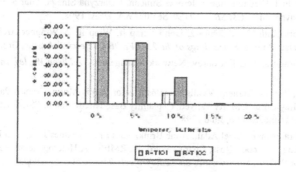

Figure 20.6. Rate of temporary buffer overflows

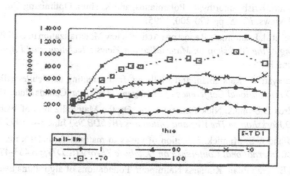

Figure 20.7. Effect of a half-life

By carefully monitoring the usage patterns of sub-queries for global queries, the proposed algorithm can determine when to invoke a new optimization process. Based on the decaying mechanism of usage patterns, their recent variation can be identified and used in an optimization process. In addition, it can generate a practically applicable implementation plan for the sub-queries based on their recent usage patterns. Although the optimum plan obtained by searching all possible plans is desirable, its efficiency is not guaranteed when its optimization takes too long. Therefore, it is possible to employ the proposed algorithm when the number of sub-queries is large. Since the set of materialized sub-queries selected by the proposed algorithm is chosen based on the relative utilization efficiency of available storage space in a mediator, it may not be optimum but practically efficient. Furthermore, the temporary storage space of a mediator is used to reduce the unnecessary invocation of an optimization process and the cost allowable ratio μ can be used to control the trade-off between the inefficiency of the current plan and the invocation frequency of a new optimization process.

References

[1] Sophie Cluet, Claude Delobel, Jerome Simeon, Katarzyna Smaga. Your Mediators Need Data Conversion!. *ACM SIGMOD '98* Seattle, WA, USA, 1998

[2] Mary Tork Roth, Peter Schwarz. Don't Scrap It, Wrap It! A Wrapper Architecture for Legacy Data Source. *Proceedings of the 23rd VLDB Conference* Athens, Greece, 1997.

[3] A. Leinwand and K. F. Conroy. Network Management. *Addison-Wesley, Inc.* pp.17-36, 1996.

[4] Chen Li, Ramana Yerneni, Vasilis Vassalos, Hector Garcia-Molina, Yannis Papakonstantinou, Jeffrey Ullman, Murty Valiveti. Capability Based Mediation in TSIMMIS. *ACM SIGMOD 98* Demo, Seattle, June 1998

[5] V.S. Subrahmanian, Sibel Adali, Anne Brink, Ross Emery, James J.Lu, Adil Rajput, Timothy J.Rogers, Robert Ross, Charles Ward. HERMES : A Heterogeneous Reasoning and Mediator System. *http://www.cs.umd.edu/projects/hermes/overview/paper*

[6] A. Y. Levy, A. Rajaraman, and J. J. Ordille. Querying Heterogeneous Information Source Using Source Description. *VLDB*, pp. 251-262, 1996.

[7] S. Chaudhuri, Krishnamurthy, S. Potamianos, and K. shim. Optimizing Queries with Materialized Views. *ICDE*, pp 190-200, 1995.

[8] Nita Goyal et al. Preliminary Report on (Active) View Materialization in GUI Programming. *proceeding of the Workshop on Materialization Views : Techniques and Applications*, pp. 56-64, June 1996.

[9] V. Harinarayan, A. Rajaraman, and J. Ulman. Implementing data cubes efficiently. *ACM SIGMOD International Conference of Management of Data*, Canada, June 1996

[10] Alexandros Labrinidis, Nick Roussopoulos. On the Materialization of WebViews. *ACM SIGMOD Workshop on The Web and Databases (WebDB '99)* June 3-4, 1999 Pennsylvania.

[11] H.Gupta and I. S. Mumick. Selection of views to materialize under a maintenance cost constraint. *International Conference on Database Theory (ICDT)*, pp.453-470, 1999.

[12] Richard E. Neapolitan, Kumarss Naimipour, Foundations of algorithms using C++ pseudocode, Jones and Bartlett publishers, 1997.

[13] Harold S.Javitz, Alfonso Valdes. The NIDES Statistical Component: Description and Justification. *SRI International* Menlo Park, California 94025. March, 1994.

[14] H. Gupta. Selection of view to materialized in a data warehouses. *ICDT*, 1997.

[15] Mark W.W. Vwemeer, Peter M.G. Apers, Query modification in object-oriented database federations, Conference on Cooperative Information Systems, 1997

[16] Abrahm Silberschatz, Peter B. Galvin, Opreating system concepts, Addison-Wesley Publishing Company, 1994.

Index